HISTORICAL PROBLEMS OF IMPERIAL AFRICA

Historical Problems
of Imperial Africa

Edited by
ROBERT O. COLLINS
JAMES McDONALD BURNS
ERIK KRISTOFER CHING

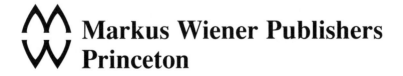 **Markus Wiener Publishers**
Princeton

Third Printing 2000

Map Design: The maps have been drawn by Jason Simpson and Michele Aurand under the leadership of Professor David Lanter of the Department of Geography at the University of California, Santa Barbara and the Director of the Digital Cartography Laboratory at UCSB.

For information write to:
  Markus Wiener Publishers
  231 Nassau Road, Princeton, NJ 08542

Library of Congress Cataloging-in-Publication Data

Historical problems of imperial Africa/Robert O. Collins, ed.
    (Topic in world history)
    Rev. ed. of: Problems in the history of colonial Africa,
1860-1960. 1970.
    Includes bibliographical references.
    ISBN 1-55876-060-1
    1. Africa—History—1884-1960.   2. Colonies—Africa—
History.   I. Collins, Robert O.   II. Collins, Robert O.   Problems
in the history of colonial Africa, 1860-1960.   III. Series.
DT29.H57   1993
960' .3—dc20   93-93-27132
                                                CIP

Printed in the United States of America on acid-free paper.

Dedication

To my colleagues and staff of the Department of History in the University of California, Santa Barbara, UCSB, who have tolerated with amusement and amicability, if not affection, one of their own for twenty-eight years. May God bless each and every one of them.

Robert O. Collins
Santa Barbara, California

Contents

Preface

In 1992 I completely revised a collection of readings originally selected in 1968 entitled *Problems in African History.* My purpose in compiling these readings was to provide, in a single compact volume, excerpts from interpretive articles, essays, and books dealing with Africa that are not readily available to the general student. I have grouped the multitude of new writings on precolonial Africa around six "problems" constructed to present controversial and conflicting interpretations as well as to provide themes for discussion and further inquiry. Although enlightening to students as to the African past, that volume does not contain any "problems" dealing with the traumatic period of transformation experienced by Africans during the European conquest and imperial rule of Africa in the twentieth century. This omission was not accidental. I deliberately excluded themes associated with Africa under colonial rule. First, students are generally less familiar with precolonial African history that has its own integral past unmarred by the Europeans. Second, I do not believe that either the precolonial or the imperial period could be appropriately presented if compressed onto one volume. I thus limited the compilation of interpretation to the precolonial period, and although this concentration made the volume more substantial, it was not completely satisfactory. The solution, however, was obvious to my fellow Africanists and to my publisher, and acting on their suggestions I have produced the following reader as a companion to *Problems in African History.*

Conforming to the methodology in *Problems in African History,* I have constructed six problems concerned with imperial rule in Africa by the European Powers. As before, the appellation on problems refers not only to those topics that at present still invoke controversy and conflicting interpretations, but also to new issues that have come to the forefront of imperial rule in Africa during the past generation. This volume, like its predecessor, identifies six problems of imperial Africa—the partition, resistance, colonial rule, education, nationalism, and exploitation or development. All of these problems remain the subject of current debate and discussion, which is the purpose of this book. I have made no attempt to present a narrative for Africa in the imperial period; that is the task of the instructor.

In choosing the selections for each problem, I have sought to include the most authoritative statements, interpretations, and analyses by well-known and distinguished scholars. Future contributions will add to our understanding of each area, but they will undoubtedly elaborate, refine or revise the basic positions that these scholars have already assumed. One may quarrel with the choice of problems and with the choice of authorities used to elucidate them. In defense I can only plead my own experience and knowledge and the favorable reaction of my students, now over many years, to my experiments in the presentation of the history of imperial Africa.

I wish to express my particular appreciation to Erik Kristofer Ching and to James McDonald Burns whose enthusiasm for the African past has evolved out of those students who have come before them but who, like their predecessors, have provided ideas, criticism, and discussion as to how to present a completely revised *Historical Problems of Imperial Africa* for students. Not only their suggestions but their skills with computers and the determination to see the project to a successful conclusion are gratefully appreciated and deserve special recognition.

I also want to express my gratitude to Professor Jack Bermingham, Dean of the Division of Social Sciences and Professor of African History at Pacific Lutheran University for his most helpful suggestions regarding many of the problems in this book. I certainly cannot forget to acknowledge the splendid cartography of Jason Simpson and Michele Aurand members of the UCSB Digital Cartographic Laboratory under the direction of Professor David Lanter, whose maps are contained in this volume.

Many thanks also go to the following authors for granting permission to reprint their works or portions thereof. Unfortunately, Michael Crowder, Hugh Deschamps, John Gallagher, Lord Hailey, Sir Frederick Lugard, Sir Harold Macmichael, Walter Rodney, and A.J.P. Taylor are dead, but their works are perhaps their finest testimonial. Fortunately all the other authors appear to be alive and well and continue to contribute to the history of imperial Africa: Raymond Betts, A. Adu Boahen, David Chanaiwa, Peter Duignan, J.D. Fage, D.K. Fieldhouse, L.H. Gann, John Hargreaves, A.G. Hopkins, John Illiffe, Thomas Jones, A.S. Kanya-Fostner, Martin Kilson, Martin D. Lewis, J.M. Lonsdale, Roger Louis, Anthony Low, Agrippah Mugomba, Abdou Moumouni, C.W. Newbury, Mougo Nyaggah, Roland Oliver, Bade Onimode, R. Cranford Pratt, T.O. Ranger, Ronald Robinson, G.N. Sanderson, Edward Steinhart, Jean Stengers, Henry Turner, and John Wilson.

I am grateful to the editors of the following periodicals who have authorized me to reprint passages from their articles: *Africa, Comparative Studies in Society and History,* and the *Journal of African History.* Finally, I wish to acknowledge the kindness of the following publishing firms which permitted me to include passages from books bearing their imprint: ABC-CLIO, Cambridge University Press, Frank Cass & Co. Ltd., Columbia University Press, Delacorte Press, Edinburgh University Press, Faber and Faber Ltd., Greenwood Publishing Group Inc., Harvard University Press, Howard University Press, Humanities Press International, Inc., Johns Hopkins University Press, The Macmillan Press Ltd., Northwestern University Press, Oxford University Press, Penguin Books Ltd., the Phelps-Stokes Fund, Frederick A Praeger, Princeton University Press, Waterlow and Sons Ltd., Yale University Press, and Zed Press.

All but the most necessary footnotes have been eliminated from the selections that follow by permission.

Robert O. Collins
Santa Barbara, California

Introduction

The history of imperial Africa is characterized by its historical brevity. Compared to the millennia of the precolonial African past, the age of the imperialists is but an historical fragment in time of little consequence if not for the traumatic changes it bestowed on African societies in so brief a period. Equipped with the tools of empire, Europe overwhelmed the Africans, despite some resolute resistance, in less than twenty-five years at the end of the nineteenth century (circa, 1875-1900) only to rule the continent for little more than half a century (circa, 1885-1960). Contemporary writers and historians have attempted to explain this phenomenon without any definitive success, and the debate continues. Indeed, after over a generation of independent Africa, in which the study of imperial Africa was regarded as irrelevant or in bad taste, there is a resurgence of interest in imperial history not only in the former colonial powers themselves but by African scholars as well. The bitterness and resentment of the Africans at being ruled by Europeans have cooled. Some Africans of an older generation even look back to the "bad old days" of colonialism with nostalgia. Moreover, most of the former rulers in Europe are now dead, and the new scholarship looks back upon their record with greater dispassion but with an extraordinary curiosity to examine the strange phenomenon known as imperialism. These new investigations of imperialism have shed the shackles of the various "schools" of colonial history that were prevalent in the first half of this century to liberate scholarly inquiry. This is not to denigrate those contributions, many of which are recorded in this volume, of the socialist, Marxist, Christian, imperial theorists and administrators or even the African scholars themselves who in the early years of African independence concentrated their research and writings on imperial themes. Indeed, African history was until 1960, to select an arbitrary date, dominated by imperial history, the history of the Europeans in Africa. A generation later this is not the case, and the history of the Africans, whether in the precolonial centuries or in the imperial period, has established its own identity and integrity, which it richly deserves. Nevertheless, the few short decades of an imperial presence in Africa cannot and can never be dismissed, for these years of European occupation and administration of Africa, for better or for worse, have changed the way of life of the African forever.

Many outside observers of the Africans in the nineteenth and early twentieth century regarded African societies as static, some even regarded them as retrogressive. This, of course, is nonsense, and although traditional African societies may have been conservative, they were also dynamic and always changing. The imposition of European rule disrupted the evolutionary panorama of the African peoples. Not only was the conquest and establishment of colonial authority sudden; it was painful. This is not to mean that Africans in the precolonial period lived in the bliss-

1

ful world of the noble savage. Africans fought, enslaved, and killed one another like everyone else, but it was rather benign compared to the ferocity and firepower of the invading Europeans. It was, in fact, somewhat of a shock to the Africans to be overwhelmed within the space of two decades particularly by peoples who did not play by their rules. It was the latter that proved to be the most disturbing and the most enduring. It was one thing to be conquered, become a vassal, a subject or a slave within the context of norms that were understood and often, but not always, acceptable. It was quite another to be coerced into an administrative system that had no relevance to the past. This is the importance of the brief imperial years in African history. They were wrenching, disturbing, turbulent years in which the Africans were subjected to new and disruptive demands in which things fell apart.

What most absorbed the historians of Africa in the first half of this century was not, however, the Africans at all; it was the manner by which the Europeans captured the continent, the Partition of Africa. The Scramble for Africa has been an astringent intellectual puzzle for many historians in their attempt to explain why in a quarter of a century the European powers would wish to stake out vast areas of African real estate. In the traditional compartmentalism of university history departments this subject was debated and written to exhaustion in ponderous tomes normally described as imperial or diplomatic history before being confronted by a curious interest in the past of the African peoples themselves. Ironically, this devilish subject by which the Europeans seized which territory for whatever reason has reemerged in recent years like a phoenix from the ashes of old scholarship by the renewed interest in imperial history now clothed in the plumage of the enormous outpouring since 1960 of histories concerned solely with the Africans. It places the Scramble for Africa in a more proper perspective without excluding the fact that the ultimate decisions to partition the African continent had to be accepted and approved in the staterooms of Europe.

The African reaction, individually as well as collectively, was no different from any society in time and place that is confronted by invaders. Upon the arrival of the Europeans in force, some Africans acquiesced, some collaborated, and some resisted. The resisters were shot down by advanced technology ruthlessly applied in the doggerel by Hilaire Belloc:

> It matters not
> What they have got,
> We have the Maxim
> And they have not.

Were the resisters to European imperialism heroes or reactionaries unable to absorb the progressive meaning of the machine gun? Perhaps, the more astute Africans were the progressive collaborators who accepted the inevitable but sought to strike a good bargain with the white devils in order to preserve their security and some of their accustomed way of living. Some of those who collaborated were intimidated by the new technology symbolized by the repeating rifle, the river steamer, the railway. Others were mesmerized by Christian missionaries bringing a new, seemingly all-powerful God to challenge the spiritual efficacy of the traditional deities. Then there were those Africans who perceived that by cooperating with these violent incomers they could negotiate a better deal for themselves and their societies than simply being gunned down in a hopeless cause. But whether resisters or collaborators, neither reactions were entirely futile. The Ethiopians destroyed the finest army of nineteenth century Italy to preserve their empire at the expense of a new Rome. Other resisters who perished before the Maxim gun have become national heroes to independent Africa. As for the collaborators, the Fanti of the Gold Coast had a long history of cooperation with the British governors to their mutual advantage against Ashanti imperialism. Many collaborators, however, became intransigent resisters when they discovered that their willingness to work with the Europeans only resulted in an unacceptable degradation of themselves and their society. The debate over this conundrum is as endless as it is emotionally and intellectually challenging.

Although historians will argue endlessly the reasons for the partition and acquisition of the African continent, with all its drama of collaboration and resistance, they become even more perplexed as to what the Europeans did with it after they got it. Intellectually, it presents challenges that were, in fact, never resolved but certainly elicited stimulating, vigorous, and often acrimonious discussion as to how to rule subject peoples. The debate was both theoretical and practical, and the theoreticians and the practitioners did not always agree. Nevertheless, there was a concerted effort to rationalize and by implication justify imperial rule by providing guidelines for "our man on the spot", the beleaguered white official sent out from Europe to administer to black Africans whose language, customs, culture, and past he did not know. Today, this attempt to take a theory of imperial rule and draft a practicum on how to do it, which would apply to every specific locality and its peoples, appears as a sterile and academic exercise divorced from reality. There is a good deal of truth to this criticism, which was ruthlessly debated in Oxford, Paris, Berlin, and Brussels, but it would be a serious mistake to underestimate the intellectual power of "indirect rule" or "assimilation", which in the heyday of European colonialism in Africa were regarded by the administrators with an awe normally reserved for Holy Writ. These were the tenets by which the Africans were governed and which profoundly shaped the official mind of the governors.

On the one hand, indirect rule implied the concept of trusteeship, which has been refined in this century through a tortuous path from the League of Nations to the United Nations and more recently the evolving concept that in a global world the international community must accept responsibility to provide security for human beings in destabilized states. On the other, indirect rule was more cynically regarded as an inexpensive means to administer millions of Africans by what many, both Africans and Europeans, regarded as a static and unprogressive system of administration.

Assimilation as practiced by the French and Portuguese produced contradictions as well. On the one hand, the idea of a hundred million Frenchmen in Africa touched a deep sentiment in the French that originated among the philosophers of the eighteenth century who held the curious idea of the oneness of mankind. This ideal has never died and has been revived in our own times by the current disenchantment with the tyranny of ethnic, religious, and national rivalries. On the other, assimilation was regarded as nothing more than a hypocritical policy whereby the French were not about to admit equality to all but a select few from their African territories to participate as citizens of France.

Despite these theories of imperial rule, their pervasive influence and their ultimate failure, the more practical results of European administration in Africa, the day-by-day, mundane decisions of the European officials, have remained in place in Africa long after the imperialists have departed. In fact, the administrative structure imposed by the Europeans to govern remains largely intact and no other manifestation of their presence has been more pronounced than the education of the West.

After the violence that accompanied the arrival of the Europeans into the interior of Africa, the African scene became one of peace and quiet under the mailed fist of European officials. The establishment of order was the very first principle of colonial policy, the foundation upon which all other objectives had to rest. Occasionally, order was not easily achieved, but by and large the imperial period in Africa was pacific, but a peace that belied the tumultuous impact of the imperial policies upon African societies. The imperial rulers were not insensitive to the fact that their very presence created new ways of doing business, but they were motivated by their own self-interest despite the fact that many officials sincerely believed they were bestowing civilization by their incorruptible, scientific administration. It was a paradox virtually inherent in colonialism, and one that was never resolved. The means by which this chasm of cultural discontinuity was starkly revealed, not by advanced technology that had dominated the conquest of Africa, but by education as defined in the context of Western learning that was quite different from the profound and traditional wisdom of the Africans. The former came slowly to Africa, and the Africans were not about to abandon what they knew and understood and that had served them well for some unknown brave new world. The Africans were not the only ones who had doubts about "educating" the African. Some administrators and many settlers regarded the importation of Western education with dismay, an enterprise that would only result in a class of "uppity niggers". The administrators were perhaps more honest. Those officials in the British colonies were concerned about sustaining traditional values as the foundation for their policies of indirect rule. Western education would only undermine those values and consequently that policy. Those in the French territories were torn between the ideals of assimilation that required a total absorption of French education and those officials who were faced with the practical affairs of daily administration that required the authority of the traditional rulers.

At first education was left largely to the missionaries who rightly perceived that the teachings of Christ could only be spread by the Word. Literacy was thus a paramount priority, but with few exceptions during the early decades of the missionary presence, education was provided usually to the unwanted in African societies—the orphans, freed slaves, outcasts. With the expansion of colonial rule, however, the demand for Africans trained as clerks and craftsmen irrepressively began to drive the institutions of education. When the mission schools could not meet the demand, the government school appeared. Still many Africans, particularly the traditional *elites,* resisted the opportunities of Western education only to discover that as one decade passed to another those Africans leaving the mission and government schools to enter the colonial money economy were not one of them, but a new powerful educated *elite* whose skills projected them into prominent positions in the affairs of the colony. By the end of the Second World War, it became abundantly clear that if the chiefs were to maintain their accustomed authority their sons would have to be educated to deal successfully with the future. The demand for Western education became insatiable. Schools sprang up like mushrooms, even universities for those Africans who could not afford to go to Europe or the United States for higher education. Everyone now understood that the path to power either within the colonial setting or beyond lay with Western education.

This education was the price not only of profitable participation in the imperial economy but the knowledge required to forge a national identity. It could be argued that nationalism was the most baleful inheritance bequeathed by Europe to Africa. In the name of the nation state, colonies, whose boundaries had been arbitrarily drawn without relevance to the ethnic or geographical realities of Africa, suddenly under the new educated African *elite* took on a life of their own. And it was the African *elite* who rose after independence to defend to the death the imperial heritage demarcated by its frontiers of convenience. In the precolonial past the African was prepared to die for his ethnic group, a society that he understood. Now the mass of Africans were being asked by the *elites* to support a new nation largely populated by those they regarded as enemies. The *elites* may have provided the leadership, but they could not have prevailed without the support of the common Africans. The educated *elites* with their new skills, whereby they could communicate with the colonial authorities, were determined to isolate the traditional leaders, not only for their personal gain, but the more commendable prospect of forging a new society that would join in the international community of nations. Consequently, a generation has passed since the plethora of African states were created from the ruins of imperial Africa. They remain unchanged in their configuration to this day, raising the question to many Africans as to the success of the nation state in the continent at a time when the nation states of Europe are struggling to subsume their own identity into a larger union.

One of the most scathing denunciations of imperial Africa has been its economic exploitation by the Europeans. To the Africans, whether of the *elites* or the traditionalists, the perception that they were the victims of European avarice was deeply rooted, an accusation that was widely shared by European liberals, socialists,

Marxists, and humanitarians. The imperialists were outraged at these charges. What the former regarded as exploitation, they argued, not without reason, was in fact the introduction of civilization in Africa by the development of its human and material resources symbolized by the schools, hospitals, railroads, roads, bridges, buildings, dams, agricultural schemes all for the purpose of bringing the African subsistence economy into the international market economy for the benefit, of course, to the Europeans but also the Africans. Nonsense, reply the critics. This so-called development not only profited the Europeans but was paid for largely by the Africans in land, taxes, and labor. Not so scream the imperialists who defend the burden of empire by its expense to the colonial power in men, money, and markets. The argument is endless, the conclusions by all parties distorted by passion, the theories as abundant as the theorists. Here, of course, lies the challenge to find one's path through the tangled undergrowth of economic theory, where the compass of one's own emotional proclivities may lead to the promised land or as frequently to preordained conclusions.

In search of empire, its governance, and its demise the only way forward into the problem of the history of imperial Africa is to begin.

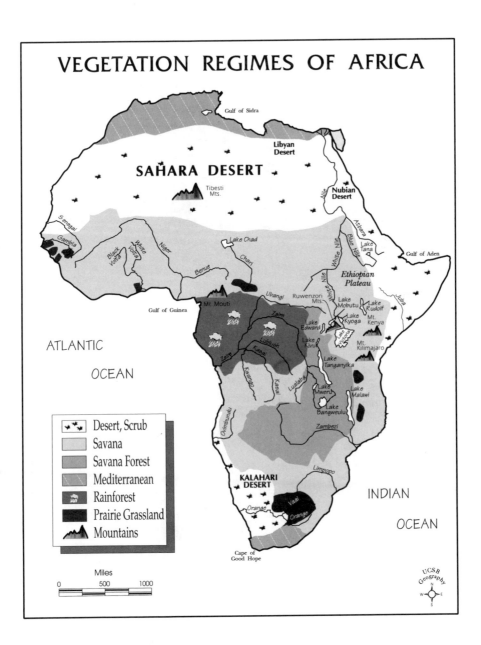

VEGETATION REGIMES OF AFRICA

Gulf of Sidra

Libyan
Desert

SAHARA DESERT

Tibesti
Mts.

Nubian
Desert

Nile

Atbara

Blue Nile

Lake
Tana

Gulf of Aden

Senegal

Gambia

Black Volta

White Volta

Niger

Lake Chad

Chari

Benue

White Nile

Ethiopian
Plateau

Juba

Gulf of Guinea

Mt Mouti

Ubangi

Ruwenzori
Mts.

Lake
Mobutu

Lake
Rudolf

Lake
Kyoga

Mt.
Kenya

Zaire

Lake
Edward

Lake
Victoria

Lubilashi

Lake
Kivu

Mt.
Kilimajaro

ATLANTIC

OCEAN

Zaire

Kasai

Lualaba

Lake
Tanganyika

Kwango

Kasai

Lake
Mweru

Lake
Malawi

Ovimbundu

Lake
Bangweulu

Zambezi

KALAHARI
DESERT

Limpopo

INDIAN

OCEAN

Orange

Vaal

Orange

Cape of
Good Hope

Desert, Scrub
Savana
Savana Forest
Mediterranean
Rainforest
Prairie Grassland
Mountains

Miles

0   500   1000

UCSB
Geography

N
W — E
S

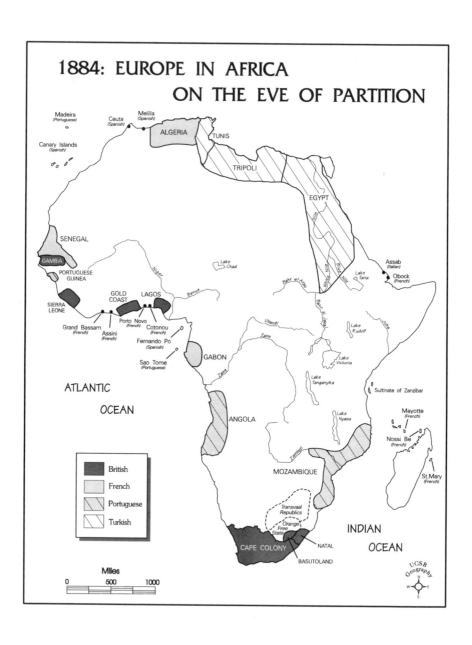

1884: EUROPE IN AFRICA
ON THE EVE OF PARTITION

Madeira
(Portuguese)

Ceuta
(Spanish)

Melilla
(Spanish)

ALGERIA

TUNIS

Canary Islands
(Spanish)

TRIPOLI

EGYPT

Nile

SENEGAL

Lake
Chad

GAMBIA

Assab
(Italian)

PORTUGUESE
GUINEA

Niger

Bahr al Arab

White Nile

Lake
Tana

Blue Nile

Obock
(French)

GOLD
COAST

LAGOS

Benue

Bahr El Jebel

SIERRA
LEONE

Grand Bassam
(French)

Porto Novo
(French)

Cotonou
(French)

Assini
(French)

Fernando Po
(Spanish)

Ubangi

Lake
Rudolf

Juba

Sao Tome
(Portuguese)

GABON

Zaire

Lake
Victoria

ATLANTIC

Lake
Tanganyika

Sultinate of Zanzibar

OCEAN

Mayotte
(French)

ANGOLA

Lake
Nyasa

Nossi Be
(French)

Zambesi

MOZAMBIQUE

St.Mary
(French)

British

French

Portuguese

Turkish

Transvaal
Republics

Orange
Free
State

INDIAN

OCEAN

CAPE COLONY

NATAL

BASUTOLAND

Miles

0   500   1000

UCSB
Geography

N
W   E
S

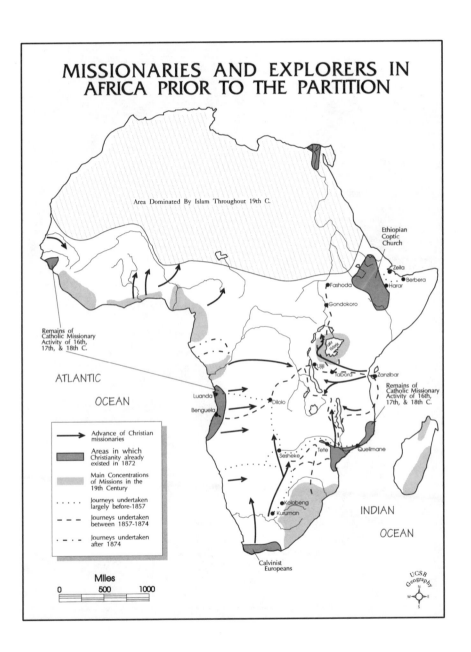

MISSIONARIES AND EXPLORERS IN AFRICA PRIOR TO THE PARTITION

Area Dominated By Islam Throughout 19th C.

Ethiopian Coptic Church

Zeila
Berbera
Fashoda
Harar
Gondokoro

Remains of Catholic Missionary Activity of 16th, 17th, & 18th C.

ATLANTIC

OCEAN

Lake Victoria
Ujiji
Tabora
Zanzibar

Remains of Catholic Missionary Activity of 16th, 17th, & 18th C.

Luanda
Dilolo
Benguela

Tete
Quelimane
Sesheke

Kolobeng
Kuruman

INDIAN

OCEAN

Legend:

→ Advance of Christian missionaries

Areas in which Christianity already existed in 1872

Main Concentrations of Missions in the 19th Century

..... Journeys undertaken largely before-1857

- - - Journeys undertaken between 1857-1874

-·-· Journeys undertaken after 1874

Calvinist Europeans

Miles
0   500   1000

UCSB Geography
N
W-O-E
S

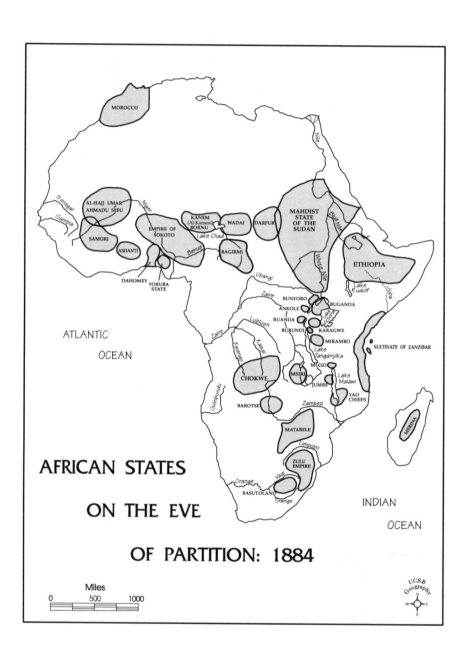

MOROCCO

AL-HAJJ UMAR
AHMADU SEFU

SAMORI

ASHANTI

DAHOMEY
YORUBA
STATE

EMPIRE OF
SOKOTO

KANEM
(Al-Kanemi)
BORNU

WADAI

DARFUR

BAGIRMI

MAHDIST
STATE
OF THE
SUDAN

ETHIOPIA

Senegal

Gambia

Niger

Benue

Lake Chad

Ubangi

Nile

Blue Nile

White Nile

Lake
Rudolf

Juba

ATLANTIC

OCEAN

Zaire

Zaire

Lublush

Kwango

Kasai

Ovimbundu

CHOKWE

BAROTSE

BUNYORO

ANKOLE

RUANDA

BURUNDI

KARAGWE

MIRAMBO

Lake
Tanganyika

MLOZI

MSIRI

JUMBE

Lake
Malawi

YAO
CHIEFS

BUGANDA

Lake Victoria

SULTINATE OF ZANZIBAR

MATABELE

Zambezi

Limpopo

ZULU
EMPIRE

Oranae

Vaal

Orange

BASUTOLAND

MERINA

INDIAN

OCEAN

AFRICAN STATES

ON THE EVE

OF PARTITION: 1884

Miles

0   500   1000

N

W   E

S

PROBLEM I

THE PARTITION OF AFRICA

During the first four centuries of contact with Africa, the European Powers had been content to restrict their holdings to a handful of scattered trading stations along the coast, the control of which passed from one state to another as each state's strength in Europe waxed or waned. Finally in the nineteenth century, European explorers penetrated into the interior and opened the enormous hinterland of Africa; yet no European government rushed to follow in their footsteps. Missionaries began to work out from the coastal enclaves, but they never regarded themselves as agents of their imperial governments. Merchants expanded their trade, but they realized that they would not necessarily gain by the intervention, occupation, and rule of any single European Power. To be sure, the presence of missionaries, merchants, explorers, and soldiers served to clear the way for the expansion of Europe in Africa, but nothing in history is inevitable until it occurs. Yet within less than twenty years, the continent was conquered and divided amidst rising national feeling at home and increasing belligerency abroad. Why? The explanations are nearly as unsatisfactory as they are numerous. The interpretations are as controversial as they are doctrinaire. The misconceptions are as enduring as they are erroneous. To scholar and student alike, the search for understanding this dynamic period, which resulted in European colonial rule in Africa and dramatically altered the future of a vast continent, is the Problem of the Partition of Africa.

There were hesitant beginnings to the Partition of Africa in the 1870s. The discovery of diamonds in South Africa in 1869 provided the incentive and capital for a large influx of Europeans that ultimately spilled across the Limpopo into Central Africa. The opening of the Suez Canal in the same year not only made the East African coast more accessible but also became the great pivot in British imperial strategy, eventually shifting British interest from Constantinople to Cairo with repercussions as far south as the great lakes of equatorial Africa and as far west as

7

Wadai and Lake Chad. In 1881, the French extended their control over Tunis, but in Tunis the French were reluctant empire builders. The repercussions to their occupation might reverberate in North Africa but not south of the Sahara. The Partition of Africa required greater stimuli than the discovery of diamonds in South Africa or political intrigue on the Mediterranean littoral. The partitioners did not have long to wait. Between 1882 and 1885 the British occupied Egypt, precipitating additional conquests that carried them as far as East Africa; Savorgnan de Brazza claimed the north bank of the Congo for France, while Leopold II, King of Belgium, began to carve out a personal fief in the vast hinterland of the Congo Basin. And not to be outdone, Otto von Bismarck decided that Imperial Germany needed colonies. Who then began the scramble for Africa—the British in Egypt, King Leopold in the Congo, the French in West Africa, or an acquisitive Bismarck? The interpretations are as numerous as the candidates.

Ronald Robinson and John Gallagher have argued that the scramble for Africa was begun, not by the intrigues of King Leopold or the heroics of Brazza, but rather by the British occupation of Egypt in 1882. Hitherto the governments of Britain and France had agreed not to permit the quarrels of their traders and officials along the coasts of Africa to become reasons for acquiring additional African territory. The British occupation of Egypt destroyed this Anglo-French collaboration. Henceforth, France consciously sought to acquire colonies elsewhere in Africa as compensation for Cairo and a means to apply diplomatic and commercial pressure on London. On the Niger and the Congo, French officials and explorers were active, and British attempts to enlist the Portuguese and King Leopold in order to check the French soon proved abortive. Moreover, Britain's occupation of Egypt provided Bismarck with the opportunity to exacerbate Anglo-French differences while carving out an African empire for Germany. From every European capital the Egyptian affair had seemed to precipitate the scramble for Africa.

Jean Stengers cannot agree. He has argued that the Partition of Africa was inaugurated neither by King Leopold nor Egypt but rather by the French, ratification of Savorgnan de Brazza's treaty with Makoko followed by the declaration of protectorates in West Africa. Chauvinism made possible French acceptance of the Makoko Treaty; economic motives resulted in the acquisition of French protectorates in West Africa. French claims to political control on the north bank of the Congo forced Leopold to assert his sovereignty on the south bank. French activity on the West African coast stirred the British to preserve their economic interests on the Niger from fear of French annexations. Driven on by the inexorable demands of public opinion, the interior markets were ready for European commercial competition which would have begun the scramble for Africa even if Egypt had never existed.

C.W. Newbury and A.S. Kanya-Forstner have agreed with Jean Stengers that the French, indeed, were responsible for precipitating the scramble for West Africa, but the ratification of the Brazza Treaty was not the turning point in French expansion nor was the British occupation of Egypt any significant influence on French acquisitions in West Africa. From the beginning Admiral Jean Jaureguiberry, the minister who was responsible for colonial affairs, sought a forward course in West Africa, not only to protect French coastal traders but to create a vast French empire in the interior of West Africa. The genesis of French imperialism in West Africa, Newbury and Kanya-Forstner argued, was not Brazza and his treaty with Makoko in 1882 but earlier in 1879-80. At that time public opinion was an important, if sporadic, factor but it did not initiate the scramble. Commercial interests were pervasive but not decisive. As with the late Victorians on the Nile, the motives for French expansion were to be found within the "official mind" of French imperialism. Both Freycinet and Jaureguiberry were prepared to commit the power of France to intervention in Africa for the purpose of future economic profits at the expense of present political control. Much of their policy was based on myth, but it was this myth which precipitated the Partition of West Africa.

Whether it was Egypt, King Leopold or the French who began the scramble for Africa, it was Bismarck who sought to take advantage of it. A.J.P. Taylor, one of Britain's most controversial and influential historians, has argued that Bismarck had no real interest in German acquisitions in Africa but expected that German colonial adventures would draw France and Germany together over imperial quarrels with Great Britain. Bismarck's map of Africa lay in Europe.

Henry A. Turner has to disagree. He remains unconvinced that Bismarck's change of policy can be attributed to considerations of European diplomacy. Turner has argued that, in fact, Bismarck simply changed his mind in 1884 and decided that Germany must expand overseas. He was motivated not so much by foreign policy as by the uncertain future of Germany in a world of predatory states. Observing these developments Bismarck simply decided that colonies were necessary more as an attempt to insure the future of Germany than as a product of any complex diplomatic maneuver.

Not only did Bismarck seize territory on both sides of the continent, but in October 1884 he joined with France to invite twelve other states to a conference in Berlin to discuss the partitioning of Africa. The conference opened in November 1884 and in 1885 passed the Berlin Act incorporating vague and pious pronouncements regarding the slave trade, free trade, and the ground rules for the occupation. In practice, they were to prove largely ineffectual, but when the Berlin Conference ended in February 1885, the scramble for Africa should have been in full swing. Paradoxically, it was not. Once having agreed on the rules for the partition, each of the contestants seemed reluctant to scramble for African territory, and it was not until the Prime Minister of Great Britain, Lord Salisbury decided that the British occupation of Egypt would have to become more permanent that the second round in the scramble began. Once the British determined to remain in Egypt, they were committed to its defense. Ronald Robinson and John Gallagher have carefully delineated the consequences of Salisbury's decision. Egypt is a desert that is made to bloom only by the waters that pour out of equatorial Africa and from the highlands of Ethiopia. No African people possessed the technological skills to interfere with the northward flow of the Nile. The European Powers did. Thus, to protect

Suez, that lifeline of empire, the British had to remain at Cairo. When they decided to take up permanent residence in Egypt, they had to defend the Nile waters, wherever they might be—Khartoum, Lake Tana, Fashoda, Uganda. Lord Salisbury first checked the Italian threat to the Nile waters by warning them to stay away from the Nile Valley. Deeply embroiled with Menelik in Ethiopia, the Italians readily agreed. Having gotten rid of the Italians, Salisbury next had to face the more powerful Germans. The conclusion of the Anglo-German (Heligoland) Agreement of 1890 resolved that problem diplomatically. But then there were the French. From 1893 until 1898 the French, fitfully at first but eventually with Gallic fervor, sought to reach the Nile at Fashoda. In July 1898 a French expedition under Captain J. P. Marchand succeeded. Throughout the nineties, successive British ministers had attempted to seal off the Nile Valley from the French by diplomacy. They all had failed, and Lord Salisbury, who had returned to power in 1885, determined that the only way to preserve the Nile Valley for Britain was to conquer it. In 1898 General H. H. Kitchener and his Anglo-Egyptian Army advanced into the heart of the Sudan, defeated the forces of the Mahdist State outside Omdurman, and raced south to meet Captain Marchand at Fashoda.

Fashoda was the greatest Anglo-French confrontation in nearly a century, and the most serious crisis in Africa between European rivals. G.N. Sanderson has demonstrated that, for France, Fashoda was the result of separate, irreconcilable, and, therefore, conflicting policies of French imperialism. Despite formidable opposition within the government to this foolhardy mission, the French sent Marchand to Fashoda in their desperate pursuit of prestige. Prestige, not economic considerations, dominated the march to Fashoda. The result only proved the folly of a policy motivated by glory and formulated in a crucible of conflicting objectives.

For Britain the great confrontation of French and British imperialism at Fashoda was the climax of half a generation of colonial rivalry. Although acknowledging that the Fashoda crisis aroused public opinion in Britain for the first time to near hysteria, Ronald Robinson and John Gallagher have regarded Fashoda as the logical conclusion of the strategic outcome of the Egyptian policy assiduously practiced for over a decade by the Englishmen who controlled affairs in Britain and Egypt. The conclusion of the Fashoda crisis virtually ended the Partition of Africa. Only a handful of states on the periphery of the continent remained free of European control and by the outbreak of World War I only two countries, Liberia and Ethiopia, maintained their independence. Two others, Morocco and Libya, had slipped under French and Italian administration respectively, but neither the Franco-German dispute over Morocco nor the Italian-Turkish struggle for Libya possessed the drama or the danger of the Fashoda crisis and were, in fact, the peripheral and rather sandy remains of the scramble for the more tropical regions further south.

Finally, A.G. Hopkins argues that the question of who began the partition of Africa distracts attention away from the scramble's place in the much broader phenomenon of nineteenth-century European imperialism. Hopkins questions the central tenet of the Robinson and Gallagher thesis—that the British occupation of

Egypt was precipitated by their concerns for the protection of the Suez Canal, the Nile waters, and for the safety of British nationals in Egypt. He argues that British fears were exaggerated by the men on the spot, and overemphasized by British ministers in London. Their actions were rather motivated by their concern for the investments of London financiers, whose interests in Egypt demanded the protection of a European administration. Hopkins observes that the acquisition of Egypt was part of a much larger global process at work. Throughout the late nineteenth century direct administration was replacing the old practice of informal empire in regions of significant European investment. Thus the scramble began not over strategic concerns regarding the protection of a sea route to India but was instead the inevitable result of a growing pattern of European expansion.

Many scholars have sought to provide a comprehensive interpretation for the Partition of Africa. Some have argued that British participation in the scramble was the result of strategic considerations arising from the British occupation of Egypt. To be sure, financial, humanitarian, and commercial interests were always present but of less influence on the official minds who made policy than the strategic requirements of the British empire. Although this interpretation has provided a more defensible explanation for the British presence at Cairo, Khartoum, and Kampala than appeals to economic inevitability, the extension of this thesis becomes less convincing when attempting to explain the partition in West and southern Africa, where personal ambitions, national prestige, and economic factors outweighed strategic consideration. Others have emphasized the complexities of the scramble for Africa that defy a general, comprehensive interpretation. European imperialism in Africa must be written only in a "polycentric fashion," for "no unitary theory will help untangle for us the richness and variety of the historical skein." [1]

---

[1] Gann, Lewis and Duignan, Peter, "Reflections on Imperialism and the Scramble for Africa," in *The History and Politics of Colonialism in Africa*, Lewis Gann and Peter Duignan eds. (Cambridge: Cambridge University Press, 1969), Vol. 1, p. 128.

Egypt and the Partition of Africa
RONALD ROBINSON AND
JOHN GALLAGHER[2]

Without the occupation of Egypt, there is no reason to suppose that any international scrambles for Africa, either west or east, would have begun when they did. There seem to have been no fresh social or economic impulses for imperial expansion which would explain why the partition of tropical Africa should have begun in the early 1880s. Gladstone's second administration was totally devoid of imperial ambitions in west Africa. Granville was unimpressed by the dingy annals of the west coast. Kimberley, at the Colonial Office, was eager to give sleeping dogs every chance of lying. The pessimistic Derby, who succeeded him in 1882, was temperamentally opposed to any suggestion, however modest, for expansion on the west coast. Finally there was Gladstone, himself, who knew little and cared little about the problem. In so far as these men possessed any coherent view of the situation in tropical Africa, it was the view sometimes of Cobden sometimes of Palmerston and the mid-Victorian imperialism of free trade. As in Gladstone's first ministry, they still concurred in looking on tropical Africa as a third-rate adjunct of the British economy, which might be worth the exertion of coastal influence, but did not justify the effort of administration inland. There was none of them likely to plant the flag in the middle of the African bush in a fit of absence of mind.

For decades all the European governments concerned with the coast of Africa both east and west had tacitly agreed not to allow the petty quarrels of their traders and officials to become occasions for empire. The ministries in London and Paris wanted nothing more than to continue their gentleman's agreement, although each faintly suspected the other of wanting to break it.

It was the British invasion of Egypt which shattered this system, because it shattered the general Anglo-French collaboration. When France came out in open opposition to the new regime in Egypt toward the end of 1882, she began to cast around for ways of putting pressure on London. There was plenty of scope for a policy of pinpricks in west Africa, and these now began in earnest. Two French firms were on the lower Niger, trading not only at the coast, but pushing into the interior. The alarming feature of this activity was that the French consular agent in the river was

[2]Robinson, Ronald and Gallagher, John, with Denny, Alice, *Africa and the Victorians: The Official Mind of Imperialism* (London: Macmillan, 1961), pp. 163, 166, 168-74. John Gallagher was a Fellow of Balliol College, Oxford, and Trinity College, Cambridge. Ronald Robinson is a former Fellow of Balliol College, Oxford, and was the Beit Professor of the History of the British Commonwealth.

now hard at work making treaties as far upstream as the kingdom of Nupe and along the Benue. In Paris they had no illusions about their chances on the lower Niger, for the British position seemed too strong. But the Minister of Marine and Colonies had high hopes for the Benue. At the same time, another British sphere looked like it was slipping away. Trade in the delta of the Congo was dominated by British firms; in the interior Lieutenant Cameron had made a set of treaties in the seventies which gave the United Kingdom an option on the inner basin of the river. Then Her Majesty's Government had rejected it. Now French and Belgian private enterprises were ready to take the Congo seriously. There was a vast river behind the mouths of the Congo, as Stanley had shown; and it had become possible to break into the hinterland, as Brazza had found. King Leopold II of the Belgians who had floated an International Association to explore central Africa at the end of the seventies, launched Stanley on another mission to open communications between the navigable Congo and Stanley Pool in the interior. At the same time Brazza too went back, acting in the name of the French section of the International Association. Here was a scramble, but only at the personal level of two explorers racing each other to the interior, each with the skimpiest of credentials. Stanley was little more than the personal agent of a petty monarch, for the International Association was a piece of mummery, and the Belgian Parliament would have nothing to do with its king's speculations. The status of Brazza was no less peculiar. He too was nominally the agent of the International Association. Although his expedition was given a tiny grant by the French government, the chief inspiration of his mission came from his own pleadings. Paris had little desire to be involved in his adventures. Brazza however had heard that Leopold intended to seize all the interior basin of the Congo, and this would cut off the French colony of Gabon from its hinterland and cast it into bankruptcy. To avoid the ruin of their colony, the French government in 1879 authorized Brazza to make a treaty at Stanley Pool. Just as the Foreign Office in the eighteen- fifties had worked to open the Niger hinterland, so the French government in the eighteen-seventies worked to open the Congo basin. They were far from wanting to extend their political control into the interior; their aim was simply to block the political extensions of others. Brazza's treaty was meant to "reserve our rights, without engaging the future."

Between 1880 and 1888 Stanley and Brazza played out their game in the Congo. This raised awkward questions for the British government. Leopold was a puny rival, and his association could be pushed into the wings if the need arose. But after Brazza had made his treaty at Stanley Pool, the Foreign Office had to rely on the French disinclination to move in central Africa. In April 1882 the British ambassador in Paris asked the Quai d'Orsay whether the Congo mission had an official character. The discussion that followed showed that in the opinion of the Ministry of Marine and Colonies, Brazza had no right to have made a treaty at all. But on the Congo, as on the Niger, all this was to change. After the Egyptian affair had reached its climax, Paris did not feel the old need to pay deference to British susceptibilities; on 10 October the Foreign Minister overrode the protest of the Marine and announced that he intended to ask the Chamber to approve the treaty. Ratification followed on 30 November. On 15 December the Foreign Office countered by recognizing Portugal's claims to the Congo and its hinterlands—claims which Britain had steadily rejected for the past forty years. In return Britain was to enjoy most favored nation treatment in the trade of the Congo, a maximum tariff rate, and the setting up of an Anglo-Portugese commission to supervise the traffic on the river. The treaty took fifteen months to complete, because the Portugese went on hoping to get better terms from France than from the United Kingdom; but its purpose was always painfully clear. When it had at last been signed, the French ambassador in London caustically defined it as:

> A security taken by Britain to prevent either France or an international syndicate directed by France from setting foot in the Congo Delta . . . The British Government . . . would rather parcel it out with Portugal, whom it can influence at will, than leave France with an open door.

That was true enough. During 1883 and 1884 the Gladstone Cabinet hoped to use the Portugese as a sort of holding company which would decently veil the preeminence of British interests. Lisbon would do the governing, London would do the trade. In fact, British optimism went further than that. It was rumored in the Foreign Office that King Leopold's own organization might become ". . . as I hear is not unlikely, an English company." Both these sanguine hopes are very revealing. As a direct result of the Egyptian occupation, British interests in the Congo were now threatened by Leopold and the French. If their sphere were to be saved, then ministers could no longer rely on the old gentleman's agreement; from now on, official acts of policy would be needed. This they understood. Yet they refused to meet the new situation by any territorial extension of their own. Instead, they fell back on a variant of their technique of informal empire. Others could administer on paper, while they enjoyed the trade. With the King of Portugal as their caretaker on the coast and the King of the Belgians as their manager in the hinterland, all might still be saved, thanks to these regal subordinates.

In fact, the British plans went astray both in the Niger and in the Congo. Ministers had their doubts already over the Anglo-Portugese Treaty. They were to end by thoroughly repenting of it. Although the treaty had been designed to guarantee the interests of British traders, they were loud in opposition to it, because of the nominal Portugese control and the actual Portugese tariff. Their protests were joined by the ancestral voices of the Anti-Slavery Society and the Baptist Union. Behind all this agitation there may have lain, as Granville suspected, the fine hand of King Leopold. The complaints of these pressure groups however were not enough to stop the treaty. That it failed was another of the consequences of the Egyptian crisis. After the occupation of Cairo, it seemed to French observers that Britain was driving for African empire. French diplomacy attacked the Anglo-Portugese arrangement, both as a way of keeping the Congo open, and of putting pressure on the British in Egypt. The treaty was signed on 26 February, 1884, and during March the Quai d'Orsay was actively inciting opposition in Belgium, Holland and the United States, the powers with trading interests in the Congo. But in his search for supporters, Ferry hooked a bigger fish than these. On 31 March he tried to get the Germans to join the resistance. This overture was to begin the partition of West Africa.

Bismarck too had his grievances against British policy. To his rooted dislike of Gladstone as a man fit only to chop down trees and make up speeches, he could now add a splenetic indignation at Granville's dawdling. In February 1888 he had enquired whether Britain would be ready to protect the German settlement at Angra Pequena; in December he repeated the enquiry. But for a further six and a half months the only reply he could get from London was a series of vague observations about British claims in that region. In part the muddle was caused by the objections of the Cape, in part by the British feeling that the colonial politicians had to be listened to, if South Africa was one day to be united around that province. But it was an important muddle. The occupation of Egypt gave Bismarck the chance to deepen the rift between Britain and France and to enter the African game. In March and April of 1884 the Germans took steps to assert their own protectorate over Angra Pequena, but the ambiguity of their statements and the imperceptiveness of Gladstone's ministers (one of whom as late as June did not know where Angra Pequena was) left the British as naively ignorant as ever about where their attitude was taking them. It was beginning to take them a long way. On 5 May Bismarck hinted at this in two messages to London, in which German colonial claims and the question of the Congo were ominously linked. By another in this chain of muddles the messages were not delivered. Thereafter Bismarck swung the weight of Germany behind the Congo revisionists and then against the whole British position in West Africa. On 7 June he let the Foreign Office know that Germany refused to recognize the Anglo-Portugese Treaty and wanted a conference to settle the Congo question. Granville was too discouraged to press on with ratification, and that was the end of the Treaty. But the retreat did not stop there. On 4 August the Germans suggested to the French that they should cooperate over West African questions generally at the impending conference, and at the end of the month the French persuaded their new collaborators to join in an onslaught against the least expendable of the British spheres, the Niger.

It seems then that any attempt to analyze British policy in terms of some one decisive factor breaks down before the facts. There is nothing for it but to approach the problem from another direction. Instead of postulating a single, necessary and sufficient cause of these events, it is well to be less pretentious and to define them as the result of an interplay between nonrecurrent factors in the early eighteen-eighties. Government policy in West Africa seems to have evolved as a by-product of three major crises, one in Egypt, another in Europe, a third in the domestic politics of Great Britain, and a minor crisis on the west coast itself. The Egyptian affair had started off the "scramble." It had ended the standstill arrangement in Africa. It had run British policy into a noose held by Bismarck. When Germany's policy swung towards France, the two of them squeezed hard on the British position in West Africa. That position was already susceptible to change, as the bases of tribal societies and economies were eroded by the gradual commercial penetration of the interior. So long as other things stayed equal, Gladstone's cabinet thought it could cope with the results of this erosion by making only small adjustments in its traditional policy. But things did not stay equal, and the Egyptian aftermath shifted the European balance, blowing these calculations sky-high.

It would seem that the claiming of the Niger in 1884 was motivated neither by increased enthusiasm enlarging the empire nor by more pressing economic need to exploit the region. The incentive to advance here was no stronger than of old. It sprang from a passing concatenation of minor trade rivalries in West Africa with major changes of front by the Powers in Europe and the Mediterranean, mainly provoked by British blunders and difficulties in Egypt. The Liberals claimed the Lower Niger merely to prevent an existing field of British trade from disappearing behind French tariff walls; and they limited their new commitment to this negative purpose. They had not decided to found an ambitious West African empire. All they had done in the face of French hostility was to make a technical change in the international status of the Lower Niger. Henceforward the Powers recognized this country as a British sphere, but government still had no serious intention of administering, developing or extending it.

King Leopold, Savorgnan de Brazza, and the Beginning of the Scramble for Africa

JEAN STENGERS[3]

Was it Leopold II who began [the scramble for Africa]? One could so imagine when reading the first treaty signed by the agents of the expedition which he sent into Africa. In this treaty--which was published in 1884 by the American Senate to whom the King had sent it--the political idea was apparently the most important: the Vivi chiefs of the lower Congo ceded their rights of sovereignty over a part of their territory of the *Comité d'Etudes* [du Haut Congo], the organ which served as a screen for the King. This was June 13, 1880. If the text was authentic, the political initiative would be striking. Unfortunately, it is not. Leopold had sent the American Senate a falsified version. The real Vivi treaty of June 12, 1880, has been found, and it does not provide for any abandonment of sovereignty.

At its beginnings, Leopold's enterprise in Africa had no political nature. This does not mean that the King, from time to time, did not envision or contemplate political projects, but they never progressed beyond the stage of ephemeral plans. The central idea, the program, in every sense of the word, of Leopold was elsewhere. It consisted in the organization of the commercial exploitation of Central Africa. To establish trading stations, to get started a big commercial enterprise, this was Leopold's first objective.

It was not until 1882 that he was forced to change direction, to impress a new orientation upon his enterprise. It was necessary to face a danger, that is, Brazza. Was he not going to plant the French flag in the regions of the Congo where Leopold II wanted to penetrate, even as far as the stations where the *Comité d'Etudes* was already established? In order to stop Brazza, to prevent his annexations, the only method was to plant another flag before his, and one which would also be the emblem of a political power. Henceforth, Leopold sought for a way to acquire sovereignty: now began the march toward the formation of the Congo State.

But all this, which began in 1882, was only a counterweight to Brazza's policies,

---

[3]Stengers, Jean, "L'Impérialisme Colonial de la Fin du XIXe Siècle; Mythe ou Réalité," *The Journal of African History,* Vol. III, No. 3 (1962), pp. 47, 91. Translated by Nell Elizabeth Painter and Robert 0. Collins. Jean Stengers is a Professor of Contemporary History at the University of Brussels and a Member of the Belgian Royal Academy.

to the intentions reputed to be Brazza's. In our search for first initiatives, should we not turn directly toward France?

It is in France, in fact, that we think the two real initiatives of the "scramble" began. The first was the conclusion of the Brazza-Makoko treaty and, even more, its ratification in 1882. The second was the protectorate policy inaugurated in West Africa in January 1883. The first episode is well known, although France's reasons for installing herself in the Congo have never been sufficiently analyzed. The second, we believe, has never been brought into focus.

In 1882 Brazza returned to France. He brought what he himself called, and what everybody would soon be calling, his "treaty" with Makoko. It was, in fact, two documents in bizarre legal form—and which were certainly not the work of a specialist in international law—dated September–October 1880. The explorer declared in the first that he had obtained from King Makoko, reigning sovereign north of Stanley Pool, the "cession of his territory to France." Makoko had put his "mark" on this declaration. In the second, he declared that he had occupied, in the name of France, part of this territory situated on the edge of Stanley Pool itself (that is to say, what became Brazzaville). This "treaty," to use Brazza's expression, installed France in a small territory whose strategic and commercial importance was great, being situated on the doorstep of the navigable Congo, but which was isolated by hundreds of kilometers from both the coast and the existing French possessions.

The government, as we have seen, would propose approval of the Brazza-Makoko treaty to Parliament. This would be accepted unanimously in November 1882, by the Chamber. "The Chamber," commented the *Temps,* "high spirited and warm hearted, has put aside all dissension: it was truly French. . . . " In this enthusiasm, it is easy to distinguish the dominant major part played by national pride. It could be felt alive everywhere. A competition was opened in Africa between two rivals: Brazza and Stanley. France supported her champion and wanted his triumph. Stanley, who had returned to Europe in 1882, attacked Brazza and declared that the treaty with Makoko was worthless. One more reason for French public opinion to form a solid block around the man who wore its colors.

While making the cause of Brazza in the Congo triumphant and achieving this victory for France, it was possible to get even with England. It is here that we rediscover the question of Egypt—but from a point of view, it must be emphasized that Robinson and Gallagher [*Africa and the Victorians,* London: Macmillan, 1961] have not noticed. After the hurt, the humiliation that the occupation of Egypt caused it, French public opinion instinctively looked for a way to compensate for the British success. It needed a French success. The Congo offered itself at this point. For us it is, wrote a Parisian newspaper, "the best and the surest revenge to the frustrations that we have just suffered." Brazza, of course, did not fail to play on these sentiments. "A speaker who preceded me," he declared during a ceremony at the Sorbonne, "said that the English have left us behind everywhere. There is, however, one place where we have put our mark before them; that is the Congo [prolonged applause notes the report]. The French flag flies over this land and the Parliament has only to say the wòrd for it to be ours forever."

In the Congo the French policy had been more chauvinistic than calculating, dictated far more by patriotic exaltation than by considerations of economic matters. In West Africa—where the second French initiative took place in January 1883—the game was completely different. It was, without interference by public opinion and without public outcry, a game calculated to promote the interests of national commerce.

Commercial interests and territorial occupation had been linked on the West Coast more than once during the nineteenth century. These were always limited occupations—responding above all to local or regional preoccupations. The last of these local maneuvers carried out "to support national commerce" had been the reestablishment in 1882 of the French protectorate over Porto-Novo.[4]

In January 1883 the designs apparently were enlarged. Texts came from the ministry of the Marine and Colonies in Paris which, when brought together, defined a new policy, and which one would be tempted this time to call grand policy.

A protectorate on the coast from the Gold Coast to Dahomey, political treaties on the Benue, agreements with the chiefs in the eastern delta of the Niger, eventually protectorates at Bonny, Old Calabar, or in that region, treaties to the south of the Cameroon estuary: one recognizes that there is here, in the treaties of January 1883, a far-reaching political program.

The plans were grand, but the means actually employed were mediocre, and all in all, the policy defined in January 1883 produced only very minor results.

To the west of Dahomey action was reduced to really very little. It was put off essentially for fear of diplomatic complications. Farther to the east, in the Niger and the Cameroon, those who tried to execute the new policy with slender means hardly succeeded at all.

Thus, between the program conceived on paper in January 1883 and its realization in West Africa, there was a world of difference. The little that the French did was sufficient however—just as the approval of the Brazza-Makoko treaty had been sufficient in Central Africa to set off the "scramble." In fact, there is no doubt, once the English documents are taken in hand, that it was the French initiatives which, taken together and, in a way, regarded by the Foreign Office and the Colonial Office, were at the origin of the decision taken by the British government to act.

Already the Brazza-Makoko treaty had begun to cause worries for West Africa, as well as for the Congo, for a "coup" like that which Brazza had succeeded in pulling off might well be repeated elsewhere, and, for example, on the Niger. "The tactics of M. de Brazza may be imitated on the Niger, and that great highway into the interior of Africa be converted into a French river," wrote a British trader to the Foreign Office, where his words were listened to. Then came the news of the reestablishment of the French protectorate at Porto-Novo, which reinforced the alarm. Then came the announcement that a French warship was at Bonny and that

[4]The declaration reestablishing a French protectorate at Porto-Novo was signed in Paris in 1882 but not carried out in Africa until April 1883, Ed.

the officers of the ship were trying to obtain a treaty from the native chiefs. Under these conditions, it became "a question of the first importance to consider how British interests are to be protected." From June 1883, Percy Anderson, in the Foreign Office, makes the point. He brought together the different elements of the French activity and particularly emphasized the last:

> The Captain of the Voltigeur is trying to induce the natives of the mouths of the Niger to accept his treaties. If he succeeds in this, the final step will have been taken, and British trade will have no chance of existence except at the mercy of French officials

The conclusion, from that point onwards:

> Action seems to be forced on us. Only one course seems possible; that is, to take on ourselves the protection of the native states at the mouth of the Oil Rivers, and on the adjoining coast protectorates are unwelcome burdens, but in this case it is a question between British protectorates, which would be unwelcome, and French protectorates, which would be fatal.

Later news from the West Coast—the treaty concluded with Passall, the activities of Mattei—did nothing but further reinforce the reasoning so well defined by Percy Anderson. This reasoning resolved the British government to act. In a second region of Africa, the "scramble" began.

In analyzing the events of 1882-1883, we see the new face of imperialism emerge, which it acquired from that moment and which it kept to the end of the parcelling of the lands that were still free in the world. Three characteristics particularly emerge: the development of colonial chauvinism; the new type of occupations designed to safeguard economic interests as their end; finally, the role of public opinion. National pride, national *amour propre,* and chauvinism entered into colonial affairs with a force which they had never before had. In this case, Brazza appeared as a great instigator. His propaganda in 1882 used, without a doubt, numerous economic arguments; it indicated to France the direction of rich and fertile lands. But Brazza would never have been acclaimed if, in a moral sense, he had not waved the national flag. It was when he invoked the tricolor which he had planted in the heart of Africa that he had his audience in his hand, that he carried off the country. Even the economists who agreed with his views did so more as patriots than as economists. Leopold, a great admirer of Paul Leroy-Beaulieu,[5] sadly reported that "chauvinism seemed to have possessed" the eminent author of *Colonisation chez les peuples modernes* [The Colonialism of Modern Peoples]. Here we see the new aspect of colonial policy, it satisfied a need for grandeur which, in more than

---

[5]Pierre Paul Leroy-Beaulieu, French economist and writer. Ed.

one case, passed well above considerations of material interest. Yves Guyet in 1885, shocked by the mental habits of the traditional economist used to serene calculations in all matters, wrote of the psychological evolution of his colleagues, and particularly of their attitude vis-a-vis the British colonial empire:

> We are jealous of that vast domain, and we want to have one like it to oppose theirs at any price. We no longer count, we listen only to passion. We want annexations, of which we see only their size, without worrying about their quality.

In virtue of the opinion it has of itself a great country must spread overseas. And thus it proves to itself and shows to others its national vigor. "One believes," said the German chancellor in 1890, "that if we only had colonies, and bought an atlas and colored Africa blue, we would then be a great people." Not to act, not to expand, is to give to oneself the label of incapacity, the prelude of political decadence. Jules Ferry proclaimed in 1885:

> It is necessary that our country put itself in a position to do what the others are doing, and because colonial expansion is the most important means at this time used by all the European powers, it is necessary that we play our part. Otherwise what happened to other nations which played a great role three centuries ago and which now find themselves, no matter how great they once were, fallen to the level of third or fourth class powers, will happen to us.

The rank: it was their rank in the world—an absolutely new phenomenon whose appearance was vainly sought before this time—which the European countries would defend by mean's of overseas partitions. This was especially so in the partitioning of Africa. There, more than in Asia or Oceania, the process is definite and well defined; it was a continent that could be taken apart piece by piece. The success of each one was visibly measured on the map. "In this partitioning, declared the *Comité de l'Afrique francaise* [Committee on French Africa], "France has the right to the largest part." And in trying to realize this program, the majority of those who supported the work of the *Comité*—secondary school students, for example, or officers, which were found in such great numbers among the subscribers—evidently thought above all of the grandeur of their homeland. On the race which was begun, economic preoccupations of course were present, but they very often changed their character in comparison with those of the past. During the period which Jules Ferry very correctly called that of "modest annexations and of little actions, of bourgeois and parsimonious conquests," a well-planned annexation was sought more than once, in order to gain economic advantages or to improve the condition of national commerce. Those were the classic and traditional objectives. French commercial houses on the west coast pushed for annexations; they wanted to procure a privi-

leged position there. The British consul in the Gulf of Benin, Hewett, recommended the protectorate policy. In his eyes the best way to stimulate national commerce
would be to establish direct commercial relations with the hinterland. Calculations
of this kind had a positive character. But after 1882–1883 the fear of annexations by
others would be substituted for positive calculations. Conquest would be made in
the name of protection to defend an area considered endangered by the interventions
of another power because it was necessary to make good one's own commercial
interests there. The "tariffs" of others: that was what became, on the economic plain,
the major obsession which seized all minds.

Finally the third new element: the role of public opinion. In the autumn of 1882,
in the affair of Brazza and the Congo, observers were unanimous in agreeing that
such an unleashing of the press and public opinion had never before been touched
off by a colonial question. Thus began in colonial matters a series of movements of
public opinion at the end of the nineteenth and the beginning of the twentieth century. It is necessary to speak in the plural of movements and not of a movement, for
it was never a question of one emotion, such as we know in politics, that literally
take over and dominate imaginations in a lasting manner. It was by sporadic spurts
that colonial enthusiasm would flare up in one country after another separated by
periods of indifference which so upset the champions of the colonial cause.

To conclude, let us come back again to Egypt. Without the occupation of Egypt,
would things have happened as they did in Africa south of the Sahara? If the
Egyptian question had not inspired a desire and a need for revenge, would French
opinion have embraced Brazza's cause as it did? When it is a question of movements of collective emotion, the "what would have had happened if," we must recognize, is nearly always a futile question. There are always too many imponderables
in emotions which escape analysis.

But the "scramble" also had a basis in economic reasons, And here there is no
doubt possible: Egypt or no Egypt, economic factors would have in any case begun
the movement sooner or later.

The fundamental element that must be kept in mind is the following: from the
moment when the economic penetration of the dark continent was begun, the temp-
tation to reserve certain advantages for oneself in the regions penetrated was strong,
even irresistible. The march toward the interior became almost of necessity synonymous, in many cases, with the acquisition of economic privileges.

Remarkably, despite his forward entrance on the scene, Leopold II did not set off
the process. From 1882, in fact, by a political about face whose genius must be
acknowledged, he abandoned his designs on a privileged exploitation to make himself, to the contrary, the champion of free trade in Central Africa. In this way he
played the card which would lead to triumph. When some of the exclusive treaties
that Stanley and his collaborators had signed at the beginning were brought to light,
they evidently made the King uncomfortable, but he was able to overcome the bad
effect they produced by burying them under torrents of solemn promises to respect
free trade. And so the bomb was dismantled.

Whether by Leopold II in the first phase, whether by Goldie, whether by the French eyeing the Benue, Africa in the 1880s, or rather, the interior markets of Africa, were opened for commercial competition, which would have engendered the "scramble" in any case. And this would have been so had Egypt never existed.

The French Policy and the Scramble for Africa

C.W. NEWBURY AND A.S. KANYA-FOSTER[6]

What was the significance of these French moves [up the Senegal, in the Niger Delta, and on the Congo]? What were their motives and the reasons for their timing? One cannot answer these questions by concentrating exclusively upon the immediate origins of the scramble for territory which they provoked. The ratification of the De Brazza treaty, for example, was not a crucial turning point in French expansion as some have pictured it. De Brazza had no official powers to negotiate and the government was reluctant to accept the results of his unauthorized diplomacy. Jaureguiberry regraded the explorer as a foreign upstart in the employ of a private organization closely linked with King Leopold of the Belgians, and he tacitly opposed the submission of the treaty to Parliament. Even after its ratification, both he and the Quai d'Orsay warned their agents:

> The question of the Congo is not the only important one. The need to concentrate our efforts at other points, the necessity to bind together our colonial empire, and the complications which it can lead to will point out the prudent limits beyond which you cannot go in a country where thus far our interests are relatively weak

As is well known, the pressure of public opinion forced the government to act. But the success of the Congo lobby's propaganda campaign and the popular enthusiasm which it aroused did not reveal "the new face of imperialism." De Brazza's supporters had done just as well with their agitation over the trans-Sahara railway three years before, and the reasons for their success were the same in both instances. Parliament ratified the de Brazza treaty because it gave France a new route into the vast and wealthy lands of the West African interior. Rouvier's report to the Chamber had a strangely familiar ring:

---

[6]Newbury, C.W. and Kanya-Foster, A.S., "French Policy and the Origins of the Scramble for West Africa," *The Journal of African History,* Vol. X, No. 2, 1969, 170-75. A.S. Kanya Fostner is Professor of History and Associate Dean of the Faculty of Graduate Studies at York University, Toronto. Colin Newbury is University Lecturer in Commonwealth History at the University of Oxford and a Fellow of Linacre College.

This vast commercial enterprise, of which one can hardly catch a glimpse of the future and of which one does not know today the measure of its extent, will certainly develop to the profit of those who first penetrate these regions barely opening them to world commerce. More a neighbor of Africa than most other nations, more directly interested in the future of this continent by her possessions of Algeria, Senegal, Gabon, and by the numerous commercial outlets which it possesses on the west coast [of Africa], France will seriously fail to recognize her interests, most certainly, if she allows others to precede her in the movement which is sweeping the civilized world toward these still mysterious regions of yesterday.

Not even the phrasing had been changed since 1879.

The repercussions of the occupation of Egypt also had little significance for French expansion in West Africa. Certainly, the British occupation had a profound effect upon the general course of Anglo-French relations, and it may have facilitated the adoption of more overtly anti-British policies, just as public reaction to the occupation may have contributed to the success of de Brazza's publicity campaign. But Jaureguiberry's protectorate policy was designed to defend French interests in West Africa, not to drive the British out of Egypt. And Anglo-French hostility was no new phenomenon; fears of British expansion had plagued Jaureguiberry ever since he first came to office in 1879. Even the suddenness of the Minister's actions in January 1883 can be explained without reference to Egypt. There is strong circumstantial evidence that he and his advisers were forced by domestic considerations to activate their plans while they still had the opportunity. At the time, France was in the grip of a serious ministerial crisis over the proposed expulsion of the princes from the armed forces. Jaureguiberry was violently opposed to the measure, and when the Government asked for discretionary powers to deal with individual cases on 19 January, he must have known that his days in the cabinet were numbered. On that same day, his proposals for the occupation of Porto-Novo and the extension of a French protectorate along the Slave Coast were sent to the Quai d'Orsay. His orders to the South Atlantic Naval Division, issued without consulting the Foreign Ministry, were actually signed two days after his resignation and the day before he was finally replaced. Those who emphasize the commercial factor in French expansion have a much stronger case. The protection of coastal trade had been a prominent theme since the 1870s, and, after the failure to reach a comprehensive settlement, the pressures to assume territorial commitments in its defence became powerful indeed. But coastal trade was not the policy-makers' sole concern. Jaureguiberry himself was much more interested in the future commercial prospects of the interior. The extension of French influence along the Niger-Benue complex was the most important element in his protectorate programme. The Benue treaties were intended to give France "the route to Lake Chad and the rich borderlands of Adamawa and Bornu." The treaties with Bonny and Calabar were intended to give

French trade, "established on the Niger up to Egga, and also on the Benue where he dreamed to carry all our efforts now, an independent outlet to the sea." The gunboats operating from Bamako were intended to give France control over the Niger as far as Bussa. Jaureguiberry's protectorates were not simply an attempt to safeguard the coastal trading interest; they were also part of a two-pronged assault aimed at the creation of a vast territorial empire in the West African interior. Admittedly, this was a long-term and a rather vague objective; the minister himself never described the occupation of Bamako and his plans for the Lower Niger as two related elements in a fully developed policy of imperial expansion. But the simultaneous advance on both fronts was clearly more than pure coincidence. Soleillet had talked of such an empire in 1876, and the Colonial Department had noted his views. Rouvier's speeches had echoed the same theme after 1879. Twenty years before them, Faidherbe had drafted detailed plans for the empire's creation, and his were the blueprints which the Ministry of Marine was using.

Certainly, there had been a revolution in French African policy: but one cannot grasp its significance by studying the diplomacy of imperialism, because this revolution preceded the diplomatic phase of the partition. The French entry into the politics of the Lower Niger and the Congo was not the start but the continuation of a new policy. By then the fascination of Sudanese wealth, the fear if not the reality of foreign rivalry, and the triumph of protectionist sentiment had already whetted their appetites for African territory and rendered the old techniques of informal expansion obsolete. The crucial change in French policy was the transition from informal to formal empire; it took place not in 1882-3 but in 1879-80.

What brought this change about? Local crises in Africa cannot provide the complete answer. The breakdown of the traditional pattern of trade along the coast may have forced the French to intervene politically; but even here their objectives were not limited to the protection of existing trade from British competition. And in the western Sudan no growth of African opposition forced them to adopt the techniques of military conquest. Tokolor resistance did not provoke the capture of Murgula or the occupation of Bamako; the fall of Murgula and the loss of Bamako did not even provoke Tokolor resistance. The conquest of the western Sudan was not an involuntary response to the pressure of local African circumstance but a determined European bid for territory. Developments in French political life can provide only a partial explanation. The stabilization of the republic after the elections of 1877 and 1879 and the resignation of MacMahon, the return of France to the diplomatic stage at the Congress of Berlin, and the new spirit of self-confidence which these developments engendered should all be kept in mind. But they merely provided the backdrop to the process of policy-making. The nationalist and expansionist sentiments of French public opinion are more directly relevant. The popularity of the trans-Saharan railway was one of its most significant characteristics; the popularity of de Brazza was his most powerful weapon. Parliament was sympathetic to all the government's West African schemes. Twenty-five million Frs were spent on the Senegal railway before the Chambers finally called a halt, and even the government's sternest critics did not dare to criticize its political objectives or to question the value of its projected African empire. But the impact of public opinion was sporadic and selective, and opinion itself was unstable; the agitation in favor of the trans-Sahara railway and de Brazza was more than matched by the furore over the Tunisian campaign. Nor can sudden bursts of nationalist fervor account for the origins of the policies pursued after 1879. Public opinion may on the whole have supported African expansion; it did not initiate the process.

Pressure from private commercial interests also played its part. Bordeaux merchants, the most influential group in Senegal, had long coveted the trade of the western Sudan. In 1851 and 1854 they campaigned for the appointment of Faidherbe and petitioned the government to open up the river *escales.* In 1879 the firm of Maurel et Prom supported the railway scheme; in 1880 it set up shop at Medine; by 1883, it had two steamers plying between Saint-Louis and Hayes. Along the southern rivers, Verminck and his associates tirelessly demanded official protection and support, as did the C.F.A.E. in the Niger Delta. Governments did not remain deaf to their appeals. But ministers like Jaureguiberry were anything but traders' cats-paws. They made a clear distinction between the national and the private interest, and it was the former, not the latter, which they tried to serve. Nor were the traders empire builders to a man. They were divided on important issues such as fiscal control and administrative responsibility. Their operations were limited to the coast and the river *escales;* even the Bordeaux merchants on the Upper Senegal were more interested in the profits to be had from supplying the expeditionary forces and transporting material for the railway than in gum or gold. And those who saw their trade threatened by the increased competition which the railway would bring, actively opposed and obstructed the government's plans. In France, moreover, the most influential commercial pressure groups, the Bordeaux and Marseille chambers of commerce, lagged far behind the government in their appreciation of Africa's future commercial importance.

Indeed, it was the local Senegalese administration which often stated the commercial arguments most forcefully. Briere de L'isle was the most insistent in his demands for the revival of mercantilist principles in French African trade and the most effective in undermining the government's commitment to peace. Once the military advance began, the military themselves became the focus of local initiative. The agents of expansion exerted the pressures which most affected the policy-makers. But French expansion in Africa was more than a case of "a little local imperialism". Senegal alone could not secure the massive capital outlay on which the Niger plan depended. And the decision to introduce the military factor was taken in Paris; Jaureguiberry was the man who sent Desbordes to the Sudan.

Ultimately, the motives for French expansion are to be found within the policy-making framework itself, within the "official mind" of French imperialism. What transformed French policy after 1879 was a change in official thinking on the vital questions of cost and military effort. Freycinet and Jaureguiberry were the ones who broke with the tradition of limited government intervention in African affairs.

Alarmed by the imagined threat of foreign competition, they made the state the principal agent of African expansion. Convinced of Africa's legendary wealth, they invested public funds in its future profitability. Discarding the old notions of informal empire, they made political control the basis for economic development, and they set out to win their empire by military means. This last was the crucial decision, and for it, the Ministry of Marine, rather than the Ministry of Foreign Affairs, was the department primarily responsible. Within the Ministry a group of dedicated and energetic officials—Legros, Dislere and the head of the Upper Senegal Bureau, Lieutenant-Colonel Bordeaux—provided a strong supporting cast; but on the evidence available, Jaureguiberry himself seems to have acted the leading part.

French expansion in West Africa had its peculiarities. Its economic objectives were all-important, but these did not derive from any profound changes within the structure of the French economy or even from any serious assessment of Africa's economic potential. The policy-makers of the 1880s, like their predecessors of the 1820s and 1830s, fell victim to the myth of Sudanese wealth. Their calculations were no more solidly based than they had been half a century before. Jaureguiberry's estimate of a Sudanese market of 80,000,000 people was hardly the product of careful study, and Jaureguiberry was by no means unique. More intelligent men like Freycinet and more sophisticated economists like Rouvier talked blandly of markets three times the size. When policies are based on myths, they can be as fanciful as the objectives they seek to attain. But this does not make them any the less significant. The age of imperialism was not an Age of Reason, and French policies were nothing if not the product of their age.

Any interpretation of the partition must take this imperialist phenomenon into account. The policies of Freycinet and Jaureguiberry contained the very essence of late-nineteenth-century imperialism; they were the Gallic doctrine of tropical African estates enunciated fifteen years before Chamberlain came to office. And this difference in timing was vital. By 1895 the scramble for West Africa was virtually over; in 1880 it had yet to begin. Chamberlain's doctrine may have "inspired the beginnings of . . . modern administration" in Britain's African territories; its French counterpart inspired the actual process of expansion. The beginnings of British imperialism in West Africa may have been a consequence of the partition; the beginnings of French imperialism were its cause.

Germany's First Bid for
African Colonies
A.J.P. TAYLOR[7]

Thirty years of European concussions came to an end at the Congress of Berlin. In the ensuing period the European Powers shrank from European conflicts, and the problems which continued to divide them were, as the French said of Alsace, "reserved for the future." European rivalries were temporarily diverted to the less dangerous field of extra-European expansion and in the years between 1881 and 1912 the European powers extended their influence or their empires over Africa and large parts of Asia.

This imperialist expansion was of two kinds. The more important was the struggle for the heritage of decaying states, themselves very often the relics of earlier epochs of imperialism. The struggle over the succession of the Turkish Empire had gone on since the end of the seventeenth century; but what distinguished the Age of Imperialism was that more of these decadent states came into the market and that the process of absorption was rendered more and more difficult by the interference of some other European (and in one case of an Asiatic) power: Thus France was able to establish her control over Tunis, Annam, and Madagascar without serious difficulty; but she extended her influence over Morocco only after coming twice to the brink of war with Germany. Great Britain annexed the Boer republics (relics of an earlier Dutch empire) after a period of conflict with Germany and she asserted her predominance in Egypt after a period of conflict with France. It was owing to the rivalry of England and Russia that Persia and Afghanistan preserved their independence. Persia nearly lost it to Russia in the last years before 1914; and, thanks to the jealousy of all the powers, China preserved her independence except for the loss of a few ports in what proved to be an abortive partition in 1898. It is not necessary to speculate at length on the reasons for these imperialist activities: the objects of conflict were going concerns; their economic and political importance was known; and in many cases they adjoined possessions or strategic routes of European Powers (Morocco on the frontier of Algiers, Egypt and Persia on the route to India, the Boer republics on the frontier of Cape Colony, and so on). The rival powers were still primarily influenced by European considerations; and though the extra-European questions provoked crises, it was the old problem of the Balkans which produced the

---

[7]Taylor, A.J.P., *Germany's First Bid for Colonies* (Hamden, CT: Archon Books, 1967). pp. 1-7. A.J.P. Taylor, 1906-1990, was one of Britain's most influential and controversial historians.

War of 1914, with the even older problem of the Franco-German frontier as a contributory cause.

The predominance of European considerations is even greater in relation to the second form of European expansion in these thirty years—the occupation of hitherto ownerless territories, or rather of territories with no ruler substantial enough to be treated as an independent power. Under this head come most of Africa and the islands of the Pacific. The enormous areas of tropical Africa appear impressive on the map; but of most of them the plain truth is that they had remained so long ownerless because they were not worth owning. The principal exception was the basin of the Congo, which, curiously enough, slipped through the hands of the two traditional colonial powers, England and France, and was secured by a royal speculator, Leopold II of Belgium, masquerading as a philanthropic society. Portugal, with a shadowy traditional claim to all Africa, managed to retain one colony on the west coast, and one on the east. France, who created a great North African empire within a few years, had intelligible political reasons for doing so: the republican government wished to demonstrate by colonial expansion that France was still a great power despite the humiliations of 1870; part of the expansion was undertaken to protect the frontiers of the existing colony of Algiers; and much of the rest aimed at opening for France an overland route to the Sudan, where it was commonly believed it would be possible to divert the upper Nile and so make the English position in Egypt untenable. France regarded Egypt as part of the heritage of Napoleon, and, in endeavoring to oust the English, was seeking to recover what had once been hers.

England had two interests in Africa, which she meant to preserve a settlement of British colonists in South Africa, and a predominant influence in Egypt, which was both valuable in itself and a vital point on the route to India. The new English acquisitions were made in order to protect what England already possessed by cutting off the Nile from foreign interference, and the Boer republics, and neighbours of Cape Colony, from foreign help. It is true that these new possessions sometimes proved to have a value of their own, such as the diamond mines of Kimberley and the cotton plantations of the Sudan; but it was not for this that they had been undertaken.

In these years of "the scramble for Africa" there was suddenly added to the old colonial rivals, France and England, a power which had hitherto confined itself strictly to the European continent. The German colonial empire, or rather the formulation of the theoretical claims, was virtually the work of a single year: the Cameroons were established in July 1884, German South West Africa in August, New Guinea in December 1884, and German East Africa was begun in May 1885 (though its frontiers were not settled until 1890); Samoa was added in 1899; otherwise apart from some minor adjustments of the Cameroons frontier at the expense of France after the second Moroccan crisis (1911) the German colonial empire was complete. The success of Germany, as previously of Prussia, had been due to freedom from all concern in non-German questions: Prussia had been able to secure the support of Russia because of her indifference to the Near East, and of Italy, because of her indifference to the maintenance of the treaty settlement of Europe. It is therefore surprising that Germany should have deliberately pushed her way into the hornets nest of colonial conflicts. The explanation of this German outburst of colonial activity has usually been found in the rising enthusiasm for colonies, and it is true that there was in Germany a certain amount of colonial agitation. Imperial Germany was a "made" state, an artificial reproduction of French nationalism tinged with echoes from the Holy Roman Empire; the new Germany had political tradition, and had therefore to ape the political traditions of others. Many Germans demanded a colonial empire simply because other great powers had colonial empires, and their demand was reinforced by the current belief that the possession of colonies was in itself a profitable thing. Many writers, not only German, at this time failed to grasp the truth about the British empire—that it had come into being as the result of British commercial enterprise and industrial success; and they asserted the reverse, that the prosperity and wealth of Great Britain were due to the existence of her empire. The German campaign for colonies rested on the simple dogma: give Germany colonies and the Germans will then be as prosperous as the English.

It is difficult to believe that this primitive outlook was shared by the German governments particularly in the days of Bismarck. It has often been suggested that Bismarck was driven into a policy of colonial expansion against his will. Lord Salisbury, who was a member of the British Foreign Office in 1884, put forward this explanation in a defence of Bismarck written some twenty years later:

> Prince Bismarck was personally opposed to German colonisation. . . .
> He therefore encouraged us to make fresh annexations on the West
> Coast of Africa, to which we had been previously indisposed; hoping
> that the clamour for such annexations by Germany would subside.
> Suddenly he found that the movement was too strong for him, and that
> his only expedient, in order to avoid a crushing Parliamentary defeat,
> was to make friends with the party which urged the acquisition of
> Colonies. He went to Lord Ampthill [the British Ambassador], ex-
> plained his dilemma, said he should have to take up the Colonial policy
> vigorously and begged that we should give him our support.

To imagine that Bismarck was influenced by public opinion, or that he was swayed by fear of "a crushing parliamentary defeat" is to transfer to Germany the conceptions of constitutional government as practiced in England or France. The Imperial German government did not depend upon a parliamentary majority, and the German press was only slightly freer than the press in Russia. There are, of course, plenty of instances—the history of the Schleswig-Holstein affair is full of them—when Bismarck gave the signal for a popular campaign to compel him to do what he wanted to do, but there seems to be no other case in which Bismarck is supposed to have bowed to the force of public opinion. Nor is it conceivable that Bismarck was suddenly converted, after years of skepticism, to a belief in the value of colonies. He was contemptuous enough of those who were ready to disturb the quiet of Europe for the sake of the "sheep stealers" of the Balkans. But even Bismarck could not have found words of condemnation strong enough for a policy which provoked a quarrel with Great Britain for the sake of the "light soil" of South-West Africa or of the headhunters of New Guinea. Bismarck's colonial policy alone seems meaningless and irrational; but when to the relations of England and Germany are added those of Germany and France, and those of France and England, Bismarck's policy in 1884 and 1885 becomes as purposeful as at any other time in his career. Such an examination shows that Bismarck quarrelled with England in order to draw closer to France; and that the method of quarrel was the deliberately provocative claim to ownerless lands, in which the German government had hitherto shown no interest. These lands had a certain negative value to Great Britain, in that they adjoined existing British colonies or lay near British strategic routes; but their value was not such as to provoke the English government into a war. Moreover, they were of no concern to any other power, and claims to them would not cause any international complications, such as would have been occasioned by German demands in China or Persia. The German colonies were the accidental by-product of an abortive Franco-German entente.

It may be asked whether the later colonial disputes and discussions between England and Germany were similarly related to the European situation. It would be rash to attempt to discover in German policy after 1890 any such persistent and successful planning as in the days of Bismarck, particularly when to the gross incompetence of his successors were added the planless impulses of William II. Moreover, with the passing of time the German colonies did acquire a spurious ideological value; they became a white elephant, a sacred relic of Bismarck's era. He could contemplate passing on their useless burden to England, and even in 1890 the German government could surrender vast theoretical claims in East Africa in exchange for the really valuable island of Heligoland. Ten years later the value of colonies was taken as an axiom by the Germans, and from the failure of their colonial ventures they drew the moral not that colonies were a mistaken luxury, but that they ought to have more, and better, colonies. In the first decade of the twentieth century the Germans demanded "a place in the sun"; by this they meant someone else's place in the sun, their own having proved too hot.

Bismarck Changes his Mind
HENRY A. TURNER[8]

It is not difficult, however, to point out circumstantial evidence that casts considerable doubt on the validity of Taylor's reasoning. For example, just prior to Bismarck's move into the colonial world his utterances to his most trusted confidants contain strong indications that he was very skeptical about the prospects for reconciling France and Germany genuinely and permanently. The attempt to placate the French was, contrary to the impression conveyed by Taylor, nothing new, having been a basic component of Bismarck's policy at least since 1878. But even while pursuing this goal, Bismarck did not cease to doubt the possibility of quickly overcoming French resentment at Germany's possession of Alsace-Lorraine. It therefore seems questionable whether the Chancellor would have been willing to saddle his new German Reich with the sort of uncertain obligations and dangers that overseas possessions entailed, solely in order to pursue a goal he suspected was unattainable in the foreseeable future. As Taylor himself admits, if Bismarck had really been looking for a quarrel with Britain in order to test the possibility of a Franco-German entente, there was a simpler and less risky alternative to the seizure of overseas possessions; he could instead have sided with France against Britain in the dispute over Egypt. Taylor dismisses this alternative in characteristically apodictic fashion. It would not, he states, have served Bismarck's purpose, "which was to convince the French that he had a grievance of his own and therefore actually needed French help. A grievance had to be created, and Bismarck turned to the colonial topics, which he had hitherto despised." However, if Bismarck had actually been seeking a rapprochement with Paris he would certainly, as a master diplomat, have sought it initially at the lowest price. Before resorting to such extravagant means as an imperialist policy he surely would have at least tried playing the Egyptian card.

More important than these objections to Taylor's theses is the fact that, like all the other interpretations that attribute Bismarck's change of policy to ulterior motives, it fails to accord with the documentary record of the Chancellor's words and actions. Some of this documentary evidence is new, having come to light only after Taylor's book was written. But much was available in print even in 1938, in German monographs and in documents published by the Reich in the 1880s. As will be shown below, these sources indicate clearly that Bismarck was not primarily motivated by any of the ulterior motives imputed to him. They reveal instead that

[8]Turner, Henry A., Jr., "Bismarck's Imperial Venture: Anti-British in Origin?", in *Britain and Germany in Africa,* Roger Louis, Prosser Gifford, and Alison Smith eds. (New Haven: Yale University Press, 1967) pp. 49-53. Henry Turner is a Professor of German History at Yale University.

he simply changed his mind and decided there must be German overseas possessions. This is not to say that Bismarck suddenly became an ardent imperialist. From
all indications he was a very reluctant convert and retained a high degree of skepticism even while presiding over the founding of Germany's overseas empire. This
was obviously because he moved to reverse his policy not by the confident expec-
tation of gaining concrete advantages but rather by a mounting concern about the
possible adverse consequences of continued abstention. He acted, that is, only in
order to avert what he feared might be the damaging effects of not doing so.
Bismarck's apprehensions stemmed initially from his growing concern lest the failure to stake out a German claim in the colonial world might have grave economic consequences. This was by no means an immediate possibility. Although
Germany's commerce with Africa and Asia had been increasing rapidly since the
mid-1870s, it remained only a minuscule fraction of the country's total foreign
trade. But the non-European world was still the great unknown factor: there was
always the chance that the extravagant predictions of the colonial zealots would
eventually be borne out. As long as the principle of free trade prevailed in the colonial world, this possibility caused Bismarck no apprehension, for there was no
reason to assume that Germany would lack access to Africa and Asia if those continents should prove to be of great economic importance. What brought Bismarck
to reconsider his policy were the multiplying signs in the early 1880s that the era of
free trade, which he himself had dealt such a heavy blow in Europe by the adoption
of the protectionist German tariff of 1879, was also drawing to a close in the colonial world. Quite clearly, his attitude began to change under a barrage of reports to
the effect that the colonial powers were beginning to favor their own nationals by
means of differential tariffs and other discriminatory policies. The Chancellor's
doubts about the wisdom of continued opposition to German overseas possessions
were further heightened by the developments that foreshadowed the partition of
Africa; beginning with the well-publicized de Brazza-Stanley race to claim territory along the Congo in the early 1880s. As long as large parts of the non-European
world were free of colonial rule, German commerce could get access to the markets
and resources of Africa and Asia regardless of the discriminatory policies of the
imperialist powers. But if those powers were to carve up all of the non-European
world, German overseas merchants would be at their mercy. And without territorial possessions of her own overseas, Germany would be unable to obtain for her subjects the sort of economic privileges the colonial powers could gain for theirs
through reciprocity agreements. The indications are that Bismarck had these
eventualities in mind and that they contributed to his decision to break with his old
policy.

    Bismarck was also not immune to the Torschlusspanik that was to play such an
important role in the partition of the non-European world—he feared that the gate
was rapidly closing and that the last chance was at hand. A major factor in his turn
to imperialism was the thought that if he failed to authorize the hoisting of the
German flag, the flag of another European power would quickly go up. In

Germany's case at least, It is impossible to account for the new imperialism of the late nineteenth century without taking into account the dynamics of the highly competitive European state system. Finally, it should be said that here was undoubtedly a domestic political dimension to Bismarck's reversal of policy. He was, after all, primarily a man of politics who instinctively sought out the political significance of almost everything that came into his purview. Still, it would be a mistake to conclude, as have some, that he limited his assessment of the political ramifications of such a major policy decision to tactical, short-range considerations such as the impact on a single election campaign. He was without question aware in 1884 that the popular colonial issue would be a useful cudgel against the anti-imperialist Radical Party in the campaign for the Reichstag elections. However, the line of argument that would attribute the origins of his imperialist venture to his concern about those elections founders on the fact that he continued to enlarge Germany's overseas commitments even after the Radicals had been dealt a resounding setback at the polls. It is far more likely that long-range considerations played. a greater role in Bismarck's assessment of the domestic aspects of overseas questions than did the campaign of 1884. This was, it must be remembered, the mature Bismarck, who was seeking to stabilize the political system he had imposed on the German people and to convince them his government really served their interests. Moreover, the early 1880s was a period when, under the impact of a severe economic depression, Bismarck had committed his government to the task of restoring and furthering the material welfare of Germany. The possible effect that continued abstention from the colonial arena might have on the attitude toward the government of such an important component of society as the business community, particularly if Africa and Asia became as important economically as the imperialists had predicted, must therefore have given the Chancellor pause. There are also indications that he was very much concerned about the effects on his own place in German history. In remarks that have an unguarded, sincere ring, he later explained that in considering whether to take the plunge into colonial affairs he had to ask himself "whether after twenty, after thirty years, people will charge that fainthearted Chancellor back then with not having the courage to ensure for us a share of what later became such valuable property."

It was this complex of economic and political considerations that brought Bismarck to reconsider his position. Formerly, he had opposed overseas possessions for Germany on the grounds that they would be a twofold liability, externally because the country lacked a fleet adequate to defend them, and internally because the costs of administering them would "widen the parliamentary parade ground" by increasing the government's financial dependence on the Reichstag. In searching for solutions to the new developments described above, however, he began to relax his rigid attitude, gradually moving away from his old position. When he finally became convinced he had found an administrative formula that circumvented at least his domestic objections, he acted to commit Germany to the imperialist scramble.

Britain's Nilotic Imperative
RONALD ROBINSON AND JOHN GALLAGHER[9]

If the strategic reasons for staying in Cairo were strong, the internal Egyptian reasons against withdrawal were overwhelming. By 1889 Baring had convinced the Prime Minister that there could be no stability or security in Cairo without occupation. As the British Agent saw it, the internal crisis which had come to a head in 1882 was still unsolved. Revolution still simmered beneath the surface tranquillity of the occupation. The chances of setting up a reliable Egyptian regime and so returning to a supremacy wielded from outside, were smaller than ever.

By June 1889, Salisbury had come round entirely to Baring's point of view. The British Agent had stated his case in these words:

> The real reason why the evacuation policy is well nigh impossible of execution is based on the utter incapacity of the ruling classes in this country . . . [They] are almost exclusively foreigners. . . . Now, all this class are detested by the people, and they are more disliked now than they ever were before . . . if he [Riaz Pasha] were left to himself he would go far to produce a revolution in six months. . . . Really, the more you look at it, the more does the evacuation policy appear to me to be impossible under any conditions."

Baring warned the Prime Minister that even if the French agreed to give the British a right of reentry, a withdrawal now would lead to anarchy and disaster for British influence. Moreover he could see another and even worse danger in evacuation. Reopening the entire Egyptian question would shatter any chance of reconciliation between Britain and France and might well lead to War.

Having reached this conclusion by the middle of 1889, Salisbury soon drew others, momentous still for the future of Africa. Within the next six months he decided at Baring's prompting that if they were to hold Egypt, they could not afford to let any other European Power obtain a hold over any part of the Nile Valley. In so doing, he took what was perhaps the critical decision of African Partition. Henceforward almost everything in Africa north of the Zambesi River was to hinge upon it. The idea that the security of Egypt depended upon the defence of the Upper Nile was as old as the pyramids; and the government had been reminded of it often

---

[9]Robinson, Ronald, and Gallagher, John with Denny, Alice, *Africa and the Victorians: The Official Mind of Imperialism* (London: Macmillan, 1961), pp. 274, 281-89.

enough. Sir Samuel Baker, the well-known explorer and once the Khedive's governor in the Sudan, wrote about it in 1884 and 1888. He pointed at the danger that a hostile power could readily dam the Upper Nile, starve Egypt of water, and so destroy the country. This had been one of the objections of the forward party to abandoning the Sudan, and for the same reason Riaz Pasha had pressed upon Baring the need to win it back. The Nile is the life of Egypt. The Nile means the Soudan. If [any European Power] . . . took possession of the banks of the Nile it would be all over with Egypt. . . . The Government of His Highness the Khedive will never willingly consent, not without compulsion, to such an attack on its existence.

But the British Agent was not at this time persuaded. He had strongly advised Salisbury against reconquering the Sudan for the time being; and the Prime Minister had agreed.

So far they had good reason to be complacent about the Upper Nile and its headwaters in Uganda and Ethiopia. As long as no other power was in sight of seizing these regions, they could have little bearing on Egyptian security. The Dervishes who held the Sudan could not cut off the flow of the river on which the life and stability of Egypt depended, for they were not engineers. No European power had yet reached the point of sending menacing expeditions towards the Upper Nile, and it was still possible that Britain would leave Egypt soon.

But things were very different by 1889. The British were certainly intending to stay. Cairo was becoming more and more the pivot of their Mediterranean strategy. A foreign power astride the Upper Nile would be in a position either to levy blackmail or to lever them out of Egypt. It was the Italians, advancing from the Red Sea towards the eastern Sudan, who presented the first threat of this kind.

In May 1889, the Italian minister, Crispi, made the Treaty of Uccialli with Ethiopia—an agreement designed to give Rome great influence in the country of the Blue Nile. He also laid claim to Kassala which commanded the Atbara tributary of the Nile. With this town as a base the Italians might edge their way towards Khartoum at the confluence of the White and the Blue Nile. Crispi's vaulting African ambition and the challenge at Kassala goaded Salisbury to make up his mind about the Nile Valley as a whole.

How long he had meditated it before putting on paper the policy of closing the Valley of the Nile, who can say? But by August 1889, the Prime Minister was anxious enough about Kassala to ask Baring what he thought about it. The reply must have been emphatically against letting foreign powers into the Nile Valley, because on 15 November, "[the Prime Minister] concurred fully as to the inviolability of the valley of the Nile even in its affluents." The doctrine was already fully formed.

The reasons for adopting this policy are plainly disclosed in Baring's correspondence with Salisbury. If the Italians took Kassala, he wrote, "They would soon strike the valley of the Nile. . . . At Khartoum the establishment of a civilized Power in the Nile Valley would be a calamity to Egypt."

When Baker and others had put forward similar views in 1888, Baring went on, he had thought them "unnecessarily alarmist," . . . "The savage tribes who now rule in the Sudan do not possess the resources or the engineering skill to do any real harm to Egypt." But the Italian threat had now converted Baring:

> The case would be very different were a civilized European power established in the Nile Valley. . . . They could so reduce the water supply as to ruin the country. . . . Whatever power holds the Upper Nile Valley must, by the mere force of its geographical situation, dominate Egypt.

There was already enough discontent inside the country without inviting foreign powers to manufacture subversion by drought. But Baring the administrator still guided Baring the strategist. He did not want Salisbury to stop the Italian advance at the expense of a premature reconquest of the Sudan, for this would disorganize the Egyptian finances which the British Agent had been at such pains to set in order. He urged the Prime Minister to keep "a strictly defensive policy" for the time being; and to keep the Italians out of the Nile Valley by diplomacy.

Just as the Prime Minister in June had concurred in Baring's counsel to stay in Egypt, so after November he took up Baring's policy of defending the occupation of the Upper Nile.

"In respect to Kassala," Salisbury wrote in March 1890, "it gives the Power occupying it command over one of the main affluents of the Nile, and therefore a power of diverting a portion of the supply which is vital to Egypt." And he agreed to such measures as may be necessary for the purpose of protecting your Nile Valley against the dominion of any outside Power." It was, he declared, "essential to the safety of Egypt" that this should be done. The policy was comprehensive. At first it applied specifically to the Italians and Kassala. But Salisbury and Baring had plainly adopted it from November 1889 as a general principle; and the principle held good for all Powers and for all parts of the Nile Valley, indeed as far south as the headwaters of the river in the Uganda country.

Thus the safety of the Nile had now become a supreme consideration, and the policy was quickly put into effect. On 7 March, 1890, Salisbury warned the Italians off the Nile, and later Baring was sent to Rome to try and set safe limits to their advance. The new strategy also forced Salisbury and Baring to reconsider the defensive policy of the past six years in the Sudan. Baring gave three reasons for doing so: in the first place, Egypt's finances had now turned the corner; secondly, "the dervish movement has been going rapidly downhill"; and thirdly, diplomacy could not be relied upon for ever to ward off other powers. In the end, occupation alone could make certain of the Upper Nile. The Prime Minister agreed that sooner or later the Sudan would have to be reconquered. But like Baring, he preferred to wait— so long as diplomacy would suffice to keep foreign rivals away. Salisbury as usual was against giving the imperialists at the Horse Guards a free hand. More important, he took it for granted that an "imperialist" advance would jar upon the prejudices of the electorate at home:

They were so deeply impressed with the disasters of six years ago, Salisbury explained, and the apparently inexorable necessity which had driven them into situations where those disasters were inevitable, that they shrink instinctively from any proposal to advance into the Egyptian desert. I do not say that this is a sufficient argument to prevent such an advance, if there is a clear balance of undoubted advantage in its favor; but in the absence of any such evidence, it must be accepted as a strong presumption. As far as I can see matters, I should say that until you have money enough to justify you in advancing to Berber, you had better remain quiet.

For the time being, diplomacy must remain the chief defence of the security of Egypt in the Nile Basin. If he was not yet ready to reoccupy the region, he made it plain that he would oppose its occupation by any other power. Having already warned off the Italians, he quickly gave the French and the German ambassadors a similar message. The new strategy was now operating.

For all the worldly wisdom which prompted this strategy, it flowed less from hard-headed reckoning than from a change of heart. Behind it lay a sea change in the Victorian spirit and the official mind. A new age was struggling to be born. To the old men who sat at the head of affairs—as old men usually do—it seemed that imperialism was entering on its greatest epoch. But European expansion was already at odds with the new forces of colonial nationalism which it had goaded into life. The dynasts were beginning to lose their way in history. The shadows were falling over the times and themes they knew best. The end of the European age was in sight. Beset with problems for which their historiography offered no solutions, the old men in the chancelleries came more and more to combat their manifestations rather than to grapple with their causes.

In any event ministers began to fear that Providence and the laws of progress were no longer working on their side. Shocked by nationalist intransigence and Oriental fanaticisms, jostled by new rivals in Africa and new enemies in the Mediterranean, they were losing their nerve. Self-confidence had carried the English to the ends of the earth. Drop by drop it was dribbling out of them.

For the Victorians at mid-century the excellence of moral suasion and free partnership had seemed self-evident. But now this belief was being shrunk by fears of subversion and disloyalty. Too often the old aspirations to liberate and improve the world had been ungratefully accepted or surlily refused. Orientals and Africans had been shown the way. They had not followed it. Boers and Irishmen had been given equal rights with Englishmen. They had misused them. Step by step, the easy British optimism modulated into an injured resentment and a harsher outlook. Since the Irish bit the hand that fed them, they should undergo twenty years of resolute government. Since the Indians could not be assimilated, the Ilbert Bill and the Indian Councils Bill were Radical treachery to the Raj. Since the King of Burma was a bad risk, he should be deposed. Having failed to find willing partners by policy, the

Victorians condemned them to be involuntary subjects.

Hence they were driven into abandoning creative policy and replacing it by cold administration and control. Prestige became all important to them. So too did insurance. Policy grew more and more committed to the warding off of hypothetical dangers by the advancing of frontiers. When Salisbury put his Nile strategy into practice, the defensive psychology which kept watch over northern India had been transplanted into Africa. The frontiers of fear were on the move.

And so the Prime Minister at the end of the eighteen-eighties had decided upon an enlarged Egyptian policy. Not that there was any popular demand for it. It had emerged from the subjective calculations of national interest made by the small group which still decided such matters. To them supremacy in Egypt was becoming crucial, as the balance in Europe and the Mediterranean shifted. In Salisbury's mind, the pivot of the British position in the Mediterranean, and therefore in the world, was moving from Constantinople and the Straits to Cairo and the Canal, from southeastern Europe and Asia Minor to the Nile Valley and Northeast Africa. The Nile Valley strategy was something of an anomaly among the traditional concepts of the national interest handed down from Pitt, Canning, and Palmerston to Salisbury. He became the first Victorian statesman to discover a vital interest in the middle of tropical Africa, but if he was the first, he was not the last, to do so. The decisions of the winter of 1889 to 1890 set the priorities of British policy for the remainder of the Partition, and the Nile Valley headed the list. Salisbury stamped his new design upon tropical Africa, but it was a new design for an old purpose. Hitherto Britain had given way to her rivals in both East and West Africa, in order to protect Egypt. Henceforward, she could yield only on the west, for the Nile Valley and its approaches from the east coast were now considered vital to Egypt. The Mediterranean and Indian interest, like a driving wheel in some vast machine, was now engaging the lesser wheels of the eastern-central Africa and connecting them one by one to its own workings. At the turn of Salisbury's strategy, these once remote and petty interests in the Sudan, Uganda and the northern hinterlands of Zanzibar were changing into safeguards of Britain's world power.

French Policy on the Upper Nile

G.N. SANDERSON[10]

Except for a moment in June 1894, the Germans always kept their action, or inaction, on the Upper Nile subordinate to their general foreign policy. In France, on the other extreme, policy towards the Upper Nile often followed a completely autonomous course which was sometimes in direct opposition to the broader trends of French diplomacy. Indeed, by 1897 the Foreign and Colonial Ministries were pursuing two separate and irreconcilable policies. Something not dissimilar occurred in London during 1897-1898, when Salisbury and Chamberlain differed radically on policy towards France in West Africa. But not even "pushing Joe" ever dared to imitate the offhand arrogance with which the Pavillion de Flore sometimes ignored the directives—indeed, almost the very existence—of the Minister for Foreign Affairs.[11]

Between 1889 and 1892 Eugene Étienne [Under-Secretary for the Colonies] had striven to introduce some order into the chaos of French activity and stagnation on the mainland of Africa. His scale of priorities, on which the upper Ubangi and the Upper Nile ranked very low, was maintained by his successor Jamais. But Jamais quite failed to control either the soldiers in West Africa, or the forces which Étienne himself had released. When Delcasse took over in January 1893, the under secretary's control over expansionist activity was little more than a legal fiction. Mizon was levying private war in Adamawa, a region which London and Berlin regarded as their private bone of contention. In West Africa the *commandant superieur* Archinard passed on Declasse's instructions to his subordinate Combes—but with explicit orders not to obey them. On the upper Ubangi the younger men were going as far as they dared in opposition to the "politique de moindre effort" for so long enforced by Paris and by de Brazza. Even Liotard, normally the most loyal of subordinates, had caught the prevailing infection when he advanced on Bangasso in March 1893. In this situation Haussmann, the Directeur Politique at the Colonies, tended to regard his function as that of a brake on local excess of zeal. In 1893 he was not looking for new adventures, above all not on the Upper Nile, but rather to liquidate old ones, especially the potentially very dangerous Adamawa affair.

[10]Sanderson, G.N., *England, Europe and the Upper Nile, 1882-1899* (Edinburgh: Edinburgh University Press, 1965), pp. 386-92. G.N. Sanderson was formerly a Professor of History at Royal Holloway College in the University of London, and Professor of History in the University of Khartoum, Sudan.

[11]Pavilion de Flore was the location of the French Colonial Ministry and "pushing Joe" was Joseph Chamberlain, British Colonial Secretary. Ed.

To these hazards Delcasse seems to have been quite indifferent. He did indeed recall Mizon, but evidently with the†greatest reluctance. He did not get to grips with the *officiers soudanais* until in December 1893 heavy pressure from press and parliament forced him to appoint a civilian governor general, Albert Grodet, with the directive that "the period of conquest and territorial expansion must be considered as definitely over." Meanwhile, influenced by Victor Prompt's dangerous hydrological speculations and perhaps by the sudden enthusiasm of d'Arenberg and Harry Alis, Delcasse launched a drive for the Nile. Leopold had promoted this idea through his agent Harry Alis, hoping to enforce a diplomatic settlement on the upper Ubangi as an indispensable preliminary to the French expedition; but to Leopold's dismay Declasse proposed to challenge the Congolese by armed force as well as to "reopen the Egyptian question" by a threat to the Nile waters of Fashoda. Meanwhile, Declasse kept even his own *Direction* as far as possible in the dark. Develle, the Foreign Minister, was no wiser, though he was on record as approving at any rate a mission "towards" the Bahr al-Ghazal. However, Delcasse invoked the assistance of the President of the Republic himself to overcome Monteil's reluctance to undertake the mission; and Sadi Carnot, usually regarded as a model of constitutional rectitude, associated himself completely with a mere *sous-ministre's* private and unauthorized project to challenge the British occupation of Egypt.

The Monteil Mission of 1893 was not so much a policy as a conspiracy in the margin of policy. It was neatly frustrated when Leopold II, a conspirator beside whom Declasse was a beginner, inspired the probably unwitting Monteil to insist on a previous agreement with the Congo State as a *sine qua non* of his departure for Africa. Declasse could not dismiss out of hand the colonialist hero of the hour and a man who still enjoyed the powerful support of Etienne. The Mission therefore languished from August 1893, when Monteil delivered the ultimatum embodying his "conditions," until it was given its quietus by Casimir-Perier early in 1894. Casimir-Perier's suppression of the mission was certainly prompted by his desire to assert his own ministerial authority against Presidential encroachment; he was moreover prepared, from whatever motives, to go to almost any length to please King Leopold. At the beginning of 1894 there were however good objective reasons for putting a sharp curb on adventures in Africa. The British had protested again Mizon's proceedings in language which, if used in any but an African dispute, might have heralded an early ultimatum. In December 1893 there had been an accidental but bloody clash between British and French troops in the hinterland of Sierra Leone. In January 1894 a French column, sent to relieve a junior officer who had advanced to Timbuktu in direct contravention of orders, was ambushed and annihilated. *Le Matin* thundered: *"Les Romains, qui furent le module des conquérants dans l'antiquité, châtiaient sans pitié l'héroïsme indiscipline."*

The early months of 1894 were the high-water mark of "héroïsme indiscipliné." Thereafter the Colonies (since April 1894 a full Ministry) seems to have exerted a more effective control over its agents overseas. The details of this process are unknown. Boulanger, despised for his lack of expert knowledge, initiated an internal reorganization of his Ministry; and this may have had some effect. The appointment of Grodet certainly went far to spike the guns of the *officiers soudanais,* in spite of—or perhaps because of—Grodet's quarrelsome, unscrupulous and generally unpleasing personality. Haussmann's rather ineffective *immobilisme* began to be eclipsed by the influence of younger men, more in sympathy with the forward policy and perhaps for that very reason better able to control it. After his return to the Pavillon de Flore in June 1894, Delcasse no longer seems to have held his Direction at arm's length; he evidently worked closely with it in opposition to the proposed Phipps-Hanotaux settlement. In the second half of 1894 the Colonial Ministry launched a series of successful missions—Decoeur, Toutee, Ballot—through the Dahomey gap towards the middle Niger. These successes, and the *esprit de suite* of the whole operation, showed a professional touch which had been lacking in the planning of the Monteil Mission; and they extorted the rueful admiration of a fellow professional Sir Percy Anderson, "It is impossible not to be struck by the admirable way in which the numerous French expeditions are conducted by capable officers." In sharp contrast to these successes, the Liotard Mission to the Upper Nile, authorized by the French Cabinet in November 1894, made no progress worthy of the name. But compared with the West African expeditions the Liotard Mission was little more than a *façon de parler.* There was no independent mission under an experienced military explorer. Instead, the drive to the Nile was entrusted to a rather pedestrian administrator already overburdened by routine tasks for which his resources were barely adequate. Delcasse's apparent satisfaction with this rather halfhearted arrangement invites speculation; it is at least possible that his policy towards the Upper Nile was no longer so headstrong as in 1893.

Delcasse's successor Chautemps was a clearheaded administrator, who took the first and decisive step towards remedying the "situation anarchique" of conflicting and overlapping jurisdictions in French West Africa. The setbacks to Delcasse's forward policy in the Ivory Coast and elsewhere had raised an outcry in the Chambers; Chautemps insured against a similar danger on the Upper Nile by simply neglecting to reinforce Liotard. This quiet reversal of Cabinet policy may not have been to the taste of his *Direction;* but no one else objected—least of all Hanotaux, who had in November 1894 openly opposed the Liotard Mission. In September 1895, Marchand, presumably with support from the permanent officials, submitted his proposals to Chautemps. Administratively, the essence of Marchand's scheme was that the Upper Nile mission should be given an organization and status similar to those of the successful West Africa expeditions. This was a technically sound proposal which Chautemps was prepared to consider; but he was not prepared to act until the political implications of Marchand's plan had been explicitly approved by the Quai d'Orsay [the French Foreign Office]. In September 1895 the relations of France with Russia, and of Russia with Germany, were moving Hanotaux actively to seek a rapprochement with England, rather than to initiate action which could, as he well knew, lead only to a violent quarrel. But he seems to have lacked the nerve to kill the project outright. Instead, he hedged and procrastinated. Meanwhile, so long as Chautemps was in office, the Colonies took no further action, and the Marchand Mission remained a paper project. The mission was finally launched, after the fall of Chautemps and Hanotaux, by those who had doubtless supported it from the first—the permanent officials, notably Ernest Roume. Approval was obtained from Guieysse, the new and professionally inexperienced Colonial Minister, when he had been only a week in office. Berthelot, the new Foreign Minister, was if anything even less qualified for his position than Guieysse. Roume found an ally at the Quai d'Orsay, presumably Benoit, the high colonialist *Directeur des protectorats.* Pleading overwhelming urgency—a plea totally belied by their later action—these men rushed Berthelot into approving a project of which the full political implications had never been explained to him. This concealment was almost certainly deliberate; and the mission to the Upper Nile, in 1895 as in 1893, was promoted by methods which can only be described as conspiratorial. But this time the conspiracy was not merely in the margin of policy; it was a conspiracy directly opposed to Berthelot's policy of amicable settlement with England, if possible even in Egypt.

In 1896 the able and aggressive Gustave Binger became *Directeur des affaires d'Afrique* at the colonial Ministry. Given a tough-minded Minister who would underwrite their policies, the bureaux of the Pavilion de Flore could now disregard the directives of a mere nonpolitical Foreign Minister like Hanotaux. The *Colonies* found their tough-minded Minister in Andre Lebon; and Hanotaux' efforts to assert his control over this formidable combination were pathetically futile. He apparently watered down Marchand's instructions by omitting all mention of the White Nile and of Fashoda, in the attempt to convert the mission from "a pistol shot on the Nile" to a means of comparatively gentle pressure in the Bahr al-Ghazal. He certainly opposed the Colonial Ministry's foolhardy and irresponsible policy—supported, however, by his own *Direction*—of enlisting the military support of the Negus Menelik. But after he had been overruled in full Cabinet on Ethiopian policy in March 1897 he seems to have admitted defeat; and he took no traceable action when early in 1897 the Pavillon de Flore issued instructions quite incompatible not only with Hanotaux' own watered-down version but with the original objects of the Mission as approved by the Quai d'Orsay. While the *Colonies* did its best to set the Nile on fire, Hanotaux pursued an expectant and unprovocative policy in this sphere, presumably hoping that "Marchand n'arriverait pas"—at least, not on the Nile itself.

The Marchand Mission was the last and most spectacular manifestation of the "imperialism of prestige" which came to dominate French colonial expansion in the eighteen nineties. In this movement, economic motives played very little part; in the Marchand Mission itself, none at all. Marchand's own motives were those common to the *officiers soudanais* who conquered a subcontinent while Ministers protested and businessmen placed their investments elsewhere: a hunger for action and adventure, ennobled by the concept of *la plus grande France,* and in Marchand's particular case (which was certainly not unique) spiced by a hearty detestation for "greedy and hypocritical" England. Until 1893 the "imperialism of prestige" had been restrained rather than encouraged, at least in its more extravagant forms, by the Office tradition at the *Colonies;* Haussmann was utterly opposed to its extension to the Nile valley. Moreover Étienne, from motives which can at least in part be just-ly described as economic, saw French expansion in Africa largely as the creation of a "Greater Algeria." To this vision the Upper Nile was quite irrelevant. But from 1894 the control of policy fell increasingly into the hands of permanent officials who were, in Monson's words, "extremely combative" towards England. To these men, always ready to assert the prestige of France by "inventing and intensifying" difficulties with England, the Nile project was very relevant indeed; for its funda-mental object was to restore French prestige in the theater where national pride had received its most grievous wound since 1871.

Precisely because the British occupation of Egypt was so widely felt as an intol-erable affront to national self-respect, the Nile project enjoyed support far outside the ranks of convinced colonialists once its connection with Egypt had been clearly established. In June 1894, at the close of the debate in which Etienne established this connection, the Chamber voted unanimously in favor of what at least appeared to be a policy of active reprisal against the Anglo-Congolese Agreement. In December 1896, when a Deputy queried the inflated upper Ubangi budget which, as almost everyone knew, concealed the credits of the Marchand Mission, even the Socialist Jean Jaures demanded *un vote nationale;* and obtained one, by an enor-mous majority. It is hardly relevant to discuss the influence of the Parliamentary Colonial Group in this connection. The Chamber needed no convincing; all that the Colonialists had to do was to make the keynote speeches and to provide any neces-sary detailed information. In 1882 the French Chamber had shrunk from the large-ly imaginary hazards of joint intervention in Egypt. In 1885 it had destroyed Jules Ferry because he had become involved in petty hostilities, for the moment unsuc-cessful, with China. But in 1894 and 1896 the Chamber gave its overwhelming approval to a policy carrying risks beside which those of 1882 and 1885 were neg-ligible. Behind this policy there was little rational calculation. It rested rather on a quite irrational conviction that a successful expedition to the Upper Nile *must* somehow lead to a favorable solution of the Egyptian question; and on the further assumption, less irrational but almost willfully erroneous, that economic interests would always keep England from making the Nile a *casus belli.* These views were not confined to an ill-informed public and parliament. Astonishingly, they were shared by French diplomatists and by the professional experts not merely in the Colonial Ministry, but in the Foreign Ministry. Even had Hanotaux' position been stronger than it was, it is doubtful whether, after his return to office in 1896, he could have halted the Marchand Mission against the combined pressure of the per-manent officials and of public opinion. Beneath the surface of events, however, the "imperialism of prestige" was losing ground to the economic imperialism of the *Union Coloniale Française.* The businessmen who formed this organization relaxed their hostility to further expansion to the extent of regarding Morocco as an indispensable acquisition; but they never had the slightest sympathy for an imperialism of prestige in the Nile valley. They well knew that in Egypt Cromer safeguarded their investments better than any conceivable alternative regime was likely to do; better, indeed, than they were safeguarded by the *fonctionnaires* in some French possessions. As for the Sudan, profits here were obviously a chimaera. In the shock and disillusion which followed Fashoda, the interests embodied in the *Union Coloniale* were able to use the influence which they had been quietly accumulating during the previous five years. If the Marchand Mission was the last grandiose fling of the old imperialism of prestige, its denouement in 1898-1899 was the first victory for an imperial policy based on more material calculations. It was at a meeting sponsored by the *Union Coloniale* that Eugene Étienne read the obituary of the imperialism of prestige; Marchand had known what he was about when he so bitterly denounced *"les coloniaux d'exploitation rationnelle."*

French policy towards the Upper Nile was certainly the outcome of a conflict of interests; indeed of a multiple conflict which even included personal interests, not always of a reputable kind, but once the Upper Nile had been publicly linked to Egypt in 1894, French intervention was sustained by a wider enthusiasm which rose to a climax in 1897 and 1898, only to collapse thereafter with a surprising rapidity. In England, too, similar conflicts played their part in the determination of policy; but here too there was a wider enthusiasm for intervention and ultimately for acquisition. Until the end of 1894 this wider enthusiasm scarcely existed so far as the Sudan was concerned; but in 1898 and 1899 it reached a peak from which it did not decline until it had undergone the chastening experience of the South African War. By 1898 it had endowed with strongly acquisitive overtones a Sudan policy which had in the later eighteen-eighties been gradually and rather reluctantly initiated as a purely defensive strategy to protect the Nile waters and so to safeguard the British position in Egypt.

The Meaning of Fashoda

RONALD ROBINSON AND JOHN GALLAGHER[12]

At first sight there is a certain absurdity about the struggle for Fashoda. The massive advance of Kitchener's army took two and a half years, and it ended by browbeating a few men marooned by the side of the Nile. There was a strange disproportion between ends and means, as there was in building two railways from points two thousand miles apart to run into the deserts of the Upper Nile. A still deeper absurdity seems to lie in the French speculation about damming the river and in the labors of the British to stop them. Even Marchand himself came to see that the scheme was harebrained, for it turned out that there was no stone within miles of Fashoda. To this extent, the great rivalry for the Upper Nile was based on a myth. The greatest absurdity of all might seem to be that for two months two great Powers stood at the brink of war for the ownership of the *sudd* and desert of the Upper Nile.

It is true that after 1895 there was an irrational fringe to the British attitude towards the Nile. It is no less true that this attitude commanded the assent of British opinion during the dramatic climax of the struggle. Nearly all the English newspapers stood firm behind the government during the crisis, and their tone was considerably more strident than that of the French press. The abstract analysis of editorials is not worth much as an evaluation of public opinion, but there is no doubt that there was plenty of warlike spirit in the country. Even the British and Foreign Arbitration Association let it be known that while they remained devoted to their doctrine they did not think that it should be applied to Fashoda.

The aggressive mood of 1898 has often been regarded as an example of the hysterical passion for aggrandizement which is supposed to have swept through Britain at the end of the century. This "new imperialism" is said to have been produced by the spread of literacy, the coming of the mass vote and the rise of the yellow press. This may be so, or it may not. At the end of the century there may have been a new imperial spirit rising in some sections of English society. Perhaps the new voters and the new readers may have applauded a policy of swagger and bluster towards the foreigner. The newly fashionable theories of Social Darwinism may have introduced a racial arrogance towards lesser breeds without the law. More people by this time may have come to believe that Africa could be made into another India.

All this may have been true; but it is not to say that new public pressures drove the government down the road to Fashoda, or that popular demand in September

---
[12]Robinson, Ronald and Gallagher, John with Denny, Alice, *Africa and the Victorians: The Official Mind of Imperialism* (London: Macmillan, 1961), pp. 376-78.

1898 compelled government to do what it would otherwise not have done. During the Fashoda crisis the leaders of both parties came out openly in favor of the Nile Valley strategy. In a speech on 12 October, Rosebery warned the French not to make a mistake" . . . which can only lead to a disastrous conflagration"; the next day Asquith spoke in the same sense; on 28 October, Harcourt spoke of the need for national unity; while Campbell-Bannerman said on 24 November that ". . . we ranged ourselves as one man in determining to resist the aggression." This chorus of patriotic union was joined by the Liberal and Radical press. Among the politicians only Morley, among the newspapers only the *Manchester Guardian* stood out against this general line of approval and support for the British government. At the time of Fashoda opinion in the country was being exhorted by two political parties both saying the same thing and both casting it in stereotypes of the national honor and the civilizing mission. It may well be true, as Chamberlain asserted, that British policy was strengthened by ". . . the spectacle of a united nation," but it does not follow that the policy was determined by that spectacle. To assert that it was, is to study the situation of 1898 from the standpoint of other centuries and, it may be, from the standpoint of other countries.

The Fashoda crisis was not the outcome of a ferocious popular will then, although it evoked signs of one. It was the logical conclusion of a strategy followed by the Foreign Office for a decade. Of the calculations and interests involved in this, the public knew very little. The leaders of both parties understood the strategy, and most of them approved of it; but time after time they refrained from any public explanation of the vital issues it involved, lest this should hinder British diplomacy abroad and provoke the intervention of the ignorant at home. Foreign policy was a matter of an elite, and they conducted it according to their own view of national interest and world policy. The British electorate found that their country now enjoyed a condominium over the Sudan, whether they liked it or not. However it may have appeared to the man in the street, to the initiated few, Fashoda was simply the climax to an old policy of imperial defence.

In the eyes of the real makers of policy, there was obviously a scramble in Africa; but it was hardly for Africa or for empire for empire's sake. Throughout the partition their overriding concern was to claim those regions of the continent which seemed vital for security in the Mediterranean and therefore in the world.

Africa and the Victorians:
The Method and the Argument
A.G. HOPKINS[13]

Academic discussion of the occupation of Egypt and of the partition of Africa as a whole has been dominated for the past twenty-five years by one study: *Africa and the Victorians.* If the early literature on this subject has suffered an unjustified neglect, Robinson and Gallagher's celebrated work has experienced a degree of well-merited publicity which might be thought to render any further exposition predictable and therefore redundant. However, the appearance of a second edition of *Africa and the Victorians,* containing some important reflections and restatements by Professor Robinson, provides historians of imperialism with an opportunity to reassess the accounts they have offered of the aims of the book, and also to review the interpretation in the light of recent research. A brief statement of the argument is nevertheless a task which remains poised between the difficult and the impossible. This is partly because the book is so substantial and well-documented, but mainly because it contains such cascades of ideas and richness of language that summaries may become distorted by failing to be as sensitive to the nuances of the problem as were the authors themselves. Any return to the text should keep this warning in mind.

In the most general terms, Robinson and Gallagher reached the conclusion that the official mind "gave much less weight to economic interests and much more to strategic factors in Africa" than they had assumed when they began their research, and similarly "more weight to local crises in Africa and less to the power of British expansion." An examination of motives showed that the "Victorians were intent on anything but building another empire in Africa." In no region, apart from the southern, did their interventions accompany, much less represent, a heightened imperial ambition in their domestic politics or a new colonizing thrust in their economy. Of the local crises, none was more important than that which arose in Egypt:

> From start to finish the partition of tropical Africa was driven by the persistent crisis in Egypt. When the British entered Egypt on their own, the Scramble began; and as long as they stayed in Cairo, it continued until there was no more Africa to divide.

[13]Hopkins, A.G., "The Victorians and Africa: A Reconsideration of the Occupation of Egypt, 1882" in *The Journal of African History,* v.27, no. 2, 1986, pp. 360-91. A.G. Hopkins is a Professor at the Graduate Institute of International Studies, Geneva.

The implications of "Gladstone's bondage in Egypt" extended far beyond the fla-
gellation of his liberal conscience. "The repercussions south of the Sahara' were
immense: they compelled Britain to make a stand in East Africa to provide additional security in the Indian Ocean for the routes to the East, and they forced her
to allow France compensation in West Africa for the rebuff she had suffered in
Egypt. . . .

It is now apparent that the much emphasized military protest of February 1879
involved only 300-600 officers whose aim was not to establish a revolutionary government but to secure their arrears of pay. Far from being a threat to order, the
demonstration was both encouraged by the khedive and resolved by him as a means
of convincing foreign interests that his power, and not merely his presence, was
indispensable to the maintenance of political stability. It was this challenge to
European influence in Egypt which led to Ismail's deposition in June of that year.
The army demonstration which took place in February 1881 was essentially a dispute between Turco-Circassian and Egyptian officers over a limited programme of
reform; it was remarkable mainly for the lack of bloodshed and the moderation of
the settlement which followed. The more important demonstration in September, far
from establishing a new military dictatorship bent on revolution, installed some
familiar conservatives in a constitutional Chamber of Delegates, which was pledged
to pursue modest internal reforms and to fulfil Egypt's international obligations,
including servicing the national debt. Indeed, the new regime achieved a rare political feat: it was both popular and stable. Even when Urabi emerged as the leading
figure in Egyptian politics in February 1882, his actions were consistent with his
pronouncements that he was loyal to the khedive and to the sultan, and that he
intended neither to eliminate European influences nor to renege on the interest payments due on Egypt's debts. Furthermore, "law and order" were maintained until
June, when rioting occurred in Alexandria. It was this event, supposedly exhibiting
the full range of atrocities known to man and masterminded by Urabi, the treacher-
ous revolutionary, which finally convinced the Liberal government that intervention
was necessary. But this account, too, has now been substantially revised: the riots
were less serious than has long been supposed, and they were probably spontaneous.
If there was premeditation, the prime suspect has to be Tewfiq, Britain's pliable
puppet, who had an interest in discrediting Urabi in order to bolster his own position. Urabi himself heard of the disturbances late in the day, and moved quickly to
quell them.

It is perhaps worth reemphasizing that the purpose of citing these examples is not
to diminish their very considerable significance in the history of Anglo-Egyptian
relations, but to demonstrate that they cannot be used for the specific intention of
showing that Egypt was sliding into anarchy. At the same time, it has to be acknowledged that false perceptions can be as important as spurs to action as accurate ones,
and it is undoubtedly true that some misunderstanding, compounded by a degree of
ignorance, entered the official mind when it came to focus on Egyptian affairs.
However, the notion that Egypt was in the grip of revolutionary disorder cannot be

explained as an unfortunate misreading of the political situation. The reporting was deliberately, as well as persistently, partisan. This happened because the Europeans faced a dilemma which in the end could be resolved only by intervention. They wanted a government which was both stable and cooperative. A stable government was one with a solid domestic power base; but the stronger its local support the greater its ability to resist or qualify external demands. The more pliable the regime, the weaker its domestic power base; the government would obey orders but could not implement them without arousing opposition. Hence a paradox emerged: strong governments were reported for noncompliance, which was equated with the erosion of orderly rule; pliable governments were given warm approval but ultimately could not sustain the stability they were said to represent. The local agents of European governments and business interests became particularly alarmed after September 1881 because the new (and stable) government included in its reform programme policies which aimed at eliminating waste by removing the excessive number of highly paid European officials and by curbing the activities of foreign adventurers. Since disorder was defined as allowing Egyptians a greater say in running their own country, it was not surprising that scare stories multiplied in number and intensity. It was not anarchy that drew the Europeans into Egypt, but the European presence which made the formula for maintaining stability increasingly complex and represented opposition as anarchy. . . .

Britain, like France, had long-standing and extensive commitments in Egypt. But, whereas French connections covered a wide span of interests, Britain's were more narrowly focused on the economy. English did not become, as French did, the second language of the country, and political sympathy for "nationalist" aspirations was diluted by Britain's need to maintain the integrity of the Ottoman empire as a barrier to Russian expansion. Moreover, Britain's economic interests commanded particular importance by virtue of their size. A detailed account of Anglo-Egyptian economic relations in the nineteenth century can be bypassed here because it is readily accessible in Owen's authoritative studies. It is sufficient to note that Egypt's external trade increased substantially from the 1840s and so too did Britain's share of it. In 1880 Britain took 80 percent of Egypt's exports and supplied 44 percent of her imports; and a notable feature of the composition of trade was the shipment of raw cotton and the sale of Manchester cotton goods. Commercial expansion was accompanied by railway and harbor construction, and by the installation of industrial machinery—all of which gave employment to British manufacturers and personnel. Export development was financed largely by external borrowing, and in this activity, too, British investors were dominant. The volume and distribution of overseas investment are subjects which have to be approached with caution. Very little is known about private investment except that it was substantial and substantially British. More than half the public debt was owed to British creditors in 1873, before the rash of short-term loans raised the proportion held by French investors; even so, the funded debt remained largely in British hands. After the successful consolidation of 1880, Egypt's total external indebtedness stood at nearly

£100 million; and the proportion held by British investors increased further as the French disposed of their unified bonds.

The fact that Britain had a sizable economic stake in Egypt does not imply an automatic connection between investment and action. Iron laws, like conspiracies, are appealing theories of history but they ought to be treated with as much skepticism as their rivals, which place excessive reliance on chance and coincidence. Professor Platt has shown that the British government, unlike the French, was anxious to avoid giving public guarantees to private investors, and the notion of Lord Salisbury cowering before a Victorian Shylock is not merely fanciful but bizarre. To accept these objections, however, is not to deny the possibility that economic considerations played a part, perhaps even a crucial part, in Britain's decision to invade Egypt. Lord Salisbury, like other ministers of the time, did not need to be blackmailed into recognizing the importance of Britain's overseas trade to her balance of payments or of her credit to her credibility. Research by Cassis on the City of London has shown just how close the personal and financial connections were between those who formulated international policy and those who financed it; and Johns has revealed the part played by these ties in helping to decide the fate of Egypt. These intimacies formed, not a conspiracy of the unworthy, but a charmed circle of the great and the good. They were overt not covert, and they effected a harmonious union between personal and national interests.

Evidence now available makes it clear that the Conservatives adopted a much more positive and unyielding stance towards the Egyptian question during their period of office (1874-80) than Robinson and Gallagher allowed. The government acquired a direct investment interest in Egypt as a result of Disraeli's purchase of the khedive's Suez Canal Company shares in 1875, and also recognized its obligation, as guarantor of loans made to the Ottoman empire in the 1850s, to ensure that Egypt's contribution towards servicing these debts was met. The sizable problems of private investors whose fortunes were tied to Egypt's national debt, and the wider impact of default on commercial and manufacturing interests in Britain, were also acknowledged and dealt with. This did not mean that ministers fell over themselves to provide bondholders with a Treasury guarantee, thus raising taxes and committing electoral suicide. But it did mean that the Conservatives were resolved to make Egypt pay its debts. And, in taking this step, the line between official neutrality and unofficial assistance became so blurred that very soon it existed only as a formality. . . . However, the evidence collated in this essay has indicated that intervention did not spring from any danger to the Canal, from the spread of anarchy, or from French ambitions, but from the conscious and sustained defence of Britain's expanding economic interests in Egypt. The official version is what was said, but it is not necessarily either the truth or the whole truth. And if the witnesses break down under cross-examination, then it also follows that the causes of actions cannot be deduced from the reasons given for them in *Africa and the Victorians*.

How, then, can the reasons cited in this essay be related to a causal explanation of the decision to occupy Egypt? In answering this question economic impulses emanating from the metropole can be emphasized without embracing either a narrow formulation of the "bondholder thesis" or a broader stereotype of the "triumph of industry." The presence of British industry was indeed felt in Egypt, most obviously through the connection with Manchester's cotton manufacturers. But Egypt also experienced the impact of an even more dynamic part of the British economy in the second half of the nineteenth century: the financial and service sector. The importance of this sector increased as its contribution to employment, purchasing power, and the balance of payments grew. There was a massive expansion in overseas lending after 1850, and a new generation of investors, magnates and middle class, were tempted into placing savings abroad by returns to be had from countries which they (and sometimes their advisers) knew little about. Egypt experienced the full weight of these forces after 1838, when the Ottoman empire was pried open and a free-trade regime established. Thereafter, foreign investment grew rapidly and foreign personnel, staffing the service sector in private and public employment, increased in number. In 1876, when the khedive was unable to meet his debt repayments, Egypt experienced a crisis which was a direct external manifestation of the particular course taken by the development of the British economy during the previous half century.

No conspiracy of bondholders is needed to account for the political expression of these economic interests. Ties between City and parliament were undoubtedly close: they spanned business and politics; they were tightened by friendships; and they were sometimes sealed by marriage. In these ways the City's voice was heard and heeded, though it was only one, albeit important, influence on policy-making. But every politician of standing was well aware that Britain played a vital and expanding role in theinternational economy; safeguarding her position was a matter of technique rather than of principle. Defence costs had to be held down and diplomatic disasters avoided; beyond that the tactics employed depended very largely upon party, personality, and the particularities of the case.

It remains, finally, to indicate the relationship between the argument advanced here and Robinson and Gallagher's claim that Britain sought to extricate herself from her Egyptian embarrassment, and that her failure to do so was, in diverse ways, the driving force behind the partition of tropical Africa.

According to one estimate, Britain made no less than sixty-six official declarations of intent to withdraw from Egypt during the period 1882-1922. There is no need to question the sincerity of these declarations, but the fact is that Britain did remain in Egypt, and some reason for her continued presence has to be found before "force of circumstances," the argument of last resort, is invoked. The explanation surely lies in the causes of intervention adduced earlier in this essay: Britain had important interests to defend in Egypt and she was prepared to withdraw only if conditions guaranteeing the security of those interests were met—and they never were. Despite doubts and anxieties, the Liberal government maintained Britain's presence in Egypt, not merely because it could not find its way from Cairo to Alexandria, or even because it became embroiled, as an Egyptian power, with sizable provincial problems in the Sudan, but because those members of the government who had pushed Gladstone into Egypt were not going to let him out until their aims had been achieved.

It is still possible, nevertheless, that Britain's continued presence in Egypt had the effect, claimed by Robinson and Gallagher of hastening the partition of tropical Africa. But this contention, too, is one that finds little support from the evidence now available.

The first part of the argument suggests that the French advance in sub-Saharan Africa was largely a response to Britain's decision to occupy Egypt. The difficulty here is that French plans for moving into West Africa were formulated in 1879, three years before the occupation of Egypt, and therefore cannot have been prompted by it. In fact, the French congratulated the British on the action they took in 1882 because it appeared to safeguard rather than to imperil French business and personnel. At that time France was heavily engaged in Tunisia, Algeria, and Indochina, and used Britain's action in Egypt to assist her there rather than in sub-Saharan Africa. It was not until 1885 that the French felt free to turn their attention to Egypt. But at that point they met an immovable object in the form of Lord Salisbury, and the pressure they were able to exert was limited by the fact that French interests had prospered under British rule. After 1882, French investors wanted to put their money into Egypt not to take it out and French cultural influences continued their successful advance. The challenge at Fashoda in 1898 was a desperate attempt to regain what was already lost. It was a wild undertaking which, though momentarily a popular success had little support in influential official and business circles.

The second part of the argument holds that, having occupied Egypt to defend the routes to India, Britain had then to extend her control over East Africa to complete her strategic purpose. Britain preferred to secure the East coast for reasons of defence than to secure the West coast for reasons of commerce. But this argument is no more easily sustained for East Africa than it is for West Africa. A reassessment of the Foreign Office memoranda on which Robinson and Gallagher rest so much of this part of their case shows that East Africa's strategic importance was considered not in relation to the Canal but in relation to the Cape, a finding which confirms Dr. Farnie's judgement cited earlier. Furthermore, the Foreign Office and sundry business interests regarded East Africa primarily as a land of economic opportunity; hence their emphasis on the interior, and not merely on the coast, on the potential for white settlement, and on the wealth which might be generated more readily there than West Africa, where disappointments were more familiar. Egypt played little part in these calculations.

This conclusion does nothing to diminish the importance of the occupation of Egypt in the history of modern imperialism. The significance of Admiral Seymour's action is not that his guns signalled the start of the partition of Africa, but that his fleet was anchored to a long chain of causation which stretched back to Britain and to specific changes in metropolitan economy and society which gathered speed in the second half of the nineteenth century. Seen from this perspective, Egypt's place in the study of imperialism is greatly enhanced: it can be linked, not to sub-Saharan Africa, but to other parts of the world—from the Mediterranean to Latin America—which experienced similar impulses and similar crises in the 1870s; and it stands out even more clearly as an example of the conditions which led minor nations with major debts to lose their independence by failing tests of credit worthiness set by external examiners. Finally, because contemporaries perceived these issues with a clarity that modern scholarship has sometimes obscured, the occupation of Egypt merits a larger place in theories of imperialism than it has been granted. It is in these ways that "spheres of interference" might be better understood; and the challenge, thrown down by Robinson and Gallagher in their brilliant book, of reformulating the problem of partition might then be picked up and dealt with to their satisfaction.

This article offers a reassessment of Britain's decision to occupy Egypt in 1882. Research published since 1961, it is suggested, does not support the view put forward by Robinson and Gallagher in their celebrated book, *Africa and the Victorians,* that Britain intervened reluctantly to safeguard the Suez Canal in response to disorder in Egypt, or that she was led on by French initiatives. Moreover, the decision to occupy Egypt did not have the effect claimed by Robinson and Gallagher of precipitating the scramble for West and East Africa. It is argued instead that the causes of intervention lay in the metropole rather than on the periphery. British interests in Egypt were both important and expanding, and they were upheld by Conservative and Liberal governments in the period following the khedive's declaration of bankruptcy in 1876. This conclusion makes the Egyptian case less important in understanding the scramble for tropical Africa but more important in understanding late nineteenth-century imperialism. The occupation illustrates how the emergence of a particular configuration of economic and political forces in Britain found expression abroad after 1850, and it does so without invoking narrow or deterministic forms of historical explanation. Finally, it is suggested that the Egyptian case deserves a more prominent place in the study of theories of imperialism than it has received, because most of the ideas which enter modern scholarly discussion of this subject can be traced to the contemporary debate over the highly controversial decision taken by Britain in 1882.

Suggested Readings

Ascherson, Neal, *The King Incorporated: Leopold the Second in the Age of Trusts* (New York: Doubleday & Co, 1963).

Brunschwig, Henri, *French Colonialism: Myths and Realities* (New York: Praeger, 1966).

Collins, R.O., *King Leopold, England. and the Upper Nile,* 1899-1909 (New Haven: Yale University Press, 1968).

Eyck, Erich, *Bismarck and the German Empire* (New York: W.W. Norton, 1964).

Forster, Stig, Mommsen, Wolfgang, and Robinson, Ronald, eds., *Bismarck, Europe, and Africa* (London: Oxford University Press, 1988).

Galbraith, J.S., *Mackinnon and East Africa, 1878-1895,* (Cambridge: Cambridge University Press, 1972).

————, *Reluctant Empire: British Policy on the South African Frontier, 1834-1854* (Berkeley: University of California Press, 1963).

Gann, L.H. and Duignan, Peter eds., *Colonialism in Africa, 1870-1960,* vol 1. "The History and Politics of Colonialism, 1870-1914." (Cambridge: Cambridge University Press, 1969).

Gifford, Prosser and Louis, Roger, eds., *Britain and Germany in Africa: Imperial Rivalry and Colonial Rule* (New Haven: Yale University Press, 1971).

Hargreaves, J., *Prelude to the Partition of West Africa* (London: McMillan, 1963).

Hopkins, A.G., *An Economic History of West Africa* (New York: Columbia University Press, 1973).

Kanya-Fostner, A.S., *The Conquest of the Western Sudan: A Study in French Military Imperialism* (London: Cambridge University Press, 1969).

Kieth, Arthur Berriedale, *The Belgian Congo and the Berlin Act* (Oxford: Oxford University Press, 1919).

Landes, D.S., *Bankers and Pashas: International Finance and Economic Imperialism in Egypt* (Cambridge: Harvard University Press, 1958).

Langer, William, *The Diplomacy of Imperialism* (New York: Knopf, 1951).

Packenham, Thomas, *The Scramble For Africa* (New York: Random House, 1991).

Roberts, Stephen, *The Economics of French Colonialism* (London: Frank Cass & Company Ltd., 1963)

PROBLEM II

COLLABORATION OR RESISTANCE TO EUROPEAN RULE

Having partitioned Africa, the European powers set out to occupy the continent. In fact Chapter VI of the General Act of the Conference of Berlin of 1884/1885, which was designed in part to regulate the scramble for Africa, stipulated the conditions by which the powers would mutually recognize what constituted an effective occupation in Africa. Although such conditions were seldom put to the test, no European state could ever claim to rule where it could not claim sovereignty. Once the technical criteria of occupation had been settled, however, the European powers were free to occupy Africa, exerting control with an ease more apparent than real. Equipped with superior weaponry and resources, a relatively small number of Europeans, usually assisted by African troops or allies, were able to impose their control over large African populations. The conspicuous facility by which the Europeans asserted their authority seemed to indicate a moral, as well as a technical, superiority, at least in the minds of the imperialists, while often obscuring the reality of African resistance. Although even the imperialists have today ceased to confuse superior morality with superior technology, the dominant role of the latter in the European occupation of Africa remains irrefutable but has eclipsed the nature of the African response. Not only have the alternatives available to Africans facing the European invaders appeared clear and distinct, but the results, favorable for the collaborators and detrimental for the resistors, seemed so obvious as to require no further inquiry. This sharp distinction between collaborators and resistors has now been challenged. The polarity with which scholars once viewed the African response has now become blurred by the growing awareness both of the complexities of human motivation and of the rational calculations made by the Africans after assessing their interests and the probable consequences to themselves and their society of collaboration or resistance. This confusion has created the historical problem of African collaboration or resistance to the imposition of European control.

Traditionally, scholars have focused their attention on the means by which vastly outnumbered whites imposed their rule over large indigenous black populations and upon those Africans whose collaboration not only insured their own survival, but enabled them to adapt successfully to the imperatives of European colonial rule. Thus, historians came to regard the resistors as romantic reactionaries, or even "protonationalists," determined to sacrifice themselves needlessly on the altar of lost causes in a futile attempt to preserve an authority that the European presence had reduced to an anachronism. Conversely, those Africans who accommodated themselves to the European incomers have been regarded by many historians as sensible realists attuned to the changing situation in Africa, as progressive and sophisticated collaborators whose cooperation secured and frequently enhanced their own authority and the well-being of their people.

Primary resistance ended with pacification and generally played little role in later nationalist appeals. Although subsequent, sporadic revolts against British rule were regarded as equally reactionary, their causes were employed to further the nationalist movement. Ronald Robinson and John Gallagher accept the negative character of African primary resistance, as well as its "protonationalist" nature. They regard the resistors as romantic reactionaries and contrast their fruitless savagery to the prudence of the collaborators who gained by accommodation what the protestors lost. Roland Oliver and John D. Fage concur, arguing that the farsighted and well-informed leaders perceived the futility of resistance. These African statesmen reaped the rewards of cooperation, while the less prescient and less well-advised leaders jeopardized their authority and often the integrity of their society by resistance.

These conclusions have, in the past, seemed so apparent, so patently obvious to historians of Africa that they appeared self-evident, requiring little elaboration or explanation no matter how fundamental to the course of European colonial rule in Africa. Today, however, historians of Africa have reexamined the period of pacification by challenging the accepted interpretations with new hypotheses. To them the division of African reactions to the imposition of colonial rule into negative resistance on the one hand and prudent collaboration on the other appeared increasingly artificial and inadequate. Rather than a simple dichotomy, the revisionists argue, African responses, including resistance as well as accommodation, can be explained as rational calculations of self-interest and not simply irrational, instinctive reactions. Indeed, African resistance can be regarded in positive terms. Thus, the very manner of resistance, as well as the results, conditioned the character of future European administration and profoundly influenced, usually to the advantage of the Africans, their relationship with the colonial rulers. Moreover, the African response was not simply a reaction to European initiatives. It was in fact a complex pattern produced by the interplay of European and African interests that were far more subtle than the arbitrary division into progressive collaborators and reactionary resistors.

The role of African resistance specifically in the history of West Africa is delineated by J.D. Hargreaves who argues that the African leaders who chose resistance were neither less far sighted nor less progressive than those who collaborated. "In fact they were often the same men." Some, like Samory, discovered that collaboration brought intolerable restrictions. Others, particularly the Fulani, found that a willingness to accommodate themselves to European overrule was an essential ingredient in preserving their privileges and perquisites as a ruling minority. Even the resistance of the Ashantehene, which ultimately led to British subjection of the Ashanti, did not lead to the end of the Ashanti nation. In fact, it regenerated Ashanti nationalism that proved such a formidable opponent to the national liberation movement of Kwame Nkrumah. In Dahomey the success of a collaborator like Tofa, with the failure of a resistor like Behanzin, cannot be sharply distinguished since the former achieved immediate but ephemeral success, while the latter met defeat but acquired lasting fame.

A.G. Hopkins reaches similar conclusions in his examination of collaboration and resistance in West Africa. He observes that in the second half of the nineteenth century West African traders were caught in the double bind of a slumping world market and the demise of the centuries-old slave trade. Hopkins recognizes separate responses to the changing economic conditions, determined by factors of geography, social and economic development. These choices represented an individual or community's careful assessment of their most effective means of responding to deteriorating terms of trade. Like Hargreaves, Hopkins sees their choice between collaboration or resistance as being determined not by early nationalist sentiments, but by rational economic calculations.

While Hopkins sees economics as dictating the choice and form of collaboration or resistance, Edward Steinhart believes that a community's decision to collaborate or resist was largely shaped by political factors. Steinhart identifies a correlation between social and political organization and collaboration. Societies that had a strong national, and relatively undivided class system, tended to resist colonial encroachment. Conversely, highly stratified societies, especially ones with an aristocratic ruling class like the Ankole, tended to reconcile themselves to colonial overrule more readily. These reactions exist on a continuum of responses. Thus collaboration or resistance are strongly influenced by preexisting social and political structures.

In East and Central Africa, T.O. Ranger has argued that the Africans were active participants, not just objects, in the "pacification," and that their actions directly conditioned the European occupation and administration. Moreover, historians have generally underrated the strength of the indigenous societies of East and Central Africa which in fact resisted European encroachment more successfully than hitherto believed. The result of their resistance did not mean the unconditional subjection of the African but a "balance of power" in which many African societies held their own against the Europeans while a few were so formidable the Europeans chose not to fight them. The Africans were thus often able to exploit the needs, weakness, and ignorance of the incomers to their own advantage. In this process they were not exclusively collaborators or resistors, but both. Indeed during the colonial period the historian frequently has had difficulty determining who were the resistors and who were the collaborators.

Although the revisionists have reexamined the rather simplistic assumptions of the past with subtlety and sophistication, their most important contribution to understanding the African response to the imposition of European rule is in dissolving the sharp differences hitherto drawn between collaboration and resistance. Nevertheless, the danger still remains of reducing historical interpretation to the peculiarities of each confrontation between African and European and replacing fallacious clarity with the chaos of precision.

Romantic Reactionaries Versus Sophisticated Collaborators
RONALD ROBINSON AND JOHN GALLAGHER[1]

Despite the astounding games of partition it played with the maps of Asia and Africa at the end of the nineteenth century, the so-called new imperialism was merely a second-order effect of the earlier work of European expansion. Colonizing the Americas and the other white dominions had been a durable achievement, constructed out of the manpower, the capital and the culture of the lands on the Atlantic seaboard. By this time their growth in self-sufficiency was throwing them outside the orbit of European control, whatever relics of that overlordship might still exist on paper, or might still be fleetingly reasserted by force of arms. Yet far from this being a period of decay for Europe, its energies were now developing their maximum thrust. The potential of the old colonies of settlement had matured so far that they were generating local expansions of their own. The Canadians and Brazilians had organized their backlands. The Americans and Australians had spilled out into the Pacific. The South Africans had driven north of the Zambezi. Whatever the flag, whatever the guise, the expansive energies of Europe were still making permanent gains for western civilization and its derivatives.

None of this was true of the gaudy empires spatch-cocked together in Asia and Africa. The advances of this new imperialism were mainly designed to plaster over the cracks in the old empires. They were linked only obliquely to the expansive impulses of Europe. They were not the objects of serious national attention. They have fallen to pieces only three-quarters of a century after being thrown together. It would be a gullible historiography which could see such gimcrack creations as necessary functions of the balance of power or as the highest stage of capitalism.

Nevertheless, the new imperialism has been a factor of the first importance for Asia and Africa. One of the side effects of European expansion had been to wear down or to crack open the casings of societies governed hitherto by traditional modes. Towards the end of the nineteenth century this had produced a social mobility which the westerners now feared to sanction and did not dare to exploit by the old method of backing the most dynamic of the emergent groups. Frontiers were pushed deeper and deeper into these two continents, but the confident calculus of early nineteenth century expansion was over and done with.

---

[1]Robinson, Ronald and Gallagher, John, "The Partition of Africa," in F.H. Hinsley, ed., *The New Cambridge Modern History* (Cambridge: Cambridge University Press, 1962), Vol. XI, ch. 22, 639-40.

It is true that the West had now advanced so far afield that there was less scope for creative interventions of the old kind. The Russians had as little chance of fruitful collaboration with the Muslim emirs of Khiva and Bokhara as the French and British were to have with the theocratic of the Sudan. When the time of troubles came to the peoples of China or Tongking or Fiji, their first response was to rally around the dynasty, just as in Africa the Moroccans and Ethiopians were to group under the charisma of the ruler. Movements of this sort were protonationalist in their results, but they were romantic, reactionary struggles against the facts, the passionate protests of societies which were shocked by the new age of change and would not be comforted. But there were more positive responses to the western question. The defter nationalisms of Egypt and the Levant, the "Scholars of New Learning" in Kuang Hsu, China, the sections which merged into the continental coalition of the Indian Congress, the separatist churches of Africa—in their different ways they all planned to reform their personalities and regain their powers by operating in the idiom of the westerners.

The responses might vary, but all these movements belonged to a common trend. However widely the potentials might range between savage resistance and sophisticated collaboration, each and every one of them contained growth points. In cuffing them out of the postures of tradition and into the exchange economy and the bureaucratic state, western strength hustled them into transformation. One by one, they were exposed to rapid social change, and with it came conflicts between rulers and subjects, the rise of new elites the transforming of values. All that the West could hear in this was distress signals. But just as its ethnocentric bias has obscured the analysis of imperialism, so its Darwinism has stressed the signs of decrepitude and crack-up in these societies at the cost of masking their growth points.

In dealing with these protonationalist awakenings, Europe was lured into its so-called age of imperialism; from them, the modern struggles against foreign rule were later to emerge. But the idiom has hidden the essence. Imperialism has been the engine of social change, but colonial nationalism has been its auxiliary. Between them, they have contrived a world revolution. Nationalism has been the continuation of imperialism by other means.

The Futility of Resistance: The Success of Collaboration

ROLAND OLIVER AND JOHN D. FAGE[2]

For the African peoples the most important factor at this stage of colonial history, however, was probably not the issue of European settlement or its absence, not the relatively concrete issues of land and labor, certainly not the difference between the policy of one colonial power and another, but the far more intangible psychological issue of whether any given society or group was left feeling that it had turned the colonial occupation to its own advantage, or alternatively that it had been humiliated. To a large extent this was a result of the accidents of occupation in each particular territory. Every occupying power inevitably made both friends and enemies. Every occupying power, before it could train a local army or police force, needed native allies and was prepared to accord substantial privileges to those who would play this part.

According to the value judgements of modern Africa, such peoples were traitors and quislings; but these categories hardly fit the circumstances of eighty years ago. Then, the primary choice lay not with individuals but with their political leaders. If these were farsighted and well-informed, and more particularly if they had access to foreign advisers such as missionaries or traders, they might well understand that nothing was to be gained by resistance and much by negotiation. If they were less farsighted, less fortunate, or less well-advised, they would see their traditional enemies siding with the invader and would themselves assume an attitude of resistance, which could all too easily end in military defeat, the deposition of chiefs, the loss of land to the native allies of the occupying power; possibly even to the political fragmentation of the society or state. In trying to see the early effects of the colonial occupation upon the African peoples. It is essential to realize that the rivalries and tensions between African communities did not end with the colonial occupation. They continued, with the colonial administrations both using them and being used by them. As with the slave trade in earlier times, there were gainers as well as losers, and both were to be found within the confines of every colonial territory.

[2]Roland Oliver and John D. Fage, *A Short History of Africa* (Harmondsworth: Penguin Books Ltd., 1964), pp. 202-3. Roland Oliver was formerly Professor of History at the School of Oriental and African Studies, University of London. John Fage is Professor Emeritus of African History at Birmingham University.

African Reaction to the Imposition of Colonial Rule in West Africa

JOHN D. HARGREAVES[3]

A common though superficial view of the partition of Africa is that Europeans, having decided to impose their power, proceeded to do so, enabled by the superior technology represented by Belloc's famous Maxim gun.[4] J.S. Keltie, author of the earliest and still the most detailed general account, believed that "we have seen the bulk of the one barbarous continent parcelled out among the most civilized powers of Europe." In such a perspective, European occupation inaugurated such a radically new phase in African history that the methods and motivations of the conquerors seemed a vastly more important subject for study than the reactions of the conquered.

From the new frontier of African historical studies, the view is rather different. We can trace how, in the centuries before the partitions, African states, entering into more or less stable relations, grew or diminished in power as a result of commerce, statecraft, war, and internal changes. The nineteenth century provided in Africa many examples of what philosophic historians might earlier have called "great revolutions and the rise and fall of states." One may see what has been described as a sort of African partition of Africa, a radical reshaping of political structures and boundaries, taking place throughout the century. It is most evident in the Muslim countries of the Western Sudan, with the great Fulani jihad in Sokoto, the consolidation of Bornu, the rise and defeat of Macina, the foundation of the Tukulor state of El Hadj Omar and later of the military empires of Samory (Samori) and Rabeh. But in coastal areas, too, many peoples were adapting their attitudes and institutions in response to the challenges presented by foreign traders, missionaries and governors. Wolof states took to peanut growing and to Islam; the Fon state in Dahomey reorganized its economy and extended its power; the "city-states" of the Oil Rivers perfected their mechanisms for controlling trade.

---

[3]Hargreaves, John D., "West African States and the European Conquest, in L.H. Gann and P. Duignan, eds., *The History and Politics of Colonialism in Africa* (Cambridge: Cambridge University Press, 1969), Vol. I, ch. 6, 199-2OO, 205-16. John Hargreaves is Professor of African History at the University of Aberdeen.
[4]Whatever happens we have got The Maxim, and they have not..

Not all such states were completely wiped from the map by European imperialism. Although some, like the Muslim empires that faced the French military in Haut Senegal Niger, were deliberately broken up by the conquerors, the cultural identity, institutional structure and ruling personnel of others survived not only under colonial rule but after its termination. The Tolon Na, traditional Dagomba chief, represented Nkrumah's radical republic of Ghana in Lagos; the ancient dynasty of Mossi played active if somewhat conservative roles in Voltaic politics during the 1940s and 1950s; rulers of small Mende and Temne chiefdoms provided much of the basis for the rule of the Sierra Leone People's Party. Most striking of all was the power wielded within the Nigerian federation by representatives of the ruling houses of the Fulani empire. It is therefore relevant to many present problems to inquire how such survivals became possible, what forces or conditions determined whether African states could retain their identity, what characteristics were needed for survival through the violent mutations induced by the European partition.

Historians of colonial policy might propose a simple hypothesis: that the decisive factor was the policy and attitudes of the occupying powers, whose material superiority was such that they could reshape the continent in accordance with their national interests and ideologies. British governors and consuls, their activities watched on the one hand by ministries drilled in the need to economize by administrative improvisation, and on the other by merchants anxious not to damage potential customers too badly, were unable to press so severely upon the African states that confronted them as ambitious French militaires, shrugging off civilian control as they sought Napoleonic conquests. One mode of expansion pointed towards the pragmatic philosophy of Indirect Rule, the other towards an integrationist ideal attainable only after French control had imposed rigorous processes of levelling and indoctrination.

Comparisons between French and British policies need to be taken no further in this discussion. Neither side embarked on the occupation of its African empire with a fixed and monolithic policy, pointing towards a single inevitable fate for the African polities in its path. If the aims and aspirations of those Europeans who led the advance sometimes implied a need for military conquest, more often they were such as could be satisfied by some form of treaty, providing access to commercial markets, denying land to rival imperialisms, laying foundations for political control. Of course, . . . there were treaties and treaties. Some were taken seriously by both signatories, some by neither; some were far reaching in their terms, others almost meaningless. After the onset of the scramble, and the enunciation by the Berlin Conference of the principle of "effective occupation," African signatories were usually required to make more far-reaching surrenders of their rights of independent action than in the days of "informal empire." Yet, since they were more liable to diplomatic challenge, these later treaties needed to be better authenticated. When the European signatory needed collaborators in policies which he was still too weak to carry out directly, there might still be genuine reciprocity of obligation. Even when imperial control had become secure, it was still necessary to find interlocutors within the colony; ex-employees of the postal department, however shrewd, did not make ideal "chiefs."

Given this range of possible attitudes on the part of the European invaders, a number of options might be open to African rulers. Among the short-term advantages obtainable from treaties or from collaboration with Europeans were not merely access to firearms and consumer goods, but opportunities to enlist powerful allies in external or internal disputes. Why then did so many African states reject such opportunities, choosing to resist the Europeans in battle? In West Africa, as in East and Central Africa, it cannot be said that those who opted for resistance were less farsighted or forward-looking than the "collaborators". In fact they were often the same men. Wobogo, for example, first received Binger cordially; became much more suspicious of the French after his accession; but only fought them after the Voulet mission had made their hostility unmistakably clear. Lat-Dior, *damel* of Cayor, a Senegalese kingdom with much longer experience of the French, was a "modernizer" in his acceptance of commercial groundnut production, and adjustment to its social consequences. After resisting Faidherbe's attempts to replace him by a more compliant ruler, he cooperated with succeeding governors on the more generous terms they offered, but finally reached the sticking point when the French began to build a railway through his country. Convinced (rightly) that this "steamship on dry land" would erode his sovereignty, he chose to die resisting in 1886.

Examples could be multiplied indefinitely. Nearly all West African states made some attempt to find a basis on which they could coexist with Europeans. Virtually all seem to have had some interests which they would defend by resistance or revolt—some conception of what can only be described as a rudimentary "national cause", anterior to, and distinct from, the national loyalties demanded by modern independent states. An analysis of the "national cause" of any specific people would need to embrace some values deeply rooted in their own culture and not very readily comprehensible to outsiders, together with some that can be universally understood—claims to territories, freedom to settle matters of internal concern without foreign interference. On this basis they would face the problem of relations with foreigners. Whether it was judged necessary to defend the national cause in battle, and at what stage, depended on variables on both sides of the Afro-European relationship, African statecraft as well as on European intentions.

In countries where African political structures had already been deeply affected by the growth of export trade, Afro-European relationships were conditioned by economic change. In the Niger delta, among the Yoruba, in coastal areas near Sierra Leone or on the Ivory Coast, political authority was diffused, and many African rulers were moved by considerations of commercial advantage or profit. Studies of "conjecture" may be needed to explain not only the pressures behind the European advance, but certain African reactions. Trading chiefs and heads of houses, as well as European merchants, sought to maintain the rate of profit in times of falling produce prices. The present discussion approaches the study of African resistance chiefly through rather simple cases, where centralized monarchies possessing the physical means of resistance, defended national causes that can be described in fairly simple terms. To extend such an analysis to West Africa as a whole will, however, involve detailed studies of the relations between trade and politics, such as the one A. G. Hopkins is undertaking for the Lagos hinterland.

One of the classical cases of military resistance seems to be that of Samory who between 1891 and 1898 fought the French with remarkable tenacity and military skill. Yet the record of his relations with France and Britain in the preceding decade shows many examples of his readiness to negotiate bases for genuine cooperation with either or both, provided that such bases safeguarded certain fundamentals of his independence. His early contacts with the French, beginning with the armed conflict at Keniera in February 1882, were indeed characterized by mutual mistrust and antagonism. But the French had to act circumspectly while building up their military force in the Niger valley, and it was only in early 1885 that Commander A.V.A. Combes's invasion of Boure (whose gold was so important to Samory's economy) revealed prematurely the full extent of their hostility.

Samory's response was to develop his contacts with the British in Sierra Leone, first established in 1879-80. After occupying Falaba in 1884 he sent emissaries to Freetown to invite the Governor "to ask the Queen to take the whole of his country under her protection." The purpose of the offer was clearly to obtain British support in warding off the French, and Governor Rowe was doubtless correct in interpreting it as a diplomatic flourish not intended to alienate sovereignty. More intent on protecting Sierra Leone's sphere of commercial and political influence among Temnes and Limbas than in seeking influence on the Niger, he did not even report the offer to London until a year later. His reply to Samory was amicable but cool, simply welcoming his promise to respect Temne country, "the Queen's garden, "and agreeing to develop friendly relations and trade.

Yet this was not without importance for Samory. Commercial contacts alone gave him a vital interest in collaboration with Freetown. Until 1892, when the Sierra Leone government enforced the licensing of arms sales according to the Brussels convention of 1890, this route provided Samory with his supply of modern breech-loading rifles, which he was increasingly aware might be needed for use against the French. Even now, Samory had not accepted armed conflict with France as inevitable. He was not leading a jihad against all Christians, nor a pan-African revolt against imperialism. He was concerned, practically, with governing and extending the empire he had conquered, with controlling its resources of gold, agricultural produce and men (including, of course, its slaves) and with enforcing the observance of Islam. It was perhaps less evident in the 1880s than later that these conditions were incompatible with the purposes of the French forces on the Niger. French relations with the Tukulor empire of Segou remained somewhat ambivalent until 1890; and the French military, desperately anxious to forestall supposed British ambitions and chafing under restraint from Paris, were reduced to signing treaties with Samory also.

In March 1886, when Colonel L.L. Frey was obliged to divert his forces against Mamadou Lamina, Samory was able to make a French mission under Captain Tournier modify the terms which they had intended to impose upon him. He secured French recognition not only of his territories on the right bank of the Niger, but of his rights over the contested districts of Boure and Kangaba. This left him more independence of action than the French were prepared to tolerate; and the following year, J.S. Gallieni (of all the French commanders the one most susceptible to the idea of protectorate relationships with Muslim rulers) sent Captain E. Peroz to negotiate new terms. Samory, although reluctant to damage his prestige by surrendering territory, wished to avoid further battles against French military power at a time when he was about to attack his archenemy Tieba, chief of Sikasso. After discussion he therefore agreed, by a treaty of 23 March 1887, to abandon the gold of Boure to the French and to accept a boundary line on the Tinkisso river. According to the French, he agreed also to place his state and any future acquisitions under their protection.

As is often the case with such treaties of protection, it is difficult to tell how far Samory was aware of having entered into some new relationship with France under the protectorate clause. Certainly he interpreted it quite differently from the French (whose immediate concern was not to define their permanent status in his territories, but to acquire a legal title against the British). There is some evidence that Samory believed that the French had undertaken to assist him to further his own designs, in particular against Tieba; counting on the alliance, he asked Binger for troops and artillery to help in his siege of Sikasso. But he certainly did not regard himself as having made an irreversible surrender of sovereignty. When the French refused to assist him, began to encroach on his territory, and tried to prevent his trading with Freetown, Samory "began to doubt whether, after all, the white man's word could be thoroughly relied upon" and tried, somewhat naively perhaps, to reverse his policy.

There still seemed to be possibilities of balancing British against French. In May 1888 Samory, while still besieging Sikasso, was visited by Major A.M. Festing, an official from Sierra Leone. This devout, garrulous, and pompous man had exaggerated faith in his personal powers of persuasion and influence. He had an unrealistic vision of Samory, with Festing as adviser, making peace with his enemies, consolidating his dominions into a genuinely united kingdom, and admitting the railway which the house of F. and A. Swanzy hoped to build from Freetown. Samory was interested, accepted the principle of a railway, and promised to sign a treaty when he returned to Bissandougou; but he refused to risk provoking a French attack before defeating Sikasso. In February 1889, indeed, he signed a new treaty with the French, accepting the Niger as the frontier everywhere, and agreeing to direct trade towards French ports; but soon afterwards he returned this treaty (though not that of 1887) to the French. He told another British travelling commissioner that he now considered himself free of obligations and ready to place his people and country under British protection; and on 24 May 1890 he signed a treaty promising not to alienate territory or undertake obligations to third powers except through the British government. It was, however, too late. London had already decided that the French protectorate treaties must be recognized, that war with France for West Africa was excluded, and had agreed with France on a partition of influence through the middle of Samory's empire. G.H. Garrett's treaty was not ratified, and Samory's partisans in Freetown tried in vain to persuade the government to work with him.

Samory's diplomacy was thus doomed to failure by the constant hostility of most French soldiers. Although some civilians wanted to avoid, or at least defer, a conflict, the ambitious and thrusting Colonel L. Archinard was hostile to any policy of tolerating Muslim empires. In April 1891 he again slipped the long rein of civilian control and attacked Kankan, intending to cut Samory's supply route to Sierra Leone. Thus the final period of armed resistance began. Until all of Yves Person's work has been published, assessment of Samory's personality and achievements can only be tentative. His dealings with the French were so marked by mutual mistrust and cultural incompatibility that a sober judgment is difficult; but it seems that Samory's attempts at coexistence were at least as seriously intended as those of the Frenchmen with whom he was dealing. For both sides, collaboration involved accepting restrictions of their rights, interests and prestige, which came to seem intolerable.

Samory's case thus hardly supports the view of Professors Oliver and Fage that "nothing was to be gained by resistance and much by negotiation"; nothing that he held important could have been permanently gained by either method. (J. Suret-Canale suggests that something might have been achieved had Samory, Amadou, and Tieba been "capable of rising above their quarrels in time to present a common front to the invader". Although such a coalition might have postponed the French conquest, however, it is doubtful whether it could have averted it.)

On the other hand, resistance—if combined at other times with willingness to accommodate and skill in doing so—could further the cause of national survival. In Northern Nigeria, most evidently, the military resistance of the Emirs did much to determine the basis of the very special relationship which their successors enjoyed with the British administration. Even here, however, D.J.M. Muffett has argued that the conflict of 1903 was due less to intransigent resistance by Sultan Attahiru than to Lugard's determination that, before the British could utilize the Fulani as a "ruling caste", the military basis of British suzerainty should be asserted by conquest. Muffett cites reports by Burton and Temple to show that before the expedition to Kano and Sokoto, Lugard was receiving "a mounting tale of evidence of the Sultan's readiness to be amenable and of the ripeness of the time for a diplomatic approach"; and he questions the translation and the dating of the famous assertion by Attahiru's predecessor that "Between you and us there are no dealings except as between Mussulmans and unbelievers—War, as God Almighty has enjoined on us." Lugard may indeed have hoped that the conquest of Kano would make that of Sokoto unnecessary. But as Attahiru saw British soldiers invading his provinces from the south, as he was joined by the stream of Tijaniyya fugitives from the

French in the west, it must have seemed increasingly clear that "the doings of the Europeans" threatened the independence of Muslim Africa. It was left for his successors to discover how much could be preserved by collaboration with the British. Ashanti, faced with ambivalent British, attitudes touched on above, may have missed opportunities of profiting by a more flexible diplomacy. Even hostile officials like W. Brandford Griffith presented a less formidable menace to African autonomy than did Combes or Archinard. Anglo-Ashanti relations have been described as "a mutual and protracted misunderstanding between peoples with fundamentally different conceptual frameworks." The freedom which British imperialists claimed to be bringing to the peoples of Ashanti were not the freedoms demanded by the resisters of 1900—freedom "to buy and sell slaves as in the old time," freedom "from demands for carriers . . . from the obligations of building houses and supplying thatch," and from the unwelcome attentions of "huxters and strangers."

Yet contradictions of this sort, which, existed along the whole front of Afro-European relations, did not inevitably have to be resolved by head-on conflict. Might not Prempeh have preserved more of Ashanti political and cultural autonomy by accepting, for example, Griffith's unauthorized Protectorate of 1891? He would have preserved the unity of the confederacy, its rights to levy customary revenue, and some, at least, of the "habits and customs of the country"; and although the Ashantehene would in many respects, no doubt, have become increasingly dependent on the British Resident who was to be appointed, an adaptable Ashantehene would doubtless have made the Residency equally dependent upon his own collaboration. In retrospect Prempeh's decision that "Ashanti must remain independent as of old" seems to have led logically on to his own deposition in 1896, to Governor Hodgson's ill-advised claim in 1900 to assume the authority of the Golden Stool, and so to the final military conflict and the subjection of Ashanti to direct British, administration.

But this was by no means the end of the Ashanti nation. In 1900 some of the outlying peoples of the Confederacy, who had not always been noted for their loyal support of ruling Ashantehenes, rallied to defend Ashanti against British aggression. Prempeh in exile became a more powerful focus of unity than he had been in Kumasi; British administrators in Ashanti, cherishing their separate status under the Governor of the Gold Coast, came better to appreciate the strength and complexity of Ashanti national feeling. The advice of R.S. Rattray, appointed as government anthropologist in the 1920s, furthered this reassessment. Ashanti began to seem a natural theater for experiments in Indirect Rule. In 1924 Prempeh returned to the country; in 1926 he was recognized as Omanhene of Kumasi. The Confederacy was restored under his nephew in 1935, and in 1943 crown lands in Kumasi were restored to the Ashantehene. One may reasonably ask whether, but for the resistance of the 1890s, Nkrumah's Convention People's Party would, over fifty years later, have faced such strenuous opposition from the National Liberation Movement, "a Kumasi centered Ashanti movement, which appealed for support in the name of the

Ashantehene, the Golden Stool, Ashanti interests, Ashanti history and Ashanti rights." References to military exploits against the British enabled the Ashanti to counter the anti-imperialist centralism of the Convention People's Party with claims to have been anti-imperialist from the first hour. In the long run, something was after all gained by resistance for the Ashanti "national cause", if not for that of a future unitary Ghanaian nation.

This conclusion is reinforced by a comparison of the experience of the Fon and the Gun during the French occupation of <u>Dahomey</u>. The Fon state of Abomey throughout the nineteenth century exhibited attitudes of proud resistance towards all European attempts to encroach upon its sovereign rights or to compel changes in a way of life which Europeans found particularly abhorrent. This does not imply that it was "hostile to modernization." King Gezo, although unable to fully meet British demands that he should cease exporting slaves and conducting the sacrificial "customs," did much to encourage and participate in the production and sale of palm oil as soon as Europeans showed interest in buying it. But although trade and diplomatic intercourse were welcome, the Dahomeans were uncomfortably aware that Europeans who entered African states to trade sometimes ended by ruling. Thus in 1876, Gelele preferred to undergo a British naval blockade rather than admit European interference in a commercial dispute which lay within his own jurisdiction. Yet he was anxious to avoid a military conflict, for "he who makes the powder wins the battle." When the French sent troops to Cotonou under a treaty of cession of 1878 (made in Gelele's name but probably without his consent), he confined himself to obstruction and protests.

Rulers of the Gun kingdom of Porto-Novo were more ready to cooperate with Europeans, both politically and commercially. In part, this attitude reflected fear of Abomey, whose armies for much of the nineteenth century constituted an intermittent threat to this smaller Aja state; in part it was caused by the desire of one of the ruling lineages to secure external support for its dynastic and territorial claims. In 1862 King Soji made an unsuccessful attempt to preserve these interests through a French protectorate. After 1874 his son, King Tofa, revived this policy. Tofa was a shrewd politician who worked with European traders to increase his wealth and power; "his succession," say the traditional historians of Porto Novo, "marked the transition into modern times." At first the French could do little to protect his territories against either Abomey or British Lagos, and Tofa showed bitter disappointment with the protectorate. But when <u>Behanzin,</u> who succeeded Gelele at the end of 1889, took more active steps to enforce his territorial claims, the French government was drawn somewhat hesitantly into military operations against him, largely through the intrigues of their ally Tofa.

How did Tofa, the "collaborator," fare by comparison with <u>Behanzin</u>, "the shark that troubled the bar"? Although Behanzin defended Dahomean rights more vigorously than Gelele had latterly done, he, like his predecessors, at first tried to avoid fighting France. In March 1891, after the initial clashes, Behanzin received French emissaries with apparently sincere expressions of friendship and desire for peace, and agreed not to make war on Porto-Novo, since the French were there. But he refused formally to renounce his title to Cotonou, or his liberty to send armies to other parts of his dominions; and he rejected as infringing his internal sovereignty French demands for the release of some of his own subjects whom he had detained during the fighting. In 1892, after receiving new arms supplies from German merchants, he proudly reaffirmed his right to coerce all the towns which he considered as his, excepting Porto-Novo, even at risk of a war with France. "I am the king of the Negroes," (he wrote to the French representative), "and white men have no concern with what I do. . . . Please remain calm, carry on your trade at Porto-Novo, and on that basis we shall remain at peace as before. If you want war I am ready."

By this time the French had come to the conclusions somewhat apprehensively and reluctantly, that war would be necessary to defend the position which their subjects had established in Dahomey. Accordingly, in 1892 the Senegalese Colonel A. A. Dodds carried out that march on Abomey which tough Dahomean diplomacy had thus far helped to postpone. But even now France hesitated to destroy the structure of the Dahomean state. During 1893 Behanzin continued to resist with much popular support; and the French, finding difficulty in identifying other *interlocuteurs valables,* contemplated accepting his offers to negotiate. In January 1894 they recognized his brother as ruler of an area corresponding roughly to the seventeenth-century rump of Abomey, and as a temporary expedient practiced a form of indirect rule until 1900. Even afterwards the dynasty continued to enjoy widespread prestige, which the French acknowledged in 1928 by arranging the ceremonial return from exile of Behanzin's ashes. (One wonders how far they had considered the implications of the analogy with the return of Napoleon's ashes to France in 1840.) Nor was this prestige confined to traditionalist circles. A clandestine newspaper published by two nationalist schoolteachers in 1915 took the name *Le Recadaire* (ceremonial messenger) *de Behanzin.*

By comparison, Tofa's policy of collaboration won certain advantages in the short run. He remained ruler of Porto-Novo under the French protectorate until his death in 1908, but with dwindling privileges and functions. He seems to have become bitterly conscious of accusations that he had sold his country to the French. With his funeral, say the traditional historians, the monarchy of Porto-Novo came to an end. His heirs, for whom he had sought French support, were mere French clients, their influence among the Gun eclipsed by others. On 28 November 1965 the author of this essay visited Tofa's successor in Porto-Novo. Elsewhere in the town revolutionary manifestations were taking place on behalf of the Gun President of the Dahomean Republic, who had been declared deposed by a Fon prime minister. Even though this constitutional conflict clearly reflected old antagonisms of Fon and Gun, however, the royal palace had become an irrelevant backwater. President S.M. Apithy, representative of the Gun "national cause," had begun his eventful political career as a young intellectual associated with the Catholic mission. But Justin Ahomadegbe leader of the Fon, spoke not merely as a trade unionist, but as a member of the house of Behanzin.

Until more research has been done on the policies and aims of individual African states, a survey of this kind must be superficial and tentative. It is hardly profound to conclude that the most important element making for the survival of African polities under colonial rule was simply a strong sense of ethnic or political identity—the attachment of their subjects to what has been called the "national cause." This sense of identity tended to be strengthened when the rulers who represented it could point to some record of resistance to imperialism. This does not mean blind or reactionary opposition. Those leaders who achieved most for the national cause, whether immediately or in the longer run, combined military action with more or less discriminating attempts to find some basis for coexistence or collaboration. Indeed, their success in keeping old national causes alive has sometimes presented problems to modern leaders who seek to represent a broader form of nationalism.

African Reaction to the Imposition of Colonial Rule in East and Central Africa

T.O. RANGER[5]

The myth of African reaction to the imposition of colonial rule in East and Central Africa in the early colonial period in Africa dies hard. Scholars have challenged the old assumptions concerning the white man's overwhelming moral force and the Africans' acquiescence to the invaders' rule. But opposing assumptions concerning the overpowering military superiority of the Europeans and the despairing inability on the part of Africans to determine their own fate have all too often taken the place of these long-standing conceptions. "The balance of power had moved right over into the European side of the scales," writes Basil Davidson. The armies and expeditions of Europe could now do pretty well whatever they liked in Africa, and go more or less wherever they pleased. Backed by their wealth and increasing mastery of science, the European kings and soldiers carried all before them. In doing so they found it easy—and convenient—to treat Africans either as savages or as helpless children.

Africans were not completely helpless, however, during the early colonial period in East and Central Africa. They could not avoid the imposition of colonial rule, but they were not simply objects or victims of processes set in motion outside Africa and sustained only by white initiative. Even in this period Africans helped to make their own history. Many scholars have shown how Africans necessarily participated in the early colonial administrative systems. Others have demonstrated how black men shared in the economic development of the new colonial territories. Here I wish to stress that the "balance of power" in East and Central Africa also allowed of African political initiative during the "pacification."

Britain and Germany of course possessed very great technical, manpower and capital resources. But they employed only a minute proportion of these for the colonization of East and Central Africa. In the first instance, responsibility for their paper spheres of influence was handed over by the two governments to chartered

---

[5]Ranger, T.O., "African Reaction to the Imposition of Colonial Rule in East and Central Africa," in L.H. Gann and P. Duignan, eds., *The History and Politics of Colonialism in Africa* (Cambridge: Cambridge University Press, 1969), Vol. I, ch. 9, 293-317, 319-21. T.O. Ranger is the Rhodes Professor of Race Relations at Saint Antony's College, Oxford..

company administrations. The power of European capital was called in to transform Africa, but European capital did not respond. Every company administration was grossly underfinanced.

Only the British South Africa Company, drawing upon Rhodes private fortune and the expanding economy of South Africa, was able to mobilize more capital and employ larger numbers of men. The 700 police and pioneers who entered Mashonaland in 1890 represented an exercise of European power quite without parallel anywhere else in East and Central Africa. But the B.S.A. Company, for all its resources, was unable to establish a strong administration in Northern Rhodesia.... Even in Southern Rhodesia the Chartered Company's resources proved inadequate to the task in hand.

These Company administrations have been severely criticized by historians. Freeman-Grenville has told us that "not one" of the employees of the German East Africa Company "appeared suitable for the task in hand." I have myself declared that Company rule in, Southern Rhodesia "was inevitably producing a society whose atmosphere was profoundly different from any conceivable crown colony, and different for the worse." But when the Company administrations were replaced in Uganda, Kenya, German East Africa, and Nyasaland with official colonial administrations, the new regimes were initially not much more efficient or powerful than the old

In Kenya, so an ex-government official tells us, the new official regime inherited "little more than an embryonic administration in the coastal belt, a few poorly garrisoned stations on the Uganda road, and an appreciation of the difficulties which had to be overcome." The arrival of the Imperial Government with all its potential resources of men and money made little immediate difference to the administration. No deliberate planned and directed operation of conquest was set on foot; none of the Commissioners was given the forces necessary to implement such a plan had one been sanctioned. As conquest was ruled out . . . and staff and forces were insufficient to establish law and order throughout the country, the handful of administrative officers had to concentrate their efforts in maintaining and improving their position in the established Posts. "Here we are," recorded R. Meinhertzhagen in his Kikuyu diary for 1902:

> three white men in the heart of Africa, with 20 Nigger soldiers and 50 Nigger police, 68 miles from doctors or reinforcements, administering and policing a district inhabited by half a million well-armed savages who have only quite recently come into touch with the white man . . . the position is most humorous to my mind.

In German East Africa the new regime was similarly short of men and money. The first Governor, Baron Von Soden, attempted wherever possible to avoid further commitments in the interior. "The establishment of military stations," he wrote, "is impossible without increased burden to the budget." Harry Johnston in Nyasaland was weaker still. "No other administration in what became British tropical Africa," writes Dr. Stokes, "started out with such slender financial and military backing. . . . Johnston lacked the power to subdue [and] was also lacking in the means to persuade."

If the power of European governments in East and Central Africa has been overestimated, the strength of some East and Central African societies has often been underrated. Many scholars have argued that the nineteenth-century history of the area was a progress to disaster which left African societies on the eve of colonization greatly weakened and divided. Perhaps the century saw a decline in terms of agricultural production, of population growth or of life expectancy. But in terms of military strength and of the ability of the stronger East and Central African societies to defend themselves, the European colonizers probably faced a more formidable task than they would have done a century earlier. The stresses of the nineteenth century had provoked reactions. Some societies at least had developed both stronger military institutions and more centralized political machinery. There were the intrusive Ngoni military systems whose decay has been greatly overestimated. There were other societies that responded to Ngoni pressure or to Ngoni example—the Bemba, the Hehe, the Sangu. There were the Swahili-Arab trading empires and enclaves and the Nyamwezi and other interior state systems which had risen to emulate them. The pastoral peoples of Kenya, especially the Nandi, had also been moving towards more effective and centralized action. Kingdoms, long established on different bases, like Buganda and Barotseland, responded successfully to the challenge of the nineteenth century and built up military and raiding systems. Some of these had increasing access to firearms; many had widespread trading or diplomatic connections which assisted them to take the white man's measure.

There were also, of course, many small-scale societies unable either to comprehend what was involved in colonization or to offer initial resistance. In armed clashes the superiority of modern weapons generally made up for lack of numbers. In any case it was always possible to supplement small numbers of whites with African "friendlies." Where the colonial power did suffer initial reverses it was provoked into committing more men and more money. The resistance of African societies was bound to be broken in the end. Nevertheless the confrontation of relatively weak colonial administrations with relatively strong African military systems did produce a practical "balance of power" very different from that described by Davidson. There were, in fact, some African societies or peoples whom the early colonial administrators could not easily afford to fight.

We may give a few out of many examples. Harry Johnston, for instance, for all his belief that the white man was destined to take over and develop the land of East and Central Africa, had to entrench the land rights of the Ganda aristocracy in 1900. He justified this policy with the explanation that he was dealing with "something like a million fairly intelligent, slightly civilized negroes of warlike tendencies and possessing about 10,000 to 12,000 guns." British officials in Kenya would not heed Sir John Kirk's call for the ending of Masai raids by "an aggressive war which to be successful must annihilate every vestige of the present Masai system." The British realized that "any premature collision could scarcely breed any but evil consequences for themselves." Administrator P.W. Forbes of North-Eastern Rhodesia subdued his desire to punish the Bemba and warned Bishop Dupont in 1897, "I would ask you always to bear in mind that although the Company will do their best to assist you in any way, we are not at present in a position to fight the whole Awemba nation." Even Rhodes chose in the end to enter Central Africa by outflanking the Ndebele rather than by confronting them.

Europeans sometimes refused to accept these facts. Some believed that they really could go where they liked and do what they liked; but they rarely believed it for long. The German East Africa Company, wrote a contemporary, "did not care to take any steps to conciliate the natives; their policy, judging from their conduct, was to treat the latter as conquered people, whose feelings it would be absurd to consider." But the Company "was quite unable to cope with the insurrection which it had deliberately incited," and its experiences served as a warning to other East and Central African administrations. In Southern Rhodesia, too, especially after the overthrow of the Ndebele in 1893, the administration acted as if Africans did not exist as a factor in the local balance of power. But the risings of 1896-97 cost the Company more than £7,000,000 and gravely endangered their Charter. The British Colonial Secretary received the news of the rising in the spirit of the more cautious and more general tradition, "Are you absolutely certain," he asked, "that the precautions you are taking will furnish force amply sufficient? The history of war with South African natives contains several disasters both to Colonial and Imperial troops." Most colonial administrators in East and Central Africa were accordingly aware of their limitations. Colonial rule, writes Professor Oliver, spread slowly, "very conscious of its military weakness and its financial dependence, never, if it could be avoided, taking more than a single bite at a time."

The colonizers' weakness, however, was by no means all to the advantage of African societies. In many ways it contributed towards making the impact of European intrusion more rather than less grievous. It could produce, for instance, exercises of force and injustice over and above those implicit in the whole process. "Under-investment in a decent administration," Mrs. de Kiewit Hemphill tells us of Kenya, "is sometimes worse than the most thoroughly arbitrary rule." The officials of the British Imperial East Africa Company were led through their lack of support or resources into "unsavoury expedients" and into penny pinching "where economy was unwise or dangerous." The Kikuyu, for example, were drawn into bitter conflicts with the whites because the British attempted to make company stations in Kikuyu country self-supporting, which led to raiding and looting by company officials. Thus British financial weakness "established a series of patterns and precedents which, for better or worse, gave direction to the subsequent history of African and European relations." In Southern Rhodesia the British South Africa Company at first tried to solve its financial difficulties by calling on unofficial white settlers and prospectors. Instead of establishing a regular machinery of native administration the company allowed unofficials to recruit their own labor, to collect taxes on the company's behalf and even to mete out justice with disastrous results. This state of affairs continued until 1896, when W. H. Milton was called in from the Cape to reorganize the Chartered Company's administration in Rhodesia and to bring about major reforms.

Colonial weakness not only resulted in violence and injustice but was also liable to shatter whole African polities. . . . The weakness of Harry Johnston's administration in Nyasaland led directly to "the rapid disintegration" of African political systems. Unlike Lugard in Northern Nigeria, who possessed a force formidable by colonial standards and was able swiftly to conquer and take over a functioning indigenous political system, Johnston faced an initial weakness in military and financial power which made it necessary to destroy rather than preserve.

Yet the colonizers' weakness was often the African's opportunity. Even in Nyasaland Johnston's step by step extension of colonial administration allowed the African peoples of the north time to come to terms with other European influences, and to escape the disintegrating effect of Johnston's policies. Recent studies of the Northern Ngoni and Tonga peoples have shown a two-way process of accommodation between black and white. The mission acted as "a foreign institution which provided certain services and which through its mere presence came to play its role in Tonga politics—a role which was to some extent independent of the intentions of the missionaries themselves." This pattern continued, once the administration had been set up. To establish itself and to extend its power, a colonial authority often required native allies. Hence there was wide scope for African initiative. Of course the position varied a good deal from region to region. When the British fought against the. Ndebele in Southern Rhodesia, they employed only a relatively small number of African auxiliaries. But the British position in Uganda depended on the British alliance with the Ganda aristocracy. . . . The Ganda could thus assert themselves as virtually equal partners and gain a position of entrenched power and privilege established in law. None of the others achieved so much; some were abandoned by the colonial administration when the value of their alliance had gone. But in every case the alliance was a two-way process; each party made use of the other.

Many recent studies have concentrated upon the use made by Africans of these situations, and the skill with which African rulers exploited the need, weakness and ignorance of the colonialists. Perhaps Mrs. Stahl's study of the Chagga has done this most clearly. "The chiefs showed through the centuries," she tells us, "a remarkable ingenuity in progressively enhancing their own powers. They made use of every new thing and every new kind of human being entering the life of Kilimanjaro to enhance their own positions." They became adept at assessing European officers, "utilizing each new officer serving a term of his career on Kilimanjaro as another element in their strategems . . . they employed a whole range of new political gambits centering on the Boma." This is a far cry from African helplessness. Such Afro-European alliances sometimes profoundly influenced the pattern of subsequent politics. Some chiefs managed to secure more power for themselves, as well as special access to new sources of prestige and profits. . . . In some areas in fact the advantages gained by cooperating ruling classes within their own society amounted to radical political change.

Advantages could also be gained by one African society over another. Some Africanists have spoken of Ganda sub-imperialism, but there was also a Lozi sub-imperialism. The extension of Lozi control to Balovale and Mankoya partially compensated the Lozi for the loss of other privileges. There was a Toro sub-imperialism, a sub-imperialism exercised by the family of Chief Mumia in Nyanza, and others. In many cases the subjects of these sub-imperialists experienced colonial rule more through their Ganda or Lozi overlords than through British control. The struggle against these sub-imperialisms forms one of the dominant themes in the modern political history of East and Central Africa. The effect of African initiative exercised through such alliances has been so far-reaching that some historians have limited their attention to African societies that chose to collaborate with the whites. Many scholars have argued that the collaborators, by influencing the pattern of pacification helped to determine the shape of colonial administration, and also gained a pathway to the future by exploiting the colonial situation. Investigators have often contrasted such societies with those that chose to resist the whites by force of arms. Oliver and Fage's general history emphasizes this point. If African political leaders, they argue, were far-sighted and well-informed, and more particularly if they had access to foreign advisers, such as missionaries or traders, they might well understand that nothing was to be gained by resistance, and much by negotiation. If they were less far-sighted, less fortunate, or less well-advised, they would see their traditional enemies siding with the invader and would themselves assume an attitude of resistance, which could all too often end in military defeat, the deposition of chiefs, the loss of land to the native allies of the occupying power, possibly even to the political fragmentation of the society and state.

Resisting societies or groups not only ran the risk of disintegration but of cutting themselves off from modernization, education and economic development. Resistances, write Robinson and Gallagher, were romantic, reactionary struggles against the facts, the passionate protest of societies which were shocked at new age of change and would not be comforted. They are to be contrasted with "the defter nationalisms" which "planned to reform their personalities and regain their powers by operating in the idiom of westernizers." Distinctions between the fortunes and potentialities of cooperating and resisting societies are thus held to be great. Hence attempts have been made to explain the disposition to resist or to cooperate in terms of profound differences in the structure of pre-colonial systems. "The more urbanized, commercial and bureaucratic the policy," Robinson and Gallagher tell us, "the more its rulers would be tempted to come to terms. . . ." On the other hand the more its unity hung together on the luxuries of slave-raiding plunder and migration, the less its aristocracy had to lose by struggle against the Europeans. In this way Robinson and Gallagher account for the co-operation of the progressive Lozi and

Ganda and the resistance of the plundering Ndebele and Ngoi.

The view of African resistance as a gallant anachronism, essentially negative and backward looking, has been challenged, especially by Soviet Africanists. "It is impossible to understand the African past without the reestablishment of the truth about this resistance," writes Professor A.B. Davidson of Moscow.

This is the main reason why it must be reestablished. And without making a study of what was the answer of one people or another to the establishment of colonial rule it is difficult to understand not only the past of that people but its present as well. It is difficult to comprehend the character of the liberation movement in the recent revolutionary years. . . . resistance left its mark on the most important internal processes of the development of the African peoples; in the course of resistance tendencies to change developed more quickly.

Soviet historians have not provided much solid evidence to buttress these conclusions, but to my mind Russian scholars have assessed the significance of African resistance to colonial rule in a more accurate fashion than their Western colleagues. The former have a better understanding of the "resisters"; the latter have a better grasp of the "collaborators." But if we are fully to understand the nature of African reactions to colonial rule, we must take account of collaboration and resistance alike. My aim in the remainder of this chapter is to show how resistance, as well as collaboration, shaped African political history.

To begin with, I disagree with many of the generalizations made by "Western" scholars. I do not consider that resisting societies were necessarily different in structure, motive or atmosphere from cooperating ones; I do not believe that cooperating societies necessarily desired modernization more than resisting societies, or even necessarily achieved it more rapidly. The foremost among the societies engaged either in resistance or in collaboration had more in common with one another in fact than with those small-scale societies that could neither resist nor exploit colonial rule. Thus the most notable resisters had some experience of foreign contact. They were centralized, sometimes highly so, and they had some capacity for intelligent choice. Again, some communities which—according to Robinson and Gallagher— should have resisted, and were expected to do so at the time, did not, in the end, do so. In certain instances, migratory military groups or societies organized for slave-raiding and looting, successfully accommodated themselves to the whites. Such communities included the Northern Ngoni of Nyasaland, the Bemba of North-Eastern Rhodesia and the Masai of Kenya.

Some resisting societies desperately attempted to avoid the necessity of resistance. Some cooperating societies made it plain that they were ready to resist if their cherished privileges were attacked. A historian has indeed a difficult task in deciding whether a specific society should be described as "resistant" or as "collaborative" over any given period of time. Many societies began in one camp and ended in the other. Virtually all African states made some attempt to find a basis on which to collaborate with the Europeans; virtually all of them had some interests or values which they were prepared to defend, if necessary, by hopeless resistance or revolt.

To illustrate this point we should consider, for instance, the contrast between Matabeleland and Barotseland. The former resisted; the latter collaborated. Superficially, the distinction seems clear. . . . The Ndebele, with their raiding system, had no interest in foreign commerce. The Lozi had an elaborate bureaucracy and were strategically placed athwart the transcontinental trade routes. The Ndebele seemed fated to clash with the whites. The Lozi were likely to take from the Europeans whatever was needed to improve the Lozi bureaucracy and to further Lozi trade. But what would the Lozi have done if, like the Ndebele, they had been faced with a white invasion of their eastern raiding grounds, if their regiments had been driven back, if they had faced at long last a white column marching on their capital? They surely would also have resisted. (The white missionaries at the Lozi court certainly expected them to do so.)

Resistance on the part of an African people did not necessarily imply a romantic, reactionary rejection of "modernity," though a lengthy war might of course occasion repudiation of European influence. Similarly, non-resistance, in the sense of abstaining from armed struggle, did not always imply a readiness to modernize. Professor Low tells us that the price exacted by the Masai for the implied alliance with the British was the preservation of the Masai way of life. "An official report of the E.A.P. Government was later to complain," he writes, "that no punitive expedition has ever been undertaken against the Masai; an omission, it said, which subsequently enabled the Masai to eschew British pressures for change."

On the other hand, some societies that did offer armed resistance, nevertheless desired contact with Europeans under their own control. Gungunhana of Gazaland had Protestant missionaries at his kraal, including an African minister. Gungunhana negotiated with Rhodes and desired increased trade while preparing to fight the Portuguese. Chief Makombe of Barwe, rebelling against the Portuguese in 1917, expressed his anxiety for continued intercourse with the British "who have enriched his subjects." Other societies developed a driving desire for modernization after the first bitter resistance was over. In terms of their eagerness for Western education, there was little to choose between the Nyasaland Tonga, who did not resist, and the Kikuyu, who did.

I must also take issue with the standard interpretation that nothing was to be gained by resistance under any circumstances. Much, of course, depended on the local situation and on the military resources and psychology of the colonizers. Herero resistance against the Germans certainly turned out to be a disaster for the Herero nation. . . . But some societies did gain benefits by demonstrating the ability to take up arms when forced to do so. The Basuto rulers wanted mission education, economic contact with the outside world and British protection. They had to fight to achieve these. It would be hard to argue that their final struggle, the so-called Gun War of 1879-81, was futile. Arising out of Basuto resistance to forced disarmament, it dragged on for seven months, cost the Cape Government £4.75 million, and ended in complete failure. . . . On March 18, 1884 the Basuto finally became British subjects directly under the Queen.

The Ndebele provide another, though rather different, example. After the Ndebele war of 1893, the Ndebele state was disrupted. The new rulers no longer recognized any indigenous authority. The regimental system was broken, cattle were confiscated, land was taken—all without any machinery of complaint or redress. In 1896 the Ndebele had little to lose from further armed resistance. It turned out that they had something to gain. Their rebellion threatened to smash the whole position of the British South Africa Company in Southern Rhodesia. Suppression exhausted the Company's financial resources; it also involved large numbers of British troops and a great extension of British political authority. Under these circumstances Rhodes was compelled to gamble on negotiating a peace settlement so as to prevent the war from dragging through the rainy season into another year, with backbreaking expense to the company and a probable British assumption of direct control. The High Commissioner had proscribed the Ndebele leaders; the settlers demanded unconditional surrender and condign punishment. But Rhodes dealt with the leaders and came to terms. The Ndebele did not get much—the recognition of rebel leaders as well as of loyalists as salaried indunas and spokesmen for the people; an apparatus of complaint and redress; a regular system of native administration; a new commitment to make more land available to them. But it was considerably more than they would have got without a rebellion. Resistance, far from preventing future political activity, helped the Ndebele to move into a new political era.

The Wahehe of Tanzania seem to be a perfect example of a people broken by futile resistance. They were crushed by military might. They did not even achieve a negotiated peace. Defeat left the people in a desperate state. . . . [But] Memories of their resistance dominated subsequent German and Wahehe thinking alike. Partly because of pride in these memories Wahehe institutions, or more accurately a Wahehe sense of identity, survived so well that Uhehe became the site of the most successful Tanganyikan experiment in indirect rule. Both the Germans and the British felt respect for the Wahehe, so that in later years Wahehe objections were taken especially seriously. Oliver and Fage tell us that for the African peoples the most important factor at this stage of colonial history was . . . the intangible psychological issue of whether any given society or group was left feeling that it had turned the colonial occupation to its own advantage, or, alternatively, that it had been humiliated.

The Wahehe can hardly be said to have turned the early colonial situation to their profit, but they did not come out with a sense of humiliation. "Today all Wahehe idolize Mkwawa," wrote a British district officer in the early Mandatory period. "This may be because he actually beat the white man in battle."

These examples have shown that the fact of resistance could influence very greatly the later political history of a particular African Society. But resistance had a wider impact. Thus it was resistance and rebellion that provoked the most extensive theoretical debates among the colonizers and had most impact on their attitudes. In territories like Tanganyika and Southern Rhodesia, which had experienced the terrifying challenge of great rebellions, memories of war or fears concerning new outbreaks dominated the white man's mind. While indigenous policies of accommodation served, on the whole, to support white assumptions of African readiness to accept white moral leadership, the rebellions challenged all easy generalizations about African gratitude and readiness to accept colonial rule, and all assurance that whites understood the Africans. Rebellions instead provoked almost anguished professions of incomprehension and disillusion. . . . African loyalty could never again be taken for granted.

Thereafter, as Dr. Iliffe has written of Tanganyika "the fear of rebellion became the decisive argument in any political debate." Freiherr Von Rechenberg always dreaded another rebellion. Von Rechenberg's successor, H. Schnee, never ceased to be afraid . . . he had never forgotten the files (on Maji Maji) and always present in his mind was the thought that it could happen again. "The principal motivation of settler politics was fear," writes John Iliffe, "after Maji-Maji settler thinking was defensive." The same was true in the Rhodesias. Officials regularly expected renewed outbreaks. In 1903 a general inquiry from Native Commissioners as to the state of African opinion found one "firmly convinced that we are in for such a row as we have not had up here yet . . . the whole attitude of the natives leads one to believe that they are going to have another slap at us." Similar fears were being expressed in 1915. Even in 1923, at the time of the change to Responsible Government, reports of instructions to Africans by priests and prophets were causing official concern. The settlers' memories of the rebellions remained vivid.

The consequences of white preoccupation with the possibility of black rebellions are hard to assess. There was much argument over the cause of past risings and over future policy to prevent further outbreaks. Some Europeans wanted the iron hand, others the velvet glove. Fear undoubtedly had much to do with the growing expression of white prejudices against the blacks. Nevertheless, particular African societies did profit by resistance, and the white man's awareness that—if pushed too far—black men could strike back also gave certain advantages to Africans as a whole. Black resistance also convinced Europeans of the importance of continued alliances with cooperative black communities. In Tanganyika, according to Dr. Iliffe, Von Rechenberg devised his economic policy to meet peasant demands, lest rebellion become the only outlet for Africans trapped in an unjust economic system.

In Southern Rhodesia the fear of rebellion led to withdrawals of over provocative measures. . . . Fear of native risings, occasioned by excessive fiscal demands, profoundly affected British official thinking. In 1904, for instance, Colonial Secretary Lyttleton remarked that in future tax questions of this kind "the attitude of the natives will have to be taken into account."

Secondly, African resistance sometimes stimulated important changes in the structure of African societies. It is already well established that such changes could be brought about by collaborating groups. Through collaboration a society, or its leaders, could gain better schools and greater economic opportunities. Historians have, in fact, distinguished a number of so-called "Christian Revolutions" in which key collaborators tried to solve some of the weaknesses of nineteenth-century African state systems, to make their bureaucracy more efficient through literacy and to render the central power independent of traditional sanctions and limitations arising out of kinship or regional groupings. "Christian Revolutions" of this kind were effected in Barotseland, Bechuanaland and Buganda. They were not, of course, identical in character, but they all tried to apply what historians have called the Christian 'great tradition' to solve problems of scale and effectiveness.

I would not deny the importance of these 'Christian Revolutions' which did effect substantial changes. But they had serious weaknesses. They provided opportunities for minority groups only. They rested upon alien sanctions and did not achieve mass commitment. They broke with traditional restraints and often weakened the mass sense of belonging. Even internal reforms designed to improve the popular lot by abolishing serfdom, forced labor and tribute may have weakened the feeling of identity between the rulers and ruled. Like these "Christian Revolutions" the modern nationalist movements of East and Central Africa attempt to erect effective bureaucratic and other institutions for a territorial state. But they also have to try to modernize at a more profound level by achieving mass commitment to reform. We can see the experiments of the "Christian Revolutions" as forerunners of one part of modern nationalism. But if we seek forerunners in the attempt to commit the masses to an effective enlargement of scale we have to turn rather to the resistance movements.

We must distinguish, of course, between short wars fought against the incoming whites and later protracted rebellions. In many instances the initial war was fought with the traditional military system. Little attempt was made to modify it, or to involve in the struggle wider social strata or neighboring African peoples. But a long drawn out rebellion was a different matter. The insurgents faced new problems and had to search for new solutions. The distinction made by Dr. Iliffe between initial tribal wars waged against the Germans in Tanganyika and the Maji Maji rising is of great significance. "Maji Maji," Dr. Iliffe says, was "a post-pacification revolt, quite different from the early resistance. That had been local and professional, soldiers against soldiers, whereas Maji Maji affected almost everyone. . . . It was a great crisis of commitment."

The point can be well illustrated for the Southern Rhodesian rebellions. The Ndebele had fought the 1893 war using their old military system. The subject peoples and the lower castes had taken no part in the fighting; neither had there been any attempt by the Ndebele to ally themselves with the peoples of Mashonaland or farther afield. The result had been disaster. The Ndebele then faced colonial pressures of greater intensity than anywhere else in East and Central Africa, except perhaps in the plantation areas of German East Africa. They desired to rebel—and this presented problems of organization and of scale. In 1896 not only the surviving members of the regiments and the adults of the royal family but also the subject peoples of Matabeleland and the tribes of Western and Central Mashonaland all joined to fight the whites.

The problem for the Shona was different. Their political fragmentation had prevented them from putting up any coordinated initial resistance to the arrival of the whites. As the implications of white rule were realized, individual paramounts began to refuse demands for taxes or labor, always ineffectively. Thus to "rebel" effectively, the Shona had to discover a principle of solidarity and to recover at least some degree of the political unity which they had once possessed. The Maji Maji rebels faced similar difficulties. It is not certain that their rising was in any sense planned. But once it had broken out, the insurgent leaders had to effect some coordination between the militarized Ngoni and the original rebels. This had to be achieved without any tradition of political centralization. Risings therefore led to political experimentation. Some rebels attempted to revive older centralizing institutions. But at the same time new men came to the front with new ideas. (The Shona, for instance, tried to revive the ancient Rozwi kingship. But younger men also elbowed aside aged paramounts.) Above all, such insurgents developed the notion of charismatic as distinct from bureaucratic or hereditary leadership.

In considering what this involved I have found helpful a recent article by M.A. Doutreloux on prophets in the Congo. He argues that the prophet cults which have been a feature of the history of the Congo from at least the early eighteenth century onwards have their roots in an essential weakness of Congolese society. This society could not find a solution to the problem of fragmentation and instability…. The prophet movements rose in order to remedy this situation. These movements were assaults not only on witchcraft but also on traditional limitations; they proclaimed a church or creed for all Africans and imposed their own regulations and codes of conduct upon believers; they endeavored to provide an indigenous Great Tradition to rival the alien Great Tradition used by the Christian revolutionaries. They pre-eminently involved the masses.

The most striking resistance movements of East and Central Africa were clearly led by prophetic figures. Among the Nandi one may trace the rise to authority of the Orkoiyot prophets in face of British pressure. I have pointed out the key role of the oracular priesthood of Mwari in Matabeleland, and of the spirit mediums in Mashonaland in the Southern Rhodesian rising of the 1890s. Prophets also played a major part in the Maji Maji rebellion. In the last two instances especially, we can discern the features described by Doutreloux. The prophets imposed new regulations and new instruction on the faithful; they brought believers into the congregation by dispensing "medicine"; they promised immunity both from witchcraft and from bullets; they promised success in this world and a return from death. They spoke to all black men. This was true in Southern Rhodesia even though the leaders involved were members of traditional religious systems with roots deep in the past. Under the stress of the rebellion situation what L.H. Gann has recently described as a "theological revolution" took place. The officers of the old cults were able to appeal to the centralizing memories with which they were associated, but they enjoyed too an extension of power and function; they asserted a new authority over chiefs and indunas; and they imposed new obligations on their followers. For a time the charismatic leadership of the prophets brought together Ndebele aristocrats, subject peoples, deposed Rozwi, Shona paramounts. As Gann puts it, "The proud Matabele chieftans now agreed to operate under the supreme direction of an ex-serf, a remarkable man who in 'normal' times would hardly have acquired much political influence."

There were many other upheavals on a smaller scale. A list of risings allegedly led by "witch doctors" in East and Central Africa amounts to some thirty-five to forty instances. These prophetic leaders appealed to notions of past unity but also attempted to reconstruct society. Religious leaders of resistances often came from outside the societies concerned and appealed for cooperation with peoples who had formerly been their rivals. Sometimes the religious leader claimed to speak in the name of a long-dead hero figure who had established a now vanished unity; sometimes he claimed to be the bearer of a new divine commandment that black men would unite.

Thus Resistance movements of this sort can hardly be regarded as tribal-conservative ones, involving as they did calls to recognize new authorities, new injunctions and cooperation on a new basis. Neither were they completely reactionary and anti-modernizing. The situation gave scope for the "new man" with specially relevant skills—like the trained Ndebele policeman in 1896. Gann has pointed out that among the followers of the chief Shona religious leader in 1896, Kagubi, were men who had been in touch with Europeans and picked up some of their skills. Kagubi's daughter was a school-girl in the Catholic mission at Chishawasha. I have myself described elsewhere how in the Makombe rising of 1917 in Portuguese East Africa there was a return to the new opportunities of leadership by men who had gone to seek their fortunes in the colonial economy, producing a "leadership of paramounts and spirit mediums and returned waiters and ex-policeman."

Of course these attempts to create a large-scale mass movement failed. Although in a single tribal situation, as with the Nandi or the Kipsigis, the charismatic leadership of the prophets continued to provide coherence even after defeat, where attempts at unity had been made over much larger areas, involving many more disparate peoples, defeat brought the new forms of cooperation to an abrupt end. In some cases, indeed, defeat led to a sudden abandonment by many of the ex-rebels of their commitment to African religious leadership and a turning instead to mission Christianity. The new religion was felt to have proved itself the more effective.

The future belonged, it seemed, to the representatives of the "defter nationalisms" which operated "in the idiom of the Westernizers." Leadership passed into the hands of the educated elite, often drawn from cooperating groups with access to modern ideas and skills.

So runs the standard argument. But this argument needs to be probed. Students of African nationalism are coming to pay increasing attention to the current of mass political emotion and to the continuity of rural radicalism, as well as to the development of *elite* leadership. Therefore we must ask if there is any continuity between expressions of mass political emotion in the twentieth century and the risings we have discussed. It can be suggested that the resistance tradition runs into modern mass nationalism just as does the tradition of the "Christian Revolution." But I do not wish to suggest an essential conflict between the *elite* solutions of the cooperating societies and the mass solutions of the resisters. The "resisters" and "collaborators" were not fundamentally distinct. There has always been a complex interplay, also, between mass and elite expressions of opposition. The establishment of colonial rule took a long time. "Primary resistance" to the whites still continued in some areas of East, Central and Southern Africa while "secondary" oppositions had already developed elsewhere. Independent churches, trade unions and welfare associations overlapped and coexisted with tribal or pan-tribal resistance. There was a fascinating interaction between them.

This sort of interplay continued into the 1920s and 1930s. African trade unionists in Bulawayo in 1929 looked to the resistant Somali as an example of successful unity; on the other hand, surviving leaders of the Ndebele rebels looked with envy at the successful collaborators, Lewanika and Khama, who had retained their land. The resistant Kikuyu looked with admiration at the institutions of the accommodating Ganda and sought at first to achieve them through a Kikuyu Paramount Chief movement. The ancestry of modern African politics in short, is a complicated one. What we can say with certainty is that its patterns do not derive merely from decisions conceived in the capitals of the colonial powers and put into effect in East and Central Africa. In so far as they derive from the period of the "Pacification" and of the establishment of the colonial administrations they derive from the participation of African societies in those processes; through both accommodation and resistance; through eager demands for modernization and stubborn defenses of a way of life.

Resistance, Collaboration, and the Transformation in the Terms of Trade

A.G. HOPKINS[6]

The evidence indicates that West Africa's external trade experienced a crisis in the last quarter of the nineteenth century. Export producers had become caught in a staple trap: the barter terms of trade had turned against them, and attempts to increase the volume of exports had either failed, or where successful, had contributed to a further decline in the terms of trade, with the result that growth had become self-defeating. Within a relatively short space of time the primary producers and traders came under severe pressure to develop alternative exports and to adopt cost-reducing innovations. This "general crisis" of the late nineteenth century led to strains, misunderstandings and conflicts between all those, Europeans as well as Africans, who in varying degrees had become dependent on legitimate commerce for their livelihood. The expansion in the volume of overseas commerce in the second half of the nineteenth century, combined with the adverse movement in the terms of trade, led to the modification or abolition of many of the early features of legitimate commerce that had been inherited from the time of the external slave trade, and also caused the European powers to discard the assumptions governing their traditional policy of limited intervention in West Africa. Just as pronounced booms have had a marked effect on the course of West African history, so, too, have serious slumps. Since the beginning of legitimate commerce there have been two periods of ten years or more when the barter terms of trade have moved against export producers and when the income terms have either fallen or remained static. The first period of depression was in the last quarter of the nineteenth century, and helped to bring the Europeans into Africa. The second period, covering the years 1930-1945, helped create the movement which was to expel them.

In some parts of the underdeveloped world the requirements of the industrial nations were consistent with the maintenance of the established social and political order. Britain's demand for Argentinean beef for example, strengthened the position of an already existing class of large landowners in that area, since cattle rearing was most efficient on sizeable units of land. Peaceful economic integration was also

    [6]Hopkins, A.G., *The Economic History of West Africa* (New York: Columbia University Press, 1973) pp. 135, 142-47.

associated with a policy of political reality in Latin America, though it was not the only reason for it. In West Africa, on the other hand, the accidents of geography and history which enabled small farmers and traders to participate efficiently in overseas commerce posed acute problems of adaptation for the traditional warrior entrepreneurs who had cooperated so profitably with European slavers during the days of the Atlantic trade. African rulers experimented with a number of modes of adaptation to their new situation, and these can be classified according to their negative or positive character. Four of the most important, which were adopted singly or in conjunction, will be dealt with here.

The first negative response was to continue exporting slaves in defiance of the ban imposed by the European nations. Little is known at present about the relative profits of slaving and legitimate commerce, but it seems that few African slave exporters turned willingly to the new trade, even though the terms of trade were more unfavorable in the second quarter of the century than they were to become later on. This reluctance may be taken as an indication that for established exporters the costs of legitimate commerce (in terms of diminished political power as well as of cash income) outweighed the returns. The predicament of Ghezo, the ruler of Abomey, was duplicated in other parts of the West Coast:

The state which he maintained was great; his army was expensive; the ceremonies and customs to be observed annually, which had been handed down to him from his forefathers, entailed upon him a vast outlay of money. These could not be abolished. The form of his government could not be suddenly changed, without causing such a revolution as would deprive him of his throne, and precipitate his kingdom into a state of anarchy.

As for the palm oil trade, that was a "slow method of making money, and brought only a very small amount of duties into his coffers." Ghezo's support of the slave trade ceased only with his death in 1858. After the withdrawal of European nations from the Atlantic trade, the shipment of slaves was handled mainly by Brazilian merchants, such as Domingo Martinez, who operated in the Bight of Benin between 1833 and 1864. The Brazilians were eventually eliminated by the naval squadron by the closure of foreign slave markets, and by their own inability to procure the necessary European trade goods. By the end of the 1860s the overseas slave trade had been reduced to a trickle. Responding to the new trade by trying to perpetuate the old was no longer possible.

Next, African rulers attempted to bolster their fortunes by means which were familiar to preindustrial governments throughout the world, namely by employing armed strength to plunder and to exact tribute from their neighbors. The kings of Senegambia used this tactic as an outlet for the energies of their hard drinking, hard fighting warrior elite (tyeddo); Ashanti mixed force with diplomacy in order to control, or secure access to, the wealth of the coastal peoples; the kings of Dahomey made annual incursions into Yoruba country; and the Yoruba states themselves fought a series of wars in which economic goals were prominent. Military operations, and, perhaps more important, the constant threat of them, led to the abandonment of fertile land, and to the creation of broad areas of neutral territory between hostile states. They perpetuated conditions which were inimical to the growth of the petty capitalism that had been fostered by legitimate commerce. They dramatized what may be called the crisis of the aristocracy in nineteenth century West Africa, a social and political crisis stemming from a contradiction between past and present relations of production. They were a last resort. and, as such, represented the ultimate failure of the ancient regime to adapt peacefully and efficiently to the demands of the industrial world.

The first of the two positive modes of adaptation was for former slave suppliers to develop an export trade in legitimate goods. Some of them became employers rather than exporters of slaves, and they used servile labor to harvest palm trees, to grow groundnuts and to transport produce to markets. The rise of legitimate commerce, far from bringing about the abolition of domestic slavery, increased the demand for cheap labor in Africa itself and so perpetuated a service industry, the supply of slaves which was detrimental to the long-term development of the natural resources of the region. The result was the growth of a small group of large export producers in areas which were near enough to the coast for the transport of bulky goods to be a feasible proposition. In Dahomey and some of the Yoruba states, for example, the rulers and important chiefs established large palm estates worked by slave labor. However these men now had to face competition at their palace gates from a multiplicity of small, efficient farmers who were only partly committed to the overseas markets, but who supplied the greater part of the produce shipped to Europe in the second half of the nineteenth century. The large producers found that they were unable to influence local export prices simply by controlling production, as they had done previously, yet at the same time they themselves were highly vulnerable to changes in the prices paid for produce by European merchants on the coast, since a sizeable part of their total incomes was derived from export earnings.

States which were not situated close to the coast had great difficulty in making constructive adjustments to legitimate commerce. Ashanti, however, is an interesting example of a partially exceptional case. Faced with a severe crisis early in the nineteenth century, the rulers of Ashanti responded by expanding their export trade to the north, selling kola nuts and buying cattle and slaves. Demand in the Hausa states had grown following the jihads of the early nineteenth century because kola was an approved stimulant in Muslim communities, which were denied alcohol. Supplies were increased partly by gathering kola nuts from wild trees, but mainly, it appears, through the establishment of plantations worked by slave labor. Good fortune, commercial skill and a highly efficient system of government helped Ashanti to adjust to the central economic problem which it faced in the nineteenth century. Yet some important questions still have to be answered before the response of Ashanti can be counted as an unqualified success. In the first place, not enough is known about the total value and the rate of profit of the northern trade to say whether its expansion in the nineteenth century fully compensated for the diminution of exports to the south. It has to be remembered that the size of the internal market was still severely limited by transport costs, and that the decline of trans-Saharan trade after 1875 might well have affected purchasing power in the north. Secondly, Ashanti still depended on the coast for supplies of munitions, salt and cotton goods, which came through satellites, such as the Fante states. These states now produced palm oil and kernels for export, and no longer relied on Ashanti for supplies of slaves for shipment overseas. Thus it is likely that there was, from the Ashanti point of view, an unfavorable shift in the balance of economic power. What is certain is that the attempt to reassert control over the Fante in the second half of the century brought Ashanti closer to conflict with the British. Finally, more research is needed into the potentially disintegrative elements within the Ashanti state: the implications for her long-term economic welfare and political stability of the existence of marked inequalities of wealth, the growth of the slave labor force, and the frustration of the merchant class, whose development was deliberately restrained, lest private enterprise should harm the national interest, as conceived by the king.

The second positive mode of adaptation was for traditional rulers to recognize the small producers as a serious new force, and to give them an increased stake in a reformed political system. For example, Lat Dior, the ruler of Cayor in Senegal, tried to forge an alliance with the groundnut farmers of his state in the 1870s in an attempt to counterbalance the power of the traditional military estate. However, support could not always be relied on, and aspirations, once encouraged, tended to multiply. The small producers used their new wealth to purchase, among other items, guns, and with these they could threaten the rulers who sought their cooperation. The new generation of export producers in West Africa had every reason to be wary of encouragement from their superiors, for rulers who allowed independent producers to develop did so in the hope of taxing their wealth. Not surprisingly, this aim became a cause of friction, particularly in the last quarter of the century, when profits from the export trade were reduced to a minimum. Furthermore, taxing small producers posed serious practical problems. Collecting tolls from a convoy of slaves travelling on an established route was easy enough, but, as the Aro of south-east Nigeria found, levying duties on palm oil was an entirely different matter, for oil was produced and traded in small quantities at many diverse points. Thus the attempt to accommodate the new capitalist class and secure the incomes of traditional rulers was a difficult operation.

The negative responses may have helped to prevent a sudden decline in incomes, but were ultimately self-defeating. The positive responses achieved better results, but were still not wholly successful. The difficulties of the progressive rulers arose first from an internal conflict of interest stemming from a basic change in the structure of export producing firms, and second from the fact that they were unable or unwilling to take the necessary adjustments in the time allowed by impatient and often unsympathetic foreigners. For a while it seemed that there was a chance of stabilizing the existing frontier between Europeans and Africans on the West Coast, but in the last quarter of the century the indigenous rulers were called on to make concessions over such matters as railways, internal tolls and slavery, which they judged, quite rightly, would undermine their political independence. At that point the dialogue over peaceful coexistence came to an end. Possessing fewer internal assets, and experiencing at the same time greater external pressures, the modernizing aristocracies of West Africa were less able to control their future than were their revolutionary counterparts in Japan after 1868.

As a general proposition, it can be said that the traditional unit of trade was less affected by the structural changes brought about by legitimate commerce than was the traditional unit of production. This was because large wholesalers were still necessary, whether the commodities to be handled were slaves or palm oil, whereas large producers were not. Many established entrepôts, such as Whydah, Lagos, Bonny and Old Calabar, substituted palm oil for slaves and survived as major ports right down to partition, and in some cases beyond. Their rulers continued to levy traditional taxes on visiting ships, and their leading merchants received credit and goods on a larger scale than ever before. Even the old trading premises survived: after abolition, the baracoons (warehouses where slaves were kept pending shipment) were used to store the new, legitimate exports. Although the entrepôts were not affected in precisely the same way as producers in the hinterland, it does not follow that they were not affected at all by the development of legitimate commerce, or that they found it any easier to establish a lasting and satisfactory relationship with their European customers. On the contrary, African rulers had to struggle in the nineteenth century to control destabilizing forces which threatened the cohesion of the entrepots, and sometimes their very existence. Some indication of the nature of these forces is necessary for an understanding of the degrees of solidarity and disunity exhibited by the middleman states which faced increased European pressure towards the close of the century. The best illustration of their problems is provided by the history of the area centering on the Niger Delta, which has been the subject of some important research in recent years.

Legitimate commerce presented opportunities to a new generation of traders, as well as producers, because it gave employment to a greater number of intermediaries, who were needed to collect export crops and to distribute manufactured goods. Entry into small-scale trade was easy because there were few barriers of capital or skill. The result was that existing wholesalers faced more competition than they had in the past, though this is not to imply that such rivalry was unimportant during the time of the Atlantic slave trade. The new traders won their most striking success in the Niger Delta. Virtually all the "city states," as Dike has called them, experienced serious political unrest between 1850 and 1875, as slaves and ex-slaves challenged the authority of the established wholesalers and rulers. This movement was personified by Ja Ja, the former slave who rose to a position of economic importance in Bonny in the 1860s, but whose social origins prevented him from attaining the highest political office. In 1869 Ja Ja formed his own state at nearby Opobo thus conferring on himself the political power which he felt his commercial success deserved. The career of Nana Olomu, the leading figure in Itsekiri trade and politics in the 1860's, provides another striking example of how advancement was becoming based on commercial achievement rather than on inherited status, though Nana's social origins were less humble than Ja Ja's, and he was able to further his political ambitions in his home territory. Ability put a man in a strong position; ability and acceptable family connections made him almost unassailable.

Indigenous commercial institutions in the Delta states were not entirely immune from change, and were affected by the alterations in personnel. At Bonny and Kalabari, for example, the rise of men whose success was a result of trading ability rather than of ascribed social position had repercussions on the traditional "canoe house" (a compact and well organized trading and fighting corporation capable of maintaining a war canoe) because increased social mobility led to a greater turnover of commercial and political authority. Jones has analyzed the history of these states in the nineteenth century in terms of a developmental cycle, which started with the expansion of a canoe house, moved on to a phase of political accretion, in which several houses coalesced, and culminated in varying degrees of disintegration, as unity broke down. For present purposes it might also be useful to think of the economic aspects of this cycle in terms of the theory of the firm, whereby a successful company expands, takes over its rivals, and achieves a local monopoly, only to find that its dominance is undermined from within, as managers leave to start their own businesses, and challenged from outside, as new competitors move in to try and secure a share of the monopoly profit.

Certain qualifications to the foregoing analysis have to be made, even at the risk of complicating the story. In the first place it should be noted that legitimate commerce speeded social change in the trading states, but did not initiate it, for social "upstarts" had also found scope for their talents during the days of the Atlantic slave trade. Secondly, some states escaped slave revolts, and in others slave risings were not always movements of the downtrodden against their masters. In Kalabari, for example, class conflict was minimized by integrating mechanisms which helped to assimilate slaves into society. In Old Calabar slave risings were partly demonstrations in support of established, rival political factions, and so served a functional purpose in reinforcing the status quo. Finally, care must be taken not to romanticize the careers of the famous Delta traders. Some scholars, understandably anxious to write African rather than Imperial history, have seen in these men the forerunners of the nationalist movements which developed in the colonial period. This interpretation bestows on the actors a motive and sense of purpose which they themselves would have had difficulty in recognizing. The leaders of the Delta states were great traders, and they certainly fought hard to maintain their independence, but their world view did not extend much beyond their local commercial interests, their vision of social justice did not include the emancipation of their own slaves, and they resisted African as well as European rivals with the true impartiality of homo economicus.

Conflict and Collaboration
EDWARD STEINHART[7]

In the study of response to colonial rule in Africa over the last decade and a half, the subject of African resistance and heroism has at last assumed its rightful place. Until the close of the colonial era it was fashionable to portray Africans as the passive and generally grateful recipients of the benefits of European authority. Independence and liberation movements have had the effect of decolonizing African historiography as well as African territory. In the process, however, some of the complexity and variety of African responses have been hidden in the long shadows cast by the heroes of resistance and the martyrs of rebellion of the early colonial era. It was in the hope of adding nuance, color, and depth to the picture emerging from the shadows that this study of conflict and collaboration was undertaken.

The societies examined in the following pages are not without their heroes and martyrs. But often far more interesting and subtle are the characters and policies of those who chose actively to cooperate with the arrival of European, in this case, British imperialism. By a "controlled comparison" of the histories of three separate but contiguous and closely related societies, I have attempted to gain insight into the responses of African political elites confronted with a forced interaction with powerful external forces. The means by which these external forces were accommodated to the domestic political scene by the leaders of the local African polity is the process I have called collaboration. It is clear that collaboration as I have used it does not mean submission, defeat, or resignation. On the contrary, it is an active policy of cooperation and compromise. In an African context, freed from the derogatory connotations and nuances of moral corruption assumed by the term in the wake of the European experience of Quisling and Petain, collaboration can be understood as one option among several open to African leadership in the situation of crisis and conflict engendered by the scramble for African territory and the colonization of the continent by the European powers. Our understanding of the role of collaboration in the history of Africa under colonial rule (and of colonial rule in Africa) seems to me to be crucial to our understanding of both Africa's place in the colonial world and of colonialism's place in the emergence of modern Africa.

---

[7]Steinhart, Edward, *Conflict and Collaboration: Kingdoms of Uganda* (Princeton: Princeton University Press, 1977) pp. vii, viii, 256-60, 266-69. Edward Steinhart is a Professor of History at the University of Texas, Austin.

Conflict and Collaboration: Some Conclusions

By the end of 1907, three kingdoms in western Uganda had made the difficult transition from independence and effective isolation to the status of remote dependencies within a worldwide empire. Some of the lesser kingdoms of the lacustrine region had disappeared in the course of the transition, others had emerged more powerful than at any time in their history. The key to a successful transition in each kingdom was the emergence of a collaborating elite who were willing to occupy the crucial roles and do the vital work of accommodating the once independent kingdoms to their new statuses. It is not surprising that similar groups came to power in what were historically and genetically related societies, sharing a great deal in the way of political culture and social structure. The fact of a common colonial overlord in addition makes possible a "controlled comparison," both implicit and explicit, in studying the events of the period from 1890 to 1907. By this comparative method, the responses of resistance and collaboration in western Uganda can be used to fill out a theory of colonial collaboration from the preliminary sketches already made.

Any theory of collaboration must first clear away some of the debris of previous meanings and connotations of that highly evocative term. First of all, collaboration has generally been taken as the polar opposite of resistance, despite the fact that the two responses have historically been closely associated in a complex pattern of reaction to colonial intrusion. To speak of "resisters" as against "collaborators" or "resisting" as against "cooperating" societies is to distort the often complex behaviors adopted by African political actors and to construe the history of Africa under colonial rule as a Manichaean melodrama. Instead, the two terms should be descriptive of a homogeneous pattern of responses operated in a subtle, sometimes violent, and often devious manner to admit to the local political arena a host of new, external, and imperial political forces. This pattern of response, in addition to the accommodation of imperial interests, served the dual role of simultaneously preserving a sphere of independent political action for the initiative of African leaders. Thus, collaboration should not be seen as a morally and politically bankrupt reaction to conditions beyond the control of the African actors. Removed from the context of World War II and the anti-Fascist resistance, collaboration with colonialism can be seen as a fluid and creative response by African ruling groups and individuals to a situation of inherent conflict and compromise. The response itself, dictated by the perceived needs and objectives of the collaborators, and the resultant accommodation of western political values and institutions occurred through a contentious process of political exchange, negotiation, and struggle, not from the mechanical imposition of those values by the colonizer or a judicious selection of preferred values by the colonized. In this view of collaboration as a political process, the African element of continuity, the gradual adaptation of local institutions and practices, emerges as the equal of the imperial element of administrative and economic exigencies in the creation of the collaborative mechanism of colonial rule.

The Emergence of Chiefly Collaboration

In western Uganda where highly stratified social systems were paired with high-ly authoritarian political systems, the emergence of a collaborative mechanism involved the transformation of the "traditional" political elite and ruling class of those societies into a collaborating class. It was the chiefs, the territorial and military leadership of the African kingdoms, who had the most to offer as collaborators as well as the most to gain by seizing the opportunity to cooperate in the institution of a new regime. As a class, they possessed the skills and attitudes that made for effective cooperation and compromise with the British overlords. Once a class of collaborators had emerged, it also had the most to lose if it failed to make the essential compromises or refused cooperation with those who had the ultimate power to remove them from authority. In general, each of the three regimes of collaboration involved not just the creation of a collaborative mechanism in the form of a recognized and rewarded hierarchy of appointed chiefs; it also involved a continual renegotiating of the terms and conditions of chiefly cooperation. This renegotiating, often accompanied by conflict, might well be deemed "resistance" by those inclined to emphasize the heroic elements in African behavior. Whatever the label, the process was one of constant maneuver for political advantage: a politics of collaboration.

Neither the social nor the political systems of the three kingdoms of western Uganda were identical in 1890. The differences in the degree of stratification and class hostility as well as the degree of authoritarianism and political domination were manifested in each kingdom's reaction to intrusion. The range of the spectrum of response exhibited by each kingdoms in its adoption of a policy of collaboration seems to have varied with the degree of stratification and domination in each system. Of course, other factors cannot be held constant in a historical study. It is therefore impossible to make categorical statements of the relationship of class domination to collaboration, but we can at least remark on what appear to be the propensities of the three systems under study.

I believe we can conclude from the examination of the responses of the three kingdoms that the more politically authoritarian and socially divided the society, the more likely a response of collaboration by the ruling elite and the less likely that elite is to mount a concerted and effective campaign of resistance. Thus, the most pastoral-dominant and class-based system—Ankole—was the most ready to adopt a policy of collaboration. The most national, least divided into hierarchical classes-Kabarega's Bunyoro—was correspondingly the most resistant to imposed changes and the slowest to develop a counterlife willing and able to make the compromises necessary to the establishment of a collaborationist regime. Toro, with its pastoral traditions and Bito dynasty, proved intermediate in its response. The schism created by rival dynastic claims in conjunction with the class division of Toro society provided the opening for the emergence not only of a collaborating elite, but of a collaborating monarch as well.

If the degree of social and political solidarity accounts for variations in the range of collaborationist response, what is the mechanism by which social statics are translated into historical dynamics? Although it is impossible to speak with certainty from the evidence of only three societies, the process that social science terms "elite recruitment" seems crucial to the understanding of the dynamics of emergent chiefly collaboration. In Ankole, where selection of the elite was highly restricted and intensely competitive within the class of potential rulers, a political culture of intrigue and factionalism for all the political offices tended to the perpetuation of those politics under a new sovereign. In Bunyoro and Toro, where the dynastic politics of the Bito clan were seen as being above the politics of competition for chiefly office, a moderating influence on factionalism seems to leave operated. The wider range of eligibility for the chiefly elite including both pastoral and agricultural groups in Bunyoro as well as a smattering of talented aliens, particularly in military service, seems to have opened the recruitment patterns in Bunyoro and promoted a degree of solidarity between classes and status groups that, if not quite nationalist in its intensity, was a great improvement on the tensions and frictions of her southern neighbors. The system of recruitment of the political elite before the colonial intrusion thus emerges as a crucial variable in the expression of the social tensions and political frictions that facilitated the emergence of a response of active collaboration with the intruders. If we are to make sense of the African history of imperialism, it is such variables within African societies as these to which we must increasingly turn.

The fact that previous patterns of elite recruitment persisted into the colonial era meant a continuation of many of the cultural and political practices of the old regime under the new. The largely self-selected elite that sought and gained recognition by the British suzerains only gradually moved away from the behaviors and practices on which their traditional authority rested. Much has been written about the conflicting values of traditional and bureaucratic chieftaincy under colonial rule. Far less has been said about the continuity of African values in relative harmony and accord with the performance of chiefly roles expected by the colonial powers. At least in the first years of colonial overrule, the most effective collaborators among the African elite were those who blended the two roles and represented in their person the collaborative mechanism that mediated the contact of two cultures, two political and economic systems. Thus Mbaguta could instigate the construction of roads and the system of regular tax collection and bookkeeping while remaining a devoted pastoralist who would ultimately retire to tend his extensive herds of cattle. He could similarly initiate a formal investigation into the assassination of a colonial official while simultaneously spreading the rumors and hatching intrigues that would cast suspicion on his political rivals and ensure his predominance in the court politics of Ankole. Like the members of the collaborating elite with a foot in both camps, the political practices of collaboration were to share elements of both the old and new regimes.

It may seem irrelevant to try to come to any conclusions regarding the failure of the African societies of western Uganda to mount effective armed struggles against the imposition of colonial rule. The overwhelming technological superiority of Britain expressed in terms of military firepower and potential manpower made the outcome of virtually any armed resistance, no matter how well organized and led, a foregone conclusion. In the end it would have been the Maxim gun, if it had gone that far. But outside of Bunyoro's struggle under Kabarega, the question was never put to the acid test of firepower. Indeed, the failure of resistance and rebellion is really a question of the failure to raise a significant movement along the populace in that direction. It is a question of the failure of political leadership and popular support, not of military strategy or tactics

Put in political terms, the failure of resistance must be seen as a function of the success of an alternative strategy by the African political leadership. Once a significant number of the political elite of each kingdom had opted for a policy of active collaboration with the imperial forces, the schisms within African society made resistance a futile and costly alternative. The divisions between the elite and the masses could not be bridged by an effort to secure popular support for armed struggle once the leadership itself was fractionated. More important, the emergence of divisions within the ruling class would have made civil war of some sort an inevitable outcome of attempts at resistance. Ultimately the successes of the collaborators in securing British support for their authority within the African kingdoms meant the demise of the initial attempts at mounting armed opposition to British intrusion in local affairs.

The successful application of a policy of collaboration goes a long way toward explaining the near total absence of immediate "post pacification" rebellions. With a locally respected and traditionally legitimate elite to administer the new systems of taxation, courts, and public works, no effective leadership could be found to champion any serious attempts at the overthrow or radical modification of the colonial system. Where opposition to colonial rule did border on rebellion, as in Bunyoro, it was focused on the participation of non-natives in the colonial system, which threatened both the loyalty of the masses and the elite's position of authority. But the very style of political confrontation represented by Nyangire brings into focus some of the deeper underlying bases for the failure of rebellion.

The politics of confrontation themselves seemed to have been contrary to African cultural and political traditions. The tendency of Africans to avoid or deflect hostility by verbal and cultural stratagems—by joking, deception, or "signifying" one thing when meaning something else was often noted by observers of African (and Afro-American) behavior. Often what was misunderstood as a propensity to lying and trickery was in fact a propensity to indirection, aimed at avoiding confrontation and rupture by preserving the semblance of amicability and agreement. For example, a European's demand for a contract of blood brotherhood would seldom be refused by an African host. Instead, the exchange of gifts that accompanied the ritual exchange of blood would be intentionally insulting or the ritual itself marred, making clear to all but the European communicant that the contract was a sham. By such cultural devices, contracts and solemn agreements were made that Europeans believed were in earnest, but that Africans felt free to ignore. Unfortunately, when the Europeans took such agreements seriously and acted upon them, the Africans often found that the cultural misunderstanding had generated a political reality that could not be ignored. By such stratagems, confrontation was deflected until it was too late to find the means to oppose openly what had come to be the reality of European dominance. Perhaps, then, at the deepest level, the root cause of the failure of African resistance and rebellion in western Uganda can be located, not in the inadequacy of their arms or martial virtues, but in the propensity within African society to schism and within African culture to pacific and indirect accommodation to potentially disruptive and explosive situations.

Suggested Readings

Bley, Helmut, *Southwest Africa Under German Rule 1889-1914* (Evanston: Northwestern University Press, 1971).

Davidson, A.B., "African Resistance and Rebellion Against the Imposition of Colonial Rule" in T.O. Ranger, *Emerging Themes in African History* (Nairobi: East Africa Publishing House, 1969).

Edgerton, Robert B., *Mau Mau: An African Crucible* (New York: Ballantine, 1989).

Flint, John, *Sir George Goldie and the Making of Nigeria* (London: Oxford University Press, 1966).

Iliffe, John, *Tanganyika Under German Rule: 1905-1912* (London: Cambridge University Press, 1969).

"The Effects of the Maji Maji Rebellion of 1905-06 on German Occupation Policy" in Gifford, Prosser and Louis, William Roger, *Britain and Germany in Africa: Imperial Rivalry and Colonial Rule* (New Haven: Yale University Press, 1967).

Morris, Donald, *The Washing of the Spears: A History of the Rise of the Zulu Nation under Shaka and its Fall in the Zulu War of 1879* (New York: Simon and Schuster, 1965).

Ranger, T.O., *Revolt in Southern Rhodesia 1896-97: a Study in African Resistance* (Evanston, Northwestern University Press, 1967).

Robinson, David, *The Holy War of Umar Tal: The Western Sudan in the mid-Nineteenth Century* (Oxford: Clarendon Press, 1985).

Wilks, Ivor, *Asante in the Nineteenth Century: the Sturcture and Evolution of a Political Order* (London: Cambridge University Press, 1975).

PROBLEM III

COLONIAL RULE
IN AFRICA

The problem of colonial administration in Africa involves a comparison of the administrative styles and techniques of the two great imperial powers, Great Britain and France. From the inception of their African empire until after World War II Britain, tried to rule through existing and traditional authorities wherever possible. This administrative expedient became codified as the doctrine of "indirect rule." The French for their part sought initially to integrate the administrations and incorporate the peoples of their new territories with France in an attempt to forge an enormous francophone empire. This policy of "assimilation" remained the official French colonial policy until the First World War. It was then replaced by the doctrine of "association", a policy that allowed the differing French territories to be administered by African authorities, utilizing techniques of administration specifically suited to each region.

Thus their are three questions regarding imperial rule in Africa. How did the British policy of indirect rule work? How did the French policy of assimilation work? And what were the differences, if any, between the later French policy of association, and British indirect rule?

The principles of indirect rule were most clearly and eloquently presented by one of Britain's greatest colonial administrators, Lord Lugard, in his book *The Dual Mandate in Tropical Africa*. Certainly no other book of its time had such a profound influence on the formulation of British colonial policy. To Lugard, the two most important administrative principles to rule subject peoples were "decentralization" and "continuity." If the foundations for rapid material and moral progress were to be established properly, the colonial government must combat the tendency to over-centralize by delegating the powers local district officers needed to maintain a balance between tradition and modernity in order to preserve law and order and, of course, British rule. At the same time, continuity must be maintained on all administrative levels. If this were not accomplished, each new official would have to start afresh. The progressive development of "primitive peoples" would thereby not be advanced and could, in fact, be retarded by administrative confusion.

If decentralization and continuity were the basic principles of Lugard's administrative system, the relationship between British officials and the native rulers was the key. This relationship must be based on cooperation and directed toward facilitating evolutionary change. The native administration must be advised rather than directed by the British administrator and allowed to develop along its own lines into a system of modern local government. Only in this manner, Lugard argued, could the proper foundations be built upon which might rise the future improvement of the colonial peoples.

Turning from principles to pragmatism, Lugard described in his *Political Memorandum* the administrative methods necessary to carry out the principles in *The Dual Mandate*. The *Political Memorandum* were detailed instructions for British administrative officers written before World War I and revised in 1919, some years before the publication of *The Dual Mandate* in 1922. Lugard intended that these detailed instructions would implant the spirit of his system while preserving the continuity it required. First of all, he stressed the importance of recognizing and ruling through the indigenous authorities. The role of the British officers, except in such critical areas as taxation, military forces, and the alienation of land, was to advise, not demand. Their task was difficult and delicate. Not only did they have to use the indigenous institutions, which were alien to British officials, but they were expected to improve them by educating the chief officials without simultaneously destroying the authority of the traditional rulers. By thus utilizing the indigenous institutions and authorities, the British officials could preserve continuity with the past while laying the foundations for the progressive improvement of the indigenous society.

Indirect rule was not the product of mere rationalization or modest expenditure. It was founded, instead, on ethics, tradition, and theory. The British expected that indirect rule would assist the African people adjust to the traumatic impact of contact with the West without losing their identity. They were skeptical that their own institutions could survive when transplanted to Africa, and they deeply believed that any system of government must take into account African institutions and traditions. Thus indirect rule permitted the full expression of "African genius" without creating chaos. What this meant in practice, observed Pratt and Low, was a demand for African development in the context of Victorian values. In theory, at least, indirect rule was a happy combination of "expediency and high purpose."

While indirect rule sought to fit British administration to the specific needs and realities of each colonial situation, the French *Mission Civilatrice* demanded one uniform, rational administrative policy for their entire African empire. Throughout the nineteenth century, French colonial theory was dominated by the doctrine of assimilation. Although the idea of assimilation is as old as the Roman Empire, the philosophical origins of French assimilation are to be found in the Enlightenment,

with its deep belief in the power of reason and the concept of the universal equality of all men. Men were, of course, different, but these differences were the result
of varying environments that reason, principally education and rational change,
could eliminate. The French Revolution provided the opportunity to translate these
ideas into action, and the *Declaration of the Rights of Man and of the Citizen* tri-
umphantly applied to all men, not just Frenchmen, who are "born and live free and
equal in rights." These egalitarian principles obviously applied to the French
colonies that were promptly incorporated as constitutional and administratively
equal parts of continental France. Despite the setback to the idea of assimilation during the First and Second Empires, assimilation as the theoretical framework for
French colonial policy continued to reemerge with greater vigor during the more
egalitarian periods of the republican government.

But what did assimilation mean? Martin Lewis has observed in *One Hundred
Million Frenchmen: The Assimilation Theory in French Colonial Policy* that
Frenchmen had widely divergent interpretations of assimilation. It was certainly
never a monolithic theory rigorously applied in Africa, and its meaning was vigorously debated, particularly in the late nineteenth century.

But even while the utility and practicality of assimilation was being debated in
France, the great French imperial proconsuls were already laying the foundations
for administration through association, which was destined to eclipse assimilation
as official French policy. Raymond Betts has traced the evolution of the association
policy, demonstrating that it, like assimilation, has its origins in the Enlightenment
but remained indistinct until the work of Louis-Léon-César Faidherbe, Joseph-
Simon Gallieni, and Louis-Hubert-Gonzalve Lyautey made association a practical
reality and a pronounced policy. In West Africa, Indochina, Madagascar, and
Morocco these three remarkable administrators established French control by first
utilizing the indigenous inhabitants in the conquest itself and then permitting them
to regulate their own affairs through their own institutions. French authority was
thus superimposed in a manner not entirely dissimilar to the indirect rule that
English administrators employed in the British African territories. Like indirect
rule, association was practical, economical, and effective, and to French colonial
theorists and practitioners, a "systematic repudiation of assimilation." Assimilation
remained official policy until just before the World War, but in reality it was
ignored throughout French Africa. By 1910, assimilation appeared dead, eclipsed
by association.

The flexible, economical, and practical characteristics of association immediately invited comparison with indirect rule, and Hubert Jules Deschamps, himself a
distinguished French colonial administrator, argued that the similarities far outweighed the differences. Deschamps regarded Lord Lugard as an intensely practical
man, a man of common sense, decency, and good faith who sought sensible solutions to the complex problem of imperial rule. Lugard was concerned foremost with
efficiency, peace, and order—not with abstractions about the universal applications
of reason or the fundamental equality of all men. Indirect rule accomplished the for-

mer while ignoring the more lofty ideals of the latter. Like Lugard, the French faced similar problems of colonial rule for which the theory of assimilation offered no ready solutions. And like Lugard, Deschamps observed, the French recognized traditional authorities and maintained indigenous institutions. Although the French frequently let some such institutions fall into disuse, they supported so many that leading colonial thinkers, like Ernest-Francoise-Maurice Delafosse, came to regard the policy of association as the French counterpart to indirect rule.

The British system of indirect rule rested on the recognition that peoples and their institutions were different and that these differences should be respected. Africa could thus evolve within traditional forms and with traditional leaders. Since no attempt was made to integrate the alien overrulers with traditional rulers and ruled, this policy, argued Deschamps, could only lead to separation and independence. Despite the acceptance and practice of association, the French still clung to the ideals of assimilation. Deschamps concluded that in the end the Lugardians and the assimilationists both won and lost. The traditional institutions vanished before modern ones, but African nationalism triumphed over political assimilation. French and British policies, so dramatically different in theory, cancelled one another to become, in practice, virtually identical. Or were they? Michael Crowder cannot agree.

Crowder argues that Deschamps does not fully appreciate the fundamental differences between the French and British systems of colonial rule. These differences clearly emerge when comparing, for instance, the way in which the British and the French employed the native authorities. On the one hand, the British emphasized the advisory role of British officials while respecting, if not enhancing, the powers of the traditional authorities and the institutions by which they ruled. On the other, the French regarded the chiefs as petty officials in the colonial administration retained for convenience and efficiency rather than from any regard for their traditional authority and institutions of governing. Despite the official policy of association, the deep belief in assimilation on the part of French officials in the field encouraged indifference if not contempt for African customs and institutions that were largely ignored in favor of French language, customs, and administration. To Frenchmen assimilation was synonymous with the civilizing mission that reduced traditional chiefs to "mouthpieces and scapegoats" and elevated Africans who learned French and accepted French culture to an elite status that practiced power in the colonies and influence in France. Conversely, in British territories the chiefs remained powerful figures dispensing decisions and justice while the educated Africans were relegated by British officials to petty positions in the bureaucracy or excluded from government and traditional society to drift with little influence over either. Although the similarities between French and British colonial rule appear superficially self-evident, below the surface the differences between the two systems were not only differences in degree but also in kind.

Principles of Native Administration

JOHN FREDERICK LUGARD[1]

The British Empire, as General Smuts has well said, has only one mission—for liberty and self-development on no standardized lines, so that all may feel that their interests and religion are safe under the British flag. Such liberty and self-development can be best secured to the native population by leaving them free to manage their own affairs through their own rulers, proportionately to their degree of advancement, under the guidance of the British staff, and subject to the laws and policy of the administration.

But apart from the administration of native affairs the local government has to preserve law and order, to develop the trade and communications of the country, and to protect the interests of the merchants and others who are engaged in the development of its commercial and mineral resources. What, then, are the functions of the British staff, and how can the machinery of Government be most efficiently constituted for the discharge of its duties in those countries in Africa which fall under British control?

The staff must necessarily be limited in numbers, for if the best class of men are to be attracted to a service which often involves separation from family and a strain on health, they must be offered adequate salaries and inducements in the way of leave, housing, medical aid, or their equivalents in money, for their maintenance in health and comfort while serving abroad, and this forms a heavy charge on the revenues. Policy and economy alike demand restriction in numbers, but the best that England can supply.

Obviously a consideration of the machinery of British administration in the tropics involves a review of its relations to the home government on the one hand, and of its local constitution and functions on the other. I will take the latter first.

The government is constituted on the analogy of the British government in England. The governor represents the king but combines the functions of the prime minister as head of the executive. The councils bear a certain resemblance to the Home Cabinet and Parliament, while the detailed work of the administration is car-

---

[1]Lugard, John Frederick, *The Dual Mandate in Tropical Africa* (London: Frank Cass & Co. Ltd., 1965, by arrangement with William Blackwood and Sons Ltd.) pp. 94-97, 102-5, 199-218. John Frederick Lugard, 1858-1945, was the Governor of British Nigeria, and one of the great proconsuls of the British Empire.

ried out by a staff which may be roughly divided into the administrative, the judicial, and the departmental branches.

The administrative branch is concerned with the supervision of the native administration and the general direction of policy; with education, and the collection and control of direct taxes, which involve assessment and close relations with the native population; with legislation and the administration of justice in courts other than the Supreme Court; and with the direct government and welfare of the non-native section of the population. The departmental staff is charged with duties in connection with transport, communications, and buildings (railways, marine, and public works); with the development of natural resources (mines, collieries, forestry, agriculture, and geology) with the auxiliary services of government (medical, secretarial, accounting, posts and telegraphs, surveys, &c.); and the collection of customs duties.

The task of the administrative branch is to foster that sympathy, mutual understanding, and cooperation between the government and the people, without which, as Sir C. Ilbert, has observed, no government is really stable and efficient. Its aim is to promote progress in civilization and justice, and to create conditions under which individual enterprise may most advantageously develop the natural resources of the country. The task of the departments, on the other hand, is to maintain the government machine in a state of efficiency, and to afford direct assistance in material development. Their motto is efficiency and economy. The two branches work together, and their duties overlap and are interdependent in every sphere. The efficient discharge of those duties in combination constitutes the white man's title to control.

There are in my estimation two vital principles which characterize the growth of a wise administration—they are decentralization and continuity. Though, as Lord Morley said of India, "perfectly efficient administration has an inevitable tendency to overcentralization," it is a tendency to be combated. It has indeed been said that the whole art of administration consists in judicious and progressive delegation, and there is much truth in the dictum, provided that delegation of duties be accompanied by public responsibility. This is not applicable to the head of the government alone or in particular, but to every single officer, from the governor to the foreman of a gang of daily laborers. The man who is charged with the accomplishment of any task, and has the ability and discrimination to select the most capable of those who are subordinate to him, and to trust them with ever-increasing responsibility, up to the limits of their capacity, will be rewarded not only with confidence and loyalty, but he will get more work done, and better done, than the man who tries to keep too much in his own hands, and is slow to recognize merit, originality, and efficiency in others. His sphere of work becomes a training school, and he is able to recommend his best men for promotion to greater responsibility than he himself can confer. The governor who delegates to his lieutenant governors, Residents, and heads of departments the widest powers compatible with his own direct responsibility to the crown, will witness the most rapid progress.

But delegation to an individual who is not equal to the responsibility obviously means disaster, and it is therefore often advisable to entrust extended powers to the individual rather than to incorporate them as a part of the duties of his office. His successor, who must obviously have less experience, and may or may not be his equal in ability, will not then automatically enjoy the same latitude, until he has proved his capacity in the higher office. Increased latitude to the individual is not, however, inconsistent with increased delegation of duties to the office, more especially in the administrative branch of the service, where posts must of necessity grow in importance as the country as a whole develops. It is a frequent ground of criticism that the Colonial Office has been somewhat backward in appreciating the value of this principle in these young and rapidly growing dependencies.

The governor, by delegating work to others, would seem to lighten his own task, but in point of fact the more he delegates the more he will find to do in coordinating the progress of the whole. Moreover, in order to have a right appreciation of the abilities, and of the personal character of each principal administrative officer and head of department, he must be in close personal touch with them, and make absolutely clear to them the essential features of his policy. He must be the directing brain, and leave the execution to others. The task he undertakes is no light one, and if he should be called on to create an administration *ab ovo,* or to lay down new lines of policy in an old one, the work may become more than the time at his command suffices for, and the personal touch with his officers may temporarily suffer from the insistent demands of his office, until he is able gradually to delegate to those in whom he has confidence.

The second of the two principles which I have described as vital in African administration is continuity, and this, like decentralization, is applicable to every department and to every officer, however junior, but above all to those officers who represent the government in its relations with the native population. The annually recurrent absence on leave, which withdraws each officer in West Africa from his post for about a third of his time, the occasional invalidings and deaths, and the constant changes rendered unavoidable of late years by a depleted and inadequate staff, have made it extremely difficult to preserve in that part of Africa any continuity whatever. The African is slow to give his confidence. He is suspicious and reticent with a newcomer, eager to resuscitate old land disputes—perhaps of half a century's standing—in the hope that the new officer in his ignorance may reverse the decision of his predecessor. The time of an officer is wasted in picking the tangled threads and informing himself of the conditions of his new post. By the time he has acquired the necessary knowledge, and has learnt the character of the people he has to deal with, and won their confidence, his leave becomes due, and if on his return he is posted elsewhere, not only is progress arrested but retrogression may result.

It is also essential that each officer should be at pains to keep full and accurate records of all important matters, especially of any conversation with native chiefs, in which any pledge or promise, implied or explicit, has been made. It is not enough that official correspondence should be filed—a summary of each subject should be made and decisions recorded and brought up to date, so that a newcomer may be able rapidly to put himself *au courant*. The higher the post occupied by an officer, the more important does the principle become. It is especially important that the decisions of the governor should be fully recorded in writing, and not merely by an initial of acquiescence or a verbal order. This involves heavy office work, but it is work which cannot be neglected if misunderstandings are to be avoided and continuity preserved. The very detailed instructions regarding the duties of each newly created department which were issued when the administration of Northern Nigeria was first inaugurated, served a very useful purpose in maintaining continuity of policy, till superseded on amalgamation by briefer general orders.

In the sphere of administration there are obviously many subjects—education, taxation, slavery and labor, native courts, land tenure—in which uniformity and continuity of policy is impossible in so large a country, unless explicit instructions are issued for guidance. By a perusal of the periodical reports of Residents, the governor could inform himself of the difficulties which presented themselves in the varying circumstances of each province, and think out the best way in which they could be met, and could note where misunderstandings or mistakes had been made. By these means a series of memoranda were compiled, and constantly revised as new problems came to light, and as progress rendered the earlier instructions obsolete. They formed the reference book and authority of the Resident and his staff.

In a country so vast, which included communities in all stages of development, and differing from each other profoundly in their customs and traditions, it was the declared policy of government that each should develop on its own lines; but this in no way lessens the need for uniformity in the broad principles of policy, or in their application where the conditions are similar. It was the aim of these memoranda to preserve this continuity and uniformity of principle and policy. . . . In Africa we are laying foundations. The superstructure may vary in its details, some of which may perhaps be ill-designed, but the stability of the edifice is unaffected. You may pull down and reerect cupolas, but you cannot alter the design of the foundations without first destroying all that has been erected upon them.

If continuity and decentralization are, as I have said, the first and most important conditions in maintaining an effective administration, cooperation is the keynote of success in its application—continuous cooperation between every link in the chain, from the head of the administration to its most junior member—cooperation between the government and the commercial community, and, above all, between the provincial staff and the native rulers. Every individual adds his share not only to the accomplishment of the ideal, but to the ideal itself. Its principles are fashioned by his quota of experience, its results are achieved by his patient and loyal application of these principles, with as little interference as possible with native customs and modes of thought.

Principles do not change, but their mode of application may and should vary with the customs, the traditions, and the prejudices of each unit. The task of the administrative officer is to clothe his principles in the garb of evolution, not of revolution;

to make it apparent alike to the educated native, the conservative Moslem, and the primitive pagan, each in his own degree, that the policy of the government is not antagonistic but progressive—sympathetic to his aspirations and the guardian of his natural rights. The governor looks to the administrative staff to keep in touch with native thought and feeling, and to report fully to himself, in order that he in turn may be able to support them and recognize their work. Lord Milner's declaration that the British policy is to rule subject races through their own chiefs is generally applauded, but the manner in which the principle should be translated into practice admits of wide differences of opinion and method. Obviously the extent to which native races are capable of controlling their own affairs must vary in proportion to their degree of development and progress in social organization, but this is a question of adaptation and not of principle. Broadly speaking, the divergent opinions regard to the application of the principle may be found to originate in three different conceptions.

The first is that the ideal of self-government can only be realized by the methods of evolution which have produced the democracies of Europe and America—viz., by representative institutions in which a comparatively small educated class shall be recognized as the natural spokesmen for the many. This method is naturally in favor with the educated African. Whether it is adapted to peoples accustomed by their own institutions to autocracy—albeit modified by a substantial expression of the popular will and circumscribed by custom—is naturally a matter on which opinions differ. The fundamental essential, however, in such a form of government is that the educated few shall at least be representative of the feelings and desires of the many—well-known to them, speaking their language, and versed in their customs and prejudices.

In present conditions in Africa the numerous separate tribes, speaking different languages, and in different stages of evolution, cannot produce representative men of education. Even were they available, the number of communities which could claim separate representation would make any central and really representative council very unwieldy. The authority vested in the representatives would be antagonistic to that of the native rulers and their councils, which are the product of the natural tendencies of tribal evolution, and would run counter to the customs and institutions of the people.

An attempt to adapt these principles of Western representative government to tropical races is now being made in India. Though the powers entrusted to the elected representatives of the people are at first restricted under the dyarchical system (which reserves certain subjects for the central authority), the principle of government by an educated minority, as opposed to government by native rulers, is fully accepted.

The experiment has so far shown much promise of success, but the real test is not merely whether the native councillors show moderation and restraint as against extremists of their own class, but whether, when legislation has to be enacted which is unpopular with the illiterate masses and the martial races of India, there may be a reluctance to accept what will be called "Babu-made law," though it would have been accepted without demur as the order of "the Sirkar"—the British Raj. It is, of course, now too late to adopt to any large extent the alternative of gradually transforming the greater part of British India into native States governed by their own hereditary dynasties, whose representatives in many cases still exist, and extending to them the principles which have so successfully guided our relations with the native states in India itself, and in Malaya in the past. It is one thing to excite an ignorant peasantry against an alien usurper, but quite another thing to challenge a native ruler.

Such a system does not exclude the educated native from participation in the government of the state to which he belongs, as a councillor to the native ruler, but it substitutes for direct British rule, not an elected oligarchy but a form of government more in accord with racial instincts and inherited traditions.

The second conception is that every advanced community should be given the widest possible powers of self-government under its own ruler, and that these powers should be rapidly increased with the object of complete independence at the earliest possible date in the not distant future. Those who hold this view generally, I think, also consider that attempts to train primitive tribes in any form of self-government are futile, and the administration must be wholly conducted by British officials. This in the past has been the principle adopted in many dependencies. It recognized no alternative between a status of independence, like the Sultans of Malaya, or the native princes of India, and the direct rule of the district commissioner.

But the attempt to create such independent states in Africa has been full of anomalies. In the case of Egbaland, where the status has been formally recognized by treaty, the extent to which the crown had jurisdiction was uncertain, yet, as we have seen, international conventions, including even that relating to the protection of wild animals, which was wholly opposed to native customary rights, were applied without the consent of the "independent" state, and powers quite incompatible with independence were exercised by the suzerain.

The paramount chief might receive ceremonial visits from time to time from the governor, and even perhaps be addressed as "Your Royal Highness," and vested with titular dignity and the tinsel insignia of office. His right to impose tolls on trade, and to exact whatever oppressive taxes he chose from his peasantry, was admitted, but his authority was subject to constant interference. The last-joined district officer, or any other official, might issue orders, if not to him, at any rate to any of his subordinate chiefs, and the native ruler had no legal and recognized means of enforcing his commands. He was necessarily forbidden to raise armed forces—on which in the last resort the authority of the law must depend—and could not therefore maintain order. The third conception is that of rule by native chiefs, unfettered in their control of their people as regards all those matters which are to them the most important attributes of rule, with scope for initiative and responsibility, but admittedly—so far as the visible horizon is concerned—subordinate to the control of the protecting power in certain well defined directions. It recognizes, in the words of the Versailles Treaty, that the subject races of Africa are not yet able to stand alone, and that it would not "conduce to the happiness of the vast bulk of the people-for whose welfare the controlling power is trustee—that the attempt should be made."

The verdict of students of history and sociology of different nationalities, such as Dr. Kidd, Dr. Stoddard, M. Beaulieu, Meredith Townsend and others is, as I have shown, unanimous that the era of complete independence is not as yet visible on the horizon of time. Practical administrators (among whom I may include my successor, Sir P. Girouard, in Northern Nigeria) have arrived at the same conclusion.

The danger of going too fast with native races is even more likely to lead to disappointment if not to disaster, than the danger of not going fast enough. The pace can best be gauged by those who have intimate acquaintance alike with the strong points and the limitations of the native peoples and rulers with whom they have to deal.

The Fulani of Northern Nigeria are, as I have said, more capable of rule than the indigenous races, but in proportion as we consider them an alien race, we are denying self-government to the people over whom they rule, and supporting an alien caste—albeit closer and more akin to the native races than a European can be. Yet capable as they are, it requires the ceaseless vigilance of the British staff to maintain a high standard of administrative integrity, and to prevent oppression of the peasantry. We are dealing with the same generation, and in many cases with the identical rulers, who were responsible for the misrule and tyranny which we found in 1902. The subject races near the capital were then serfs, and the victims of constant extortion. Those dwelling at a distance were raided for slaves, and could not count their women, their cattle, or their crops their own. Punishments were most barbarous, and included impalement, mutilation, and burying alive. Many generations have passed since British rule was established among the more intellectual people of India—the inheritors of centuries of Eastern civilization-yet only today are we tentatively seeking to confer on them a measure of self-government. "*Festina lente*" ["make haste slowly," ed.] is a motto which the Colonial Office will do well to remember in its dealings with Africa.

The system adopted in Nigeria is therefore only a particular method of the application of these principles—more especially as regards "advanced communities,"— and since I am familiar with it I will use it as illustrative of the methods which in my opinion should characterize the dealings of the controlling power with subject races.

The object in view is to make each "emir" or paramount chief, assisted by his judicial council, an effective ruler over his own people. He presides over a "native administration" organized throughout as a unit of local government. The area over which he exercises jurisdiction is divided into districts under the control of "headmen," who collect the taxes in the name of the ruler, and pay them into the "native treasury," conducted by a native treasurer and staff under the supervision of the chief at his capital. Here, too, is the prison for native court prisoners, and probably the school, which I shall describe more fully in the chapter on education. Large cities are divided into wards for purposes of control and taxation. The district head-man, usually a territorial magnate with local connections, is the chief executive offi-cer in the area under his charge. He controls the village headmen, and is responsible for the assessment of the tax, which he collects through their agency. He must reside in his district and not at the capital. He is not allowed to pose as a chief with a retinue of his own and duplicate officials, and is summoned from time to time to report to his chief. If, as is the case with some of the ancient emirates, the commu-nity is a small one but independent of any other native rule, the chief may be his own district headman.

A province under a Resident may contain several separate "native administra-tions," whether they be Moslem emirates or pagan communities. A "division" under a British district officer may include one or more headmen's districts, or more than one small emirate or independent pagan tribe, but as a rule no emirate is partly in one division and partly in another. The Resident acts as sympathetic adviser and counsellor to the native chief, being careful not to interfere so as to lower his pres-tige, or cause him to lose interest in his work. His advice on matters of general pol-icy must be followed, but the native ruler issues his own instructions to his subordinate chiefs and district heads—not as the orders of the Resident but as his own—and he is encouraged to work through them, instead of centralizing every-thing in himself—a system which in the past had produced such great abuses. The British district officers supervise and assist the native district headmen, through whom they convey any instructions to village heads, and make any arrangements necessary for carrying on the work of the government departments, but important orders emanate from the emir, whose messenger usually accompanies and acts as mouthpiece of a district officer.

The tax—which supersedes all former "tribute," irregular imposts, and forced labor—is, in a sense, the basis of the whole system, since it supplies the means to pay the emir and all his officials. The district and village heads are effectively super-vised and assisted in its assessment by the British staff. The native treasury retains the proportion assigned to it (in advanced communities a half), and pays the remain-der into colonial revenue.

There are fifty such treasuries in the northern provinces of Nigeria, and every independent chief, however small, is encouraged to have his own. The appropria-tion by the native administration of market dues, slaughterhouse fees, forest licens-es, etc., is authorized by ordinance, and the native administration receives also the fines and fees of native courts. From these funds are paid the salaries of the emir and his council, the native court judges, the district and village heads, police, prison warders, and other employees. The surplus is devoted to the construction and main-tenance of dispensaries, leper settlements, schools, roads, courthouses, and other buildings. Such works may be carried out wholly or in part by a government depart-ment if the native administration requires technical assistance, the cost being borne the native treasury. The native treasurer keeps an accounts of receipts and expenditure, and the emir, with the assistance of the Resident, annually prepares a budget, which is formally approved by the lieutenant governor.

In these advanced communities the judges of the native courts—which I shall describe in a later chapter—administer native law and custom, and exercise their jurisdiction independently of the native executive, but under the supervision of the British staff, and subject to the general control of the emir, whose Judicial Council consists of his principal officers of state, and is vested with executive as well as juridical powers. No punishment may be inflicted by a native authority, except through a regular tribunal. The ordinances of government are operative everywhere, but the native authority may make bylaws in modification of native custom, e.g., on matters of sanitation, etc., and these, when approved by the governor, are enforced by the native courts.

The authority of the emir over his own people is absolute, and the profession of an alien creed does not absolve a native from the obligation to obey his lawful orders; but aliens—other than natives domiciled in the emirate and accepting the jurisdiction of the native authority and courts—are under the direct control of the British staff. Townships are excluded from the native jurisdiction.

The village is the administrative unit. It is not always easy to define, since the security to life and property which has followed the British administration has caused an exodus from the cities and large villages, and the creation of innumerable hamlets, sometimes only of one or two huts, on the agricultural lands. The peasantry of the advanced communities, though ignorant, yet differs from that of the backward tribes in that they recognize the authority of the emir, and are more ready to listen to the village head and the Council of Elders, on which the Nigerian system is based.

Subject, therefore, to the limitations which I shall presently discuss, the native authority is thus *de facto* and *de jure* ruler over his own people. He appoints and dismisses his subordinate chiefs and officials. He exercises the power of allocation of lands, and with the aid of the native courts, of adjudication in land disputes and expropriation for offenses against the community; these are the essential functions upon which, in the opinion of the West African Lands Committee, the prestige of the native authority depends. The lawful orders which he may give are carefully defined by ordinance, and in the last resort are enforced by government.

Since native authority, especially if exercised by alien conquerors, is inevitably weakened by the first impact of civilized rule, it is made clear to the elements of disorder, who regard force as conferring the only right to demand obedience, that government, by the use of force if necessary, intends to support the native chief. To enable him to maintain order he employs a body of unarmed police, and if the occasion demands the display of superior force he looks to the government as, for instance, if a community combines to break the law or shield criminals from justice—a rare event in the advanced communities. The native ruler derives his power from the suzerian, and is responsible that it is not misused. He is equally with British officers amenable to the law, but his authority does not depend on the caprice of an executive officer. To intrigue against him is an offence punishable, if necessary, in a provincial court. Thus both British and native courts are invoked to uphold his authority.

The essential feature of the system (as I wrote at the time of its inauguration) is that the native chiefs are constituted

> as an integral part of the machinery of the administration. There are not two sets of rulers—British and native—working either separately or in cooperation, but a single government in which the native chiefs have well-defined duties and an acknowledged status equally with British officials. Their duties should never conflict, and should overlap as little as possible. They should be complementary to each other, and the chief himself must understand that he has no right to place and power unless he renders his proper services to the state.

The ruling classes are no longer either demi-gods, or parasites preying on the community. They must work for the stipends and position they enjoy. They are the trusted delegates of the governor, exercising in the Moslem states the well-understood powers of "wakils" in conformity with their own Islamic system, and recognizing the king's representative as their acknowledged suzerain.

There is here no need of "dyarchy," for the lines of development of the native administration run parallel to, and do not intersect, those of the central government. It is the consistent aim of the British staff to maintain and increase the prestige of the native ruler, to encourage his initiative, and to support his authority. That the chiefs are satisfied with the autonomy they enjoy in the matters which really interest and concern them may be judged by their loyalty and the prosperity of their country.

The limitations to independence which are frankly inherent in this conception of native rule—not as temporary restraints to be removed as soon as may be, but as powers which rightly belong to the controlling power as trustee for the welfare of the masses, and as being responsible for the defence of the country and the cost of its central administration—are such as do not involve interference with the authority of the chiefs or the social organization of the people. They have been accepted by the Fulani emirs as natural and proper to the controlling power, and their reservation in the hands of the governor has never interfered with the loyalty of the ruling chiefs, or, so far as I am aware, been resented by them. The limitations are as follows:

1. Native rulers are not permitted to raise and control armed forces, or to grant permission to carry arms. To this in principle Great Britain stands pledged under the Brussels Act. The evils which result in Africa from an armed population were evident in Uganda before it fell under British control, and are very evident in Abyssinia today. No one with experience will

deny the necessity of maintaining the strictest military discipline over armed forces or police in Africa if misuse of power is to be avoided, and they are not to become a menace and a terror to the native population and a danger in case of religious excitement—a discipline which an African ruler is incapable of appreciating or applying. For this reason native levies should never be employed in substitution for or in aid of troops. On the other hand, the government armed police are never quartered in native towns, where their presence would interfere with the authority of the chiefs. Like the regular troops, they are employed as escorts and on duty in the townships. The native administration maintain a police, who wear a uniform but do not carry firearms.

2. The sole right to impose taxation in any form is reserved to the suzerain power. This fulfills the bilateral understanding that the peasantry—provided they pay the authorized tax (the adjustment of which to all classes of the population is a responsibility which rests with the central government)—should be free of all other exactions whatsoever (including—unpaid labor), while a sufficient proportion of the tax is assigned to the native treasuries to meet the expenditure of the native administration. Special sanction by ordinance—or rule approved by the governor—is therefore required to enable the native authority to levy any special dues, etc.

3. The right to legislate, is reserved. That this should remain in the hands of the central government—itself limited by the control of the Colonial Office, as I have described—cannot be questioned. The native authority, however, exercises very considerable power in this regard. A native ruler, and the native courts, are empowered to enforce native law and custom, provided it is not repugnant to humanity, or in opposition to any ordinance. This practically meets all needs, but the native authority may also make rules on any subject, provided they are approved by the governor.

4. The right to appropriate land on equitable terms for public purposes and for commercial requirements is vested in the governor. In the northern provinces of Nigeria (but not in the South) the right of disposing of native lands is reserved to the governor by ordinance. In practice this does not interfere with the power of the native ruler (as the delegate of the governor) to assign lands to the natives under his rule, in accordance with native law and custom, or restrict him or the native courts from adjudicating between natives regarding occupancy rights in land. No rents are levied on lands in occupation by indigenous natives. Leases to aliens are granted by the central government.

If the pressure of population in one community makes it necessary to assign to it a portion of the land belonging to a neighbor with a small and decreasing population the governor (to whom appeal may be made) would decide the matter. These reservations were set out in the formal letter of appointment given to each chief in Northern Nigeria.

5. In order to maintain intact the control of the central government over all aliens, and to avoid friction and difficulties, it has been the recognized rule that the employees of the native administration should consist entirely of natives subject to the native authority. If aliens are required for any skilled work by the native administration, government servants may be employed and their salaries reimbursed by the native treasury. For a like reason, whenever possible, all non-natives and natives not subject to the local native jurisdiction live in the "township," from which natives subject to the native administration are as far as possible excluded. This exclusive control of aliens by the central government partakes rather of the nature of "extra-territorial jurisdiction" than of dualism.

6. Finally, in the interests of good government, the right of confirming or otherwise the choice of the people of the successor to a chiefship, and of deposing any ruler for misrule or other adequate cause, is reserved to the governor.

The habits of a people are not changed in a decade, and when powerful despots are deprived of the pastime of war and slave-raiding, and when even the weak begin to forget their former sufferings to grow weary of a life without excitement and to resent the petty restrictions which have replaced the cruelties of the old despotism, it must be the aim of government to provide new interests and rivalries in civilized progress, in education, in material prosperity and trade, and even in sport.

There were indeed many who, with the picture of Fulani misrule fresh in their memory, regarded this system when it was first inaugurated with much misgiving, and believed that though the hostility of the rulers to the British might be concealed, and their vices disguised, neither could be eradicated, and they would always remain hostile at heart. They thought that the Fulani as an alien race of conquerors, who had in turn been conquered, had not the same claims for consideration as those whom they had displaced, even though they had become so identified with the people that they could no longer be called aliens.

But there can be no doubt that such races form an invaluable medium between the British staff and the native peasantry. Nor can the difficulty of finding any one capable of taking their place, or the danger they would constitute to the state if ousted from their positions, be ignored. Their traditions of rule, their monotheistic religion, and their intelligence enable them to appreciate more readily than the negro population the wider objects of British policy, while their close touch with the masses—with whom they live in daily intercourse—mark them out as destined to play an important part in the future, as they have done in the past, in the development of the tropics.

Both the Arabs in the east and the Fulani in the west are Mohamedans, and by supporting their rule we unavoidably encourage the spread of Islam, which from the purely administrative point of view has the disadvantage of being subject to waves of fanaticism, bounded by no political frontiers. In Nigeria it has been the rule that their power should not be re-established over tribes which had made good their independence, or imposed upon those who had successfully resisted domination. On the other hand, the personal interests of the rulers must rapidly become identified with those of the controlling power. The forces of disorder do not distinguish between them, and the rulers soon recognize that any upheaval against the British, would equally make an end of them. Once this community of interest is established, the central government cannot be taken by surprise, for it is impossible that the native rulers should not be aware of any disaffection.

This identification of the ruling class with the government accentuates the corresponding obligation to check malpractices on their part. The task of educating them in the duties of a ruler becomes more than ever insistent; of inculcating a sense of responsibility; of convincing their intelligence of the advantages which accrue from the material prosperity of the peasantry, from free labor and initiative; of the necessity of delegating powers to trusted subordinates; of the evils of favoritism and bribery; of the importance of education, especially for the ruling class, and for the filling of lucrative posts under government; of the benefits of sanitation, vaccination, and isolation of infection in checking mortality; and finally, of impressing upon them how greatly they may benefit their country by personal interest in such matters, and by the application of labor-saving devices and of scientific methods in agriculture.

Unintentional misuse of the system of native administration must also be guarded against. It is not, for instance, the duty of a native administration to purchase supplies for native troops, or to enlist and pay labor for public works, though its agency within carefully defined limits may be useful in making known government requirements, and seeing that markets are well supplied. Nor should it be directed to collect licenses, fees, and rents due to government, nor should its funds be used for any purpose not solely connected with and prompted by its own needs.

I have throughout these pages continually emphasized the necessity of recognizing, as a cardinal principle of British policy in dealing with, native races, that institutions and methods, in order to command success and promote the happiness and welfare of the people, must be deeprooted in their traditions and prejudices. Obviously in no sphere of administration is this more essential than in that under discussion, and a slavish adherence to any particular type, however successful it may have proved elsewhere, may, if unadapted to the local environment, be as ill-suited and as foreign to its conceptions as direct British rule would be. The type suited to a community which has long grown accustomed to the social organization of the Moslem state may or may not be suitable to advance pagan communities, which have evolved a social system of their own, such as the Yorubas, the Benis, the Egbas or the Ashantis in the West, or the Waganda, the Wanyoro, the Watoro, and others in the East. The history, the traditions, the idiosyncrasies, and the prejudices of each must be studied by the Resident and his staff, in order that the form adopted shall accord with natural evolution, and shall ensure the ready cooperation of the chiefs and people. Native etiquette and ceremonial must be carefully studied and observed in order that unintentional offense may be avoided. Great importance is attached to them, and a like observance in accordance with native custom is demanded towards British officers. Chiefs are treated with respect and courtesy. Native races alike in India and Africa are quick to discriminate between natural dignity and assumed superiority. Vulgar familiarity is no more a passport to their friendship than an assumption of self-importance is to their respect. The English gentleman needs no prompting in such a matter-his instinct is never wrong. Native titles of rank are adopted, and only native dress is worn, whether by chiefs or by schoolboys. Principal chiefs accused of serious crimes are tried by a British court, and are not imprisoned before trial, unless in very exceptional circumstances. Minor chiefs and native officials appointed by an emir may be tried by his Judicial Council. If the offence does not involve deprivation of office, the offender may be fined, without public trial, if he prefers it, in order to avoid humiliation and loss of influence.

Succession is governed by native law and custom, subject in the case of important chiefs to the approval of the governor in order that the most capable claimant may be chosen. It is important to ascertain the customary law and to follow it when possible, for the appointment of a chief who is not the recognized heir, or who is disliked by the people, may give rise to trouble, and in any case the new chief would have much difficulty in asserting his authority, and would fear to check abuses lest he should alienate his supporters. In Moslem countries the law is fairly clearly defined, being a useful combination of the hereditary principle, tempered by selection, and in many cases in Nigeria the ingenious device is maintained of having two rival dynasties, from each of which the successor is selected alternately.

In pagan communities the method varies; but there is no rigid rule, and a margin for selection is allowed. The formal approval of the governor after a short period of probation is a useful precaution, so that if the designated chief proves himself unsuitable, the selection may be revised without difficulty. Minor chiefs are usually selected by popular vote, subject to the approval of the Paramount Chief. It is a rule in Nigeria that no slave may be appointed as a chief or district headman. If one is nominated he must first be publicly freed.

Small and isolated communities, living within the jurisdiction of a chief, but owing allegiance to the chief of their place of origin—a common source of trouble in Africa—should gradually be absorbed into the territorial jurisdiction. Aliens who have settled in a district for their own purposes would be subject to the local jurisdiction.

There are some who consider that however desirable it may be to rule through the native chiefs of advanced communities, such a policy is misplaced, if not impossible, among the backward tribes. Here, they would say, the Resident and his staff must necessarily be the direct rulers, since among the most primitive peoples there are no recognized chiefs capable of exercising rule. The imposition of a tax is in their view premature, since (they say) the natives derive no corresponding benefit, and learn to regard the district officer merely as a tax collector. Moreover, refusal to pay necessitates coercive expeditions—scarcely distinguishable from the raids of old times. To attempt to adapt such methods—however suitable to the Moslem communities—to the conditions of primitive tribes, would be to foist upon them a system foreign to their conceptions. In the criticisms I have read no *via media* is indicated between those who are accounted to rank as advanced communities, entitled before long to independence, and direct rule by the British staff. Let us realize that the advanced communities form a very minute proportion of the population of British Tropical Africa. The vast majority are in the primitive or early tribal stages of development. To abandon the policy of ruling them through their own chiefs, and to substitute the direct rule of the British officer, is to forgo the high ideal of leading the backward races, by their own efforts, in their own way, to raise themselves to a higher plane of social organization, and tends to perpetuate and stereotype existing conditions.

We must realize also two other important facts. First, that the British staff, exercising direct rule, cannot be otherwise than very small in comparison to the area and population of which they are in charge. That rule cannot generally mean the benevolent autocracy of a particular district officer, well versed in the language and customs of the people, but rule by a series of different white men, conveying their orders by police and couriers and alien native subordinates, and the quartering of police detachments in native villages. Experience has shown the difficulty in such conditions of detecting and checking cases of abuse of office, and of acquisition of land by alien and absentee native landlords. There is a marked tendency to litigation, and the entire decay of such tribal authority as may previously have existed.

The changed conditions of African life is the second important fact for consideration. The advent of Europeans cannot fail to have a disintegrating effect on tribal authority and institutions, and on the conditions of native life. This is due in part to the unavoidable restrictions imposed on the exercise of their power by the native chiefs. They may no longer inflict barbarous and inhuman punishments on the individual, or take reprisals by force of arms on aggressive neighbors or a disobedient section of the community. The concentration of force in the hands of the suzerain power, and the amenability of the chiefs to that power for acts of oppression and misrule, are evidence to primitive folk that the power of the chiefs has gone. This decay of tribal authority has unfortunately too often been accentuated by the tendency of British officers to deal direct with petty chiefs, and to ignore, and allow their subordinates to ignore, the principal chief. It has been increased in many cases by the influx of alien natives, who, when it suited them, set at naught the native authority, and refused to pay the tribute which the chiefs were given no means of enforcing, or acquired lands which they held in defiance of native customary tenure.

Here, then, in my view, lies our present task in Africa. It becomes impossible to maintain the old order—the urgent need is for adaptation to the new—to build up a tribal authority with a recognized and legal standing, which may avert social chaos.

It cannot be accomplished by superseding—by the direct rule of the white man—such ideas of discipline and organization as exist, nor yet by "stereotyping customs anti institutions among backward races which are not consistent with progress."

The first step is to hasten the transition from the patriarchal to the tribal stage, and induce those who acknowledge no other authority than the head of the family to recognize a common chief. Where this stage has already been reached, the object is to group together small tribes, or sections of a tribe, so as to form a single administrative unit, whose chiefs severally, or in council as a "native court," may be constituted a "native authority," with defined powers over native aliens, through whom the district officer can work instead of through alien subordinates. His task is to strengthen the authority of the chiefs, and encourage them to show initiative; to learn their difficulties at first hand, and to assist them in adapting the new conditions to the old—maintaining and developing what is best, avoiding everything that has a tendency to denationalization and servile imitation. He can guide and control several such units, and endeavor gradually to bring them to the standard of an advanced community. In brief, tribal cohesion, and the education of the tribal heads in the duties of rulers, are the watchwords of the policy in regard to these backward races. As the unit shows itself more and more capable of conducting its own affairs, the direct rule, which at first is temporarily unavoidable among the most backward of all, will decrease, and the community will acquire a legal status, which the European and the native agent of material development must recognize. "The old easygoing days, when the probity of the individual was sufficient to rule, are gone. . . ." Intelligent interest, imagination, comprehension of alien minds—these are the demands of today.

Methods of Native Administration: Political Officers and Native Rulers

JOHN FREDERICK LUGARD[2]

THE OBJECT IN VIEW

The British role here is to bring to the country all the gains of civilization by applied science (whether in the development of material resources, or the eradication of disease, etc.), with as little interference as possible with native customs and modes of thought. Where new ideas are to be presented to the native mind, patient explanation of the objects in view will be well rewarded, and new methods may often be clothed in a familiar garb.

CONNOTATION OF NAMES OF RANKS

The term "Resident" implies duties rather of a Political or advisory nature, while the term "commissioner" connotes functions of a more directly administrative character. The former is therefore applicable to the Chief Government Officer in a province of which large areas are under the immediate rule of a Paramount Chief, who, with native officials, himself administers a form of government. The latter is more adapted to provinces, or parts of provinces, less advanced in civilization, where the authority of the native chiefs is small, and a large measure of direct administration must devolve upon the protectorate government. The term "commissioner" is, however, already used in so many other connections, viz., a commissioner of the supreme or provincial court, a member of a commission of inquiry, a police commissioner, etc., that for the sake both of distinction and of brevity, the term Resident has been adopted to denote the two highest grades in the administrative or political department, and the term "district officer" though strictly applicable only to the next two grades will be used in this memorandum to include an assistant district officer:

[2]Lugard, John Frederick, *Revisions of Instructions to Political Officers on Subjects Chiefly Political and Administrative* (London: Waterlow and Sons, Ltd., 1919), pp. 296-305

GENERAL NATURE OF ADMINISTRATIVE OFFICER'S DUTIES

It is the duty of Residents to carry out loyally the policy of the governor, and not to inaugurate policies of their own. The governor, through the lieutenant-governor, is at all times ready and anxious to hear, and to give full and careful consideration to the views of Residents, but, when once a decision has been arrived at, he expects Residents to give effect to it in a thorough and loyal spirit, and to inculcate the same spirit in their juniors. This does not mean a rigid adherence to the letter of a ruling. Among such diverse races in widely varying degrees of advancement, it is inevitable and desirable that there should be diversity in the application of a general policy by the Resident, who knows the local conditions and feelings of his people. It does mean, however, that the principles underlying the policy are to be observed and the Resident in modifying their application will fully inform and obtain the approval of the governor.

FESTINA LENTE ["Make haste slowly," ed.]

Festina Lente is a motto very applicable to Africa, provided that the coach is not set on the wrong rail, so that a wrong course—temporarily easy—is inaugurated. By shirking initial difficulties and yielding to prejudice far greater difficulties must be encountered later. The government relies on its administrative officers to keep in close touch with native opinion and feeling, and to report for the information of the governor. It is thus only that we can produce the best results, that the governor the lieutenant-governors can keep in touch and gain information, and the political officer can count on support and on recognition of his work.

DIFFERENCE OF METHOD IN ADVANCED OR BACKWARD COMMUNITIES

(a) **Advanced tribes**—The degree to which a Political Officer may be called upon to act in an administrative capacity will thus depend upon the influence and ability of the native chiefs in each part of the province, though in every case he will endeavor to rule through the Native Chiefs. In those parts of provinces which are under the immediate authority of a Chief of the first or of the second grade, the primary duty and object of a political officer will be to educate them in the duties of rulers according to a civilized standard; to convince them that oppression of the people is not sound policy, or to the eventual benefit of the rulers; to bring home to their intelligence, as far as may be, the evils attendant on a system which holds the lower classes in a state of slavery or serfdom, and so destroys individual responsibility, ambition, and development amongst them; to impress upon them the advantage of delegating the control of districts to subordinate chiefs, and of trusting and encouraging these subordinates, while keeping a strict supervision over them; to see that there is no favoritism in such appointments and to inculcate the unspeakable benefit of justice, free from bribery and open to all.

Where taxation exists the consequent duty of assessing all the towns and villages himself will throw upon the political officer a considerable amount of purely administrative work. In his work he should invite the co-operation of the chief, and endeavor to enlist his cordial assistance by making it clear to him that his own interests are deeply involved.

(b) Backward tribes—In districts where there is no chief of the first or second grade, a political officer's functions become more largely administrative, and among uncivilized pagan tribes he must assume the full extent to which time and opportunity permit. In such communities he will constantly endeavor to support the authority of the chief, and encourage him to show initiative. If there is no chief who exercises authority beyond his own village, he will encourage any village chief of influence and character to control a group of villages, with a view to making him chief of a district later if he shows ability for the charge. Native court clerks or scribes, constables or couriers will never be allowed to usurp the authority of the native chief or village head.

POSITION AND DUTIES OF RESIDENT IN CHARGE.

The Resident is, the senior government official in the province, and represents the lieutenant-governor in all administrative matters. In the absence of a responsible officer of any department it is his duty to report any dereliction of duty on the part of any departmental subordinate to the head of his department, or if of a serious nature to the lieutenant-governor. All such officers will be guided by the instructions and wishes of the Resident, so far as they are not incompatible with the orders they have received from the head of their department, to whom they will report the matter if the Resident's instructions conflict with departmental orders. The head of a department issues his instructions direct to his subordinate officer, and it is the duty of the subordinate to keep the Resident fully informed of any orders he receives which it may be useful for him to know, as, for instance, a Public Works Department officer who had received orders to commence the repair of houses, etc. If the subordinate is a native clerk, the district officer will be regarded as the local representative, and communications from the head of the department will be addressed to him. The first and most essential duties of a Resident and his staff are those in connection with the conduct of native administration, including the close supervision of the native courts and the assessment for taxation. This work is sufficiently onerous, and it cannot be adequately performed if a Resident is charged in addition with work and correspondence of a general administrative nature. As the senior representative of government in his province, he cannot be entirely relieved of all general administrative duties, but in the scheme of administration in Nigeria for which I am responsible, it has been my endeavor to relieve him of them as far as possible (a) by the creation of lieutenant-governors with an adequate secretariat to undertake it, and (b) by the appointment of station magistrates charged with the police court work at large centers, and with the conduct of nonpolitical questions and correspondence.

JUNIOR STAFF

Residents will spare no efforts to instruct young officers posted to their staff, and will see that all are familiar with the ordinances, regulations general orders, and political memos. These constitute the laws and usages of the protectorate, which all political Officers are bound by their oath to enforce impartially. District officers in charge of divisions will send full reports to the Resident from which he will extract any information useful for his half-yearly and annual report to the lieutenant governor, to whom he will forward all assessment reports and any particular report, or quote paragraphs from it, if of particular interest, so as to afford the lieutenant governor an opportunity of gauging the abilities of junior officers. Assistant district officers will submit their reports to or through their divisional officer, as the Resident may direct. Junior officers will not be employed at headquarters on clerical or accounting work which the native staff is capable of performing. District officers will reside at the administrative center of the division to which they are posted, and not at the capital of the province. Whenever there are any assistant district officers in excess of the establishment, they will be temporarily posted to the secretariat for six months training.

NECESSITY FOR CONSTANT TRAVELLING

Political officers must endeavor to preserve a proper equilibrium between their judicial and executive duties, neither allowing the former to engross all their time and to detail them at their headquarters nor becoming so absorbed in assessment, and other executive work, as to neglect judicial duties and leave cases to the native courts which would be more advisedly tried by the provincial court.

"The work done by a political officer," said Sir H. Lawrence, "in his district, surrounded by the people, is greatly superior to the work done in office surrounded by untrustworthy officials." A district officer should pass from place to place and endeavor to lessen oppression and bribery, and to watch over and improve the native tribunals. He should when possible be accompanied by the local chief or district head. He will of course at the same time hold his court wherever he may be, and take opportunity to do so in a formal manner in the principal towns.

The primary object of travelling through the province is, that the political officer may show himself to the people and hear their complaints at first hand, not trusting to the reports which reach him at headquarters, where the villagers may possibly often fear to carry complaints, especially if they refer to some petty oppression or illegal exaction by the chiefs. It is only by the advent of a British officer that scoundrels, misrepresenting the government action, or extorting what they will from the natives in the name of government, can be caught; for the villagers in their ignorance, supposing them to be genuine, dare not as a rule complain.

It has been abundantly shown by experience that "unrest," resulting in, murders and outrages, and eventually necessitating the use of force, inevitably takes place among primitive tribes when districts are not regularly and systematically visited. By frequent touring, abuses are redressed before they become formidable, the law abiding people are encouraged to restrain the turbulent and lawless elements, and trust and confidence in government is fostered.

In provinces where there is direct taxation, officials should be constantly passing from place to place, for the purpose of carrying out the assessment of every village . . . or verifying and revising the initial assessment. But whether there is direct taxation or not, it is equally the duty of a political officer to travel constantly, in order to record, or to add to the statistics required for the provincial records; to verify or fix the areas of jurisdiction of each ally acquainted with the various peoples in his district. These duties are of primary importance in the early stage of administration and organization.

Travelling, it must be remembered, costs money for transport, and is not undertaken for pleasure. Each journey, therefore, should achieve some definite and useful result.

A veterinary or forestry officer, or Public Works Department officer, inspecting roads and buildings, and any other departmental officer who has occasion to travel in a province should seize the opportunity of accompanying a political officer on tour. It is not, however, essential that a departmental officer should be accompanied by a political officer, since such a course would frequently result in mutual delay, but he would generally be accompanied by one of the native political staff to facilitate his work.

LANGUAGES

All officers of the political staff are required to pass an examination in the Ordinances and Regulations of Nigeria, in the General Orders, and in one of the chief native languages of Nigeria. Proficiency in a native language is an important qualification for promotion. Promotion will ordinarily be provisional only unless an officer has passed, and he will be liable to revert if he does not do so within the period prescribed. Assistant district officers must pass the Lower Standard to qualify for promotion, and a Resident should have passed the Higher Standard, especially if the language he has adopted is Hausa.

CONTINUITY ESSENTIAL IN AFRICA

I regard continuity of administration as a matter of paramount and indeed of vital importance in African administration. It is only after many years of personal contact that the African—naturally reserved and suspicious towards strangers—will give his confidence unreservedly. More can often be accomplished in half an hour by an officer well known and trusted by the people, than by another, though his superior in ability, after months of patient effort.

It has, therefore, been my general rule, that the more senior an officer becomes the less liable he is for transfer from his province. An assistant district officer may be posted to two or three provinces in succession, in order that he may gain experience, and the lieutenant governor may decide whether his abilities are best adapted for work in an advanced, or a backward province. As a second class district officer he has become more of a fixture, and finally when he becomes Resident in substantive charge of a province he is never taken away from it.

These rules are of course liable to violation owing to sudden vacancies, etc., more especially of late under war conditions, but though a senior officer may be removed for a time he will be restored to the province he knows and to the people who know and trust him as soon as circumstances permit. Now that there is an administrative roster for all Nigeria, a Southern Provinces officer may find himself posted on promotion to the Northern Provinces and vice versa . But here again the change will not as a rule be permanent, especially amongst the senior officers, and I should endeavor to restore an officer to the people whose language he has learnt and among whom he can do more efficient work, as soon as an exchange could be effected. Residents in like manner will avoid changing their staff from one division to another if it can be helped.

RELATIONS OF DEPARTMENTAL OFFICERS WITH RESIDENT AND NATIVE ADMINISTRATION

The political officer is the channel of communication between all departmental officers and the native administration. It is essential that a Resident shall be fully informed of any project which a departmental officer proposes to inaugurate, and he will inform the emir and enlist his assistance. If after consulting the emir he considers that the project—or the manner in which it is proposed to carry it out-™is inadvisable he will refer to the lieutenant governor, and it will be held in abeyance until a reply is received. The general scope of the work having thus been discussed and approved, the departmental officer is at liberty to give orders as to details, but if he desires to introduce any new principle he will again consult the Resident. If the work is to be carried out at some distance from the capital, a responsible native official will usually be attached to the departmental officer, through whom he can make his requisitions for labor, etc., and issue his instructions. If the matter is urgent, and the departmental officer finds it necessary to issue instructions without delay, he will fully inform the Resident, in order that he in turn may inform the native administration.

While these instructions are of especial importance where the expenditure of native administration funds is involved, the general principle will also be observed in the execution of duties or works which are paid for from departmental notes. In the former case the native administration has the right to determine the priority in which different works shall be carried out, and the method, subject to any technical objections. Thus, if with the approval of the governor the native administration provides funds for the construction of several different sections of roads, the construction of which is placed in the hands of the Public Works Department, it is admissible that the native administration should decide which road should take priority and if it is itself capable of carrying out the earthworks, it may request the Public Works Department to deal with the alignment, bridges, and culverts, and only to exercise a general supervision over the remainder. Since, however, the road may eventually become a metalled motor track under the Public Works Department charge, it is clear that the construction must be in accordance with technical instructions. On the other hand a departmental officer carrying out government work from departmental notes such as the repair of telegraphs will look to the district officer to assist him in procuring the necessary labor and supplies, usually, as I have said, through the medium of an official of the native administration. Departmental officers must bear in mind that, in order to obtain the full benefit of native cooperation, the orders must be given not by the Resident or any of his staff, but by the head chief.

Where the duties of a departmental officer are educational, e.g., medical and sanitary, forestry, agriculture, and veterinary, and he is engaged on a tour of instruction, it is desirable that he should inform the Resident of the nature of the advice he proposes to give, especially if it involves a specific course of action, in order that the Resident may instruct his staff and the native administration to cooperate, and also in order that there may be no conflict of instructions. I recollect an instance in which two departmental officers, visiting the same town within a short time of each other, each with a different object in view gave diametrically opposite instructions on a specific point to the local chief. In such a case the Resident would have been able to discuss the matter with both and to arrive at a clear course of action. Political officers are, moreover, able to put a departmental officer in possession of local conditions and prejudices, and so to assist him in his objects.

JUDICIAL FUNCTIONS

The Resident in charge of a province has exofficio full powers as judge of the provincial court of the province, of which his European staff are "commissioners." The judicial powers of a commissioner may be increased at the discretion of the lieutenant governor, irrespective of his rank, on the recommendation of the Resident and of the Legal Adviser, in accordance with the ability he shows in his judicial work. Evidence of judicial ability will necessarily count much in selection for promotion.

NATIVE COURTS

A Resident will establish a native court in every city or district where it appears advisable to do so, and will constantly supervise its work, especially in the lower grades of courts. He must of course carefully study the Native Courts Ordinance and Memo, 8. In courts of grades A and B he will watch the integrity of the native judges, and note their comparative ability for promotion to more important centers, and see that their sentences are in accord with British conceptions of humanity. In the lower grades he will take care that the initiative of the chiefs who compose the court is not interfered with by the clerk or scribe, that they do not exceed their powers, and that their sentences and findings are free from bias.

THE "PROVINCE," "DIVISION," AND "DISTRICT."

A province is a single entity under the control of the Resident in charge. It is divided into divisions under district officers responsible to the Resident. The divisions must not be confused with the "districts" under native headmen. The more important divisions will be under first-class, and the less important under second-class district officers. The charge of a first or second-class division is an appointment notified in the Gazette, which forms the treasurer's authority to disburse the duty pay which attaches to it.

The division in which the headquarters of the province is situated will usually be in charge of a district officer, like any other division, so far as its routine work is concerned, but it is, I think, of great importance that in the more advanced provinces the paramount chief should deal direct with the Resident, and he is apt to feel slighted if referred to a subordinate officer. He should not only have free access to the Resident at all times, it should not be debarred from consulting him in any matter, even of detail, regarding the "emirate division" even though the matter may eventually and properly be dealt with by the district officer. In provinces where there is no paramount chief and only an embryonic native administration, the Resident will generally be able to take charge of the headquarter division himself with the assistance of a district officer who can take his place when on tour.

The number of divisions in a province is subject to the approval of the governor, and they will be notified in the Gazette, but their boundaries may at any time be altered by the lieutenant governor subject to the stipulations in this paragraph. One or more assistant district officers will be attached to each division, either generally or to a particular district, as the Resident may decide. Each divisional officer will tour constantly in his division hearing complaints, recording statistics, inspecting native courts, checking native agents, surveying, and assessing, and supervising the collection of taxes where these are imposed. He will reside near the principal town of the division, and each division in turn will be visited by the Resident. The divisional headquarters (involving the erection of new buildings, as well as political considerations) will not be transferred to another place without the prior concurrence of the governor. The Resident himself will reside at the provincial capital, which will also usually be the headquarters of the military detachment (if any) and of the medical and police officers. Wherever he wishes to go on tour the district officer in charge of the headquarter division will deal with any urgent correspondence addressed to him or any urgent matter as may be directed by the Resident, unless the "relief Resident" is present.

A province, or even a division, may comprise various units of native administration, but in no case will such a unit be comprised partly in one province and partly in another; and the same applies as a rule to a division. The limits of the jurisdiction and authority of native chiefs may not be altered, or one emirate or chieftainship placed under another, without the sanction of the lieutenant governor, who will in any case of importance consult the governor. Such reference is necessary when it is proposed to subordinate a chief hitherto independent, and more especially an independent pagan community to a Moslem emirate which should very rarely, if ever, be done.

DEPARTMENTAL FUNCTIONS OF POLITICAL OFFICERS

A political officer has to represent various departments and to exercise divers functions in the province to which he belongs. He acts as postal officer, in the absence of an European officer of the department, and is responsible for the despatch of mails in transit, and for the various duties laid down in the regulations under the Postal Ordinance. The postal and telegraph clerks, under his general supervision, will undertake the duties of issuing stamps, and preparing receipts for parcels and registered letters, etc.

The police in his province are under the general orders of the Resident, whose relation to them and to the commissioner or assistant commissioner of police is laid down in Police Regulations and in General Orders and elsewhere. Isolated police constables should never be stationed in villages since it deprives the village headman of responsibility and initiative; and men placed in such a position of power are apt to misuse their authority. Detachments without a European are always to be deprecated. When in charge of the government prison, the district officer will inspect it frequently and check the prisoners with the warrants at least once a month.

Political officers will also assist the customs on those inland frontiers where it is not possible for the department to have an European representative, and also in the collection of customs dues on postal parcels; and in such capacity they exercise the powers of customs officers, and any preventive staff is under their orders.

British Colonial Policy and Tribal Rulers

D.A. LOW AND R.C. PRATT[3]

Until recently British thinking on the administration of African peoples has been marked by a near unanimous adherence to a policy known as indirect rule. It has never been a precise concept. The form in which it was applied in any area depended on many variables, amongst the most important of which was the degree of centralized authority that existed in the tribal political system. Thus, in some areas indirect rule involved the appointment of councils of traditional elders whose rule hardly extended beyond the boundaries of a single village and who had laboriously to be induced to federate with neighboring authorities. In other areas, indirect rule meant the recognition of a powerful native ruler with an acknowledged authority over hundreds of thousands of subjects. A measure of the vagueness of the concept was the disagreement between successive governors of Uganda over whether the term applied to the type of administration in practice in Buganda. Sir Philip Mitchell, governor from 1935 to 1940, denied that Buganda was under indirect rule. His successor, Sir Charles Dundas, in contrast, regarded Buganda as the prototype of the whole idea.

However, in all the various types of local rule to which the term was applied, the local administration was entrusted to those native chiefs and headmen whose position was rooted in custom and who thus commanded the loyalty of the people. In contrast to any system of "direct rule," either through British officers or through Africans appointed without reference to local traditional claims to authority, "indirect rule" meant the appointment of traditional tribal chiefs as agents of local rule, the use in local government of those men whom the people were accustomed to obey. This principle of native administration was exceedingly influential throughout British Africa in the inter-war period. A careful study of the arguments used to defend it and of its implications and limitations is essential to an understanding of British colonial policy in almost any African territory during that period. In the case of Buganda there is additional interest in noting and explaining not only the influence of the concept but the significant variations in Buganda from the normal indirect rule pattern.

---

[3]Low, D.A. and Pratt, R.C., *Buganda and British Overrule: 1900-1955* (Kampala, Uganda: copyright 1969, Makerere Institute of Social Research; first published by Oxford University Press, 1960), pp. 163-176 D.A. Low is the President of Clare Hall, Cambridge. R.C. Pratt is a Professor of Political Science at the University of Toronto.

Initially its attractions were, mainly administrative. It was necessary to seek some other instrument to complete the chain of communication as between the government and the people . . . what more natural than that we should use for this purpose if we can find them the tribal institutions of the people themselves. What more natural indeed. With insufficient troops and a limited number of administrative officers the use of local personnel as agents of British rule was essential. The decision to enlist the tribal chiefs where possible was a natural one. They were the accepted leaders. Their presence on the British side would greatly lessen the danger of serious opposition to British rule. In a very real sense, too, there could be no substitute for them. As long as the tribal chief received the unquestioned loyalty of his people, not only would no alternative strike roots, but the chiefs themselves, unrecognized and ignored, would be a threat and a danger to the occupying power. In contrast, under indirect rule, with its instructions reaching the people through the authorities they had traditionally accepted, government would be more likely to be both accepted and effective. Lugard illustrated this point when he argued:

> Though the Suzerain power imposes the taxes and the general rate is fixed by the governor the actual assessment is in the hands of the native ruler and his representatives. . . . It therefore appears to the tax payer as a tax imposed by his own native ruler.

Rule through traditional institutions was seen to have a further advantage. It permitted the continued enforcement along traditional lines of the customary laws of the tribe. Though purged of elements that gave offence to Christian morality and "natural justice," these laws, especially when enforced by those who traditionally dispensed justice, would still provide a framework of ordered social life far more effective than any externally imposed system. With special reference to Tanganyika, Sir Donald Cameron in 1931 argued these matters as follows:

> Except in the detribalized areas and areas which were broken up by the Arabs and Germans a native is subject to a system of law and custom which he understands . . . and I claim . . . that it is because we have determined to uphold that system of law and discipline which he knows that the native in Tanganyika as a whole is so amenable. If you set up native councils which are not tribal, strictly speaking, you may call them tribal institutions because they are within a tribe but if they have not got the sanctions which I have mentioned, the sanctions of custom and usage, they are not regarded by the people with the same degree of veneration as if they were indigenous institutions of the people. . . . If you set up an artificial system of native councils which are not based on tribal authority you have got that tribal authority working underneath the whole time and then you express surprise that you do not make any progress in attaching the natives to the artificial system which you have set up.

Indirect rule soon came to rest on more than convenience and utility. In its defence were developed arguments of principle and social philosophy. The first of these expressed the fear that any other policy might destroy an established social order before alternative institutions, social controls, and values had become firmly rooted. This was seen as undesirable for both the welfare of the Africans and the security of the British rule. This combination of expediency and high purpose, often regarded by their detractors as a specifically British characteristic, clearly influenced the thinking of many British administrators. As early as 1898 it was expressed by Sir George Goldie when he wrote, "If the welfare of the native is to be considered, if dangerous revolts are to be avoided, the general policy of ruling on African principles through native rulers must be followed." Sir Percy Girouard wrote that:

> There are not lacking those who favor direct rule, but if we allow the tribal authority to be ignored or broken it will mean that we who numerically form a small minority of the country shall be obliged to deal with a rabble with thousands of persons in a savage or semi-savage state all acting on their own impulses and making themselves a danger to society generally.

Sir Philip Mitchell later argued that if the traditional communities were broken up, if the old loyalties were destroyed, other organizations, less responsible, less loyal, and more dangerous, might take their place.

It would be wrong to dismiss this as a thinly disguised self-interest. Certainly, the influence of indirect rule ideas was greatly increased because it offered practical as well as ethical advantages. The ethical considerations, however, were not mere shallow rationalizations. At the time the alternative to indirect rule was not the rapid absorption of Africans. Rather it was their direct rule by European officers and African subordinates. This, the supporters of indirect rule argued, would rapidly shatter the whole social fabric of African communities and reduce Africans to a disorganized mass of helots. Indirect rule was offered as a means of aiding these communities to stand with dignity and autonomy against the impact of western ways and ideas, adjusting to them but not being overwhelmed by them. This argument was well and strongly put in a memorandum submitted to the Joint Select Committee on Closer Union by the Tanganyika government:

> We believe that for the present and for many years to come the only way in which we can prevent the natives from "going under" and becoming a servile people (a condition desired for them by a large number of white folk in East Africa); the only way of keeping his society together; the only way in which he can be trained in public affairs—however simply in the early years—is by the system of indirect or tribal administration.

This quotation also suggests a further important observation. In the inter-war years there was strong hostility between the proponents of two main approaches to African development. One of these groups stressed the need for widespread European participation in the economic and agricultural development of the territories and for European political leadership and, eventually, control by the local European population. The second group was wary of too much European settlement and suspicious of local European political leadership. Instead it stressed that the primary responsibility of Britain was to her subject peoples, and that she held power as a trustee for these people until they developed to a position where they could rule themselves. There is no doubt that in the inter-war period almost all British supporters of this second "trusteeship" attitude towards Britain's colonial responsibilities believed that indirect rule represented the application of this trusteeship principle to the rule of African peoples. In Tanganyika, for example, Sir Donald Cameron's vigorous application of indirect rule principles was not felt to be in any way hostile to Britain's responsibilities under the mandate. Rather, quite the reverse. Cameron argued, and the Permanent Mandates Commission concurred, that Tanganyika's native administration system was compatible with both the letter and the spirit of this mandate.

Further support for indirect rule came from a conviction, widely and deeply held in the inter-war years, that European political institutions were unsuitable for Africans. This was not out of a sentiment that these institutions were too good for the African. Rather, as the Victorian confidence in the unquestioned value of Christianity, education, and commerce declined, a type of liberal racialism developed which felt that European institutions might be inappropriate in Africa. It was not argued that tribalism could be preserved indefinitely. The fact of change was recognized. Even Lugard recognized the inevitability of rapid and disintegrating change in Africa. Indirect rule was offered as a technique of social change, a means of bringing African communities into closer contact and harmony with the modern world and of raising their standards of life without any resulting social chaos. If sheltered against a too rapid disintegration, it was hoped that the indigenous institutions would adapt themselves successfully while yet remaining in basic harmony with the African temperament and environment.

In all this there was a fundamental Burkean conservatism—a skepticism of constitution-mongering, a fear of imposed changes, a belief that each people has its character and traditions and must itself evolve political institutions suitable thereto. Expressions of these sentiments were many. In 1929 the Hilton Young Commission, for example, regarded as an open question whether representative institutions would ever be suitable for African peoples. Sir Donald Cameron, with reference to the place of elections in native political development, said, "As far as I am concerned I would leave that to their genius. I would not force it upon them." And again, "Whether the native . . . will turn to a western system of government with the vote and the ballot I do not know. Again I saw that must be left to his own genius."

It might now be expected that the use which was made of traditional chiefs in the administration of the African territories would have been regarded in the United Kingdom as a technical administrative matter, of interest to very, very few. It is true that its main protagonists have always been colonial administrators. However, interest in and support for indirect rule was in fact strong and influential amongst a much wider circle. Two sources of this support can be noted briefly.

Firstly, after 1918, not only did interest in the colonies increase greatly in the United Kingdom but also large sections of important opinion came to hold a greatly enhanced sense of responsibility towards their inhabitants. Those who felt concern for the welfare and rights of the colonial peoples almost invariably supported the indirect rule approach to local administration in Africa. The backwardness of the continent precluded any consideration of independence, but it was widely felt that some autonomy and recognition should nevertheless be given to the social and political institutions which the people knew and felt to be their own. Indirect rule was thus the native administration side of a major body of British thought about Britain's responsibilities as a colonial power.

Secondly, indirect rule benefited greatly by the support which it received from British anthropologists in the inter-war years. Their judgement, with its obvious claim to being impartial and "scientific," further influenced important opinion in Britain. At any time, anthropologists are sensitive to the social costs of rapid change. They are more likely to see worth and utility in institutions and habits of life about which others might be impatient and critical. In addition, under the particular stimulus of Malinowski and Radcliffe-Brown, many British anthropologists in the 1920s and 1930s had become interested in "culture contact." Here, inevitably, interest tended to focus on the disintegrating and negative effect of the western impact. A.I. Richards made the point in 1944 in these words, "To view colonial administration as a force attacking a native society has perhaps caused too great a concentration on the disruptive processes and too little on the forces of integration which are also at work."

Thus, though approaching colonial administration from a different standpoint, the anthropologists ended with much the same opinion as most of the officials. "My own opinion," wrote Malinowski in 1929, "is that indirect rule or dependent rule is infinitely preferable."

The real difference . . . consists in the fact that direct rule assumes that you can create at one go an entirely new order, that you can transform Africans into semi-civilized pseudo-European citizens within a few years. Indirect rule on the other hand recognizes that no such magical rapid transformation can take place, that in reality all social development is very slow and that it is infinitely preferable to achieve it by a slow and gradual change coming from within. Contributing to this general reluctance to impose European institutions upon Africans was the traditional preference of the British for the unsophisticated. It is an attitude that is found frequently in British writings on African themes. It appears as a preference for the Masai over the Kikuyu, the northern peoples over the coastal tribes, the uneducated pagan over the mission-trained clerk, the Chief over the London graduate. Cameron exhibited this general attitude when he wrote:

> Our desire is to make him a good African, and we shall not achieve this
> if we destroy all the institutions, all the traditions, all the habits of the
> people. When I write that our desire is to make the native "a good
> African" I mean that he should be trained in accordance with his envi-
> ronment instead of being given a European veneer out of keeping with
> conditions under which he must live in Africa.

A consequence of this attitude was that indirect rule supporters were highly critical of any system under which the British officers in fact dominated the local scene.
Lugard, for example, was convinced that the native states of India had a more secure
political future than the areas under direct rule. In Africa, he wrote, "It must be in
fact remembered that the policy is to support native rule . . . and not to impose a
form of British rule with the support of native chiefs." By example, by encouragement, by advice, the chiefs must be led to an enthusiasm for justice and the progress
of their peoples. A Resident too enthusiastic for specific reforms and projects might
make more rapid progress initially, but if he fails to convince the chief of their value, if the native authority supports him only reluctantly and hesitatingly, then the
reforms will be unlikely to have lasting value. Always the primary stress, therefore,
should be on the education of the rulers. Lugard from the beginning recognized that
this would not be an easy task. In 1906 he wrote:

> Residents must bear in mind that the irksomeness of the new regime
> may weigh very heavily upon the native chiefs. The powerful are
> deprived of the pastime of wars and raids and even the weak may feel
> . . . that, "There can be too much even of security." Lack of any form of
> excitement and rivalry between neighboring emirates may induce a
> spirit of ennui caused by the Pax Britannica. Our object should be to
> give them an interest and an object beyond the routine performance of
> their duties, to interest them in the scheme of government, to teach them
> to recognize the new order of things, to show them common interests,
> to engage their sympathy for our efforts in secular education, and to
> promote a legitimate rivalry in civilized progress and even in sports.

This whole section suggests that while the supporters of indirect rule were anxious to encourage the African to adapt and develop his institutions along lines of his
own choosing, there were certain manly, Christian, and Victorian virtues to which
he must be led. Native authorities might choose, if they wished, to be autocratic, to
ignore such western institutions as elections and to scorn the idea that they should
be in any direct sense responsible to their people, but they could not choose to be
disinterested in progress, they could not choose blatant nepotism or a too corrupt
rule. They were, in other words, to be encouraged to promote, along traditional

lines, the values and objectives of Victorian England. An interesting minor reflection of this odd combination of values appears in Lugard's references to the education of the chiefs' sons:

> I hope that they would thus be taught not merely to read and write but to acquire an English public schoolboy's ideas of honor, loyalty and above all responsibility. It is by such means that I hope the next generation of Fulani rulers may become really efficient, reliable and honest cooperators with the British in the administration of the protectorate.

The Native Authorities and the Central Government

Indirect rule in British Africa was not only a set of values and attitudes. It is most usefully discussed in terms of the definite legal form which it first received in Northern Nigeria, and which later was copied in the Native Authority Ordinances of many other British territories in Africa.

Under these ordinances, chiefs were recognized and appointed by the governor as native authorities. As such, their primary responsibility became the maintenance of law and order in their area. To this end their authority, derived from customary law, was sanctioned in so far as it conflicted neither with any ordinance of the territory nor with "natural justice" or Christian morality. In addition, the authorities were normally empowered to issue rules and orders on a long list of matters in which, clearly, the administration was especially interested. This list would normally include such matters as the possession of firearms, gambling, the migration of labor, the cultivation of food crops, porterage and food for administrative officers on tour, and the manufacture and consumption of intoxicating liquor.

These powers which the chiefs enjoyed as native authorities had their severe limits. There was, of course, a ban on all exercises of chiefly power which were a danger to law and order or which were offensive to Christian morality and western standards of justice. In addition, Lugard insisted on four further limitations. He withheld for the colonial power the raising of taxes, the promulgating of legislation, the disposal of land, and the levying of native troops.

In addition to such general prohibitions as these, there was placed over the chiefs a senior administrative officer, a "Resident" as Lugard termed him, or a "district commissioner" as, frequently, he was called in other territories. Although Lugard referred to these officers as the sympathetic advisers and counsellors of the chiefs, it is clear that their authority far exceeded that of mere advisers. The various Native Authority Ordinances left no doubt about this. On matters of general policy his advice had to be taken, while such matters as the disposal of revenue, the issuing of rules and orders, and the appointment and dismissal of subordinate officials were not only subject to his guidance and advice but were open to his direct intervention if he judged it necessary. Finally the governor was always able to replace an unco-operative chief. There was no doubt on either side about the officers superior authority. Sir Percy Girouard wrote, "I have impressed emirs with the idea that they are my Wakila in their emirates but they must be guided by the word of the Resident who speaks for me." These close controls suggest a further aspect of indirect rule. It had been no part of the original intention of the early indirect rule supporters to preserve a series of semi-independent native states. On this point Lord Lugard could hardly have been more categorical:

> The essential feature of the system is that the native chiefs are consti-tuted as an integral part of the machinery of the administration. There are not two sets of rulers, British and native, working either separately or in cooperation but a single government in which the native chiefs have well-defined duties and an acknowledged status equally with the British official, their duties should never conflict and should overlap as little as possible. They should be complementary to each other and the chief must understand that he has no right to place or power unless he reaches his proper services to the state.

The legal position of chiefs substantiated this. Once the framework of adminis-tration had been established, colonial governments usually introduced legislation defining the responsibilities and powers of native chiefs. To be sure, their powers were not derived from an ordinance of the central government. They might have strong local authority in their own right and much deference might be paid to them. Indeed, indirect rule was based on the premise that this would be the case. Legally, however, they were the agents of the central government, enjoying only those pow-ers which it chose to delegate or recognize and subject to control and direction.

The limitations placed on the power of the native authorities were thus very great. It was, nevertheless, the hope of indirect rule supporters that the chiefs would accept these limitations and work under them without a deep sense of grievance. Indeed, it was more than a hope. Lugard judged in 1921 that the limitations had been accepted by the chiefs "as natural and proper to the controlling power and their reservation in the hands of the governor has never interfered with the loyalty of the ruling chiefs." It was a judgement which several decades of experience had sub-stantiated.

A major part of any explanation of this is the inter-war adherence of colonial administrators to the indirect rule approach to native administration. The various articles in the Native Authorities Ordinances which sanctioned direct interference and control by government officers were regarded as emergency provisions. The whole bent, however, of official thinking deprecated any blunt assertion of the administrative officers' superior powers. "The ideal of the highest efficiency and rapidity of execution," to quote Sir Donald Cameron, "must be subordinate to the main policy of encouraging and training the administration." The chiefs thus enjoyed a wider autonomy than any mere reading of the relevant ordinances would suggest, a fact which surely contributed to making these ordinances more acceptable to them.

To assure that this acceptance continued, Lugard advanced two main recommendations. The first was that governments could and must leave to the chief those functions which were most important to the maintenance of his position of authority with his people. The chief should appoint and dismiss his subordinates; he and his courts should enforce the customary law. In those territories without a settled European minority, the crown need rarely assert its rights over land alienation. The traditional system therefore should continue, with the chief retaining any powers in matters of land allocation and adjudication which were traditionally his own. Over the appointment of native authorities, there was a similar contrast between the legal powers held by the government and the powers which its officers normally asserted. Despite the reservation to the governor of the right of appointment, the traditional rules of succession were followed in almost all cases. The Residents' influence over appointments was thus almost always confined either to a rare final veto or to the indirect influence which they might exercise within the framework of the customary process of selection on behalf of one of the contenders to a chieftainship. It would obviously be a basic contradiction of the whole indirect rule philosophy for the administration to do more than this, except in rare occasions of crisis.

Secondly, Lugard laid great stress on the behavior of the administrative officers. At all times they must be careful to preserve and to enhance the dignity of the chief. Chiefs were not to be rebuked in public, instructions to their subordinates were to be given through them, and a most detailed protocol was to be followed by officers in their dealings with chiefs. Always the pomp and ceremony of office were to be preserved. Finally and most important, the Resident must have in himself a "natural dignity" that would command respect. "Vulgar familiarity" and "assumed self-importance" were to be avoided. Happily for his peace of mind, Lugard was able to assume that, "The English gentleman needs no prompting in such a matter—his instinct is never wrong."

Perhaps, however, we may suggest further reasons for the early success of indirect rule in addition to the limited autonomy retained by the chief in some tribal matters and the gentlemanly behavior of the British officers. The first must be the superior power of the British. The alternatives before a chief were cooperation or deposition. In Uganda, for example, there was an obvious moral in the contrast between Apollo Kaggwa who cooperated, continued as the leading official in Buganda, and later received the K.C.M.G.; and Kaberega, the king of neighboring Bunyoro, who did not cooperate and who spent his last years in exile on the Seychelles. However, indirect rule received more than a sullen and reluctant acquiescence. Many chiefs, overawed by the skills and knowledge of the European, were anxious to cooperate to secure the prestige which was gained by such association and to gain for themselves and their people the advantages which they hoped such association would bring. Moreover, indirect rule was not always detrimental to the chief's position. It was normally the chief alone who was recognized as the native authority. Such customary limitations to his power as councils of elders and lower chiefs received no legal recognition and inevitably, therefore, tended to be less effective. Also, the maintenance of law and order by the colonial power removed the threat of rebellion, frequently a very real check on the exercise of power in the indigenous system. Where any of these factors were at work, the chief was inclined to be sympathetically disposed to indirect rule.

Finally, in time, the interests of the chiefs and the government became more closely interwoven. They collected government taxes, heard cases that involved statute law as well as customary law, received fixed salaries and promoted centrally initiated policies. More and more were they associated in the public's mind with the administration and more did they also associate their own interests with those of the ruling power. Lugard's hope that the chiefs should become an integral part of the machinery of government was becoming a reality.

Such then have been the general values and attitudes that marked British thinking on native administration throughout most of this century. They appealed to the liberal by the paramountcy they gave to African interests. They appealed to the conservative by the organic view of society which they implied, and by their stress on gradual adaptation rather than rapid change. The ideas of indirect rule acquired enormous influence in British Africa. In territory after territory in the inter-war period native administrations were reorganized to fit this indirect rule model. Again and again the Northern and Western Nigerian and the Tanganyika Native Authority Ordinances were transposed to other territories, with a minimum of accommodation to local peculiarities and differences. Even the extremely atomistic indigenous political systems of Eastern Nigeria were searched for indigenous authorities who could be the basis of an indirect rule system. "Indirect rule," to quote Lord Hailey, "passed through three stages, first of a useful administrative device, then that of a political doctrine, and finally that of a religious dogma."

One Hundred Million Frenchmen: The Assimilation Theory in French Colonial Policy

MARTIN D. LEWIS[4]

During World War II, Jacques Stern, a former French Minister of Colonies, wrote almost lyrically of the "patient labor of assimilation" by which France had been "consolidating the moral and material ties which bind together forty million continental Frenchmen and sixty million overseas Frenchmen, white and colored" in the French Empire. And yet between 1946 and 1960 the French Empire had virtually disappeared. What went wrong? Assuredly, in the collapse of colonialism a variety of factors have been at work, many of which were quite independent of the particular policies which happened to be followed by the imperial powers. But some light may be thrown on the failure of assimilation by an examination of its place in the development of French colonial theory.

To begin with the obvious question, what does the term "assimilation" mean? While virtually all writings on modern French colonial policy use the word, confusion abounds as to its meaning. Some writers present it as the dominant and continuing characteristic of French colonial policy throughout the entire era of imperialism, as the distinctive manifestation of the French genius. Others hold that it was abandoned early in the twentieth century, and replaced by a quite different policy of "association." It is easy to show that this latter term first appeared in the literature of French colonialism as a proposed alternative to "assimilation," but it is equally true that the two words did not long remain differentiated.

Some counterpose "assimilation" to "autonomy," these two terms suggesting goals supposedly characteristic of French and British colonial policy respectively incorporation within the body politic of the mother country, on the one hand, and colonial self-government, on the other. Yet French critics of "assimilation" based their attack on the folly of extending European democratic institutions to the "inferior races" comprising the populations of the colonies and argued that the British did not engage in such irresponsible foolishness.

Some advocates of "assimilation" have given the term a purely legalistic consti-

---
[4]Lewis, Martin D., "One Hundred Million Frenchmen: The 'Assimilation' Theory in French Colonial Policy," (*Comparative Studies in Society and History,* IV, 1962). pp. 129-149. Martin Lewis is a Professor of History at the University of Indiana.

tutional meaning, with colonial representation in the metropolitan parliament as its most important manifestation. Others have used it in the much broader sense of making over non-European peoples in the "civilized" image of Europeans. Some have suggested that its true significance lies in the French acceptance of racial equality, as contrasted with the "colour bar" drawn by the British. Others have employed it in a narrowly administrative sense to refer to a highly centralized direct rule in the colonies; yet the supposedly assimilation-minded French employed the protectorate technique in many of their colonies. Also in an administrative context, assimilation has been considered to mean applying a uniform set of rules in *all* colonies without taking into account differences in size, distance from France, social organization, religious patterns, economic development, etc.

Culturally, assimilation might mean the propagation of the French language among non-European peoples; but have not the English done the same with their own tongue? Finally, to complete the confusion, one finds the odd phrase "tariff assimilation" used to describe French customs policy towards the Empire.

This melange cannot be blamed solely on the failure of scholars to define their terms, however much one might feel that it should be a part of their responsibility. At the height of the debate over assimilation as a colonial policy, a delegate to the *Congres Colonial National* of 1889-90 complained that "among the partisans of assimilation there are not two who agree on the meaning of that expression." A decade later, virtually the same thought was expressed by a participant in the *Congres International de Sociologie Coloniale* of 1900 who observed that "there are so many meanings given to 'assimilation' that it has become one of the most dangerous words of our colonial vocabulary." In 1895 Arthur Girault published his *Principes de Colonisation et de Legislation Coloniale* in which, with a true Gallic passion for order, he gave a systematic presentation to the ideas of assimilation as he understood them. His definition, while no more "correct" than any other, provides a useful point of departure for our discussion. Furthermore, his work, written as a text for law students, was restated in edition after edition, revised and expanded but always retaining the same organization in its discussion of general theoretical principles. Its influence in the training of French officialdom must have been substantial indeed.

His presentation rests on an abstract schematization involving three possible alternative colonial policies: subjection, autonomy, and assimilation. Each, he cautions, is an "abstract type and none have ever been realized in their entirety anywhere." Nevertheless, he leaves the reader in no doubt as to his own preference for assimilation, so long as its application is both "moderate" and "eclectic." Its ideal he considers "the constantly more intimate union between the colonial territory and the metropolitan territory." Colonies "are considered as a simple prolongation of the soil of the mother country," merely as *departments* more distant than the rest." The goal is "the progressive subjection to the same rules of the different parts of the territory" and "the progressive creation of veritable French *departments.*"

To Girault, "the principal result and visible sign of assimilation" is the represen-

tation of the colony in the legislature of the mother country. Other practical measures include the following, "A single body of legislation governs all parts of the
territory without distinction," and all new laws in the mother country apply automatically in all the colonies unless specific exception is made. The administrative
procedures and subdivisions that exist in the metropolis are duplicated exactly in the
colonies. The very existence of a colonial ministry may be opposed, since all the
various aspects of colonial administration would properly fall under one or another
of the home ministries: interior, justice, education, etc. No distinct colonial military
forces exist, and colonists are subject to military obligations identical with those of
citizens at home. Similarly, taxes, tariffs, and financial administration will be identical, as will the extent of civil liberties, reflecting the regime in power in the mother country.

Significantly, he comments that "the assimilation of the natives is a possible consequence, but not at all the only possible one, of the principle of assimilation of
colonies":

> If it is hoped to be able to inculcate them with our ideas and our cus-
> toms, then one works zealously to make them into Frenchmen: they are
> educated, they are granted the right of suffrage, they are dressed in the
> European mode, our laws are substituted for their customs, and in a
> word, native assimilation is pursued. But if one despairs of arriving at
> this result, if they show themselves refractory toward our civilization,
> then, to prevent them from injecting a discordant note in the midst of the
> general uniformity, they are exterminated or pushed back.

As a participant in the discussions at the colonial congress of 1900, he insisted
that "assimilation of the natives" and "political and administrative assimilation"
must be recognized as "two distinct ideas." In the third edition of this text, he commented that assimilation "has often been asked for opposite reasons, and with a
view to entirely different results":

> There are those who, when speaking of assimilation, are thinking pri-
> marily of the natives, and who imagine that it is the policy to be fol-
> lowed towards them which is in question, when in reality it is an
> entirely different matter. The assimilation of the colonies is so little that
> of the natives that in Algeria the pushing back of the latter is precisely
> what is asked by the colonists who would assimilate that country com-
> pletely with France.

Obviously, Girault's interpretation was not shared by all partisans of assimilation, but it is important to be aware of it as we seek to trace the development of the
concept.

Late in the nineteenth century a great debate developed in France over assimilation as the nation, having won and then lost its first great colonial empire in the seventeenth and eighteenth centuries, entered vigorously on a new imperial career under the aegis of the Third Republic. The foundations of the theory, however, lay in the past, and in particular in the treatment accorded the surviving fragments of the first French empire during the Revolution of 1789. . . . "The policy of assimilation," wrote Girault a century later, "was in the logic of the revolution":

> The Revolution had established the equality of all Frenchmen, and the rights which it proclaimed were in its thought the same for all men without distinction of latitude. What could have been more natural.

Of course, the "natural" implication of the Revolution might equally have been to extend to the colonies the right to choose their own form of government, as France itself was doing, even if that entailed their independence and separation from France. Unreal though the alternative might seem, in 1793 Jeremy Bentham had called on the Convention to do just that, in a pamphlet entitled "Emancipate Your Colonies."

The foundations of assimilationist theory can be traced to the arguments of the philosophe's. In Condorcet's famous phrase, "a good law is good for all men, just as a sound logical proposition is sound everywhere." Whatever their philosophical background, however, assimilationist practices were discarded with the rise of Bonaparte's star, and there began a process that would continue throughout the nineteenth century—assimilative measures became associated with republican governments, their abolition with the overthrow of these governments.

On Napoleon's [III] downfall in 1870, the government of National Defense, acting almost by republican reflex, restored colonial representation. It was some years, however, before the Third Republic was sufficiently stabilized to permit much attention to colonial problems. Before a new republican theory on the colonial question could be fully worked out, men of action had transformed the very nature of the question by the rapid extension of the empire in the 1880s. The forward push in Algeria and the new acquisitions in Indochina, Madagascar, West Africa, and Tunisia provoked controversy. Twice, in 1881 and 1885, Jules Ferry was forced from office by storms of public and parliamentary protest. But alongside those who thought imperialist ventures ill became a republican government were others who saw in the new territories a field for spreading the glories of the French tradition (as well, of course, as those who sought more mundane advantages for French capitalism).

The publication in 1874 by Paul Leroy-Beaulieu of his volume, *De la Colonisation chez les Peuples Modernes,* had attracted little attention, but by the time of its reissue in 1882, colonial policy had become a burning question. While his book was primarily historical, in dealing with Algeria he ventured to discuss the merits of current policy:

The indigenous population is at least 2,500,000. What should be done with these 2,500,000 individuals? Three possibilities exist: to push the natives back beyond the Atlas Mountains, even into the Sahara; to fuse them with the European population by imposing on them, forcibly or by propagating our customs, our laws and perhaps even our religion; or to respect all their customs, make their property inviolable, and remove the Europeans from frequent contact with them. These three systems may be defined in three words: refoulement, fusion [i.e., assimilation, ed.], abstention.

He found elements of each approach in past policy, but complained that after fifty years of French power no clear choice had yet been made. Such a decision, he felt, was urgently required, but what should it be?

The first path he considered "unjust" and therefore unthinkable. The third, "complete respect for the customs, traditions, and manners" of the Arab populations "would, if it were applied with logic, require that our army and our colonists should quit Algeria." Obviously, this too was not to be considered. "Thus, there remains only the second path, the fusion of the indigenous element with the European element." Such fusion need not mean a complete absorption of the natives, to the point that there would remain no difference in manners or customs. All that would be needed would be to create a state of affairs in which the two populations of different origin would be placed under the same economic and social regime, obeying the same general laws, and following the same impulse in the productive order. For a long time, perhaps forever, there would of course remain distinctions of habits and beliefs; but there would be an identity of interests from the economic, political, and social point of view; and properly considered, that is the only harmony that is indispensable from the viewpoint of peace, prosperity, and civilization.

The debate on assimilation that developed in the late 1880s found its focus in the sessions of the *Congres Colonial International de Paris* of July and August, 1889, and the *Congres Colonial National* which met in December, 1889, and again in February and March, 1890. Both meetings were attended by many high officials from various branches of the French government at home and abroad, as well as by scholars, explorers, and other private individuals interested in colonial questions. The first of the sessions, the international congress of 1889, was attended also by delegates from Spain, Portugal, Belgium, and the Netherlands. Its most prominent feature was the clash of opinions which took place between Gustave Le Bon, the explorer, and Alexandre Isaac, senator from the Caribbean island *department* of Guadeloupe and one of the two vice presidents of the Congress.

At the opening general session, Le Bon presented a report "On the Influence of Education and European Institutions on the Indigenous Populations of the Colonies." It was a slashing attack on "the fatal results of the system known as assimilation":

Daily, people speak of "Frenchifying" the Arabs of Algeria, the yellow peoples of Indochina, the Negroes of Martinique, of giving to all these colonies the institutions, the laws, and an organization identical to that of our French *departments*.

For such ideas he had nothing but scorn. His discourse was studded with such phrases as "inferior races," "savages," "half-civilized peoples," "barbarians." He satirized the French "taste for uniformity": "Our institutions of the moment seem to us always as the best, and our temperament, which tomorrow will lead us to over-turn them entirely, today impels us to impose them on everybody":

These theoretical views have led us and are leading us more and more to organize our colonies as French *departments*. It matters little what their population may be: Negroes, savages, Arabs, yellow peoples, should benefit from the Declaration of the Rights of Man and that which we are pleased to call our great principles. All have universal suffrage, municipal councils, arrondissement councils, general councils, tribunals of all degrees, deputies and senators to represent them in our assem-blies. Negroes, scarcely emancipated, whose cerebral development cor-responds hardly to that of our Stone Age ancestors, have jumped into all the complexities of our formidable modern administrative machines.

In passing, we should note that this was a considerable exaggeration with respect to the existing state of affairs on universal suffrage and parliamentary representa-tion; yet undeniably it was true for parts of the empire. He was particularly exer-cised by attempts to extend French education to the colonial territories. He denied any enmity for education as such, but argued that "the kind of instruction applica-ble to civilized men is not at all applicable to half-civilized man. The British expe-rience with European-style education in India provided him with a dramatic example of the pitfalls awaiting France. It had done no more, he claimed, "than unbalance the Hindus and take away from them their aptitude for reasoning, not to speak of a frightful lowering of morality."

The discussion of the report was heated. As a native of the Antilles, Senator Isaac expressed his embarrassment at attempting a reply, "Perhaps I myself am included among those natives who should not be given European education":

I cannot understand how, a hundred years after the Revolution, when if I am not mistaken it is a question of restoring to light the truths affirmed in that great epoch, it can be held that education is a bad thing; that between a colonizing people and the inhabitants of the colonial country there should be only a relationship of domination; that the customs, the language, the knowledge of European nations are a reserved patrimony which the natives should not be permitted to touch; that, finally, in the external territories of which these nations have taken possession, there should be only subjects, never citizens.

It reminded him, he said, of the days of the monarchy when the kings instructed colonial governors not to develop the spirit of the colonists too much, "because in giving the colonists a certain degree of culture they would be diverted from labors profitable to the metropolis." At that time, he continued, "there were also men in Europe who were crushed under the weight of a society based on restrictions of precisely the same nature. Were the Rights of Man proclaimed for them alone?"

How better could one make friends of a colonial people "than by establishing between them and the colonizers a community of language and interests?" Otherwise, if the native population "possesses a civilization to which you wish to confine them, that civilization will become more and more hostile to your own." And if, on the contrary, they have no civilization, "you may be blamed for having wanted to perpetuate their inferiority."

To say that it is necessary to keep people ignorant in countries under European domination, because instruction brought by the dominant people will make the natives wicked, or enemies, is to make that charge against European civilization itself. If that doctrine should prevail, it would be necessary to suppress all that has been done up to the present, and to turn boldly toward the past. It would be necessary to declare that slavery was a beneficial institution, and that there is but one means of maintaining the metropolitan authority . . . force.

Frank Puaux, a member of the Superior Colonial Council, found himself "overcome by a profound melancholy" while listening to Le Bon:

> Suppose that if on the conquest of Gaul, some savant of that time had maintained that the Gauls should be left in barbarism; that singular philanthropist might have been needed. Would we be here today, if the Romans had followed his counsel? Do not forget, messieurs, that we have become what we are because a people of superior civilization communicated their light, their arts, and their laws to our ancestors. Have we the right to keep this rich heritage for ourselves? Can we refuse to do today for others what the Romans did for us nearly two thousand years ago?

Others conceded some points to Le Bon's argument, but the general tenor of the discussion was critical of his viewpoint. Dr. Poitou-Duplessy, retired chief physician of the navy, recognized "just as the stomach requires food appropriate to its age and kind, so the brain requires nourishment suitable to the degree of development which it has attained." The brain of orientals, he agreed, is not yet capable "of partaking of our intellectual nourishment without cerebral indigestion." Nevertheless, he would not accept the view that assimilation was impossible, if approached slowly and carefully, as a parent teaches a child. Furthermore, even in an inferior race, "some men's brains are equal to the average among ourselves," and are thus capable of European education. "To refuse it to them would seem to me difficult and unjust."

When Le Bon cited a recent anthropological study as proof that the impossibility of civilizing Negroes was "well settled," that to attempt it was "pure aberration," Admiral Vallon, former governor of Senegal replied that "the blacks lacked neither intelligence nor natural gifts, and in that respect they sometimes put us in the shade." He considered that educating the natives was not only France's moral obligation but was in the interest of France as well. "We are in the same situation with respect to these colored peoples as we are with respect to our peasants. We owe education to the former as to the latter." "It is true," he added sarcastically, "that some persons think that in sending our peasants to school, we are making them enemies of society."

Several speakers criticized Le Bon's assumption that assimilation meant an attempt to transform, "natives into Frenchmen overnight. The remarks of Senator Barbey, former Minister of Marine and Colonies and the president of the congress, seemed to sum up the predominant view:

> I believe I am able to say that no one here is the enemy of the natives,
> or the adversary of those who wish to civilize them. The whole problem
> is to find the best methods for doing that . . . From this point of view,
> there remains much to be done: We have to free ourselves of a great
> number of prejudices, to better recognize the proper aptitudes of the
> various races, to determine the degree of development to which each of
> them is susceptible. . . . It is necessary above all to recognize that such
> a work will require much time. We will achieve nothing without
> patience, and, I may add, without generosity. Only by treating the
> natives benevolently and by giving them a good example can we win
> them to our ideas.

Senator Isaac's own role in the congress was the presentation of a report, "On Methods of Government in the Colonies." His main theme was the necessity of bringing the colonial regime "into harmony with the present institutions of the metropolis." He was sharply critical of the continued existence of rule by decree [*senatus consultes*] as established under the Second Empire, and asked that the colonies already represented in parliament be brought more completely under the rule of laws. Where colonial representation had not yet been established, and where that fact justified a maintenance of decree rule, he felt "it would nevertheless be bad and sometimes dangerous if the exercise of that regime were not tempered by the organization of some mode of consultation with the interested populations.

He based his argument on an extensive examination of the history of French colonial administration, designed to show that assimilation was the policy truly characteristic of republican France, and even, to some degree, of France before the

Revolution.

"What is a colony?" he asked. "Is it a simple field of exploitation? An instrument of work composed of the territory and of those who inhabit it? Is it an establishment which has completely answered the purpose of its creation when it brings to the metropolis a benefit, when there has been procured the means of draining off its products?" . . . He insisted that "we do not intend to formulate an absolute rule equally applicable to all the colonies. Common sense would indicate that was impossible. . . . Their institutions will be more or less similar or different according to their age, their geographical situation, the composition of their population." It was, he implied, only the tendency and direction of development that was essential.

In the discussion which followed his report, Paul Dislere, councillor of state and another vice president of the congress, sought to pin down his meaning. Total assimilation, it seemed to Dislere, could be achieved only "at the cost of veritable political or economic revolutions." In the "old colonies," those revolutions had taken place; "the evil is past; now there is only good to be drawn from it." He saw no impediment to their complete assimilation, giving them "all our rights," and also the same burden of taxes as in the metropolis. But he boggled at the implication that "assimilation" implied the right of all colonies, everywhere, to be represented in the national parliament, and asked what this would mean in those colonies "where a very small number of French citizens found themselves in the midst of a considerable native population." Senator Isaac hastened to reply that he had never asked that all colonies should be assimilated:

> I have, on the contrary, constantly made a distinction between assimilable colonies and those which are not suited to assimilation. . . . By assimilation I mean a situation in which the French citizens of a colony enjoy all the legal guarantees accorded to the French of the metropolis, on condition that they bear equivalent charges proportionately to their ability.
>
> The *Congres Colonial National* was organized in seven sections, the first to consider general questions of colonial organization, the others to discuss problems of specific areas: Algeria and Tunis, the American colonies, the colonies on the west coast of Africa, in the Indian Ocean, in Oceania, and finally of Indochina.

The national congress was notable for the absence of critics of assimilation among its leadership, although participants in discussion frequently challenged the proposals made and forced modifications. Senator Isaac, in charge of the discussion on general organization, sought the commitment of the congress to the general principle of assimilation, which he defended (as in the earlier congress) by an appeal to history and the French tradition. When a critic objected that discussion of pure theory would lead the congress into sterile debates and obscure the real task of finding "practical means" to improve colonial organization, he insisted that nothing worthwhile could be accomplished without an adequate theory. "Unless we are to abandon everything in the colonial domain to chance and empiricism, it is indispensable to declare ourselves for a system and to set forth its principles." To do so, he reiterated, would not mean either attempting an overnight transformation of the colonies or the imposition of a uniform approach everywhere. "One does not transform a society with the wave of a wand." One must find "a general formula which can be given diverse applications." The resolution which finally emerged with the approval of the congress declared that "in all the overseas lands under French authority, the efforts of colonization should propagate among the natives the language, the methods of work, and, progressively, the spirit and the civilization of France."

There was no dissent on the question of language, but before the provision on "methods of work" was accepted it was necessary to quiet the fears of some delegates. Commander Perisse pointed out that there was "no intention of introducing into our colonies the complicated industries which can only exist in the home country. . . . The only goal that it is possible to attain is to lead the natives progressively to cultivate certain useful trades, or to make use of more perfected implements than the rudimentary tools which they now employ."

Senator Isaac agreed, "No one would think, for example, of transporting to the Sudan this or that one of our metropolitan industries which would not find nourishment in that country. Manifestly, everywhere one should be inspired by the resources, the possibilities, the local needs." Even greater concern was expressed at the provision for spreading "the spirit and the civilization of France." In Isaac's original draft resolution he had used the word "customs" (*moeurs*), and many delegates voiced their doubt that this could ever be achieved. After the substitution of phrasing, however, and Isaac's assurances that "assimilation does not consist of substituting from one day to the next the customs and institutions of a European people for the customs and institutions of a native people," the clause was adopted.

The second general resolution adopted by the congress advocated a special regime for each colony, taking account of "different geographical, political, and economic conditions." This regime, however, should be defined by an organic law. "French laws should as much as possible be applied to Frenchmen residing in the colony," while "the native laws and customs should be respected insofar as they are compatible with the *mission civilisatrice* of France." This last provision, though modified somewhat in language from the original proposal to "guarantee in principle" the respect of native laws and customs, of course still glossed over the key dilemma in the idea of assimilation as a benevolent colonial policy.

The third general resolution called for parliamentary representation of all colonies "where the French establishment is sufficiently developed, both in the number of nationals [i.e., Frenchmen from France] . . . and the importance of their interests," and declared that voting for such representatives should be by "all French citizens" of the colony. "The native populations should be led gradually to the exercise of political rights, taking account of their state of civilization." The fourth resolution attacked the *senatus consultes* of 1854 and 1866 as "not in accord with the principles of the present Constitution" and declared that "rule by decree is not rec-oncilable with parliamentary representation of the colonies." The fifth called for the establishment, for the benefit of those colonies as yet unrepresented in parliament, of a special system of consultation in the form of a reorganized Superior Colonial Council.

The assimilationists have been misrepresented by their critics, both political and scholarly, as insisting "on a rigid universality" of their theory, making no allow-ances for variations between one colony and another. The inaccuracy of this is shown by the general resolutions, but it is even more clear from the special resolu-tions dealing with specific areas. . . . In the West African territories as yet unan-nexed, the congress felt a protectorate regime would be "more favorable than annexation to the development of our influence and more appropriate to the customs and interests of the natives."

Algeria was recognized as a special case. The congress declared that it was *une terre française,* not a colony, and that France should "strive to inspire French senti-ments among the natives, to favor French colonization by all possible means, to assimilate the European foreigners." It opposed naturalization of the natives *en bloc* but felt "it would be useful" to offer "a special naturalization compatible with the maintenance of their personal status (under Moslem law) to those who fulfill certain conditions and offer certain guarantees." If this were done, these newly created Moslem citizens of France should be allowed to vote in the elections for Algerian senators and deputies, and "to become entitled after a delay of ten years to occupy a place in the metropolitan chambers."

In the light of the general program of the assimilationists what seems significant is not the sweeping character of the measures, but their timidity. In no instance was a further extension of parliamentary representation called for, although the mainte-nance of existing colonial representation was defended even where the native pop-ulation was excluded from the franchise. For Algeria the congress recommended that "sufficient financial resources should be created" to make French education "accessible to the entire school-age population," but for Indochina the congress sug-gested only that the government "should study ways of encouraging the learning of French and making them accessible at small cost to the native population."

The resolution on the West African establishments also favored the encourage-ment of missionaries to teach French, and urged "that the sons of influential native chiefs should be brought to France, where they could be familiarized with our civi-lization and prepared to become valuable auxiliaries for French policy in Africa." Finally, with regard to Madagascar, where French control was not yet complete, the congress seemed most concerned that the government should maintain energetical-ly the political supremacy of France . . . *vis-a-vis* foreign powers. Assimilation came into the picture only in the request that France should "give as much support as pos-sible to the French missionaries and their *mission civilisatrice*" in the island.

The resolutions of the 1889-90 congress appear to have had little practical effect on the actual conduct of colonial affairs. Specifically, despite Senator Isaac's concern with ending decree rule, the *senatus-consultes* of 1854 and 1866 continued in force without change. The importance of the congress lay rather in providing a generally accepted definition of goals for colonial policy, a definition which stood unchallenged for some time. Around the turn of the century, however, a concerted attack on the ideas of assimilation began to develop.

In 1899, Leopold de Saussure attempted, in his *Psychologie de la Colonisation Française, dans ses Rapports avec les Sociétés Indigenes,* to demonstrate that assimilation was an impossibility. The core of his argument was a pseudo-scientific theory of "the heredity of mental characteristics." (He was, of course, far from alone at the time in considering this to be profound scientific truth. "The Frenchman," complained Saussure, "is persuaded that the several human species differ only as a result of education. The profound mental differences which separate the races seem superficial to him; . . . he persists in a futile struggle against the laws of heredity."

Approvingly, he quoted Gustave Le Bon's statement that "a Negro or a Japanese can accumulate all the diplomas possible without ever arriving at the level of an ordinary European." He reviewed the experience of the freed Negro in the West Indies and the United States to demonstrate the "organic incapacity" of that race. Successful examples of assimilation never involved whole races but were limited to individuals, usually of mixed ancestry. The fact that the 1889-90 congress was moderate in its demands for assimilation made it all the more dangerous, as it would "create illusions and reassure some minds."

Saussure's negative attack on assimilation was matched a few years later by a more positive statement of what colonial policy should be. Joseph Chailley-Bert, in *Dix Années de Politique Coloniale* (1902), argued that the real need of the day was a "native policy" adapted to the existing situation in the newly acquired territories which, properly speaking, were not colonies but possessions. Such a policy should recognize "the differences of race, of genius, of aspirations and of needs between the native inhabitants of a possession and their European masters" and should see in these differences the need for different institutions. The European could not work in the tropics; he could "accomplish nothing without a cheap and abundant labor supply" provided by the native population. What was needed was a policy which would "limit the introduction of European ideas to those which can serve the progress of commerce and civilization." The proper role for the European colonist was to supply capital, "not to work with his hands . . . but to direct the labor of the natives."

The new ideas were most fully elaborated by Jules Harmand in his *Domination et Colonisation* (1910). Harmand, a man of much colonial experience, had been developing his views over a quarter of a century before their final publication in book form. In 1887 he had first put forward the notion of "association" between conqueror and conquered as the proper basis for colonial policy, and by the first decade of the twentieth century this new term had virtually replaced "assimilation" as the catchword to describe French policy. In Harmand's view, "association" meant "scrupulous respect for the manners, customs, and religion of the natives," replacing simple exploitation and expropriation of the native by a policy of "mutual assistance." The purpose of the policy would be to make European domination work more smoothly and productively, reducing the need for force to a minimum. It would seek to ameliorate the condition of the native "by allowing him to evolve along his own lines," leaving his habits and traditions untouched as much as possible and employing his own forms of social organization.

Such a policy Harmand considered to be a "systematic repudiation of assimilation," substituting "indirect administration" which would conserve native institutions for the "necessarily rigid and oppressive regime of direct administration." At the same time, he was careful to note, it would "preserve with unshakable firmness all the rights of domination. . . . It does not aim to prepare for the realization of an equality which cannot be possible, but to establish a certain equivalence or compensation of reciprocal services." . . . He admitted that it was "bad" to deprive a people of their independence, but he considered it "one of the manifestations of that universal law of the struggle for life." Civilized nations could not permit "vast and fertile regions of the globe" to remain undeveloped by virtue of "the incapacity of those who hold them." He recognized that "expansion by conquest . . seems particularly unjust and disquieting to the conscience of democracies" because it leads to "a regime *ipso facto* aristocratic."

France has tried to resolve this paradox by assimilation, which is based on a preconceived faith in the equality of all men and their rapid perfectibility. The time has come to substitute for this utopian idea conceptions which may be less generous but which are surely more useful and more productive of results, since they will be in conformity with the nature of things.

The first duty of the conqueror "is to maintain his domination and to assure that it will last; everything is good which has the effect of consolidating and guaranteeing it, everything is bad that may weaken or compromise it." It was time, he said, to put aside illusions about the "natural rights of man." He mocked what he called "the revolutionary syllogism: All Frenchmen are equal. The inhabitants of the colonies are all Frenchmen. All Frenchmen have the right to send deputies to the Assembly. Therefore the colonies cannot be deprived of this right." The colonial representation which resulted from this reasoning "has caused the greatest evils." . . . Limiting voting rights to the small group of white settlers only aids "the spoliation of the native majority by the European minority" and fosters dissension and hatred. But in the old plantation colonies of the Caribbean, where suffrage had been extended to the liberated slaves, "the inferior majority oppresses the superior minority. "An Annamite, a Negro, an Arab" could not become a Frenchman by "the adoption of certain European habits, the knowledge of the language and literature of the conqueror. This culture would only make him "an enemy better armed against us . . . . Wisdom tells us not to forget the lessons of Santo Domingo."

In the light of what would follow it is interesting to note Harmand's warning that his policy of "association" should not be construed with "excessive liberalism" so as to put the native "on the same footing as ourselves" and lead him to believe that he had "the same rights in the association" as the French. Some, he feared, already tried to use the new term" association" to give a "new virginity" to that old passion of assimilation.

Association in French Colonial Theory

RAYMOND R. BETTS[5]

Although denunciations of traditional French colonial policy and doctrine often appeared to be more ardent than attempts to substitute a new policy for the old, several new, if not original, plans for native administration did emerge at the beginning of the twentieth century. Essentially all resembled one another and were more often than not grouped together under the name of "association." Because of the almost generic sense in which it was used, the term, never sharply defined, was often fused with the idea of the colonial protectorate and was at times simply seized upon as a convenient catchword. Despite these shortcomings there was wide agreement on the general ideas which the term was to embrace.

The great virtue of this policy was proclaimed to lie in its simplicity, flexibility, and practicality. Opposed to the rigidity and universalism of the condemned doctrine of assimilation, the policy of association emphasized the need for variation in colonial practice. One of its essential tenets was the idea that the determining factors in all colonial policy should be the geographic and ethnic characteristics and the state of social development of the particular region submitted to foreign control. Evolution of native groups along their own lines was the key.

Underlying these thoughts was the realization that a strong type of cooperation between colonial and native was imperative. This would be best achieved, ran the accepted argument, through the retention of native institutions. All French efforts were to be directed toward developing the region; in this task French and natives would be "associated," each doing what best suited its abilities and stage of development.

Such a program necessitated a degree of autonomy in colonial administration unknown in France prior to the Third Republic. The doctrine of assimilation naturally implied centralization, and throughout her modern colonial history France had attempted to control colonial administration from Paris. Now, however, the demand for flexibility in actual practice made the former policy seem untenable. The block theory of colonialism was condemned. Not an empire, unified and homogeneous, but a series of unrelated possessions existed, and these demanded separate adminis-

[5]Betts, Raymond R., *Assimilation and Association in French Colonial Theory, 1990-1911* (New York: Columbia University Press, 1961) pp.106-28. Raymond Betts is a Professor of History at Grinnell College.

tration. As a consequence the administrator on the spot and the officials in his charge were to assume far more responsibility for the direction of the possession's affairs than heretofore, and the task of the Minister of Colonies, it was said, was to be limited solely to coordination of general colonial policy. In short, the tradition of colonial assimilation was being discarded.

The idea of association was, of course, not entirely new, and even the use of the term, often credited first to Jules Harmand, had an old history. Rene Maunier, in his work, *The Sociology of Colonies,* traced the origin and growth of the idea. The type of association which he called "hierarchic partnership" dovetailed with that discussed by the theorists at the beginning of the twentieth century. Maunier explained that colonial partnership went through three phases, phases which he considered in an ascendant order and in which first the idea and spirit of humanitarianism were expressed, then those of equality, and finally those of fraternity. It is in the first phase that association develops; here "there is no equality, but there is humanity and moderation. There is collaboration and cooperation, but of superior and inferior."

While inklings of this idea existed before the eighteenth century, it is at the end of that century that the idea became evident. In 1789 Robinet, in the *Dictionnaire universel des sciences morales,* expressed his desire for association between colonizer and native, and in 1821 the Comte de Laborde published his *L'Esprit d'association dans tous les intérêts de la communaute,* a work which discussed the colonial situation in Santo Domingo. Then Saint Simon's chief disciple, Enfantin, described his own idealistic concept of association in the word "affamiliation," which connoted intimate ties established between ruler and ruled.

Germinated in the fertile soil of the Enlightenment, as were so many humanitarian ideas, and fed by the stream of thought emanating from the Quakers, association then implied mutual trust and friendly cooperation, but of two differently developed peoples whose relationship was described as one of teacher or of "governor" in the sense of preceptor and pupil. The idea was, perhaps, a variation on the theme of the noble savage. And it is interesting to note that the ideas of colonial association and of assimilation were largely inspired by common ideas. But whereas a conscious lineal development in the instance of the doctrine of assimilation can be easily traced, this cannot be done for association. None of the colonial theorists were aware—at least they made no indication that they were—of an earlier use of the term "association" or of the idea as such. One among them did state that the "formula is not new," but the others who interested themselves in the issue saw the origin and growth of the term and idea as being commensurate with the growth of an interest in native policy and the concept of the colonial protectorate. The native policy which France so sorely lacked, according to contemporary observers, was evolved in the last few decades of the nineteenth century by several colonial administrators, but most forcefully by two men in particular: Gallieni and Lyautey. To understand more fully the discussion of colonial theory in France, it is necessary to analyze briefly the methods of these two colonial officers. To appreciate their methods, it is advisable to begin the story with a few words about their predecessor,

Faidherbe.

Far from the effects of volatile public opinion and from the interference of a Chamber of Deputies often hostile to colonial undertakings, the new empire builders, best exemplified by Faidherbe, Gallieni, and Lyautey were able to act as they saw fit. They were their own masters. Thus they were able to analyze the colonial situation with a detachment unknown in France and were able to pursue a personal policy relatively unhindered by changing national political pressures. On the scene, free from tradition and historic polemics, they realized what many Frenchmen did not: the essential difference between modern imperialism and the earlier forms of French colonial activity.

France was not building another "New France." No colonies *de peuplement* were necessary or desirable. With her static population and her citizens' traditional love of their native soil, France was spared the problem of searching for outlets for emigration. Moreover, her newly acquired possessions were largely unsuited to white populations. Located in the tropics for the most part, these regions, with their profuse vegetation and hostile climate, were not the sort to induce colonization. As many colonial administrators clearly perceived, the true problem for France was of an entirely different sort: the relationship between a native mass and a white ruling minority. In the second colonial empire this problem was relatively new.

The beginnings of a sound native policy can be traced back to Dupleix in India or Montcalm in Canada. Nevertheless, it was not until a century later that the French colonial administrators as a group became cognizant of the virtues or even of the need of a native policy based on mutual respect between themselves and the populations they sought to rule. It could be said that they had no other choice, and indeed their policy was expedient. But it was also humane: the outstanding French colonial figures of this period were men who loved the life they followed, approached the native populations in their charge with sympathy—of a condescending sort, perhaps—and devoted themselves to the welfare of these peoples almost as much as to the welfare of the state they served. There were scoundrels, it is true, but there were also people like Auguste Pavie. That remarkable Frenchman, who sought to be as much a part of the native life in Indochina as was possible, casts his shadow across the annals of French colonial history in the late nineteenth century. Pavie spoke of the *conquête des coeurs,* and his was really such a policy. It was not limited to him, however.

The French Third Republic in the second and third decades of its existence produced a type of military officer who found in the pacification and administration of France's overseas possessions the opportunity to practice an art not suited to the European battlefield. Organization and administration were the activities in which he showed his skill, not in military strategy. In such endeavors Gallieni and Lyautey were the outstanding figures. Although they were two of the greatest administrators of colonial policy during the Third Republic, their methods followed in the tradition of native policy which had been encouraged by Leon Faidherbe.

A professional soldier trained in colonial warfare and activities during his service with General Bugeaud in Algeria, Faidherbe developed his own methods in the Senegal where he first took up his duties in 1852 as officer in the Corps of Engineers. From this date, he devoted his life to the population of the Senegal and to the problems besetting it. So successful were his initial efforts that, upon the retirement of Governor Protet, the merchants of Saint Louis suggested Faidherbe as the likely candidate for the position. In 1854 he was appointed governor-general. Under his effective leadership the internecine wars between the various local native elements were soon checked, thus enabling the French to turn their full attention to matters of political organization and administration.

Imbued with traditional French principles of justice which led him to respect peoples of other races, Faidherbe struggled to improve the native's state while he subdued the region for France. It was his policy to use force only at the moment when peaceful methods did not bring the desired results. He assumed a position in opposition to many of the colonial administrators of his day, for he rejected the French love of abstract principles and taste for complicated bureaucracy; instead he followed a practical and simple program which was based on the needs of the local population and its environment. Wherever and to whatever extent possible he avoided any interference with the customs and habits of the local population. To his aides he solemnly declared, "The first requisite is to administer the conquered populations well. . . . Because of differences of race and religion, it is necessary to let them regulate their own affairs as much as possible."

What Faidherbe was implementing in the Senegal was a policy of penetration with the aid of the native populations. Thus he sought to maintain whatever effective native institutions he found to be of advantage. When Gallieni arrived in the Senegal, he saw before him the excellent results of Faidherbe's native policy.

Ardent republican a man of thought and of action, endowed with acute intelligence, Gallieni left France in 1877 for the Senegal where his vocation of colonizer opened before him. "I love this life," he said, and he applied himself to colonial problems with the same enthusiasm that characterized Faidherbe. Although ten years after his arrival there he was named commandant of the French Sudan, his real talents became manifested more clearly in Tonkin. When Gallieni arrived in Tonkin in 1892, the French colonial government there was shaken by the struggles and piracy carried on by Chinese bands in spite of the fact that France had earlier made peace with China. Under the initiative of Governor-General Lanessan, an able administrator who also contributed to French colonial theory, the Upper Tonkin, where these struggles were most evident, was divided into four military districts. One of these territories was confided to Gallieni. His lightning-like achievements led Lanessan to give him the most troubled region, that which centered around Langson. Gallieni ended the pirate problem by a careful application of his own colonial policy:

To occupy the country firmly, to win over the natives and to make them participate in the effort we are undertaking, such were essentially the principles to be applied in order to save the Upper Tonkin from the anarchy from which it suffered.

Gallieni's method was simple, a combination of good sense and basic psychology. To protect the country against further pirate attacks, he had a chain of military posts constructed. These were made of concrete to convince the local natives of the French intention to stay and thus to rally them to the French side. He took the "inhabitants of the country as chief collaborators" against his enemies, and he employed them as often as possible in the local administration of the region.

This policy, first undertaken in Tonkin, reached its final form at Madagascar, where Gallieni gained his greatest reputation. In no region were the French more confused or insecure than on this island, the occupation of which had begun during the second ministry of Jules Ferry. Anarchy still reigned, stimulated by continual insurrection and assisted by the lack of experience among the French in charge of the occupation. These were the reasons for which Gallieni was called to Madagascar in 1896. Immediately charged with the task of pacifying the island, he destroyed the Hova Kingdom, which occupied the central plateau of the island. Then he liberated the other native peoples formerly under Hova control, confiding the region of the extreme south to Lyatey. With speed that amazed the French government Gallieni subdued all of Madagascar and, in 1905, when he left and retired from colonial life, the island was peaceful and on the way to prosperity.

It was during his mission to Madagascar that Gallieni perfected his colonial policy. The best explanations of this policy are to be found in the proclamations that he wrote at the time. Gallieni's method was founded on the immediate, the necessary, and the opinion that: "the administrative organization of a new country must be in perfect rapport with its resources, its geographic configurations, the mentality of its inhabitants, and the goal that one proposes to attain." In his instructions of May 22, 1898, on the pacification of Madagascar he declared that the best means of attaining this goal was to employ the combined action of force and politics. This he explained in two expressions which soon became famous: *la tâche d'huile* and the *politique des races*.

According to Gallieni it was best to use force in a limited way only. Immediately after the pacification of some territory, permanent posts, political centers, and means of communication were to be established. Then the advance would continue slowly; the region would be cleared with the help of the local inhabitants now won over to the French cause and duly armed for their new task. Provisional posts would be established in the newly acquired regions, and the process would thus continue until the whole region had been conquered and pacified. "This is the method of the *tâche d'huile*. New territory is not acquired until all that in the rear had been completely organized."

If force was needed as a means of assuring colonial control, political action, was still more important. . . . A knowledge of the country and of its inhabitants was imperative, for upon these elements depended the type of government which would be instituted and, consequently, the very success of this government. Gallieni believed that not only were there customs which had to be respected but also there were hates and rivalries among the peoples which could be exploited. Like every clever and able leader, he knew the value of the old adage, *divide et impera.*

Following this empirical program Gallieni pacified Madagascar. In the process he developed the second of his famous principles, the *politique des races.* As a general rule he assumed that "all administrative organization must follow the country in its natural development." The native bureaucracy was to be left intact wherever possible; administration was to be flexible and based on the needs of each region; and, finally, all reforms were to be carefully studied in terms of native needs so as to avoid the disastrous results obtained in colonies where European institutions had been introduced *en bloc.* This *politique des races* was progressive in nature and based upon means as well as ends. As Gallieni himself wrote:

> Nothing is more damaging . . . in colonial affairs than preconceived formulas, imported principles, which, based most often on European ideas, do not apply to the environments, situations, or occasions for which one has wanted to adapt them. Common sense, knowledge of the country and of its inhabitants, prudent initiative directed toward the general goal desired, these must be the guides of our civilian and military administrators.

Nothing could be farther from the traditional doctrine of assimilation. No method seemed more attractive to the colonial officers who were then winning new regions for the French empire. Among these officers, one incorporated Gallieni's ideas with his own, proved their worth, and won himself a name as a genius in colonial affairs. This was Lyautey.

Gallieni had no disciple more devoted than Hubert Lyautey, even though their personal backgrounds contrasted markedly. A member of a well-known monarchist family which had produced good soldiers for monarchy and empire alike, Lyautey served the Third Republic well. If Gallieni had simple tastes and prided himself on his republican sentiments, Lyautey remained a traditionalist and a lover of the refined way of life. Yet both men possessed a humanitarian spirit. In the service of Gallieni in Tonkin, Lyautey found his reason for being: he was seduced by colonial life. He admired Gallieni as man and administrator, and he hastened to adopt Gallieni's methods. The close friendship between the two men developed in Tonkin, where Gallieni asked for and received Lyautey as his chief of staff. From this period, Lyautey's devotion for his chief continued to grow. The novice soon acquired experience and won the admiration of his senior, who took him with him when he was given the task of pacifying Madagascar.

At Madagascar Lyautey's abilities were soon recognized and, in 1900, Gallieni entrusted the high command of the south, a heavy responsibility at the time, to Lyautey. Lyautey's own development of a native policy can be dated from this period. It is the policy of Gallieni with greater emphasis placed on the idea of the protectorate. After vanquishing the rebel chief, Rabezavena, and then winning him over to the French side, Lyautey exclaimed, "*Vive la méthode Gallieni!* Here again it has proved itself; it certainly is the true colonial method." During the entire campaign in the south Lyautey applied Gallieni's techniques with success, and, when the region was completely pacified, he defined his version of the policy in the following words:

> To adopt the policy and administration of the protectorate signifies: to maintain as much as possible in their entirely native governmental machinery, institutions, and customs; to use the traditional leaders, to let them control the police, the administration—even justice—and the collection of taxes, under the simple control of a single agent residing close to the chief.

What was here suggested was to be the basis of the administrative policy which was applied with success in Morocco. In fact, Lyautey's elaboration of the protectorate regime, his respect for Moslem customs, and his retention of the old Cherifian government—if only as a facade—proved so efficacious that, at the beginning of the First World War, he could proudly send the better part of his French troops to Europe.

In 1924, at the termination of his remarkable career in Morocco, Lyautey lauded the method developed by Gallieni and perfected by himself, when, in a speech at Casablanca, he declared:

> This agreeable and candid association of the two races is the best and strongest guarantee of the future in Morocco. Nothing durable is based on force. The intelligent and hardworking people we have found here have quickly realized all the material benefits we have brought them as well as the assurance of peace and order, business security, and economic equipment we have brought. But that which has brought us still more good will is the fact that we have shown our esteem for this people by having respected all they respect, by assuring them the retention of their traditional institutions. In a word we have placed our hand in theirs.

Although the colonial officers here briefly mentioned were among the best known of those who asserted a new colonial policy, they were not alone. For instance, General Pennequin, who had originally served under Pavie in Indochina, acquired two admirers in Gallieni and Lyautey by his practice of a sound native policy and the use of indigenous troops in the conquest of the area around the Red

River in 1892. Pennequin's superior, governor-general Jean-L. de Lanessan (1891-94), was one of the first to see the need for a well-followed policy of association. Seeking to avoid the heavy administrative machinery with which the French often weighted their colonies, he envisaged a form of indirect rule which would utilize existing native elites by associating them with the French effort. He suggested that the French leave local administration in the hands of the Annamite officials, "whom we will guide by our counsels and surround with our control." While Indochina remained the experimental grounds for a new and vigorous colonial policy pushed by a small group of resolved men, even in the depths of Africa, where the native problem might seem to be of a different order, the need for cooperation was asserted. Savorgnan de Brazza wrote in his *Correspondences,* "To make use of the natives, to identify their interest and ours, to make them our natural allies, this was one of the most important aims of my mission in my opinion."

If the ideas and practices of these men had been adumbrated by others before them, the growing range of agreement is of considerable importance. At home the theorists and popularizers were engaged in giving verbal expression to the body of knowledge, which the colonial administrators were using. This was a time when the methods already followed in the overseas regions profoundly influenced the theories in France. Practice seemed to be preceding theory.

The ideas generally included in the policy of association for the most part mirrored the methods practiced by Gallieni and Lyautey. The true significance of "association" is found in the belief that the economic betterment of the region was to be undertaken by native and Frenchmen within the general framework of native institutions. It was a policy based on the acceptance of mutual interests and on a sort of fraternity, but not of equality.

No more interesting an explanation of the policy of association is to be found than that given by Jules Harmand in his *Domination et Colonisation.* For Harmand, association was synonymous with cooperation, a policy by which the conqueror would be most able to develop the conquered region economically, but also one in which the conqueror realized his responsibility to the native and concerned himself with that person's mental and physical well-being. While he believed association could be applied almost anywhere as an economic principle or moral guide, Harmand insisted that as a political instrument association would be most satisfactory where a homogeneous and relatively civilized population was to be found, and where, as he frankly admitted, submission to foreign control would be most difficult to achieve.

As with all advocates of association, Harmand listed among the policy's salient features tolerance, respect for native customs and laws, cooperation and assistance in place of exploitation. The base upon which Harmand's idea of association was to be established was order. According to him the chief factor lacking in the more advanced native societies was stable, orderly government. Afflicted by a shortage of capital, a lack of scientific know-how, by external threats and internal corruption, the native governments found it impossible to emerge from their sad state. A foreign government both strong and efficient could do what the native government could not in assuring peace and prosperity. And it seems that in offering this argument Harmand sought to justify the act of force which he insisted imperialism was.

The most novel idea that Harmand had to offer was one which seemed to be inferred in the policy of association but which was first clearly stated by him: association involved a sort of contractual agreement. It was a contract which "envisages the coexistence and cooperation of two profoundly different societies placed in contact in a manner as brusque as it is artificial." In practice the arrangement would give the European responsibility to produce material benefits valuable to native civilization. For his part, the native, gradually reflecting on the values derived from his forced subordination, would begin to cooperate more fully with the European. In short, the policy was, in Harmand's opinion, the "systematic repudiation of assimilation," for it encouraged the retention of native institutions and implied a large degree of administrative autonomy.

Although Harmand praised the policy of association as the best of all available colonial policies for control of native populations, he did caution about a possible danger in its application. The acknowledged French tendency in colonial administration might easily lead to "excessive liberalism." While the idea of a contract did exist, this contract implied no equality among the participants, Harmand affirmed. The occupying power had to retain its primacy.

The policy of association, realistic and intelligent, reserves with unshakable firmness all rights of domination and takes into account all its exigencies. It does not at all attempt to prepare and achieve an equality forever impossible, but rather it attempts to establish a certain equivalence or compensation of reciprocal services. Far from letting the domination weaken, this policy wants to reinforce it by making it less offensive and repugnant.

In no way, however, did the newly proposed policy of association as explained by Harmand and others completely repudiate France's traditional *mission civilisatrice;* in the first place the occupation of a colonial region still implied a moral obligation which was to be fulfilled by the improvement of the native's material and cultural status. However, rather than repeat the errors of assimilation by attempting to utilize methods little in accord with local customs, the French were gradually to introduce institutions and benefits which would be advantageous to the natives and appreciated by them. In the second place, so that their economic goals would be reached, the French would be compelled to impose certain institutions on the inhabitants of the subdued region. Nevertheless, these too were to be introduced, wherever necessary within the framework of native society. Thus, in theory the policy of association differed from that of assimilation in that the former sought the improvement of the native's condition without severely altering his way of life, while the latter sought the reorganization of native society in the light of French civilization.

To the ardent adherents of the new theory practical application appeared easy, provided certain necessary conditions existed. First, respect between Frenchman and native had to be assured so that rapid cooperation between the two would ensue.

Second, realization of the responsibility of the one group to the other for the betterment of the region was necessary. Third, a sufficiently developed native administration was indispensable if the natives were to govern themselves adequately so that economic cooperation and development could take place under peaceful, even harmonious, conditions. For this last reason association was usually considered most feasible for Indochina.

Although Jules Harmand was the theorist credited with first advancing the policy of association as such, it was the Minister of Colonies, Clementel, who may be considered the first to give this policy official sanction and to forward it. In 1905, speaking on several occasions to the ardent supporters of French imperialism, he signaled the need of a native policy which made the native an associate of the Frenchman in his task of improving the colonial region. "This policy of collaboration, of association is, moreover, a necessary policy. It constitutes not only a policy of justice but also a policy of foresight and of security."

Clementel did not limit himself to words but sought to put such a policy into effect. In December, 1905, he inaugurated his colonial program with two letters of instruction to the governors of Indochina and Madagascar. Of Indochina he wrote that its betterment had to be achieved through "the protection, education, and association of the native." These were also the means by which he hoped to gain the confidence and support of the native populations: "Participating directly in all the efforts of this nature, reassured by employment of men of their own race, they [the populations] will soon realize that the goal sought is neither contrary to their customs nor beyond their capacities." As for Madagascar, Clementel wished to continue Gallieni's policies there. The native bureaucrats were to be increased in number and associated in the work carried on by the French in the various provinces. In addition, greater local administrative autonomy was to be granted.

Clementel tried to introduce this new colonial policy at the same time that the colonial congresses were urging the policy themselves. These congresses, of importance because they brought together the "colonial party," were the scenes of many discussions of colonial theory. Although this particular problem received no more treatment than any other, the various publications of proceedings indicate that warm approval was given to the policy of association. At the French Colonial Congress of 1905, Joseph Caillaux insisted that "our policy must gradually be a policy of association." Again in 1906, at the large Colonial Congress of Marseilles, the policy of association was acclaimed. Finally, in 1907, at the annual French Colonial Congress it was said with confidence, "The entire colonial group is in agreement on the necessity of following this policy of association." Paul Deschanel added that the doctrine of assimilation had seen its day, and "we are today about to apply this formula of association which the colonial congresses have already determined and illuminated."

This brief indication of the ideas expressed during the colonial congresses—in large measure the barometer of the imperialist faction in France—shows that the policy of association was now being accepted. Nevertheless, extensive studies or explanations of this policy were not to be found. By its very nature association had to be vague; it was a general policy, not a detailed program. And it was as much a solution to France's colonial problems as would be any colonial policy short of withdrawal.

Like the doctrine of assimilation before it, association was willingly accepted; it appeared to be a practical and simple idea which sold itself without the need of extensive advertising. . .

Association and Indirect Rule
HUBERT JULES DESCHAMPS[6]

Ladies and Gentlemen,

When the executive council of the International African Institute conferred upon me the honor of giving the Lugard Memorial Lecture, I was so awe-stricken by the mere name of Lugard that the possibility of any other subject matter was immediately chased from my mind. I do not know if our President, when he gave his remarkable address to the memory of the great Lord, his predecessor, in the same city in 1952, was the victim of a similar obsession. As for me, I quickly discovered that I had something to say to Lord Lugard for a long time and that I would never have a better opportunity to do so. Please allow me then to speak to him in your presence.

Undoubtedly, being a Frenchman raised on Descartes and Voltaire, and moreover a product of this wondrous and yet abominable twentieth century, I do not especially believe in ghosts. However, my Celtic origins and my profession of historian have accustomed me to their frequentation. Therefore, in your midst and in the full light of day, and with no recourse to the subterfuges of spiritualism, I am now going to conjure up my former and highly esteemed colleague, Lord Lugard of Abinger, and address myself with respect and honesty to this venerable spirit who is so dear to us.

Lord Lugard, please be so kind to forgive me if I dare to have you come back for a moment to this abusive planet. But, knowing you quite well now, thanks to the grandiose and detailed monument of 1948 pages with which Miss Margery Perham honored you, I cannot believe that you have lost all interest in what was once the passion of your life. I rather imagine that beneath the myrtle and laurel bushes of the Elysian Fields, you are pursuing doctrinal controversies with our countless departed colleagues used to govern colonies from the time of Julius Caesar and Pontius Pilate. It is true that today the colonies themselves belong to the realm of ghosts. Therefore, l invite you to take part in a fictional dispute on an outdated topic of an eminently academic sort but serious nonetheless.

Here you are in front of me, not the Lugard of his younger days, with his unforgettable thin wolf-like face, with his nose as thin and as straight as a sword, with his

---

[6]Lecture given in Brussels on June 20, 1963 under the auspices of the Eighth Lugard Memorial Lecture. "*Et Maintenant,* Lord Lugard?", *Africa,* October 1963, vol XXXIII, No. 4, 293-305. Translated by Mary Paquette. Hubert Jules Deschamps was a governor of the French Ivory Coast.

awesome Turkish saber-like mustache, and with his shining dark eyes exuding a savage energy from within their deep sockets. I would no more address that Lugard than I would a black panther.

No, the Lugard who has condescended to come back among us is the founder of our Institute, its president for twenty years, a solid old gentleman—bald, calm, pale enlightened by his lengthy experience among men. I evoke your indulgent smile for I am going to need it.

Lord Lugard, I was once your enemy. Oh, a very small enemy, so microscopic that you never chanced to see him, and one who never did you any harm. Moreover, my grudge was not against you but rather against your doctrine. You were the great victorious champion and almost the sovereign pontiff of the "indirect administration" in the 1930s when I was trying unsuccessfully to bring back assimilation.

Most of your compatriots with a refreshing naivete, still believe that assimilation has always been the unequivocal goal of French colonization. For example, in a recent short work, quite good, by the way, on Senegal, an English author wrote, "The French had for their goal the political and cultural integration of the colonial peoples whereas the British have always had as their final goal the preparation of their colonies for self-government and independence." Does this evident Manichaeism really take reality into account?

Has the English colonial doctrine really ever had this monolithic continuity? Our British colleagues would answer this question much better than I would. We Frenchmen who see it from the outside have a tendency to take it in as a whole and therefore to exaggerate its apparent simplicity. We find in it the spirit of Great Britain's institutions made up at the same time of respect of old institutions, of an optimistic liberalism and of a realistic empiricism. The Englishman seems to us to frown on great platonic constructions, he does not trust abstraction but rather puts his faith in nature. He sees the various peoples—the societies, and the institutions as living beings that he allows to grow, ready to tend to their needs, to orient them, and to use them for the best. His outlook is that of the naturalist or of the gardener. It is also the businessman's view: watch over the profits and limit the general expenses. This point of view requires that the various branches and the main office never merge. "The triumph of the British policy," writes Seeley "consists of having separated the destiny of the colonies from that of the parent state and of having reduced to a minimum their mutual interference."

That such tendencies have had as their outcome self-government and independence is apparent to us Frenchmen, impenitent reasoners. I doubt that the good English gardener, in the golden age of colonization, concerned himself much with these outcomes. Life does not follow logic. It was enough to watch over the general development of the plants, to provide for their particular needs at the various stages of their growth, taking care to avoid any absurd and oppressive generalization. God would see to the rest for He is the only master of all ultimate ends.

I may be wrong, but that is how the promising leaf mould in which your doctrine quite naturally grew and flourished appears to me. Lord Lugard, you were acquainted with the models in India where you not only hunted the tiger with rifle but the wild boar with spear. When, after your impassioned but fruitless struggle with the slavers of Lake Nyassa, you were sent to Uganda, you displayed your skill with weapons and your persuasive authority, not to abolish the native kingdoms, but to consolidate them. You enlarged the limits of Buganda, you reconstituted the Toro and reestablished its sovereign. You refused to take the place of their rulers and you acknowledged their tribal justice. Upon your return in 1893, you formulated in *The Rise of Our East African Empire,* your inflexible principle, "The object to be aimed at in the administration of this country is to rule through its own executive government."

This was the time when the French did not like you. The intervention of your Maxim machine guns in the religious wars of Uganda, then your audacious trek to Borgu, and the treaty made with the king of Nikki fifteen days before the arrival of the French officer in charge of this very same thing made you the scapegoat of our chauvinistic journalistic attacks. Thus did France have some share in your reputation, for at the same time, your compatriots discovered what you were: a hero of the empire. Chamberlain charged you with the creation of the "West Africa Frontier Force" which was to play a decisive role in the establishment of the Nigerian frontier; Bussa, where Mungo Park met his death, was to remain English. At the turn of the century, you were at the height of your glory. Kirk and Goldie were your friends; Flora Shaw sang your praise. Your eyes had lost their disquieting flame. At the age of 42, calmer but still tireless, you gained access to the government of Northern Nigeria. You had to conquer her, to organize her. Your methods were to be applied unfailingly, they were to be clarified and defined. There they were to find their perfect testing ground, a little too perfect perhaps, because later you were to try and apply this model in different situations.

It is quite useless, except perhaps for the French public, quite ignorant about British colonization (the reverse is also true), to recall your Kano, Sokoto and Katsina expeditions. What is important here is that you maintained the Fulani emirs in spite of how recent and questionable their power in Hausa territory might have seemed. You felt a certain repulsion for disorder, a need for efficacy and at the same time, a certain weakness in your means that caused you to be preoccupied primarily with "stopping disintegration." In 1906, you defined your principles in the *Political Memoranda:* recognize the native administration as an integral part of the governmental machine, while directing it in the direction of the abolition of slavery and of oppression, and also towards economic development. The British governor and the district commissioner were really to be advisors and overseers. Thanks to your methods, when a revolt broke out, the emirs remained faithful. The virtue of indirect rule, at least where pacification is concerned, is thereby demonstrated.

After an instructive stay in faroff Hong Kong, you came back, from 1912 to 1918, as governor general to bind together the North and the South, and to create Nigeria, a world, an African India. You discovered certain new elements, the anarchical structures of the South East and evolutionists of Lagos who did not fit into your plan and who irritated you. You tried painfully to make the former enter into your system and you struck up contact with the latter. You had ideals, but you were first of all a great man of action, and difficulties scared you no more than bullets. You knew how to use them to enrich your outlook.

The latter, in a partial retirement very much occupied with the League of Nations, was revealed to us in your great work: *The Dual Mandate in British Tropical Africa.* It is a classic and I will limit myself to mentioning only certain formulas from it, "Principles do not change, but their mode of application may and should vary with the customs, the traditions and the prejudices of each unit." You evoke independence without condemning it, but while showing the dangers of proceeding too quickly. One must rely upon the traditional chieftains while changing their role. "The ruling classes are no longer either demi-gods, or parasites preying on the community. They must work for the stipends and position they enjoy. They are the trusted delegates of the governor."

You evoke "the high ideal of leading the backward races, by their own efforts, in their own way, to raise themselves to a higher plane of social organization." The endeavor is to prevent denationalization, or to develop along indigenous lines.

You were not purely an intellectual, Lord Lugard; you did not attend any university. You invented no disquieting geopolitical generalizations, such as the "Cape to Cairo" (route) of Cecil Rhodes. You did not, just as your subordinate Temple did, push the consequences of your doctrine to the point of the conviction that the natives must follow (I quote Temple), "the natural evolution of their races, clearly different from those of the white man." You did not believe that it was necessary to place a moral barbed wire fence around the black world in order to prevent entry into it by politicians and missionaries. You, a practical man, are in search of methods of action for a humane advancement within the measure of man. You are not a doctrinarian. As I shall say later on, I attacked "Lugardism." But, Lord Lugard, you were no more a "Lugardist" than Marx was a Marxist, and even less so. You were simply a man of good faith searching for sensible solutions to safeguard the present and prepare the future. Lord Lugard, I am sorry, but through you, I was attacking certain French positions.

Assimilation, as I shall demonstrate later, was only rarely the official colonial doctrine of France. But it is quite true that it satisfies certain deeply rooted and constant tendencies of the French people, tendencies with origins going back thousands of years, but which the classicism of the seventeenth and eighteenth centuries expressed perfectly.

Our ancestors, the Gauls, according to all the explorers of their time, were avidly interested in novelty and were openly receptive to strangers; the Greeks referred to them as "philhellenics" or lovers of Greeks. After resisting conquest, they became subjects and then avid Roman citizens, to the point of abandoning their own language for Latin. The taste for Roman architecture and law became second nature to them. They passed this heritage on to us. We like the logical reasoning, the monuments with their sober but not cold lines, the institutions based on simple and clear principles. The Roman Empire, in uniting the various countries, left us a model and a certain regret. Moreover, all this Romanism is built on a base of Celtic anarchy with a certain flair for change and the exotic. We are quite familiar with strangers no matter to what race they belong. Add to that a dose of equalitarian and universal Christianity capping a rather pagan vivaciousness, and you will have an approximate portrait of the typical Frenchman—such, at least, as I see him in myself and in many others, either living or dead.

The first colonial efforts by France were imbued with this spirit. The expansion of the kingdom, the conversion of the savages, the absence of racism, these were the signs. But, with Colbert, mercantile success took precedence. Slavery was about to change the small insular societies, racism was introduced, the colonists were going to seek an autonomy which would safeguard their authority. In India, Dupleix developed a system of influence and suzerainty over the Hindu princes. Autonomy and protectorate, we were soon to find these formulas in English policies. Similar local situations led the two peoples to identical positions.

But the metropolitan tendencies were those of classicism. Descartes declared reason to be universal. The "interior man," the same in all latitudes, became the cornerstone of all philosophers reasoning. From then on, institutions recognized as good and reasonable were applicable to all of humanity. Spiritual and sentimental assimilation attacked slavery and tyranny. These ideas triumphed with the revolutionary Republic. The Convention abolished slavery. The Directory decreed "the human person is not a transferable property. . . . The French Republic is one and indivisible. . . . The Colonies are an integral part and therefore subject to the same laws."

We were never to know the merits of that system because the colonies were quickly lost. This loss was to be attributed to the excesses of assimilation, and from then on, the French for more than a century, were looking for a colonial policy. The first original effort was that of Napoleon in Egypt. An advocate of empire without ideology, and taking inspiration only from the necessity of the moment, he ordered that the Egyptian notables be kept with "the greatest possible latitude in their internal affairs"; he attended Moslem ceremonies and thanked the Prophet for his victories. But the Prophet did not protect him from Nelson.

In 1830, the French again met up with Islam in Algeria, and their first act was to ensure its protection. The local institutions were preserved on the whole. The Second Republic had only a vague recourse to assimilation. Slavery was once again and this time definitively abolished, the colonies elected deputies to the French parliament. But no attempt was made to assimilate the Algerians. Napoleon III declared that Algeria was an Arab kingdom. The particularity of colonial legislation was recognized, and it was put into the hands of the executive and taken away from the parliament; this rule lasted a century, almost the entire duration of the colonial Empire.

A change took place at the same time in French thought. The classical and abstract concept of the "interior man" who is invariable, a product of the mathematician Descartes, started to lose ground before the discoveries of the nineteenth century. Geography, history, and sociology were on the rise. The diversity of countries, of men, and of societies was recognized. Assimilation was then as much condemned in its intellectual roots as it had already been in practice. To the universal application of principles was easily to be substituted the method based on facts. It was the colonials, the governors, the officers, and the administrators who were going to elaborate their own terms and conditions of action according to local needs.

In Senegal, Faidherbe had already based his policy on the local chieftains. He had created a "school for chieftains" to instruct the successors. Cambon, in 1881, inaugurated the policy of the protectorate in Tunisia; he maintained the Tunisian government and administration while controlling them. Lyautey, quite a bit later, used the same system in Morocco with a modernistic trend allied with an esthetic taste for the old institutions. "I am the sultan's head servant," he liked to say, and it was true. His royalist feelings, which were of no more use in France, had found their use overseas.

In Black Africa, wherever we find kings, and except in the extreme cases of open struggle or a lack of traditional attachments, we maintained them, set them up on thrones, and made them our chief agents, just as did the English, and for the same reasons: the facilitation of conquest and of economic administration. The only difference was that we were not tempted as you were, Lord Lugard, to modernize these antiquated states, nor to create embryos of states where none existed. We did not conscientiously seek to create the future out of the past. We preserved the latter because it was convenient, and we often let it deteriorate to the advantage of direct administration. In the same way, education, wherever it existed, was carried on in French, but that was due more to the multiplicity of languages, and to the desire to form useful clerks than to a pronounced desire for assimilation.

For assimilation was then dead as far as French doctrine was concerned. Arthur Girault, the greatest of our experts on colonial law, rather grimly established that as early as 1903. The hypocritical expression of the "policy of association" born in Indochina was substituted for it. The word "association" seemed to affirm the existence of a contract between the dominating power and the subjects, whereas it really conjured up the idea of the association that exists between a man and his horse. Your expression of the "dual mandate" was at least more honest: it indicated a mutual benefit. Your work, between the two wars, began to be recognized and praised in France. A man as authoritative as Maurice Delafosse taught us at the Colonial School as late as 1926, the year of his death, a doctrine similar to yours: To protect the native institutions and to have them evolve slowly within their natural limits, and not to create mere caricatures of Europe.

There, once more I apologize because I must enter onto the scene, and that might seem especially presumptuous since I was at that time in 1930, a young assistant administrator, lost in the Malagasy underbrush, a not too-typical figure, rather insignificant and ineffective. But among the concert of praises for your doctrine, mine was the only dissenting voice. I led a solitary attack, quite unnoticed, but firmly convinced that I incarnated the future.

I had deeply loved Delafosse, both the man and his work, but I was the unruly disciple, the one who reacted the most violently to the teachings of the master by setting myself in opposition to him. Raised in the leftist, Republican tradition, and a militant socialist, I was hardly favorable to chieftains and kings. (However, I must admit that ten years later when I myself had authority over kings, I got along splendidly with them.) Assimilation and universalism had since taken refuge with that part of the Left that, since it was not in power, could criticize the methods and the doctrines of those who were. Colonization did not seem justified to me except in the words of Jaures, in so far as a "duty to proceed by degrees towards the unification of the whole human race." Add to that the fact that I was in Madagascar, a country where the traditional chieftains had been eliminated through a century of colonization, Merina and then French, and then replaced by a direct administration. That was where with all the fiery spirit of uncompromising youth, I was slowly preparing an article entitled "Education and Colonization" that the *Grande Revue,* highly praised in university circles, agreed to publish in October 1932. Since then I have written a little more than twenty works, some very long, but these few pages which remained relatively obscure were my greatest struggle.

I maintained that the native society differed from ours not by their nature but rather by their degree of evolution. Now, because of contact with us, they are in the process of evolving at an accelerated rate. Trade, the monetary economy, the plantations, mines, and the migration of workers, the creation of cities, all these have upset the traditional societies more than did the teachers and the missionaries. The breakdown of political structures is flagrant, and it is a good thing, because they were not adapted to the new age. Education must create new social classes, already apparent, and which will serve as the instruments of the future. "Colonization equals education," I wrote; even etymologically speaking, since culture naturally follows colonization . . . We still seem to control the new native societies according to principles created for primitive societies that have disappeared today. (I want to make it clear that I was not yet an ethnologist!) The idea of making them evolve "in their own milieu," without any exterior influence, is false, reactionary and racist. "Any archaeological shoring up of tottering ruins cannot be a living and lasting work." The "imported" dogma of "indirect rule" is ill-fated. Let us turn away from the English example to meditate on that of the Roman Empire which caused us to rise from barbarism. Let us welcome the natives to us, since they are coming towards us anyway, and let us build the French nation extending to Africa. In my thesis, that I was beginning to write, I enlarged my universalism to a degree most acceptable today by concluding, "Let us be good educators and prepare good Europeans."

I did not quote you, Lord Lugard, but I attacked you in each sentence. Actually, I did not hurt you very much. As far as I know, my article was read by only one person, my colleague Geismar, who was an avid fan of yours. Between Senegal and Madagascar, we exchanged a few long impassioned letters. Indirect rule was none the worse for it. I was beaten by silence, and assimilation remained buried. It arose again much later in 1945, but really, I had nothing to do with it. My glory was purely personal, that of an unknown predecessor. And at the same time, I had a vague feeling that it was too late, and that on a planet in the process of rapid change, our great doctrinal battles over colonization would soon be relegated to ancient history with not much diffusion. You never knew this stage. In the same year, 1945, which marked the end of your era, you set out for another world leaving behind in this one an unforgettable memory.

And now, Lord Lugard? Let us try and find the moral of this story. Time has judged the merits of our opposite views. We have to confront these views with the events that followed. Who was wrong? What remains of these monuments today? And what is their share in present-day Africa?

Here we are then in the court of History. The two parties appear: On one side standing proudly is indirect rule of long and glorious memory, accompanied by his two daughters, the conservation of African institutions and the controlled evolution of the role of chieftains who owe so much to you. On the opposing side, the group is less distinct: one can scarcely detect the French administrative policy previous to 1945; it differed from yours (at least in Black Africa) only in its more familiar style and less clearly defined goals. Your opposition is rather the assimilative tendency of the French people, however vague and intermittent its application to the colonies may have been, its juridical structure, its leaning towards vast rational constructs which led to the French Union and then to the Community of French Nations; add to it education in French, the steadfast belief in humanity, the distrust of the feudal, the nostalgia for the Roman Empire, the romantic vision of France the Liberator, all in all, a simplistic temperament plus naive convictions, all of this combination of obscure virtualities that I had tried to express with rigorous energy. To sum them up in a symbolic figure, I would say that it is assimilation, that is, the Revolution of 1789 sneaking into Africa rather late on tiptoe.

To judge fairly, we must examine not only the intrinsic virtues of both systems, but also their contact with the facts, that is, the evolution of Africa since 1945, and the present outcome.

Indirect rule was a convenient formula for submission. It caused the least possible disturbance. It tried to keep Africa on the African ancestral path. Therefore, the need to know the country, to take inventory of its peoples, its political resources, its legal customs. It was the golden age of ethnologists and administrators quite taken with the exotic and the picturesque. These traditional societies, perfectly preserved, with their ancient structures, their colorful ceremonies, their noble demeanor, their palanquins, their crowns, their sacred thrones, their perfect adaptation to nature, their order, their serenity, all these presented to romantic minds an idealized image of long ago, the African version of Walter Scott. The lure of the past, the charm of an escape from a Europe invaded by industrial slavery and demographic inflation, were irresistible to the intellectuals captivated by esthetics. Even I, as revolutionary as I was in thought, was sentimentally seduced by this perfume of mankind of the early ages to the point, on my return to France, of giving a scandalous lecture whose theme was, "To save humanity, let us return to the neolithic age!" I suppose that my British colleagues, faithful to the crown and the venerable institutions surrounding it, must have succumbed even more so in this anachronistic universe miraculously preserved, and over which they watched with as much love as over the natural reserves. Thus they preserved the chieftains and increased the number of rhinoceri.

Unfortunately, the chieftains, as opposed to the rhinoceri, were not merely colorful. They were scarcely inclined to modify a state of affairs that was favorable to them. The careful control, where you had seen the panacea of progress, undoubtedly suppressed the most blatant abuses, the horror of the sultans' prisons, the razzias, the slave trade; it had regularized administration and justice; it had allowed material changes while maintaining social conservatism. The native societies, too well protected, continued to live apart, without any active participation in the modern world.

Evolution came from elsewhere, as I had predicted it would, and contrary to your system. The "gentlemen of the bush" that you respected as squires and the House of Lords were outdated, outclassed, and finally looked down upon as completely antiquated by the rising new class of people who were not at all titled and hereditary gentlemen, the businessmen, the store clerks, the civil servants, the wealthy planters, the influential church members, the trade unionists, the townspeople, and I should not hesitate to include in this enumeration those at the head, the intellectuals, the reasoners who will not content themselves with passive obedience. I must say that it was the honor of England to have facilitated in its universities, and sooner than us, the formation of this unruly intelligentsia. For happily, your country also had sincere liberalism in its traditions.

And Great Britain set out resolutely on this liberal path as soon as she realized, with her magnificent empiricism, on which side the forces of the future lay. She did this by taking her parliamentary traditions to Africa, with all their historic decorum: the gavel, the wig, the speaker and the opposition of his majesty. That was the English form of assimilation. As was to be expected, the original function did not last long. "Laws," said Montesquieu, "must be so suited to the people for whom they were made that it is mere chance if those of one nation are suitable for another." Which did not prevent the above mentioned Montesquieu from having us adopt the English system which, in France, as you know, all too often has caused great difficulties. In England, the new institutions, the house and popular vote, had grown up little by little from a system inherited from the Middle Ages. To transfer them abruptly to Africa was bound to bring about conflicts, all the more serious because they clashed with the power of the chieftains developed by indirect rule. Your system was based on tribalism, on the ancient nations, conformable to the limits of traditional ethnic divisions. It constituted a resistance to nationalism, to the will of the new African politicians to create states, new and enlarged nations whose limits would be left by the colonizer. The two English traditions of liberalism and conservatism, so perfectly balanced in your country through a constant and harmonious exchange of power were bound to clash in Africa and complicate the birth of the new nations.

Undoubtedly, a certain regionalism corresponds in general to the nature of affairs and feelings. It binds people together in a more intimate and a more maternal way than the state, this "cold monster" does, as Nietzsche said. As a good provincial from the Southwest, I have always regretted that in our great Revolution, federalism was guillotined with the Girondins, and that Paris, that hypertrophied heart, had, for the most part, sapped the' provinces of a great deal of their strength. But in Africa, the nation had to be built from one day to the next, and the young chief of state could no more respect the fortresses of the past, reinforced through your efforts, than Richelieu and the Jacobins in our country could tolerate the feudal insolences and the Vendee insurrections. The choice lay between the new state and institutional disorder.

Indeed, the conflicts were lively but rarely bloody. The state triumphed over the tribes and the chieftains, sometimes by force, sometimes by settlement, often with the aid of an English diplomatic intermediary. Some great aggregates, of artificial origin, are maintained, such as Nigeria whose unity you cemented, and where the northern chieftains exist along side of the more equalitarian systems of the South. In spite of the differences in the political regimes and the cultural evolution that indirect rule had consolidated, the nations were born, and they have taken their first steps forward. British liberalism helped them and also a typically British insular attitude; a certain detachment, a certain modest reserve with regard to other peoples; an attitude where some suffered from an adolescent timidity and others from an invincible pride; and all were undoubtedly right. It does not matter, really. The result of this reserve, of this insularity, of this reluctance to be on the lookout, was that autonomy and secession were relatively easy for you. Thus the centrifugal forces were quicker to start up in your territories than in ours, at least in West Africa. The emancipation of Ghana caused a furor, and from then on, all the neighboring countries, whether they were under the British or the French, sought to line themselves up behind independence.

On the other hand, the French system, before it died, made a last attempt at assimilation. Platonic, legalistic, and steeped in geometry, the French Constituent Assembly tried in 1945, to raise a noble architectural structure built to last for centuries, where both blacks and whites could find shelter. One dreamed rather vaguely of a new Roman Empire after Caracalla, of a French world transcending continents and races. This noble illusion, made up of a mixture of traditional French chauvinism and of a very sincere anti-racist ecumenism, had been born at the Liberation. It was a question for France of assuming, after her temporary loss of stature, at the same time, a lasting greatness in the eyes of the world (for ever since Louis XIV and Napoleon, these ideas of greatness have kept coming back to us from time to time), and of liberating her black children while making citizens out of them. The word "liberation" under the sign of which the debates of the two constituent assemblies took place, could have a double meaning, and lead to one of two divergent paths: the first one was the emancipation of individuals into a vast whole which would make them equal citizens, this was republican assimilation, the principle of the First Republic and the leftist parties; the second path would be the birth of new autonomous nations, a path recommended by the charter of San Francisco and the two great victorious federations; the United States and the U.S.S.R. One of the notable consequences of the French cultural assimilation was (except for the people of Malagasy forever conscious of their individualism) that the African deputies themselves attached more importance to the first tendency than to the second. The Constitution of 1946, which created the French Union, gave freedom of the city to all blacks, with deputies in the three Parisian assemblies, where government and the laws were created. Incorporated or attached to French parties, the African parliamentary members blossomed forth in the friendly atmosphere behind the scenes; they passed their political apprenticeship in a French atmosphere, interdependent with their colleagues like the black and white keys of the famous piano of Doctor Aggrey.

Nothing there that recalled the differences and limits among peoples so dear to your disciples, Lord Lugard, and to the ethnologists. In the National Assembly, in the Senate, in the National Assembly of the French Union, there were only men dressed in suits or costumes, speaking French, and who were divided not along ethnic lines, nor according to territories, but according to their political parties. Had assimilation then won? Descartes and the "interior man," were they to triumph after a century and a half of unobtrusiveness?

No, we know that today. Assimilation came too late, at a time and in a world where the Asiatic and then the African were going to start a chain reaction. The African parliamentary members could not overlook the emancipation of India, of Indonesia, and later, the Bandung Conference and the autonomy of Ghana. They slowly broke away from the metropolitan parties which were dragging them into internal quarrels of little interest to them. They regrouped into autonomous parties that knew how to obtain, by bargaining their support, not only places in the government, but political concessions and economic advantages in Africa itself. The Constitution had added, moreover, to its assimilative sauce a few nationalistic ingredients such as the recognition of "peoples" and of "civilizations" in the plural, such as the creation of the Territorial Assemblies given much wider powers than our departmental councils. Thus, little by little, the tendency grew stronger, not towards independence which no one was seeking then, but towards federalism; what Mr. Senghor called with a slightly comical touch, "the Republic one and divisible." The Community of Nations of 1958 went further to the point of establishing a kind of Commonwealth rather than a very liberal and somewhat vague club like the British Commonwealth, but a carefully juridical edifice according to French idiosyncrasy. It was only a brief stop on the long slippery slide down. From 1960, in the image of Ghana, all the French speaking republics had become independent.

Thus, of the two aspects of assimilation that I had advocated in 1932 and that had been applied too late in 1945, one, the constitution of a political entity transcending the nations, finally failed; the other, modernism opposed to tradition had won.

Those who honestly believed in assimilation, (they were especially on the left) held the notion in the simplicity of their hearts that the age of nationalisms had passed, and that as in the U.S.S.R., we were going towards the formation of great entities which were the prelude to world unity. In fact, not only did nothing like that happen, but paradoxically, assimilation was the prelude to independence. It prepared limits for it. We learned thus that nationalism was the stage of the developing of an awareness in the peoples, this adolescent crisis that none can avoid on their way to maturity. The planetary government that many young people, myself included, had thought to be realized in 1919 thanks to President Wilson, will be realized one day, I am sure, in spite of everything. But it does seem that it will come about from the union of nations and not of denationalized individuals. And this especially in Africa where the individual is barely emerging from the communal society. The English, in treating the peoples as biological entities and not as legal abstractions, have shown their usual realism.

On the other hand, our nonchalant French practice with regard to the chiefdoms had in the long run a more positive effect on the construction of new nations than did your ingenious doctrine of the evolution of the old structures and your maternal solicitude over a good education. In our territories, the kingdoms and the chiefdoms abandoned to their old age by our indifference, fell apart painlessly or were easily neutralized; sometimes the old institutions were suppressed, only to be retrieved into the administrations of the most modernistic chieftains; often they were simply neutralized and left to die their own death. The religious attachment to the chieftains did not evoke the favor that certain ethnological studies might have led one to believe; it even happened that in order to hasten an evolution judged to be progressing too slowly, the subjects themselves as in the Bamileke country, had the chieftains' headquarters burned after having massacred the chieftains. Except for this and other rare examples, the 1789 of French speaking Africa took place quite painlessly. A sign that your colorful Middle Ages had their day.

To your account must be tallied, on the contrary, the desire to create local basic constitutions, the "native authorities" and "native councils" that you often had so much difficulty in establishing in countries where anarchies abounded. The French system facilitated change but did not promote initiative. The administration, our country, was a paternal king (in the best and most common cases) but almost an absolute one. The last of the absolute kings and one who gave no thought to abdicating. One became concerned—and much too late—after 1945, and in too few territories, with creating rural communes to give to the people of Malagasy and to the Africans the basic sense of responsibilities. So that the new nations in our sector inherited rudimentary or worthless substructures. It is still the administrative system inherited from us and made African which governs the whole, often with the help of sections of the governmental party. There is a serious deficiency there; the habit of responsibility is not taken on in a day; its absence allows tyranny, or at least, it causes the leaders to increase their power since they have to face everything.

Finally, since we are counting the points, here is another in favor of assimilation;

it is the diffusion of the French language and culture. I do not mean to make an allusion here to the great intellectuals. Without a doubt, men like Senghor or Alioune Diop, to mention only two, do great honor at the same time to the French University and to Africa. But the English speaking universities also knew how to form men of the best caliber. The originality of our system is probably the diffusion of teaching in French to the primary level. "The knowledge of French," states my friend Charton, "becomes common and popular among the youngest and most active elements. It is upon a popular base of French cultural implantation that the formation of the classes and the ascension of the elite has been able to develop." Thus we have often avoided the divorce between the masses that remain traditional and the elite that have received a foreign education. The French language has become the means of intellectual emancipation and the path that leads to unity. During a recent stay in Gabon, I found, in the smallest villages in the virgin forest, people both young and old, who would speak with me in French, and a Gabonese minister declared, "The United States chose English, we have chosen French." This without French speaking Africa having the feeling of giving up something of themselves. It goes without saying that the English speaking peoples could say the same thing. A comparative study would be interesting, but difficult. In any case, the diffusion of our languages causes the linguists, after the ethnologists, to pass from applied science to pure science and history. The latter has absorbed your world and ours with all our methods and colonial doctrines. It is history who will now act as judge and decide the points.

Let us sum up the results of the match between indirect rule and assimilation; to simplify things, let us say between you and me, which magnifies my importance greatly.

Your system rested on the conviction of the differences between peoples and a respect for their ways. You believed in the possibility of making Africa evolve within the forms of the past and with the men of the past. This life apart would only lead in the future to separation. Even if you were not consciously aware of it, this centrifugal movement was the normal outcome of your premises.

The belief of the eighteenth century and of the French Revolution that I took up in my article and that the French Union tried later on to realize, postulated, on the contrary, the basic similarity of the human species and its possibility of evolving on a single plane. Africa could only find its place in the modern world by an accelerated revolution replacing the old structures with modern forms. From then on, there could be no obstacle to assimilation in a same political entity.

And now let us count up the points:

You lost on the evolution in the traditional forms, but you won on African autonomy.

I won for the victory of men and of modern institutions; I lost on political assimilation.

One to one, Lord Lugard. Match void.

Actually, we were both deceived by having too absolute of viewpoints. Men are at the same time different and similar. The Africans reacted in a normal way; they sought the same political forms as the Europeans while defending the originality of their cultures. According to Senghor, they wanted to "assimilate, not to be assimilated." The advantage that Africa had in this double point of view was that the European domination was at the same time long enough to cause a shock and an awakening, and short enough for Africa not to have enough time to be abolished and yet to assimilate the new points brought in from the exterior without succumbing.

Some could well ask if this colonial period were not too short? If the grafting of European institutions onto the African plants will have enough strength to withstand and to make progress possible? The importance of time cannot be denied and the past cannot be wiped out in a single stroke. One can only guess that the preparation of the Africans for their new tasks, for the exercising of power and for the creation of nations has often been insufficient.

It is not the time we were lacking but the application to the tasks of the future. What I was calling for against you in 1932 was not to waste our forces by maintaining an outmoded past, but rather to set ourselves through education to laying the foundation for a modern future. We all realized this only in 1945, and a mere fifteen years of formation were not sufficient. It is not the fault of the Africans, but our own for we developed too late an ultimate policy goal. We were fairly skilled operators and not those rare geniuses, such as Alexander the Great, who cut the Gordian knot and who consciously create new worlds by seeing problems in a new light. We were honest organizers and not gods. Thus evolution, although born of our contact and our action, for the most part, escaped us and caught us by surprise.

The evolution that put an end to our empires is only beginning today. Economically and politically, socially and culturally, Africa is just starting to develop and transform. We cannot predict the future. Besides, that is not part of the role of the historian, and this speech (which I am going to bring to an end, please be assured!) was an historical sketch, a conjuring up of the past in the light of the present. May Lord Lugard pardon me for having drawn him away from the realm of the departed for a few moments. That is the lot of great men. May his ghost not come to haunt your dreams, and thank you all for having followed me so kindly this evening in this very serious phantasmagoria.

Indirect Rule—
French and British Style
MICHAEL CROWDER[7]

In his witty and thought-provoking Lugard Memorial Lecture, "*Et maintenant, Lord Lugard?*" Gouverneur Deschamps has provided us with an excellent general appraisal of the relative achievements and failures of French and British "native" administration in Africa. But he does not do full justice to the fundamental differences between the two systems. Though he hints at these differences on several occasions in his lecture, he contends that, far from what is generally supposed, the two were in practice very similar, since they both reposed indigenous chiefs[8]. He insists that "the only difference was that we were not tempted as you were, Lord Lugard, to modernize these antiquated states, nor to create embryos of states where none existed; or [our administrative practice] differed from yours (at least, in Black Africa) only in its more familiar style and less clearly defined goals." This seems seriously to underestimate the nature of the differences between the two systems, parts of East Africa and in parts of which were rather those of kind than of degree. M. Deschamps rightly insists that there has been a tendency on both sides of the Channel to oversimplify the basic characteristics of systems of colonial administration in Africa. Nevertheless there were such fundamental differences between the French and British systems that, even if both did make use of "chiefs," it is not possible to place the French System of native administration in the same category as British indirect rule. It is true that both powers had little alternative to the use of existing political authorities as a means of governing their vast African empires, and in most cases these authorities were headed by chiefs. What *is* important is the very different way in which these authorities were used. The nature of the position and power of the chief in the two systems was totally different and, as a corollary, So were the relations between the chief and the political officer, who was inspired in each case by very different ideals.

The British in Northern Nigeria, which became the model for indirect rule, believed that it was their task to conserve what was good in indigenous institutions

---

[7]Crowder, Michael, "Indirect Rule French and British Style," *Africa,* XXIV, No. 3 (1964), 197-205. Michael Crowder was one of Britain's most distinguished and respected Africanists who has written extensively on the African past. He died in 1990.

[8]In the summary of the lecture in English it is put more explicitly, "Indirect rule has been practised by local governors at least since the second empire; from the end of the nineteenth century the official policy was that of 'Association-very close to Lugard's ideas.'

and assist them to develop on their own lines. The relation between the British political officer and the chief was in general that of an adviser who only in extreme circumstances interfered with the chief and the native authority under him. However,
where chiefs governed small political units, and in particular where their traditional executive authority was questionable, the political officer found himself interfer-
ing in native authority affairs more frequently than ideally he should. This was true
in many Yorubaland, where the borderline between "advisory" and "supervisory" in
the activities of the political officer was not always clear. Though indirect rule
reposed primarily on a chief as executive, its aim was not to preserve the institution
of chieftaincy as such, but to encourage local self-government through indigenous
political institutions, whether these were headed by a single executive authority, or
by a council of elders. In Northern Nigeria a policy of minimal interference with the
chiefs and their traditional forms of government was pursued. But Lugard himself
had insisted on a reform of the indigenous taxation system and of the administration
of native justice when he was governor of Northern Nigeria and believed that, while
the colonial government should repose on the chiefs, their administration should be
progressively modernized. And, though his successors left them largely to themselves, Sir Donald Cameron, Governor of Nigeria from 1931 to 1935, who had
introduced indirect rule to Tanganyika and held similar beliefs to those of Lugard,
was shocked by the situation in Northern Nigeria, where he felt the emirates were
fast developing into Indian-style native states.

Indeed, in the earliest inter-war period many emirs and chiefs ruled as "sole
native authorities," a position which gave them for practical purposes more power
than they had in precolonial days, where they were either subject to control by a
council or liable to deposition if they became too unpopular. They were permitted
to administer traditional justice, which, in the case of certain emirs, included trying
cases of murder for which the death sentence, subject to confirmation by the governor, could be passed. They administered political units that corresponded to those
they would have administered before the arrival of the colonial power. They were
elected to office by traditional methods of selection, and only in the case of the election of a patently unsuitable candidate to office, would the colonial power refuse
recognition. There was thus a minimal undermining of the traditional sources of
authority. The main change for the Fulani emirs of Northern Nigeria, for instance,
was that they now owed allegiance to the British government rather than to the
Sultan of Sokoto, and collected taxes on its behalf, though they retained, in most
cases, 70 percent of the amount collected for the administration of their native
authority.

This system of indirect rule was, with modifications, practised wherever possible in Britain's colonies in West Africa and in most of her other African territories.
There were notable exceptions, especially in Eastern Nigeria, where the absence of
identifiable executive authority in most communities made indirect rule as practised
in Northern Nigeria almost impossible to apply. In such societies, British assiduity
in trying to discover chiefs, or invent them, might lend colour to M. Deschamps's

argument; but, in practice, the goal of ruling through traditional political units on whom local self-government could be devolved was maintained, and after much trial and error a system of democratically elected councils was formulated as most closely corresponding to the traditional methods of delegating authority.

If, taking into account such variations, we use indirect rule in Northern Nigeria as a model we shall see just how greatly the French system of administration in Black Africa differed from that of the British.

The British system depended on the advisory relationship between the political officer and the native authority, usually a chief, heading a local government unit that corresponded to a precolonial political unit. The French system placed the chief in an entirely subordinate role to the political officer. M. Deschamps alludes only briefly to the role of the French political officer towards the end of his article, where he hints at the nature of his status as a *roi* paternel or *Roi absolu*. But it is important to stress that the chief in relation to the French political officer was a mere agent of the central colonial government with clearly defined duties and powers. He did not head a local government unit, nor did the area which he administered on behalf of the government necessarily correspond to a precolonial political unit. In the interests of conformity the French divided the country up administratively into cantons which frequently cut across precolonial political boundaries. Chiefs did not remain chiefs of their old political units but of the new cantons, though sometimes the two coincided. In certain cases the French deliberately broke up the old political units, as in the case of the Futa Jallon where their policy was "the progressive suppression of the chiefs and the parcelling out of their authority." Most important of all, chiefs were not necessarily those who would have been selected according to customary procedures; more often than not they were those who had shown loyalty to the French or had obtained some education. While the British were scrupulous in their respect for traditional methods of selection of chiefs, the French, conceiving of them as agents of the administration, were more concerned with their potential efficiency than their legitimacy. We need not wonder then that as a young French administrator, after serving in Senegal and Dahomey, M. Robert Delavignette should have been astonished, on his way to duty in Niger, to find that the British political officer in Kano actually called on the emir when he had business with him and paid him the compliment of learning Hausa so that he could speak to him direct. "For the young French administrator, such a way of administration had the charm of a tale from *A Thousand and One Nights*. Contrast the position of the emir of Kano with that of the Alaketu of Ketu in Dahomey. By tradition he was one of the seven most important rulers in Yorubaland, on an equal footing with the Oni of Ife and the Alafin of Oyo. A friend who visited him while Dahomey was still under French rule found him waiting outside the French Chef de Subdivision's office. He mentioned the fact that the King was waiting to the French administrator, who replied, "Is it going to kill him to wait out there?" and kept him waiting a little longer.

It is clear then that the French explicitly changed the very nature of the powers of the chief and that "his functions were reduced to that of a mouthpiece for orders emanating from outside." This is brought out clearly, for example, in the *Arrete of 28th December 1936 on the organisation and regulation of the Local indigenous administration in French Equatorial Africa* in the section dealing with *Chefs de Canton* (or *de Terre* or *de Tribu*). *The Chefs de Canton* (etc.) are recruited:

(i) for preference from among the descendants of old families traditionally or customarily destined to command,

(ii) from among notable natives, literate if possible, who have rendered services to the French cause and who are fitted to fill these functions by their authority or influence in the country,

(iii) from among the *Chefs de Canton* (etc.) who have satisfactorily carried out their functions for at least four years,

(iv) from among old soldiers who have completed more than the normal terms of service and who qualify for special treatment,

(v) from among local civil servants (clerks, interpreters, etc.) who have worked satisfactorily for at least four years in the public service.

The following are the disciplinary measures applicable to *Chefs de Canton* (etc.):

(i) reprimand by the Chef de Department

(ii) temporary withholding of salary

(iii) temporary interdiction

(iv) reduction of salary

(v) dismissal

Since the chiefs did not, except in rare cases, represent traditional authority and, since they were the agents of the colonial power for carrying out its more unpopular measures, such as collecting taxes and recruiting for labour, they were resented in most parts of French West Africa. While they retained no traditional judicial authority such as that of their counterparts in British West Africa in their native courts, they were agents of the law, in this case the unpopular system of summary administrative justice known as the indigenat.[9] In many areas in the postwar period they became identified with pro-French administrative parties, particularly in Soudan (Mali). Hence it was not surprising that when, in 1957, just before the independence of Guinea, Sekou Toure (then Vice President du Conseil) decided to do

---

[9]Concessions were made to customary law prior to 1946, when native penal law was abolished and all inhabitants of French Tropical Africa became subject to the French code. Before that time, only those Africans who were French citizens could claim justice under the Code. The vast majority of *sujets* were subject to the indigenat already "referred to and to customary law." Customary law, however, was not administered by the chief, but by the French administrator, who was assisted by two notables of the area who were versed in tradition. These courts could try both penal and civil cases. Now customary law survives in questions of inheritance, marriage, and land.

away with chiefs, the operation was effected with remarkably little protest from either the indigenous population or from the French administration that had made use of them. Of the twenty-two Commandants de Cercle, still mostly French, called to Conakry to discuss the proposed removal of the chiefs (from 25 to 27 July only four felt that the *chefs de canton* had a useful role to fulfil in the territory), and nearly all confirmed that the chiefs no longer possessed political traditional authority and had become mere agents of the administration. As far as the Commandant de Cercle for Labs was concerned: "As for me, whether they are there or not, it is the same thing." This is a far cry from Nigeria of the day, where in the North the opposition party (N.E.P.U.) were trying unsuccessfully to rouse the people against the chiefs and where the government of Eastern Nigeria, an area in which traditionally most societies did not have chiefs, commissioned a former expatriate administrative officer to "investigate the position, status and influence of chiefs and natural rulers in the Eastern Region, and make recommendations as to the necessity or otherwise of legislation regulating their appointment, recognition and deposition." In African countries where the British had imposed chiefs, as in Eastern Nigeria and parts of Uganda, their prestige had in fact gone up, but this has certainly not been true in the former French territories.

In formulating these general models it is once again essential to recognize exceptions to the general rule. For example, the kings of the Mossi in Upper Volta, the Fulani emirs of the northern provinces of Cameroun, and a number of chiefs in Niger retained some power. But in general the French system of administration deliberately sapped the traditional powers of the chiefs in the interest of uniformity of administrative system, not only within individual territories but throughout the two great federations of West and Equatorial Africa. Thus it seems somewhat of an understatement to describe the French attitude, as Gouverneur Deschamps does, as "our practical unconcern with respect to the chiefs." Robert Delavignette in *Freedom and Authority in West Africa* (London, 1950) bears this out in his chapter on the commandant. "The man who really personified the Cercle was the commandant. . . . He was the chief of a clearly defined country called Damaragam (Zinder in Niger), and chief in everything that concerned that country. Yet this was the Damaragam once ruled over by the powerful sultans of Zinder, who are now reduced to little more than exotic showpieces of traditional Africa." So too does Geoffrey Gorer in *Africa Dances* (London, 1935), when he writes of the "*Chefs de Canton*":

> In theory these local chiefs rule under the guidance of the local administrator: in practice they are the scapegoats who are made responsible for the collection of money and men. While they enjoy the administrator's favour they have certain privileges, usually good houses and land and in a few cases subsidies; but unless they are completely subservient they risk dismissal, prison and exile.

Gorer draws attention to a phenomenon that bears out just how much the French had changed the nature of chiefs in West Africa. In Ivory Coast, if a *Chef de Canton* with no traditional rights to "rule" were imposed by the administration, the people often elected in secret a "real" chief. Delavignette also notes this in *Freedom and Authority in French West Africa.*[10]

Why this great difference in approach by the two powers to the question of native administration, given that both for reasons of economy had to administer their vast African possessions with the aid of chiefs? The difference has much to do with difference in national character and political traditions. While few would disagree that the British were inspired by the concept of separate development for their African territories, there is still much debate as to how far the French were inspired by the concept of assimilation even after its formal abandonment as official policy in favor of *a politique d'association* only by an examination of the extent of the survival of assimilationist goals in French colonial policy can we understand the reasons for the difference in the two approaches to native administration. This survival showed itself at two levels: as a dominant feature of the *politique d'association* and in the personal ethos of the French political officer.

One of the problems here is to define assimilation. M.D. Lewis has drawn attention to the many definitions of assimilation in use:

(1) assimilation as the dominant colonial policy of France, i.e. its dominant and continuing characteristics;

(2) assimilation as the policy abandoned in favor of association;

(3) assimilation as opposed to autonomy, i.e. integration versus devolution;

(4) assimilation as a legalistic definition, i.e. representation in the mother of parliaments;

(5) assimilation as civilization;

(6) assimilation as representing racial equality as against British tendency to the colour bar;

(7) assimilation as a highly centralized form of direct rule of colonies. It is of course difficult to choose any one definition as the satisfactory one.

Assimilation as practiced in the four communes of Senegal, the only instance of its full-scale application in French Tropical Africa, had the following distinctive features: political assimilation to the metropolitan country through the representation of Senegal in the *Chambre des Députiés*; administrative assimilation by creat-

---

[10] A somewhat extreme point of view with regard to the French attitude to chiefs is held by J. Suret-Canale in "Guinea under the Colonial System," *Présence Africaine*, no. 29, p. 53 (English edition): In reality, these chiefs in their role and in the powers devolved upon them had absolutely nothing traditional or customary; designed to ensure the cheapest execution (under their own responsibility) of the multiple tasks of administration, taxation, forced labour, recruitment etc. They were the exact counterpart of the *caids* of Algeria, subordinate administrators.

ing a Conseil-General for Senegal modelled on the *Conseils du Department* of France, and by the establishment of municipal councils on the French model; the personal assimilation of Senegalese in the communes by according them the status of French citizens, though they were allowed to retain their *statut personnel;* the extension of French educational facilities as part of the French *mission civilisatrice.* This policy was abandoned not so much because men like Lyautey and Jules Harmand advocated Lugardian ideas about the relationship between the colonial power and African peoples, but because, to use Lewis's phrase, the French were "not prepared to undertake the massive work of social transformation which alone could make it a reality." But the *Politique d'association* that succeeded it was certainly not that advocated by Jules Harmand, whereby the colonial power would respect the manners, customs, and religion of the natives and follow a policy of mutual assistance rather than exploitation. Rather it was one in which, while recognition was given to the impracticability of applying a full-scale policy of assimilation to African societies, a number of assimilationist characteristics were retained. First, the goal of creating French citizens out of Africans was not abandoned; it was just made more distant and much more difficult of achievement. Second, there was a high degree of administrative centralization on the mother country, which was not compatible with a true *Politique d'association.* We have already seen that the French made little concession to indigenous political units in dividing up their African territories for administrative purposes. Third, the French civilizing mission was not abandoned, and though education might be sparse, it was modelled on the French system. Children spoke French from the day they entered school. No concession was made to teaching in the vernacular as in the British territories. Fourth, individual territories were not considered as having special characters, so that the same administrative organization was imposed on them all. Political officers would be posted from one territory to the other sometimes every other year, which gave them little time to learn the local language or ethnography. On the other hand the British political officer remained in the same territory for a long period of time, and in the case of Nigeria, in the same region; and promotion depended in part on the ability of the political officers to learn indigenous languages. Thus under the French system the one constant for the political officer could only be French culture, while for the British officer every encouragement was given to him to understand the local culture. As a corollary the French did give some encouragement to the formation of a native elite, which was absorbed into the territorial and federal administrative services, albeit not on a very large scale. The British, on the other hand, in the twenties and thirties actively discouraged the formation of a class of Europeanized Africans, particularly at the level of the central colonial administration. Miss Perham in the late thirties was advocating that no African should be appointed to the administrative service, which she regarded as an alien superstructure. Rather they should be encouraged to work with the native administration. Nigeria was, in the words of Sir Hugh Clifford, governor from 1919 to 1925, a "collection of self-contained and mutually independent native states" which the educated Nigerian had no more business coordinating than the British administration. Thus Nigerians were by and large excluded from the senior service of government, while a number of French colonials reached high posts in the administration. Professor Lucy Mair writing in 1936 about the status of the educated African in the French colonies remarked that:

> The assumption which governs the whole attitude of France towards native development is that French civilisation is necessarily the best and need only be presented to the intelligent African for him to adopt it. Once he has done so, no avenue is to be closed to him. If he proves himself capable of assimilating French education, he may enter any profession, may rise to the dignity of Under-Secretary for the Colonies, and will be received as an equal by French society. This attitude towards the educated native arouses the bitter envy of his counterpart in neighboring British colonies.

Jean Daniel Meyer in *Desert Doctor* (London, 1960) writes of his experiences in French Soudan in the Army Colonial Medical Service before the Second World War, "My colleague was a full-blooded Senegalese. He had studied medicine in France, attending the Bordeaux Naval School, and had the rank of lieutenant." Fifth, the African colonies were considered economic extensions of the metropolitan country, and as Albert Sarraut insisted in his *La Mise en valeur de nos colonies* (Paris, 1923) the colonies should provide assistance to France in the form of raw materials for her industry, and, in addition to this, troops in time of war, in return for which the African would benefit from French civilization. Colonial policy in the inter-war period was to be "a doctrine of colonisation starting from a conception of power or profit for the metropolis, but instinctively impregnated with altruism."

Finally it was at the level of the political officer himself that the tendency to assimilation so often manifested itself. Whatever official colonial policy may have been concerning the status of chiefs and the necessity to respect indigenous institutions, it is clear that the majority of French political officers believed sincerely in the French civilizing mission and that it was their role to bring "enlightenment" to the African. They certainly did not believe that indigenous culture or institutions had anything of value to offer except as a stopgap. L. Gray Cowan writing in 1958 observed, "The young *chef de subdivision* in bush is still a proponent of assimilation through the very fact of his education as a Frenchman although it is no longer a part of official policy." The administrator from republican France, particularly in the inter-war period, had little time for the notion of chiefs holding power other than that derived from the administration itself. This provides a marked contrast with the average British administrator, who believed sincerely that for Africans their own traditional methods of government were the most suitable, provided they were shorn of certain features that did not correspond to his sense of justice. Coming from a country which still maintained a monarchy that had done little to democratize itself on the lines of the Scandinavian monarchies, he had a basic respect for the institution of kingship and the panoply of ritual that surrounded it. The British officer respected his Chief as separate but equal, though certainly not somebody with whom he could establish personal social relations. It was the educated African before whom he felt uneasy. Indeed many political officers openly expressed their contempt for the "savvy boy" or "trousered African." In Nigeria, even as late as 1954, one could hear such epithets used by Northern political officers about Southern politicians. The African's place was in the emir's court, not at Lincoln's Inn or Oxford.

The French political officer, on the other hand, was able to establish relationships with the educated African. M. Delavignette has published in *L'Afrique noire et son destin* (1962) a revealing letter which he received from Ouezzin-Coulibaly, late Prime Minister of Upper Volta, in 1939, concerning his application for French citizenship. Ouezzin-Coulibaly, then a young teacher in Upper Volta, had been friendly with Delavignette at that time for some ten years and expresses his devotion to France and her cause in the war in the warmest terms:

> I was at Sindou and there the news of mobilization reached me on August 29, 1939. I was able to observe in a corner of the bush the affection which the natives had for France. The mobilization was carried out quietly and with a rapidity which assumed a certain understanding of duty. I was amazed' and that was your work, the work of all those who had passed by there and who had inculcated the native peasant, who we wrongly consider unsophisticated, the idea of France and of the Fatherland.

It would be difficult to find such an intimate relationship between a British political officer and a Nigerian teacher at that period. Even as late as 1954, such contact would have been rare. It would be interesting to make a comparison of the philosophy of the colonial service training courses of France, which were much longer established, with that of the British Devonshire courses.

In conclusion, the differences between the French and British systems of administration in Africa were not only differences in degree but in kind. Both may have used chiefs, but the position of the chief in each system was radically different. The basis for these differences may be sought in the fact that though assimilation as an official policy was abandoned after the early experiment in Senegal, it continued to be a most important inspiration both for the *politique d'association* and for the political officer charged with carrying it out. An understanding of the nature of these differences is not only essential to an understanding of colonial history in Africa, but also to an appreciation of the differences between the two main language blocks in independent Africa today.

Suggested Readings

Akpan, Ntieyong, *Epitaph to Indirect Rule: A Discourse on Local Government In Africa* (London: Cassell & Company, Ltd., 1956).

Austen, Ralph, "The Official Mind of Indirect Rule: British Policy in Tanganyika 1916-1939" in Gifford and Louis, *Britain and Germany in Africa* (New Haven: Yale University Press, 1969).

Cameron, Donald, *The Principles of Native Administration and Their Application* (Lagos: Government Printer, 1934).

Cary, Joyce, *The Case for African Freedom* (Austin: Texas University Press, 1961).

Coquery-Vidrovitch, Catherine, "French Colonization in Africa to 1920: Administration and Economic Development" in Gann and Duignan, *Colonialism in Africa 1870-1960* volume 1. (New York: Cambridge University Press, 1969).

Crocker, W.R., *Nigeria: A Critique of British Colonial Administration* (London: George Allen and Unwin, Ltd., 1936).

Crowder, Michael, *Senegal: A Study of the French Assimilation Policy* (London: Metheun, 1967).

Fields, Karen, *Revival and Rebellion in Colonial Central Africa* (Princeton: Princeton University Press, 1985).

Gifford, Prosser, "Indirect Rule: Touchstone or Tombstone for Colonial Policy" in Gifford and Louis, *Britain and Germanv in Africa* (New Haven: Yale University Press, 1969).

Kirk-Greene, Anthony, H.M., *The Principles of Native Administration in Nigeria* (London: Oxford University Press, 1965).

Perham, Margery, *Lord Lugard: The Years of Authority 1898-1945* (Collins: London, 1960)

"A Restatement of Indirect Rule" in *Africa* VII (London: Oxford University Press, 1934).

Suret Canale, Jean, *French Colonialism in Africa: 1900-1945* (Pica Press: New York, 1971)

PROBLEM IV

EDUCATING THE AFRICAN

Every African of every ethnic group was educated in the context of his or her society. This was not only natural but normal to impress upon the young who would soon become adults and leaders of their patrimony and thereby assume responsibilities that were expected, accepted and deeply ingrained from birth. This traditional and eminently environmental curriculum evolved over centuries to meet the needs of their individual societies whether they represented simple villages as in southern Tanzania or more centralized states in the land of the Ashanti, the Baganda or the Kingdom of the Monomatapa. The conquest and occupation of Africa at the latter half of the nineteenth century introduced alien rulers to whom the traditional education within African societies was unproductive, unprogressive, and not always relevant to the needs of the imperial homeland. Thus education to those who were responsible for the administration of the colonies, which had been largely taken by force, was first of all to provide a multilingual servant to act as an intermediary between the imperial rulers and the ruled. Those who knew the indigenous languages as well as those of the conquerors, who could do sums, keep accounts, and read the English, French, or Portuguese of their rulers were best suited to reconcile traditional lore with the imposed legal code and civil regulations of the incomers which could only be accomplished by a Western education, which enhanced their value to the rulers.

This confrontation between traditional education, which was characterized by a full sense of memory so essential in a non-literate society rather than paper and records and now computers, was challenged first by Christian missionaries who could, like Muslims, only spread the faith by the reading of the Bible or the Quran, which required literacy. But literacy opened many avenues to a new world for the clerk in the mundane office of accounts or to the more exalted students at the universities whether they be in Khartoum, Ibadan, Paris, London or Rome—perhaps even Harvard or Berkeley. This confrontation between the traditional education of Africa and the new knowledge introduced by the conquistadors created tensions within the traditional societies and the opportunities in a world beyond the forests, pastures, and the rift.

Education is an expensive but productive, not in a capitalist sense of profit and loss, but in the provisions of skills to generate those profits from the wisdom of Muhammad, the Prophet of God, Shakespeare, and the theoretical physicists. This troubled colonial authorities like Sir Harold MacMichael, who was haunted by the "half-educated man," who had sufficient knowledge to lead his people from their educational traditions but did not know whether to take them. This was a colossal problem for the Africans, who did not know into which world they belonged, and the European colonial administrators who never resolved the dichotomy between the wisdom of the traditional learning with the new power of the education of the West.

As early as the 1920s, private philanthropical organizations, missionary societies, as well as the imperial governments, began to investigate the duty of the colonial powers to advance the level of education that they were offering by that time. In general, these investigative committees concluded that the colonial governments had to take a more active and influential role in education. Although their findings and recommendations were taken seriously, they appear never to have been widely implemented.

One example of these reports is provided by the Phelps-Stokes Committee. This Committee was comprised of a six member international team that examined eight sub-Saharan colonies between 1920 and 1921. The Report concluded that more education in Africa was both necessary and feasible. It viewed Africans in two distinct groups, the "masses" and the "leaders." For the former, teaching would occur in day schools, middle schools, and at the community level in order to provide agricultural, industrial and health education. The leaders would have access to this and more—college level training in African, European, and American universities. The Phelps-Stokes Report was the first major report of its kind and it forced the colonial powers to reform their ill-defined educational programs.

A similar committee of inquiry was led by Lord Hailey to investigate education in African colonies in 1935. Like the first study, Hailey's report concluded that colonial governments needed to take a more active role in making education available to a greater number of their African subjects. However, Hailey's report concluded that, in general, the educational mission was proceeding with success. Whereas the British had previously guided their educational mission on the basis of bureaucratic expediency, they now regarded education as valuable and important in its own right and proceeded to extend educational services and opportunities. Moreover, the French were particularly insistent to extend their educational mission to the few who would qualify in French in their administrative policy of assimilation.

Writing in 1966, John Wilson is more skeptical than Lord Hailey as to the successful implementation of the goals embodied in the Phelps-Stokes Report. The motives of the Report were indeed worthy and the colonial governments were not particularly resistant to the expansion of educational opportunities, but the Phelps-Stokes Report, perhaps because it came from an American foundation with considerable experience in African-American education, failed to create a plan that would actually work in Africa during the formative inter-war period. It was during this period that Africa and her peoples were experiencing a massive economic and social transformation. The Phelps-Stokes Report envisioned an Africa that would remain economically semi-stagnant where education could be administered gradually at the community level over time. However, as some men migrated for work, and as others became successful producers of cocoa, coffee, and other cash crops, the traditional communities were disrupted through urbanization and industrialization. In short, Wilson concludes that the Phelps-Stokes Report was a good idea gone bad by the economic success of Africa in the inter-war period.

Walter Rodney disagrees. Rather than a good plan gone awry by poor planning, colonial education was never really meant to educate. Education was part and parcel of the colonial powers' efforts to subjugate Africa and her peoples. To provide more than limited education to few clerks and junior officers to aid in the pillage of Africa, would have been unwise for the educated class would merely see their own subjugation at the hands of the Europeans and turn on their former teachers. Perhaps the most important aspect of colonial education to Rodney, was not its benign inability to educate Africans, but rather the qualitatively destructive "miseducation" that it did provide. Africans were taught to identify with a culture and mentality that were not their own. To Walter Rodney, colonial education led to economic and cultural underdevelopment.

Abdou Moumouni agrees with Walter Rodney, but is willing to acknowledge at least one positive aspect to colonial education as well. This is perhaps most evident in the emergence of Africa's nationalist leaders. Almost to the last man—Nelson Mandela, Kwame Nkrumah, Jomo Kenyatta, and Amilcar Cabral included—African nationalists were trained in European-based schools or missions—sometimes in the mother country itself. In fact, it was that very education that provided the future nationalist with the knowledge and experience to recognize the oppression under which their people were suffering and articulate methods for its abolishment.

David Chanaiwa, who has spent many years teaching in the West, is more skeptical. In his examination of colonial education in Southern Africa, Chanaiwa claims that on the one hand, racism and ethnocentrism guided the educational mission, whereas on the other hand, the colonial powers faced a constant need for the human capital that Africans could provide. Therefore, Africans were trained as clerks, etc., and were taught to become good capitalist consumers. Like Walter Rodney, Chanaiwa argues that those Africans educated by the colonial powers were taught to see the inherent value of Western industry and culture, at the expense of their African identities. However, Chanaiwa agrees with Abdou Moumouni in that at the same time, education taught Africans the values of nonracialism, pluralism, and nonviolence, which naturally led them to see the hypocrisy in their colonized status. Therefore, the nationalist leaders of Southern Africa—and the powerful symbols of freedom that they have become—came from the educated classes. But, Chanaiwa firmly distances himself from Moumouni's claim that this can be credited to colonial education. Because colonial education was designed and administered with the intent of suppressing Africans, not liberating them, nationalism emerged in spite of colonial education, not because of it.

Education and Its Results
HAROLD MACMICHAEL[1]

I would like to discuss briefly the results of the education given in schools in the Sudan. These are the most difficult to assess because they cannot be isolated from the results of the numerous other factors which are simultaneously operative. It is only possible to give in outline some general idea of the outlook of the educated classes of the present day and leave to the reader the task of estimating how much of that outlook is due to education in its technical sense and how much to the wider educative influence of contact with Western civilization.

By the "educated classes" is meant, roughly speaking, the townsmen of Khartoum, Omdurman and a few similar centers, who have passed through the governmental schools or, exceptionally, acquired an intelligent interest in the outside world by other means. They number in all, perhaps, some 12,000 including, say, 1,300 graduates of the Gordon College, 2,500 from the primary schools, 400-500 officers and ex-officers and 7,000-8,000 merchants.

In pre-war days the older generation were men who had learned their wisdom in a hard school and retained a lively memory of the rigors of the dervish regime and the crowning mercy of Omdurman. The younger generation, who had been children in 1898, were absorbing political ideas but were sufficiently under the restraint of their hard-bitten elders to retain some measure of diffidence. The postwar period was marked by sudden economic expansion and an intensification of the activities of the Egyptian politicians. The younger generation was now in the ascendent, and events in Egypt and the Near East were followed with enthralled interest. To the student class of this period belongs the conception of "the Sudan" as a national unit, the rapid development of the alluring pastime of fishing in the troubled waters of politics and the cult of modernism on the model of the Wafd. The evacuation of the Egyptian Army at the end of 1924 and the sudden realization that Egypt was a broken reed was followed by a certain correction of political perspective in one direction, but also by a decrease in diffidence and an increase in self-sufficiency and avidity for unearned increment. The idea of "The Sudan for the Sudanese' was

[1]MacMichael, Harold, *The Anglo-Egyptian Sudan* (London: Faber and Faber, 1934). Excerpts taken from pages 267-70. Harold MacMichael was born in 1882 and educated at Cambridge. As a member of the Sudan Political Service, he served throughout Africa and particularly in the Sudan. His postings included Kordofan (1905-12), Blue Nile (1912-13), and Khartoum (1913-15). He later went on to become Governor and Commander-in-Chief of Tanganyika (1934-38) and High Commissioner and Commander-in-Chief of Palestine (1938-44). He was a prolific author and was generally regarded as one of the most intelligent, yet aloof, of the British civil servants..

voiced, and a form of patriotism which was generally indistinguishable from a desire for office became popular in the towns. The claims advanced by Egypt during the treaty negotiations of 1930 to sovereignty over the Sudan were resented as implying a right to prevent the Sudanese from working out their own national salvation. This growth of a sense of nationhood is the natural and inevitable result of the acquisition of an intelligent interest in the affairs of the outside world through the medium of education, whether the word be used in the broad or the narrow sense. Were it accompanied by a corresponding development in the sense of perspective it would be entirely praiseworthy—but it would also be without parallel in history.

The teaching of English has given access to a vast new range of literature and there has resulted a ferment of ideas which have not been assimilated. There is intelligence and a craving to absorb new knowledge, but no critical faculty has developed to tone down crudity of thought or preserve balance, and no study of historical foundations and cultural backgrounds has served to correct the tendency to facile generalization and the assumption that those who direct the destinies of the country are animated by purely selfish motives. Thus there has arisen among the younger generation an intellectual malaise, which draws inspiration from parallel movements in other Eastern countries, an attitude of mind which in its lowest form is envy and in its worthier form a sense of thwarted aspiration and romanticism. The young modernist sees himself in a dream as a brilliant member and potential leader of a progressive and enlightened community, and the possessor of wealth enough to bring all the resources and pleasures of civilization within his reach. In reality he is a minor employee on modest pay born into a primitive social group which he despises, bound in his domestic life by the fetters of unenlightened custom and conscious in his hidden heart of hearts that his culture is a veneer and his daydreams things of fantasy. He invents, in compensation for a consciousness of subjection, a legend of a glorious renaissance; but he cannot realize that the true welfare of the country is capable of dissociation from his own immediate personal interests. In studying history he notes with glistening eye the ultimate achievements of those whom he is pleased to regard as his prototypes; but he pays scant attention to the long-labored process of endeavor and disappointment by which characters have been molded and wisdom learned before the final reaping of the harvest.

Education in Africa

THOMAS JESSE JONES[2]

Education must be planned with full regard both for the elevation of the masses and for the development and training of native leaders. At present many missions do not seem to be conscious of this necessary differentiation. Some have been intent on offering education and religion to the masses of the people seemingly with no provision for native leadership. Others are maintaining schools of the so-called "higher types" with little evidence of preparing their students to serve the masses of the people. A fundamental requisite of effective training of the masses is the determination to produce native leaders of moral force who will help extend education far and wide. Equally fundamental is the requisite that the education of native leadership shall be definitely rooted in the needs of the masses of the people. The interdependence of these two educational ends is certain and inevitable. Lower schools must open wide the door of educational development, the upper schools must be vitally sympathetic to the oncoming group, and both higher and lower schools must have real regard for the life of the people and the community.

Consciousness of the native millions seems to be realized as yet only by a very few. The immensity of numbers, the extensive areas of population, and the primitive and sometimes barbarous character of the people often seem to constitute an overwhelming responsibility to both missions and governments. However difficult the task, it must be undertaken if the possibilities of the people and country are to be realized. Resources of soil, minerals, and waterpower depend for their development upon the effective education of all the people. Economic prosperity and the educational development of the people are inextricably interwoven. The ultimate test of colonization is not, however, in the exploitation of physical resources. The final test is in the civilization of the native people.

The colonial . . . governments and missions have . . . really made only a beginning. In determining the extent of educational influence the Commission has accept-

[2]Jones, Thomas Jesse, *Education in Africa: A Study of West, South and Equatorial Africa by the African Education Commission, under the Auspices of the Phelps-Stokes Fund and Foreign Mission Societies of North America and Europe* (New York: Phelps-Stokes, 1921). Excerpts taken from pages 57-60, 65, and 69-79. The Phelps-Stokes fund was a private philanthropic fund based in New York and administered by a board of trustees. The Phelps-Stokes fund financed a variety of committees which evaluated a range of social issues in Africa, the Caribbean, and the United States. The particular committee for this report was comprised of six individuals from Africa, Europe, and the United States. In order to gather the information that is contained in its 300 page report, the committee travelled to Africa for one year between 1920 and 1921 and examined many countries in West and Central Africa including Sierra Leone, Liberia, Gold Coast, Nigeria, Cameroons, Belgian Congo, Angola, and South Africa.

ed the proportion of the total population usually regarded as of school age. According to statistical usage the children between six and fourteen years of age constitute about one-fifth of the total population. This represents the minimum number of children for which civilized nations require educational facilities. In South Africa, where school facilities are at their best, only one-fifth of this number are in school. In banner colonies like the Gold Coast, provision is made for only one-tenth of the minimum required in civilized countries. In others the proportion of the native youth in any kind of school is almost negligible. Even on the quantitative test, educational facilities in Africa are really only a promise of what should and what can be done for the masses in this great continent. A qualitative test of education according to the principle of adaptation to the needs of the people would turn out still less favorably.

There has also been much confusion as to the place and value of native leaders in colonial development. The tendency to discount the native leadership of a primitive people is almost universal. Such depreciation often exists on the part of one civilized group toward another as well as among uncivilized groups in intertribal relations. It is not strange that Europeans of education and power should fail to understand the possibilities of natives as guides of their own people. Some Europeans seem even to resent the suggestion of native participation in the leadership of their own people. These antagonistic attitudes toward native leadership and even any degree of education for the native people are based in part upon the general tendency to undervalue primitive peoples; but they are also due to the type of education that has been too often attempted in the past. It is difficult to imagine greater errors than those that have been committed in the name of education not only in Africa, but also in Europe and America. . . . If the training of the youth of civilized countries depended entirely upon the schools the results would often be very disappointing. The training of civilized youth is the combined result of the home, the church, the shop, the farm, the government, and numerous other social institutions potent in their influence. Among primitive people the school and the mission are almost alone in the task of molding the life of the youth, and whatever failures may occur are directly chargeable to them. Educationists are now actively changing education in Europe and America. Thoughtful natives are beginning to realize that they have not had the broader type of education they needed and also that fundamental qualities of their own groups have not only been disregarded but often condemned.

Education of the Masses

The principal agencies for the education of the masses are first, the local day schools and the middle schools; second, various forms of community extension activities; third, the government departments concerned with the general welfare of the colony. Hitherto there does not seem to have been a very clearly defined effort to extend the issuance of these agencies to the people as a whole. The first step in the extension of education to the masses of the people is to realize the possibilities presented by these agencies and to work out these possibilities so far as funds and personnel are available. The usual comment made by colonial administrators to this recommendation is that neither government nor missions have sufficient funds to carry out an extensive program. It is true that the complete program requires considerable money. It is to be understood, however, that the program may be initiated at a comparatively small cost by the use of organizations and facilities already in existence. In fact it is best that the extension work shall be begun modestly and developed normally. When the existing facilities are being used to their utmost, the simpler forms of extension activities may be added. The most important consideration of all in determining cost is the fact that the right form of mass education increases the productivity of local communities so substantially as to more than recompense the government for the expenditures made.

LOCAL DAY SCHOOL

The local day school is undoubtedly the most effective institution for the education of the masses. It is essentially the frontier station of education. To realize its full possibilities in reaching the masses it is important that educators shall decide to use the school in its subnormal status as well as in its full development. . . . Recognition of the value of the subnormal standard of the local day school must be accompanied by a determination to provide adequate supervision . . . [in terms of] the qualities of the teacher, the program, and the equipment.

Education of the Native Leadership

The various forms of native leadership in . . . colonial education involve, first, those who are to be teachers and religious workers; second, those who are to specialize in agriculture and industry; third, those who are to enter the professions of medicine, theology, engineering, or law. These teachers and leaders have been trained in mission and government schools, and in European or American institutions. . . . It is certain that the adequate training of native leadership requires, first, the organization of secondary schools accessible to native youth in every colony; second, an arrangement whereby those who are prepared to advance still further may enter colleges in Africa, Europe, or America.

SECONDARY LEADERSHIP

As the elementary school is the pioneer station for education for the masses, so the secondary school is the all-important institution for training almost every type of leader required in Africa. It is therefore essential that the activities of the secondary school be determined with the utmost regard for the needs of such leadership. The type of secondary education should vary with the needs of the community. It is apparent that an effective institution in the rural districts must be organized with reference to the agricultural life of the people. A city school should likewise have regard for the industrial, hygienic, and education needs of the urban community. There are also schools that select special objectives, such as the training of teachers, ministers, farmers, or industrial workers.

TRAINING IN TRADES AND HANDICRAFTS

Training in trades and handicrafts has for its purpose not only industrial skill, but also the development of mind and character. It is increasingly recognized that education is not limited to the transfer of facts. Every part of the body is to be used as an approach to the mind. . . . Training in handicrafts is at present offered in three forms, first, mechanical practice and household arts as part of elementary and secondary school instruction; second, trade departments or schools preparing technical teachers and tradesmen; and third, industrial schools of elementary grade preparing mechanics for actual service in villages or in the less skilled activities of industrial concerns.

AGRICULTURAL EDUCATION

Agricultural education is in many respects more vital to Africa than any other kind and neglect of it is one of the most unfortunate failures of government and mission education. Some training has been given as an incident to the life of the mission stations and the work of the colonial government, but very little has been done as a regular part of the school activities. The forms in which agricultural education may be given are, first, the supplementary training of elementary and secondary pupils; second, departments or schools of agriculture to prepare teachers and specialists in agriculture; and third, short courses to train farmers to cultivate more effectively their plots of ground to work on the large plantations.

COLLEGE EDUCATION

Though college education for African youth is limited to two institutions in Africa and to the opportunities for study in Europe and America, it is certain that the development of native leadership will require more college facilities as the standards of education advance. If college education is of any value to any group, it is to those who are to be the native guides of African people whose existence is beset with so many perplexing problems. Only a broad-minded leadership with a thorough grasp of human development can understand the peculiar difficulties attending the rise of a primitive people. The misunderstandings that seem to result necessarily from the entrance of European ideas of government and life can be explained only by native leaders capable of sympathetic appreciation of both African and European life. . . . More and more leadership of the Africans is devolving upon the strong and capable native men and women. Successful leadership requires the best lessons of sociology, economics, and education. Without such leadership, misunderstandings will multiply and increase in perplexity. The Africans must have physicians with real skill and the spirit of service to lead against the insanitary conditions that are threatening the colonies. They must have religious teachers who can relate religion to individual morals and to the common activities of the community. They must have teachers of secondary schools who have had college training in the modern sciences and in the historical development of civilization.

Unfortunately the college curriculum has only recently begun to change the traditional character of the subjects taught. The large place given to the classical languages has limited or excluded the necessary time for social and physical science, sometimes even for history. Africans have too readily believed that the culture and character of Oxford University graduates can be realized most successfully through the study of the classical languages. Many European and American supporters of classical learning now concede that the effective study of social and physical science results in equal culture and character with the additional important result of capacity to serve society along some of the definite lines of its modern requirements. All will readily grant that the classics have made a vital contribution to the development of humanity, but this recognition of the classics is in no respect antagonistic to the conviction that culture, character, and useful human service can be attained by a recognition of the results of modern scientific research. It seems necessary to state these convictions because the influence of the classical requirements of some European universities is distorting many phases of education in African schools.

There are now significant changes under consideration in European colleges and universities. The curricula are being broadened to provide for new subjects immediately concerned with the problems of the twentieth century. Even conservative institutions of learning have added departments or colleges of agriculture, forestry, and engineering. There is a realization that college activities are subject to the test of service to the community in exactly the same degree as any other activity that seeks social support. Matriculation requirements now often include such secondary subjects as agriculture, science, commercial subjects, practical mathematics, physiology and hygiene, and music. The courses leading to the B. A. degree have everywhere been broadened, and new degrees, such as Bachelor of Science, have been introduced which require no Greek and little or no Latin. European universities can render a most vital service to Africa by extending to such African students as seem qualified the benefits of this broader conception.

AN AFRICAN SURVEY
WILLIAM MALCOLM HAILEY[3]

A General Review of Education

Education in Africa should have a double function, namely, to provide the African with a better equipment for dealing with his own environment, and to prepare him for the changes to which that environment will in increasing measure be subject. It is clear that in the British areas in Africa, attention at the outset was concentrated so largely on the second of these two purposes as almost to exclude the first. The beginnings of education in Africa were laid in an age which assumed without question the intrinsic value of European civilization; African institutions were judged purely in terms of their resemblance to those already known, and concern for the improvement of African conditions manifested itself in the effort to make them approximate as closely as possible to those of Europe. To many who held that view, the Christian religion was an essential element in the introduction of the African to civilization; hence the importance of mission schools, and the official encouragement given to missions.

Popular Education

Although in some respects education in British areas at the present day is by no means free from the burden of its earlier traditions, there has been a significant change in the direction of policy. Emphasis is now laid on the first of the two purposes of education mentioned above, and attention is concentrated on the attempt to fit the African for dealing with his own environment. Many influences have contributed to this result. An age of positive values has been succeeded by one which recognizes that the worth of an institution must be judged in relation to the condi-

---

[3]Hailey, William Malcolm, *An African Survey: A Study of the Problems Arising in Africa South of the Sahara* (London: Oxford University Press, 1939). Excerpts taken from pages 1278-83, and 1286-90. Lord Hailey was born in Neport Pagnell, England in 1872. An English colonial administrator in India, he was a chief commissioner (1912-28) of Delhi, Governor of the Punjab (1924-8) and of the United Provinces (1928-30, 1931-4), and was a member of the Permanent Mandates Commission of the League of Nations. He is also the author of *Britain and her Dependencies* (New York: Longmans Green, 1943), *The Future of Colonial Peoples* (London: Oxford University Press, 1944), *Native Administration in British African Territories* (London: H.M.S. Stationery Office, 1953), and *Africa in the Modern World* (Chicago: University of Chicago Press, 1955). *An African Survey* was actually part of an inquiry committee—of which Lord Hailey was the Director—funded by the Carnegie Corporation to understand the scale of Africa's problems and the effects of colonial rule.

tions in which it operates, and, as a necessary consequence, there is a growing appreciation of the need for sociological study of the reaction of primitive peoples to the introduction of new institutions. The general agreement that education cannot be confined to a few, but must progressively extend to the mass of the population, has focused attention on the problem of finding a suitable content for "popular" instruction, which must bear a close relation to the realities of African life. The report of the Union Interdepartmental Committee on Native Education of 1935 is a significant mark of the change of South African opinion under the influence of this consideration. In the British colonies the new conception of the function of education seems to have been a consequence of the growth of the system of indirect rule, which is itself less a type of political institution than a philosophy based on an appreciation of the needs of native life. The new outlook found concrete expression in the memoranda of the Advisory Committee of the Colonial Office, which have not only had their effect on government policy, but have served to give direction to the activities of missionary bodies. The result has been an increased use of the vernacular as a medium of instruction, the production of more textbooks suited to African pupils, the introduction of agriculture and of manual training as part of the school course, the spread of teaching of the type associated with the Jeanes schools, and the substitution, at the secondary stage, of training of a vocational nature for literary instruction.

The political philosophy underlying the French method makes it difficult to apply the same standards as have been used in examining the British. Education is the main instrument for carrying out the French policy of association. . . . This system is designed, on the one hand, to create an *elite,* inspired by French ideals of civilization, which will be fitted to take its part in the administrative life of the territory, and, on the other, to provide a popular form of instruction suited to the needs of the masses. The method chosen for the education of the *elite* is logically planned, and appears successful in attaining its purpose. The French pay greater regard to African conditions in their system of education for the masses: the rural school aims at improving the native as an agriculturist, and the urban school at assisting him to gain his livelihood in the towns. Through the fact that all education is free, equality of opportunity is secured, as it cannot be when the pupil's chances of completing his course depend upon his father's income. It is doubtful, however, if this dual system can be maintained in practice. The French political ideal prescribes the use of the French languages as a universal medium of instruction. The use of French in the popular schools, and the interest in French culture which it stimulates, must tend to give the pupil an outlook which will differ only in degree from that of the *elite.* The whole trend of the French method is in effect towards the production of a civilization essentially non-African in character.

The Belgian system shows no such clearly marked tendencies. Its two distinctive features are a utilitarian outlook and a close association with religious teaching; the Catholic Church is mainly responsible for education, and has a predominating influence in the majority of the schools. There is no planned effort to create an *elite,* and, wherever possible, the vernacular is used in the earlier stages of instruction; manual training is given a prominent place, and almost all post-primary education is vocational. It is necessary, however, to remember that the present educational system, like most other administrative institutions in the Belgian Congo, is a postwar creation, and the official Belgian attitude towards the introduction of the African to a European form of culture is not yet clearly determined.

The Portuguese educational policy, so far as its features can be distinguished, would seem to aim at Europeanizing the African; but it does not at present display the same force or directness as the French system, and it is perhaps unlikely that it will in the future. In any case, the conception of a "European" form of civilization would hardly be the same in the Portuguese as in the French colonies.

The Payment of Fees

In French territories, where . . . education forms part of a policy of political and economic development, education is free, but the authorities limit the numbers of pupils who are allowed to attend the higher courses. In British areas the usual policy is to charge fees, and in government and missionary boarding schools, such as those at Fort Hare, Achimota, Budo, Makerere, and elsewhere, charges are made which, in the absence of bursaries or exemptions, would preclude any but the more well-to-do Africans from attending the courses. . . . It is said that the imposition of small school fees and payment for school books counteracts irregularity in attendance, which otherwise is prevalent. It has to be remembered that, except in the form of experiments in limited areas, compulsory education does not exist, and as children assist their parents in the house and garden they are not willingly spared for long periods. On the other hand, it is objected that the payment of fees often precludes comparatively poor chiefs and headmen from sending their children to boarding schools, while wealthy salaried employees find no difficulty in meeting the expense; and thus, in some areas, the educated class may be inadequately represented among the ruling families.

The question of payment of fees is of considerable importance in connection with comparatively expensive higher education, and if the best pupils are to be brought forward for training for the public services, or for service in the native administrations, bursaries or scholarships, or grants from government or local funds, would appear to be necessary, to cover not only board and school fees but also travelling.

Higher Education

The considerations which decide the character of higher education are largely political, for the type of instruction given depends on the view held of the place in society which the educated African may be expected to fill. As has more than once been remarked, the French look on the more highly educated African as a member of an *elite* whose specialized training fits him to assist the administration in carrying out its own ideals of civilization. By limiting themselves to this objective, the French have clearly defined the educational issue, and have evolved a system well adapted to its purpose. At present, the educated French West African takes an important but usually subordinate part in the administration. Though persons of African origin are represented in the colonial administrative cadre, the majority come from West Indian colonies, and have qualified for service by completing their education in France. That West Africans are not yet represented in any number is due to the fact that on passing out of the local professional schools they have been at once absorbed into the specific employment for which they have been trained. French policy has not favored the appearance of the educated African at the local bar; in the absence of a legislature he has not the political opportunities which are open in the British Gold Coast or Nigeria, nor has he attained the same importance in journalism. On the other hand, the absence of color prejudice makes it possible for the educated African to live in some considerable measure on equal terms with the Frenchman, and the colonial aspirant can hope also to secure a place in the activities of the mother country.

British policy as yet exhibits no clear view of the future of the educated African. Though, as has been shown, there has of recent years been a movement in favor of vocational rather than general education, it has not been carried to the length of confining education to vocational courses or restricting the number of those entitled to receive them. At the present stage in the evolution of educational policy, it is of importance to know what position it is intended to assign to the African in the service of the administration. On this point, however, there has been no declaration of general policy. There have been some expressions of opinion by local authorities on the subject, as, for instance, that all posts in government service, except those of political officers and judges, are in the future to be open to Africans who have reached the required standard of education, or that, on grounds of both justice and economy, the general interest requires that there should be a progressive substitution of an African for a European establishment. That no principle of general application has been formulated by the Colonial Office is not, as has sometimes been suggested, due only to the difficulty of forecasting the precise form of the political and administrative structure which will be evolved under the influence of the theory of indirect rule. There are few instances in British colonial history when the future of the educated native has been consciously determined, or the educational system deliberately adjusted to fit him for it. Accepting the general value of an education based on the European model, British governments have been content to wait until the product of that type of education has asserted his claim to a position in the political or administrative life of the country; when the position has been finally accorded it is more often in recognition of a claim which has been tacitly encouraged than as a result of a predetermined plan. It may be justifiable to conclude that for some time at least it is unlikely that British administrations in Africa will commit themselves to a definite view of the future of the educated African and give a decisive direction to the educational system. . . . For the present, therefore, there is likely to be an increasing emphasis on the vocational character of higher instruction, on grounds of expediency if not of general principle. The relative part to be played by types of instruction which seek to meet existing demands for specific knowledge, and those which are more concerned to create a philosophy of life, must await a decision as to the degree of responsibility which it is intended ultimately to give to the African in the management of his own affairs.

Problems in Applying the Phelps-Stokes Report

JOHN WILSON[4]

Of the constructiveness of the thinking of the Phelps-Stokes Commission there can be little doubt. But a further question arises as to whether this thinking issued inaction in Africa? . . . In practice, the attempts of the schools to relate themselves to the community resulted merely in accretion of activities and not in a genuine reorientation and reorganization of the whole school administration, curriculum, and method. Thus, education so far as the school was concerned was not genuinely reformed and the principles of the Phelps-Stokes Commission were not truly applied, first, largely because of failure to re-educate and reorganize the teaching profession.

Another factor which made teachers, parents, and the intelligentsia reluctant to accept the precepts and practice of the Phelps-Stokes Commission was that bookish education in the three R's, followed by an academic secondary and higher education, seemed eminently desirable to African people themselves for the simple reason that it provided a ladder to an altogether different world of increased financial reward and enhanced social status. Despite growing unemployment among some of the products of this education, African people had a firmer faith in it than was to be shaken by the Phelps-Stokes recommendations. Indeed the fear began to take shape in the minds of West Africans among both the uneducated and "young men" that perhaps the Europeans who dominated education departments and missions were not being entirely frank or disinterested in putting forward the findings of the Commission. To them it appeared that the West, which had achieved such power, privilege, and health, had done so, apparently, as a result of a bookish and classical education. Africans of a political cast of mind, in a position to influence opinion, felt that the recommendations of the Commission constituted an attempt to withhold the very education that was perhaps the secret of Western supremacy, so that Africans would be kept permanently in subjection. The emphasis of the Commission on agriculture of a kind typical of low economy subsistence farming even if in a community setting, smacked of an education for hewers of wood and

[4]Wilson, John, *Education and Changing West African Culture* (London: Oxford University Press, 1966). Excerpts taken from pages 34, and 38-43. At the time he wrote this piece, John Wilson was a Senior Lecturer of Education in Tropical Areas at the University of London's Institute of Education. He is also the author of *The Teaching of English as the Language of Instruction in Secondary Education* (London: Faber and Faber, 1967).

drawers of water.

The Phelps-Stokes Commission was not unaware of the fact that one of the obstacles to change was likely to be resistance of this kind. It was for this reason, among others, that their education was aimed at the whole community, children, youth, and adults. Indeed a most important element in their ideas was of education as something applied to a whole community and not, as it had come to be conceived in Africa, as a bookish process applied to individuals in childhood and youth for purposes of aiding escape from the hard facts of economic and social environment, as they bore upon the mass of the community, to personal wealth and status. In the Commission's view, the school took its rightful place only in relationship to the education of the whole community and education was to be applied to adults as well as to the young. This, as we have seen, was one of the functions of education in the preliterate indigenous society. The Commission wished education to be aimed at helping the whole community to adapt to circumstances including adaptation to change.

The education of adults would obviously be as important as the education of the young in teaching adaptation and particularly in teaching adaptation to change, for it is the older adult section of any community that is notoriously resistant to change. Yet the hard fact is that this all-important section of the Phelps-Stokes Report indicating the need for adult education was left almost completely without implementation by both government and mission, except, as has been noted, only in so far as the puny efforts of the school itself attempted to influence the community. Indeed, the Commission itself probably erred in believing that the school could powerfully influence the community, a rather persistent present-day error.

This was most unfortunate and prevented any rich immediate harvest resulting from the Commission, for it is quite obvious that the element of adult education applied to the community was an absolute essential to adult understanding and acceptance of any reform of the school itself. As has been indicated, the West African adult population opposed, usually passively, the Commission's new measures in the school, suspecting a Western desire to inhibit African development. The main measure, namely, adult education, which could have dispelled such suspicion, was central to the recommendations of the Commission but was left almost entirely in neglect.

It is very much open to question whether the Phelps-Stokes Commission had a full appreciation of the factors of change and of the speed of change operating in Africa, particularly in West Africa in the decade following the First World War. Certainly they had no vision of the impressive acceleration in the speed of change that was to occur in the 1930s and 1940s and for this they can scarcely be blamed. Such a vision would have required foresight of a well-nigh impossible order, for history has scarcely seen the like even in the Renaissance. That the Commission had not grasped the order of change of the 1920s soon became apparent in the Gold Coast. Less than a decade after the Commission, the Education Department of that country suspected that some of the recommendations of the Commission, significant as they were in terms of education for change, were not fully sensitive to speed of change.

One of the recommendations of the Commission had been the suitability for reproduction in Africa of the Jeanes school as seen in southern United States of America. In this system the schoolteacher and his wife specifically divided their time between school work and the education of the community, the teacher and his wife being themselves the model farmer and farmer's wife, as well as school teachers. The Jeanes school found more favor in Rhodesia and Central Africa generally than it ever did in West Africa. Indeed, no Jeanes school in the full sense was ever established in the Gold Coast, and much the same is true of Gambia, Sierra Leone, and Nigeria. Early in the 1930s, Mr. Tom Cranston, Assistant Director of Education in the Gold Coast and a personal friend of Dr. and Mrs. Wilkie, visited Rhodesia to examine the Jeanes schools. On his return to the Gold Coast he expressed his opinion that it was much too late for this kind of thing in the Gold Coast. This was a significant statement. What really was beginning to appear was the Phelps-Stokes Report, in examining certain aspects of Negro education in the southern United States, had really seen societies moving forward economically, much more gradually than the pace of economic change that, during the eight years immediately following the Commission, affected West Africa and, more particularly, certain areas of the Gold Coast.

Thus, in the Gold Coast, all during the 1920s the cash crop, cocoa, had been in ever growing demand and represented a rapidly increasing source of revenue to the country, a rapidly growing source of wealth to African dealers in the crop and even to the peasant farmers in extensive areas of the country. As a result, important and extensive areas of low-level subsistence farming came to be neglected in favor of, or at least rated secondary to, the cash crop.

Yet the Phelps-Stokes Commission had in mind education for a community of farmers largely engaged in food-cropping advancing only gradually. Even more in contrast, perhaps, with the conditions assumed in the report of the Commission, mining areas recently established, producing gold and manganese, rose into such prominence in the Gold Coast that to serve them a new port, Takoradi, was literally carved out of virgin coast and there were settled African harbor and railway operatives, electricians, technicians of all kinds, clerks, stock clerks, cable and radio employees. There came with them the shopkeepers, traders, market-sellers, transport owners, truck drivers, and all the other persons required to supply and service a township. It is a staggering fact that no schools were provided for this new township and it was only towards the end of its first decade in existence that a select few in this modern town got even a minimum amount of schooling. It was thirteen years later that a start was made with technical education.

Virtually the same is true of the mining areas served by the port. So exclusive was the preoccupation with providing education for the low-economy rural areas envisaged by the Commission that no one seemed prepared for the economic change initiated and foreshadowed by the emergence of these new quasi-industrialized areas with their accompanying urbanization. Furthermore, it will be recalled that, under the British system of indirect rule, the authority of native chiefs and indigenous political systems were the chosen instruments of government. Great importance was attached to the capital seats of these chiefs.

In the small township, or rather expanded village, of one of these Gold Coast chiefs, there were in 1930 and had been for some years two important government schools, one a trade school financed exclusively by the same central government which at that time boggled at providing one single school in the quasi-industrial urban area of Takoradi which the self-same government had willed into existence during the 1920s. Takoradi, despite its commercial pre-eminence and vast capital investment, being virtually carved from the bush, had no place in the system of indirect rule. Sir Gordon Guggisberg, the then governor of the Gold Coast, had been most forward in promoting Takoradi. He had also been something of an enthusiast for the Phelps-Stokes Commission. The Phelps-Stokes Commission had not quite foreseen this kind of thing, nor had the system of indirect rule allowed for it.

Signs and portents in the 1920s such as Takoradi were only the beginning of things. They were the result of quite a phenomenal period of high economic activity throughout the world. Vast and violent changes were in the making. Before the decade was out the world experienced a sudden and almost universal economic recession. This was followed by a world war in the aftermath of which the world now labors. Such swift and violent change tempts one to the aphorism that the only thing we can count as permanent, in the present day and age, is change proceeding at a breathless pace in almost catastrophic dimensions. Here is a new force, bearing on that nexus—the economic, social and political, which makes it even more difficult than ever to hold them in relationship and which presents to education a new problem, or an old problem in entirely new dimensions.

Adaptation of education to the economic and social environment through school and adult education geared to one another was the principle underlying the philosophy and recommendations of the Phelps-Stokes Commission. In its new form, the problem posed is how to adapt education, through school and community, to a rapidly changing economic, social, and political environment so that education itself will provide mankind with some kind of readiness for and adaptability to change while yet exercising constructive discrimination and control. The problem is universal. In Africa it is aggravated by the impact of rapid change on developing territories with a developing educational system, in contrast with the more advanced Western societies that have highly developed educational provision.

Education for Underdevelopment
WALTER RODNEY[5]

The main purpose of the colonial school system was to train Africans to help man the local administration at the lowest ranks and to staff the private capitalist firms owned by Europeans. In effect, that meant selecting a few Africans to participate in the domination and exploitation of the continent as a whole. It was not an educational system that grew out of the African environment or one that was designed to promote the most rational use of material and social resources. It was not an educational system designed to give young people confidence and pride as members of African societies, but one which sought to instill a sense of deference towards all that was European and capitalist. Education in Europe was dominated by the capitalist class. The same class bias was automatically transferred to Africa; and to make matters worse the racism and cultural boastfulness harbored by capitalism were also included in the package of colonial education. Colonial schooling was education for subordination, exploitation, the creation of mental confusion, and the development of underdevelopment.

A European-type school system hardly operated during the first forty years or so of colonialism. In that period, missionaries gave schooling for their own Christianizing purposes, and it was in the 1920s that the colonizing powers carried out a series of investigations into educational possibilities in Africa. Thereafter, colonial education became systematic and measurable, though it approached its maximum dimensions only in the post-Second World War era.

Colonial education was a series of limitations inside other limitations. The first practical limitation was politico-financial, which means that political policy, rather than the actual availability of money, guided financial expenditure. The metropolitan governments and their African administrators [constantly] claimed that there

[5]Rodney, Walter, *How Europe Underdeveloped Africa* (Washington, D.C.: Howard University Press, 1982). Excerpts taken from pages 240-1, 243, 245-7, 249-53, and 260-1. Historian, educator, and political activist Walter Rodney (1942-1980) was certainly one of the world's most renowned scholars. Rodney was born in British Guyana, educated in England, and began his teaching career in the history department at the University of the West Indies at Mona, Jamaica. Deemed subversive by the Jamaican government he was forced to leave in 1968. From 1969-72 Rodney taught history at the University of Dar es Salaam in Tanzania before returning to his home, Guyana, to accept the chairmanship in the history department at the University of Guyana. His position was later revoked, evidently under government pressure. Later, Rodney became the leader of the Working People's Alliance, a radical political party opposed to Guyana's Prime Minister, Forbes Burnham. In 1980 Rodney was killed in a car bomb explosion. Despite his shortened career, Dr. Rodney left a lasting legacy of scholarship. His Marxist writings attacked capitalism and imperialism of which his *How Europe Underdeveloped Africa* stands as a testament.

was not enough money for education.

Africans were being educated inside colonial schools to become junior clerks and messengers. Too much learning would have been both superfluous and dangerous for clerks and messengers. Therefore, secondary education was rare and other forms of higher education were virtually nonexistent throughout most of the colonial epoch. That which was provided went mainly to non-Africans. As late as 1959, Uganda spent about 11 pounds per African pupil, 38 pounds per Indian, and 186 pounds on each European child—the difference being due largely to the availability of secondary education for the children of the capitalists and the middlemen. In Kenya, the discrimination was worse and the number of European children involved was high.

Educators often refer to "the educational pyramid," comprising primary education as the base and going upwards through secondary, teacher-training, higher technical, and university facilities—the last named being so small that it could be represented as the point at the top of the pyramid. Throughout Africa, the primary base was narrow and yet the pyramid sloped shallowly because so few of the primary students could continue beyond that level. . . . The imperialist whites snigger at Africans for being "illiterate natives" and they would argue that illiteracy is part of "the vicious circle of poverty." Yet, the same people boast proudly that they have educated Africa. It is difficult to see how they can have it both ways. If independent Africa is still without the benefits of modern education (as it is), then seventy-five years of colonial exploitation undoubtedly have something to do with the state of affairs; and the absurdity is so much the greater when one contemplates how much Africa produced in that period and how much of that went to develop all aspects of European capitalist society, including their educational institutions.

Those Africans who had access to education were faced with certain qualitative problems. The quality was poor by prevailing European standards. The books, the methods of teaching, and the discipline were all brought to Africa in the nineteenth century; and, on the whole, colonial schools remained sublimely indifferent to the twentieth century. New ideas that were incorporated in the capitalist metropoles never reached the colonies. In particular, the fantastic changes in science did not reach African classrooms, for there were few schools where science subjects were taught. Similarly, the evolution of higher technical education did not have any counterpart in colonial Africa.

Some of the contradictions between the content of colonial education and the reality of Africa were really incongruous. On a hot afternoon in some tropical African school, a class of black shining faces would listen to their geography lesson on the seasons of the year—spring, summer, autumn, and winter. They would learn about the Alps and the river Rhine but nothing about the Atlas Mountains of North Africa or the river Zambezi. If those students were in a British colony, they would dutifully write that "we defeated the Spanish Armada in 1588"—at a time when Hawkins was stealing Africans and being knighted by Queen Elizabeth I for so doing. If they were in a French colony, they would learn that "the Gauls, our ancestors, had blue eyes," and they would be convinced that "Napoleon was our greatest general," the same Napoleon who reinstituted slavery in the Caribbean island of Guadeloupe and was only prevented from doing the same in Haiti because his forces were defeated by an even greater strategist and tactician, the African Toussaint L'Ouverture.

There is no getting away from the conclusion reached by the African educationalist Abdou Moumini that "colonial education corrupted the thinking and sensibilities of the African and filled him with abnormal complexes." It followed that those who were Europeanized were to that extent de-Africanized, as a consequence of the colonial education and the general atmosphere of colonial life. Many examples are cited in present-day Africa of the insulting treatment of aspects of African culture in the colonial period based on cultural imperialism and white racism.

Not all colonial educators and administrators were consciously taking up the position that the African should be educated the better to be enslaved. On the contrary, most of them thought that they were doing Africans a great favor; and there were a few who were enlightened enough to realize that there was scope for devising a school program which was less divorced from African reality. In 1928, even the French education minister was shocked to learn that Africans were taught that the Gauls, their ancestors, had blue eyes. From the 1920s, both Britain and France produced colonial educators and education commissions which urged greater relevance of teaching programs in Africa. They also put forward suggestions such as the use of local languages in primary schools, more education for girls, and an end to the white-collar orientation of schooling. However, the seemingly progressive nature of those recommendations could not change the fact that colonial education was an instrument to serve the European capitalist class in its exploitation of Africa. Whatever colonial educators thought or did could not change that basic fact.

To recommend that African girls should go to school is more than just an educational policy. It has tremendous social implications, and it presupposes that the society will usefully employ the educated woman. Metropolitan capitalist society itself had failed to liberate women, to offer them equal educational opportunities, or to provide them with responsible jobs at equal rates of pay with men. That being the case, it was wishful thinking to imagine that the colonial educational system would take any serious interest in African women, especially since the colonialists would have had to transform the consciousness on that matter which was characteristic of feudal and pre-feudal societies. Nowhere did the cash-crop economy or the export of basic ores make provision for educated women. As in the capitalist metropoles it was assumed that the civil service was for men. Therefore, the extremely limited employment sector in the colonies had nothing to offer educated women, and modern education remained a luxury with which few African women came into contact.

Another progressive suggestion made by some colonial educationists was for more agricultural and technical schooling. But, genuine technical education was ruled out, because the fundamental purpose of the colonial economy did not permit the development of industry and skills within Africa. Only in rare cases, such as in the Congo, was there an objective necessity for technically trained Africans. In the later stages of colonial rule in Congo, mineral exploitation had developed to such a point that there was practical need for extensive rudimentary technical skills among African workers. A few Katangese and other Congolese also received technical training of a secondary equivalent. Significantly enough, in such cases, the private companies took the initiative, since their profits were at stake, and the technical schools were extensions of their production processes. However, for the most part, whatever skilled jobs needed to be done within the restricted field of mining and industry in Africa were met by the importation of Europeans.

Early educational commissions also accorded high priority to religious and moral flavoring of instruction—something that was disappearing in Europe itself. The role of the Christian church in the educational process obviously needs special attention. The Christian missionaries were as much part of the colonizing forces as were the explorers, traders, and soldiers. There may be room for arguing whether in a given colony the missionaries brought the other colonialist forces or vice versa, but there is no doubting the fact that missionaries were agents of colonialism in the practical sense, whether or not they saw themselves in that light. The imperialist adventurer Sir Harry Johnston disliked missionaries, but he conceded in praise of them that "each mission station is an exercise in colonization."

Whatever the church taught in any capacity may be considered as a contribution to formal and informal education in colonial Africa, and its teachings must be placed within a social context. The church's role was primarily to preserve the social relations of colonialism, as an extension of the role it played in preserving the social relations of capitalism in Europe. Therefore, the Christian church stressed humility, docility, and acceptance. Ever since the days of slavery in the West Indies, the church had been brought in on condition that it should not excite the African slaves with doctrines of equality before God. In those days, they taught slaves to sing that all things were bright and beautiful, and that the slavemaster in his castle was to be accepted as God's work just like the slave living in a miserable hovel and working twenty hours per day under the whip. Similarly, in colonial Africa, churches could be relied upon to preach turning the other cheek in the face of exploitation, and they drove home the message that everything would be right in the next world.

In retrospect, it is now very clear that one of the most significant aspects of the colonial educational system was that provided by the armed forces and police. Colonial armies such as the King's African Rifles, the French Free Army, and the Congolese Force Publique produced sergeants who later became the majors and generals of independent Africa, and in several instances the heads of states. Policemen also achieved similar rapid promotion, although their political position has been rather weaker than the military proper. Like their civilian counterparts, the future police and military *elite* were at one time trained to be simply low-level assistants to the colonial overlords; but once independence was in sight they were judged by the colonizers to have the requisite qualities of colonial cadres—fit to be part of the ruling class of new-colonial Africa. In a few instances, the colonial powers towards the latter part of the colonial period rushed to train a few Africans at the metropolitan higher institutions of scientific violence, notably Sandhurst Military Academy and Hendon Police School in Britain and St. Cyr Military Academy in France. Those few who were selected for such training became the cream of the military *elite*, corresponding to those African civilians who were sent to university either in Africa or abroad.

Most of what emerged from the colonial educational system was not unique. Educational systems are designed to function as props to a given society, and the educated in the young age groups automatically carry over their values when their turn comes to make decisions in the society. In Africa, the colonialists were training low-level administrators, teachers, NCOs, railroad booking clerks, for the preservation of colonial relations; and it is not surprising that such individuals would carry over colonial values into the period after independence was regained. The colonialists meanwhile took action wherever possible to insure that persons most favorable to their position continued to man African administrations and assumed new political and state police powers. Such a presentation of events would be termed one-sided by many Europeans and Africans, too. In a sense, that is true, and the one-sidedness is deliberate. It is a presentation of what the colonial educational system achieved *in terms of what it set itself to achieve.* The other side of the matter is not the good with which colonial educators can be credited, but rather the good that emerged in spite of the efforts and intentions of the colonizers and because of the struggles of African people.

Education in Africa
ABDOU MOUMOUNI[6]

It would be unfair and untrue to see only the negative aspects of colonialism. It may have succeeded in general in its essential objects and obtained "satisfying" results in its efforts to destroy systematically national awareness and pride in many civil servants. But for some civil servants, their education implanted a thirst for more knowledge and a desire to understand their objective situation. They have come to a fairly rapid understanding of the total bewilderment of their people, and of the falsity of the "axioms" and racist affirmations of colonial propaganda. With a great deal of courage they have refused the humiliation of obsequiousness and "bending the knee" and have behaved in a manner worthy of true patriots. They have been called "bad influences," to be "closely watched," and suffered all kinds of personal humiliations and persecutions; transfers, suspensions, demotions in position, dismissals, prison and exile. The colonial system was implacable towards them because it could not afford to have doubt cast on its dogmas, or allow behavior which might erode the foundation of the social hierarchy and "scale of values" it was attempting to impose on the African peoples.

In any case, the very existence of such individuals played an extremely positive role during the colonial era. They were a living and constant reproach to the "zealous," loyal civil servants with "upright characters." They were also an example to many others who, in spite of everything, had kept their awareness as Africans intact, even if their situation was not very encouraging. To a certain extent, the behavior of the few, so radically different from that of the great mass of African civil servants and colonial administrators, contributed to the gradual awakening of the majority. Also, by forcing their superiors to respect, admire or even fear them, the "bad influences" helped to restrain, in a small but important way, the extent of the abuses of all kinds perpetrated daily by the colonialists or their native servants. Above all, by involving themselves in the fate of the African masses and helping them to the small extent that they were able, they inspired confidence in the people, reassured them, acquired their trust, and thereby inaugurated the process towards the future unification of all the groups and classes of our countries in the struggle against foreign domination.

Other aspects of colonial education also played a positive and not unimportant role. In spite of the great agility with which the colonial power ingeniously limited

[6]Moumouni, Abdou, *Education in Africa* (New York: Frederick A. Praeger Publishers, 1968). Excerpts taken from pages 50-3.

the diffusion of learning, and kept education on a fairly low level, the internal logic of the expansion of the colonial system—ever greater economic exploitation of
the colonies, and therefore constant expansion of the administrative apparatus and
the infrastructure indispensable to its normal functioning, constant battle against
major endemic diseases—forced colonialism to train an ever increasing number of
subordinate officials, in more and more fields, and with higher and higher qualifications. All these facts are closely allied with the fact that the colonies of Black
Africa, barring exceptions, were essentially colonies for exploitation, climatic conditions being unsuitable for large scale immigration of Europeans.

In any case the number of students gradually increased, and the degree of spe-
cialization became gradually, if relatively, higher. The very existence of native
cadres, even subordinate ones, did not fail to have numerous and varied consequences, firstly on the cadres themselves. Despite their limited training, the daily
practice of their profession and the experience they gained, particularly in relations
with European superiors, could only contradict and gradually demolish for them the
false ideas propagated by colonial ideology. They soon realized that in general it
was the Africans who did the work and the "bosses" who simply signed, that the
Europeans often learned their jobs from working alongside the Africans, or even
that Africans could know more on the technical level than the "whites."

At the same time, the African masses, from the very fact of the existence of
native cadres and the very conspicuous role they played in the daily interchanges
between the people and the various cogs of the administration, and in trade and other colonial enterprises, gradually became conscious of and were astonished at the
capabilities, knowledge and technical ability of the African civil servants and white
collar workers (clerks, hospital attendants, doctors, veterinaries, chauffeurs,
mechanics, and specialized workers). Slowly but surely the masses began to have
doubts about the paradoxical teachings coming from these same African cadres
about the "incapacity of the Negro." Even if this process was a limited one, and cannot be considered as having played a principal role in the slow political awakening
of the peoples of Black Africa, it nevertheless made an undeniable contribution in
that direction.

In all its aspects, colonial education exercised a constant influence, from day to
day and in contradictory directions, as much on those who benefitted directly as on
the rest of the population. Although its influence had an immediate effect in one
sense, its significance cannot be limited only to those effects seen at any precise
moment. It is a phenomenon which has been spread out over the entire evolution of
the colonial regime, and furthermore, its different effects have accumulated objectively and subjectively, reacting on each other and participating in the birth of more
and more profound changes in the individual and collective awakening of the colonized African.

Other aspects of colonial education have not become fully clear except over a
long period of time, and therefore have exercised and continue to exercise a more
lasting influence on the general evolution of the life and struggles of the African

peoples.

Colonial education between the two wars in some ways participated in the appearance and maturing of conditions which permitted the rise of the national liberation struggle in Black Africa at the end of the Second World War.

It was those same subordinate officials, trained by the hundreds in the regional schools, advanced primary schools and federal schools, originally destined to supply the civil servants and officials needed for the administrative and economic apparatus of foreign imperialism which dominated and exploited the African peoples, who, in the new international situation following the victory over Hitlerian fascism and the awakening of colonized peoples, became the first political cadres needed to create the various mass organizations (political parties, unions, youth and women's organizations) which started the struggle for liberation of our countries. Furthermore, many of these leaders had attended the same territorial or federal schools, and consequently there was a mixture of people from the same territory (in schools of advanced primary education or in professional) or from different colonies (in federal schools). Counter to the colonial motto of "divide and rule," this encouraged ties of friendship, solidarity and fraternity between students from different regions of the same territory or from different colonies of a federation. These circumstances contributed a good deal in the development of the national movement in Black Africa, particularly in organizing different organizations in a single colony at first, and then grouping these on the federal level. . . . In this way peoples oppressed by the same imperialism were able to struggle against it as a unit.

Colonial Education in
Southern Africa
DAVID CHANAIWA[7]

The colonial education of the British, Boers, or Portuguese, and in missionary, government, or African-run schools, was largely a function of the socioeconomic formations of the particular settler-type colonialism in southern Africa. . . . Socioeconomic realities demanded that some Africans be educated to occupy secondary positions in government, missions, industries, farming, transport, and communications. As teachers, ministers, secretaries, clerks, interpreters, messengers, drivers, nurses, orderlies, foremen, and soldiers, Africans were indispensable auxiliaries in the administration and economic exploitation of the colonies. Therefore, the political and economic principles required that the settlers provide at least elementary and technical education for the simple reason that the colonies would not develop economically and could not be managed politically if the vast African majority remained traditionalist. . . . The ideal of colonial education was to produce efficient but subservient semiskilled laborers and capitalist-oriented consumers.

On the other hand, the economic principle had to be reconciled with the racist principle. Ideologically, colonialism in southern Africa was based on the raciocultural principle of white supremacy. The notorious Boer policy of apartheid, the Portuguese policy of assimilation, the English policies of the Cape franchise in South Africa, and partnership in Zimbabwe, Malawi, and Zambia were all derived from the presumed raciocultural superiority of the white race. Furthermore, being tiny alien white minorities in the midst of overwhelming and fast-growing African populations, the settlers were particularly fearful of what they perceived as the Black Peril—meaning racial integration, "miscegenation," and cultural absorption. Consequently, all regional structures, institutions, and values were based on the racist principle.

Another ideal of colonial education was to produce the "good African," by a caste educational system that indoctrinated the African to accept white superiority

[7]*Mugomba, Agrippah, and Nyaggah,* Mougo, *Independence With Freedom: The Political Economy of Colonial Education in Southern Africa* (Santa Barbara: ABC-Clio, 1980). Excerpts taken from pages 228-237. David Chanaiwa is Zimbabwean and currently works in the private sector in Zimbabwe. He is the former Professor of History at California State University, Northridge, and author of many books including, Profiles of Self-Determination: African Responses to European Colonialism in Southern Africa, 1652 to Present (1976), and The Occupation of Southern Rhodesia: A Study of Economic Imperialism (Nairobi, Kenya: E. African Publishing House, 1978).

and supremacy, to submitting to and serving the whites as well as despising himself, his fellow Africans, and his heritage. In addition to its overall purpose of perpetrating white supremacy, colonial education sought to depersonalize the African. The educated African was supposed to be a self-deprecating, blackskinned European and a docile tool of settler colonialism whose highest ambition was to live like the settler in whose image he had been molded.

In missionary, government, and even African-run schools the student was removed from his parents and peers whom he was taught to despise. At boarding school, he was taught the settlers' history and culture and instilled with their capitalist individualism, materialism, and ethics. Thus, removed from his village, people, and values, and living on imported ideas, the culturally "born-again" African became alienated from himself and his heritage. Often, this alienation created a serious identity crisis.

In addition to the economic and racist principles, there was the political principle. Politically, the settlers wanted an educational curriculum that would be revolutionary in creating efficient workers and dependent consumers out of the Africans, but conservative in matters of politics and civil rights. The settlers did not want to compete for jobs and promotions with the educated Africans. While they saw the need for African doctors, engineers, teachers, ministers, and administrators to relieve the problem of manpower among white minorities, they did not want these educated Africans to question colonial rule and morality, to qualify as voters, and to provide leadership for the African masses.

In all the colonies, African education officially was separate from and unequal to white education and was deliberately and disproportionately underfinanced, understaffed and underdeveloped. In each colony there were national education for whites and special (Bantu) education for Africans. The deliberate educational differentiation and impoverishment of the Africans were, in turn, used as evidential justification for job reservation, disenfranchisement, and racial discrimination. African education was never free or compulsory, unlike white education.

The settler/missionary alliance on African education stemmed from the convergence of their interests. Both shared the ideology of racism, cultural imperialism, white supremacy, and capitalist materialism fashionable among Europeans. Settler capitalists, soldiers, and administrators patronized missionary churches and schools because of the driving psychological need to justify and legitimize white supremacy and privilege in the name of the "white man's burden." Because of his commitment to cultural imperialism and the desire to attach a significance to his labors among the so-called heathens, the missionary unscrupulously glamorized the "ignominious backwardness" and "inherent inferiority" of the Africans. Consequently, the missionary sanctified the colonial machinery as humanitarianism and as a "civilizing mission." He anointed settler industrialists, farmers, merchants, soldiers, administrators, and housewives as superior custodians of civilization, values, morals, and ethics. Hence, colonialism was no longer simply an economic process of capitalist exploitation of African resources and labor; but a noble and moral act of sacrifice for the rest of humanity. The missionary, therefore, was the best agent to produce the efficient, law abiding, subservient African laborers and consumers, through a "good Christian education."

However. . . the same missionaries also taught Africans universalism, nonracialism, nonviolence, individualism, and capitalist free enterprise that exposed the flagrant contradictions between the myths and realities of the "white man's burden." The missionary's Christianity established the universalist equality and brotherhood of mankind; his doctrine of a capitalist, materialistic, and middle-class work ethic presumed fair play, nonracialism, and social mobility which were denied in the settler society. The missionary's underlying educational principles of cultural assimilation and economic prosperity ran head-on with the settlers' self interests of white supremacy and exclusive privilege.

Consequently, mission education became the nemesis of settler colonialism in southern Africa because it essentially was education for frustration. By exposing the Africans to the idealistic universalism, nonracialism, and individualism of Western society, which the colonized African in turn took too seriously, the missionaries unwittingly were sowing the seeds for the eventual destruction of white supremacy by the educated African *elite*. The inherent contradiction between Christianity and education on the one hand and settler colonialism on the other constituted an inescapable embarrassment to the colonizers.

The denial of racial equality and economic opportunity as logical corollaries of the Western Christianity and education to which the African *elite* had been exposed did not lend itself to the expected African subordination and docility. By colonial standards, the educated *elite* waged a progressively militant revolt which was antithetical to white supremacy.

Because of the combined cultural assault from Western Christianity and education, African societies, villages, and families were split into Christians and "heathens," the school and the "bush," and into the urbanites and "country" people. Politically, Africans found themselves with two types of leadership: the traditionalist leadership of kings, chiefs, headmen, parents, and medical practitioners, and the Western-oriented leadership of teachers, ministers, doctors, and politicians. Christianity and education also led to new socioeconomic class formations within the African societies, typified by the *assimilados* in Angola and Mozambique.

The "choice" was between acceptance of Christianity and, thus, Western education on the other hand, and remaining traditionalist and illiterate on the other. In practice, however, the more the African acquired colonial education, the more he was able to enjoy the socioeconomic opportunities accruing from colonialism and vice versa. Having acquired an extensive knowledge of the colonial socioeconomic system, including its individualistic, materialistic work ethic, the educated *elite* also were more enterprising and efficient than the traditionalists. Many of the mission-educated *elite* went into private business and agriculture. Consequently, in the major urban areas like Johannesburg, Salisbury, and Luanda, there was a colonial African upper class of professionals and businessmen, a middle class of teachers, nurses, policemen, small businessmen, and junior civil servants, and a lower class of wage earners and peasants. In contrast, there still was the traditionalist aristocracy of chiefs, subchiefs, and headmen, and a commoner class of subsistence-level farmers in the rural areas.

More important, Christianity and colonial education have had profoundly disorganizing and divisive effects on the African value system and moral fibre. To appreciate these effects, it is necessary to take into account the formal missionary governmental education . . . as well as the massive informal education by advertisement in newspapers, radio, television, movies, display windows, and billboards, and examples from life-styles of the African and settler bourgeoisie. Informal education impressed upon every African the contrast between the "superior" clothes, cars, trains, airplanes, canned foods, tea, and alcohol of the white world and the "inferior" African world of "heathenism" and "superstition." Teachers, ministers, and the media told Africans their traditional technologies and economic systems of shifting cultivation and nomadic pastoralism were backward, irrational, inefficient, and precarious; European industrial goods were in fact always superior to African handicrafts; and capitalist production, consumption, and values were always superior, progressive, beneficial and universal. The overall message was that all people share a universal desire for the Western model of possession and high standard of living; African communalism, kinship, and reciprocity were viewed as elements of ignorance and retardation due to lack of educational exposure to the superior technological alternatives offered by the Western industrial civilization.

Consequently, African traditions became peripheral and subordinate to the dominant Western values derived from capitalism and individualism, and from the idea of "progress" measured primarily by the levels of material consumption. Africans were enticed into abstaining from polygamous marriages, traditional rituals, beer parties, *lobola,* diviners, and practitioners. This led to the emergence of individuals and groups whose beliefs, values, and life-styles were quite alien and antithetical to African traditions. Some from the boarding schools and urban townships have considered going back to their rural villages and kinfolk a temporary relapse into "primitivity," and have learned to despise traditional forms of dress, cosmetics, entertainment, and etiquette. Simultaneously, those Africans who have not acquired formal education, hence good jobs and material possessions, due to either traditionalism or lack of money and schools, are made to feel inferior and worthless.

Between these two extremes, the Westernized *elite* and the traditionalists, are the vast majority of the partially transformed Africans who have roots in both the African and settler cultures, languages, and value systems. The continuity of African traditions was due to the resilience of African value systems, to the shortcomings of the colonial educational systems . . . and to the racioeconomic principles of the settlers, which mitigated against total cultural assimilation of the Africans. This continuity then was reinforced by post-World War II African nationalism and negritude, both of which advocated a return to the basic African value systems.

However, modern African leadership and nationalism stemmed from an ideological and cultural environment created by Western Christianity, education, and capitalism. The average modern African nationalist leader was miseducated by the colonizers [and] ended up living in three worlds: the utopian world of universalism, nonracialism, nonviolence, and antimaterialism which they sought to establish here on earth; the practical world of settler colonialism which they misunderstood; and the traditionalist African world which they despised and from which they attempted to escape.

Viewed from the modern African scene of anticolonialism, political independence, and racial and cultural pride, the ideas and activities of the colonial-educated *elite* appear extremely neocolonialist. The personalities were essentially Christian intellectuals, preachers, teachers, lawyers, businessmen, and administrators educated in either mission or government schools. They perceived settler colonialism as a matter of providence; admired whites for their technology, religion, power and wealth; and aimed at advancing Africans through Christianity, education, and economic self-help. They accepted the supposed cultural inferiority of the black race. They also shared the puritanism and utopianism of missionaries and philanthropists, as well as the political liberalism of some settlers.

Their responses to settler colonialism were constrained by their dichotomous status—they were rejected by the settler class and alienated from their African masses and culture. First, they acquiesced to colonial expansion and conquest because they erroneously associated settler capitalism with the spread of Christianity, education, and economic prosperity. Some attempted to register their protests against racist, colonialist restrictions by vindication of the black potential. They sought to establish African economic self-determination and even self-sufficiency through vocational education under which they inculcated Western bourgeois attitudes, work ethic, and consumptive principles.

Politically, these *elite* were awfully naive and accommodationist. They failed to understand the underlying principles of settler colonialism in general. They lost a power base when they despised African traditionalism and discouraged African historical and racial consciousness. In the face of their own powerlessness and the settlers intransigence they adopted utopianism, which made them natural allies of their equally powerless but privileged missionary mentors and white liberals. The possibility of conspiracy, as opposed to commitment to color-blind humanism, by some missionary and settler liberals to alienate the African *elite* from the masses and, thus, arrest the emergence of African nationalism, cannot be overlooked. In spite of their limitations, the educated *elite* made an essential contribution to the overall continuum of African nationalism and the liberation struggle in southern Africa. They were the forerunners of modern African cross-ethnic unity, leadership, and Pan-Africanism. They were the first leaders to undermine the ethnic, collaborationist potential of the chiefs. Furthermore, the bitter experiences of both the *elite* and the masses partially account for the post-World War II revolutionary flavor in southern Africa. Comparatively, modern African nationalists have abandoned the reformist, capitalist approaches of the previous *elite* for a militant struggle against Western colonialism, racism, and values that have demeaned and shackled the African.

For the educators and intellectuals, the real historical significance of the educated *elite* lies in their literary legacy. Their sound educational training, their commitment to high intellectual standards, coupled with their personal and eyewitness experiences, enabled them to combine in their voluminous writings anecdotes of their authentic experiences and the actual machinations of settler colonialism.

The educated *elite* had the political and moral support of the African masses, especially the partially transformed urban proletariats. Formal and informal education had established the dominance of Western socioeconomic formations among the Africans. Thus, the capitalistic self-determination and education . . . found support among the masses, who saw in the self-confidence, self-help, individualism, courage, and success of the educated *elite* the embodiment of their own dreams and expectations. Until they had learned from bitter experiences and frustrations, the masses generally went along with the utopian ideals of universalism, nonracialism, and nonviolence because of missionary indoctrination and their own conviction that the utopianism was a viable antithesis to the racioeconomic world of white supremacy. The failure of utopianism partially accounts for the militant demands and armed struggle in southern Africa, which began in earnest in the 1960s.

It is probably due as much, if not more, to Christianity and colonial education as to the sense of security deriving from their numerical majority that African nationalist movements and post-independence governments have never advocated exclusively black nation-states, associations, or privileges. On the other hand, the progression from accommodation and nonviolence to militancy and violence was characterized by corresponding decrease in religiosity, materialism, and elitism. Thus, contrary to conventional Eurocentric analyses, missionary Christianity and education did not "produce" modern African nationalism and leadership. The goals, structures, and curricula of missionary churches and schools were set up to create an African population that was economically efficient and consumptive and politically acquiescent to white supremacy. Therefore, modern African nationalism developed in spite of Christianity and colonial education.

Suggested Readings

Advisory Committee on Education in the Colonies, *Mass Education in the Colonies,* Col. No. 186 (London: H.M.S.O., 1943).

Advisory Committee on Native Education in the British Tropical African Dependencies, *Education Policy in British Tropical Africa,* Command Paper 2374 (London: H.M.S.O., 1925).

Akindele, J.A.O., *History of Education in Nigeria* (Oyo: Atoro Prints, 1967).

Battle, Vincent, *Essays in the History of African Education* (New York: Teachers College Press, 1970).

Bennett, George, *Kenya: A Political History: The Colonial Period* (London: Oxford University Press, 1963).

Bermingham, Jack, "Perspectives on Colonial Education in Botswana," in Mugomba, Agrippah, and Nyaggah, Mougo, *Independence Without Freedom: The Political Economy of Colonial Education in Southern Africa* (Santa Barbara, CA: ABC Clio, 1980) pp. 172-190.

Clignet, Remi, and Foster, Philip, "French and British Colonial Education in Africa," *Comparative Education Review* 8, no. 3, (1964), 1918.

Fajana, Adewunmi, *Education in Nigeria, 1842-1939: An Historical Analysis* (Lagos: Longman, 1978).

Foster, Philip, *Education and Social Change in Ghana* (London: Routledge and Kegan, 1965).

Furley, O.W., *A History of Education in East Africa* (New York: NOK Publications, 1978).

Heyman, Richard, *Studies in Educational Change* (Minneapolis: Winston, 1972).

Heyneman, Stephen, *The Conflict Over What is to be Learned in Schools* (Syracuse: Syracuse University Press, 1971).

Hilliard, F.H., *A Short History of Education in British West Africa* (London: T. Nelson, 1957).

Hodgkin, Thomas, *Nationalism in Colonial Africa* (New York: New York University Press, 1957).

Howell, Muriel, *African Education* (Johannesberg: South African Institute of Race Relations, 1963).

Lugamba, S.M.E., *A History of Education in East Africa, 1900-1973* (Kampala, Uganda: Kampala Bookshop, 1973).

Lugard, Frederick, *The Dual Mandate in British Tropical Africa* (London: F. Cass, 1965).

Mungazi, Dickson, *Education and Government Control in Zimbabwe* (New York: Praeger, 1990).

To Honor the Sacred Trust of Civilization: History, Politics and Education in

Southern Africa (Cambridge, MA: Schenkman Pub. Co., 1983).

The Underdevelopment of African Education: A Black Zimbabwean Perspective (Washington, D.C.: University Press of America, 1982).

Oliver, Roland, *The Missionary Factor in East Africa* (London: Longmans, Green and Co., 1966).

Sifuna, Daniel, *Development of Education in Africa: The Kenyan Experience* (Kenya: Initiatives, 1990).

Thomas, Jesse Jones, *Education in East Africa* (London: Edinburgh House Press, 1925).

Yates, Barbara, "Church, State and Education in Belgian Africa," in Kelly, Gail, and Elliott, Carolyn, eds., *Women's Education in the Third World: Comparative Perspectives* (Albany: State University of New York Press, 1982) pp.127-51.

"Colonialism, Education and Work," in Bay, Edna, ed., *Women and Work in Africa* (Boulder: Westview Press, 1982).

PROBLEM V
FORGING A
NATIONAL IDENTITY

After the victories for democracy in the Second World War the creation of the United Nations and the demise of the empires of Britain and France, African nationalism arose. Out of a Brave New World from the ashes of the greatest war in history, nationalism was led by Africans educated largely in the democracies of the West and influenced by the Socialist and Marxist doctrines of the East. Whether democratic or autocratic, the power of the idea of freedom to choose one's destiny was overwhelming and could no longer be denied by empires in decline whether in Asia, the Indian subcontinent, or Africa. It should surprise no one that the Africans wanted the right to determine their own future and to become members of the community of nations rather than aggregates of ethnic groups amalgamated into colonies of disintegrating empires.

The question of forging a national identity was made more difficult in Africa by traditional ethnic rivalries and traditional leadership so deeply enshrined in a respected and beloved culture unacceptable to the new African *elite*, many of whom had roots and birth in traditional society but had become converts to the vision of a new nation from their education and exposure to the West. To them nationalism would transform a continent of peripheral and competitive ethnic groups that had little appeal to the masses but had left them undeveloped, unrecognized, and unimportant.

Professor T.O. Ranger argues that African nationalism was not simply a phenomenon of the aftermath of the Second World War, the Atlantic Charter and the United Nations. Rather, Africans set aside traditional differences in the determination to evict the imperial invaders from Africa, their homeland, conquered by Europeans at the end of the nineteenth century. He argues that since the traditional leaders had either capitulated or had been defeated, a new class of leadership emerged, the priests of the indigenous religions to unite previously antagonistic groups against the invaders. Ranger argues that this "primary" nationalistic resistance led directly to the mass nationalism of the post Second World War that resulted in the end of the colonial era.

This view of African freedom is exhilarating and effervescent, but John Iliffe in his study of the Maji Maji rebellion in Tanganykia in 1905-07 may agree with Ranger that resistance to imperial rule transcended traditional "tribal" authority under the tutelage of religious leaders, but points out that the rebellion withered when it entered those areas where the priests held less influence than the traditional leaders. As the Maji Maji Rebellion diminished before the determination and weaponry of the vengeful Germans and their African askaris, it could hardly be thought of as a national uprising. Iliffe raises the question about the spontaneous opposition to the demands of German colonialism whether it be in the fields of cotton or sisal rather than the more intellectual understanding of those who were shot down by the Maxim gun. Hatred by the demands of the Germans and their surrogates, the Akidas (Swahili from the coast associated in the minds of Africans with the slave trade) appear more paramount to the Africans than any ideas of modern mass nationalism which Ranger perceives emerging from the peoples of Tanzania against German oppression.

Like many, Martin Kilson regards African nationalism as emerging from the international wreckage of the Second World War led by those individuals who were respected not only in the colonial society as emerging African *elite*, but also in the traditional societies, of which they were often descendants and by the social and political bridges that they constructed and struggled to maintain. The nationalists straddled both worlds and were able to unite opposition to colonial rule through political shrewdness that, in the end, challenged the traditional authorities and allowed them to harness the benefits of modernization for the betterment of themselves and their new African nations.

John Lonsdale agrees with Martin Kilson that nationalism was a post-WWII phenomenon, but he emphatically denies that it was led by the newly emerging African *elite* trained in European society and recently turned nationalist. Rather, nationalism was a mass-based movement in which the masses of Africans dictated the direction of nationalism and those who would lead it.

Lastly, since the methodological approach of this volume revolves around creating "problems," William Roger Louis and Ronald Robinson provide an interesting dynamic to the emergence of nationalism in Africa. Louis and Robinson argue that nationalism was essentially non-existent as late as 1947. However, Britain's global hegemony was in jeopardy vis a vis the United States and the economic ability and political desire to maintain empire was rapidly diminishing. Therefore, it was only when the British began to disengage from their African empire and became more willing to grant concessions to potential African politicians, that Africans saw the light at the end of tunnel and were able to unite themselves into a mass nationalist movement.

Early Nationalism in East and Central Africa

T. O. RANGER[1]

On the particular [question of primary resistance and modern mass nationalism] there has been very considerable scholarly disagreement. One school of thought would emphatically differentiate the initial violent reactions from later manifestations of opposition and particularly from nationalism. Nationalist movements, they contend, are essentially modernist in outlook and directed towards the concept of a territorial loyalty. Primary resistance movements, on the other hand, were, inherently backward looking and traditional; not only tribal but emphasizing the most 'reactionary' elements in tribal life. Such movements, it is held, repudiated those within African societies who wished to come to terms with modernization and to accept education, the missionary influence, and the new commercial and technical opportunities. Resistance movements of the early colonial period were romantic, reactionary struggles against the facts, the passionate protest of societies which were shocked by a new age of change and would not be comforted.[2]

[I disagree with this argument and] it seems worth while to see if it is not possi-

---

[1]Ranger, T.O., "Connections Between Primary Resistance Movements and Modern Mass Nationalism in East and Central Africa: Part 1," *The Journal of African History* 9, no.3 (1968), 437-53. Part 2 in *The Journal of African History* 9, no.4 (1968), 631-41. Excerpts taken from pages 438, 439-40, 442-51, and 631-7. T.O. Ranger was born in 1929 and educated at Oxford where he received his D.Phil. in 1959. He later went on to teach at the College of Rhodesia and Nyasaland, Salisbury, Rhodesia, University College in Dar es Salaam (1963-9), UCLA (1969-74), the University of Manchester, and is currently the Professor of Race Relations at St. Antony's College, Oxford University. Ranger is perhaps best known for his position at the University at Dar es Salaam where he and an influential body of scholars around him were strong supporters of African nationalism in the 1960s. Ranger is a recognized authority on religious movements in Africa, specifically in East and Central Africa. Much of his scholarship argues that early religious leaders and movements were the initial sources of mass nationalism in Africa. Such is the central thesis of his book *Revolt in Southern Rhodesia* (Evanston: Northwestern University Press, 1967). It must be noted however, that Ranger's thesis in this book has been challenged by other scholars, see Beach, D.N., "Chimurenga: The Shona Uprising of 1896-7," *The Journal of African History* 20, no. 3, (1979), 395-420; and Cobbing, Julian, "The Absent Priesthood: Another Look at the Rhodesian Rising of 1896-7," *The Journal of African History* 18, no. 1, (1977), 61-84. Ranger is also the author of *African Churches of Tanzania* (Nairobi: East African Publishing House, 1968), *An African Voice in Southern Rhodesia 1898, 1930* (Nairobi: East African Publishing House, 1970), and *Peasant Consciousness and Guerrilla War in Zimbabwe* (London: James Currey, 1985).
[2]Here Ranger is referring principally to the argument of Robinson and Gallagher. For a brief example of their thesis see Robinson and Gallagher, "The Partition of Africa," in *The New Cambridge Modern History,* Vol 11, (Cambridge: Cambridge University Press, 1962) p. 640.

ble to establish some "historic connections" between primary and secondary resistance. No such argument has yet been propounded for East and Central Africa, and probably no argument in the same sort of terms can be propounded. But it seems worth while to see if it is not possible to challenge the assumption of hiatus in East and Central Africa also, and to establish some "historic connections" between primary and secondary resistance. This paper is an initial exploration of such possibilities.

The argument for East and Central Africa has to begin, I think, by establishing what is perhaps an obvious but yet insufficiently appreciated fact; namely that the environment in which later African politics developed was shaped not only by European initiatives and policy or by African cooperation and passivity, but also by African resistance. In this sense at least there is certainly an important connection between resistance and later political developments.

An example of this which I have elaborated elsewhere is that of the Ndebele of Southern Rhodesia. Their uprising in 1896 was defeated but they came out of it with some political gains. Before 1896 the Ndebele state had been in ruins; its white rulers had broken up all its institutions; confiscated all Ndebele land and nearly all Ndebele cattle; disregarded every Ndebele political authority. The 1896 rising at least showed the whites that this had been unwise. The Ndebele were still a formidable military foe; it took many men and much money to defeat their rising; and even then it had not been convincingly defeated by the end of the 1896 dry season. Rhodes faced a long drawn out war of attrition in which the authority of the British South Africa Company might well have collapsed through bankruptcy or British political intervention. So he negotiated with the Ndebele. They thus won in 1896 what they had not had in 1893—a voice in the settlement. The policy of the British South Africa Company was one defined as being to restore to the Ndebele indunas as much of the powers they had possessed under Lobengula as was possible; they received official salaries. So was struck an alliance between the Ndebele chiefs and the Rhodesian administration which still has important political consequences today.

But it was not only the attitudes of defeated African societies and those of apprehensive white settlers which were affected by resistance and rebellion. There was a complex interplay between so-called "primary" resistance and manifestations of "secondary" opposition. We have seen above that many scholars have employed a rather rigid periodization in their approach to African nationalist historiography. The period of resistance is followed by hiatus; then arises the new leadership. But we must remember that the effective establishment of colonial rule throughout southern, central and eastern Africa took a very long time to achieve. Primary resistance to it was still going on in some areas while "secondary" movements were developing elsewhere. Independent churches, trade unions, welfare associations, Pan-Africanist movements all existed at the same time as expressions of tribal or pan-tribal resistance. This fact was important in forming the attitudes of the more radical "secondary" politicians.

[I refer once again] to the Rhodesian case, one which refers back to Ndebele resistance. In June 1929 the first militant African trade union was holding its meetings in Bulawayo; weekend after weekend it hammered away on the theme of African unity, appealing not only to the pan-tribal union movements of South Africa but also to successful examples of continuing armed resistance. "If Lobengula had wanted to he could have called every nation to help him. He did not. That is why he was conquered. In Somaliland they are still fighting. That is because they are united. Let us be united."

It will be seen therefore that there is a long ancestry behind the attention currently paid by nationalist leaders to the heroic myths of primary resistance. When a man like Nelson Mandela seeks inspiration in tales "of the wars fought by our ancestors in defense of the fatherland" and sees them not as part merely of tribal history, but "as the pride and glory of the entire African nation," he is echoing the response of many of his predecessors.

In all these ways, then, resistances formed part of the complex interaction of events which produced the environment for modern nationalist politics. I now want to turn to a more complex and interesting argument. This argument runs that during the course of the resistances, or some of them, types of political organization or inspiration emerged which looked important ways to the future, which in some cases are directly, and in others indirectly, linked with later manifestations of African opposition.

The point can be well illustrated in the cases of the two greatest rebellions in East and Central Africa, the Ndebele-Shona risings of 1896-7 and the Maji Maji rising of 1905. The main problem about these risings is not so much why they happened as how they happened. How was it possible for the Ndebele and their subject peoples to rise together in 1896 when in [their previous war against the settlers in] 1893 the subject peoples had abandoned their overlords? How was it possible for the Ndebele and the western and central Shona to cooperate in the risings in view of their long history of hostility? How was it possible for the Shona groups to cooperate among themselves in view of their nineteenth century history of disunity? How was it possible for the very diverse peoples of southern Tanzania to become involved in a single resistance to the Germans? Finally, how was it that these apparently odd and patch-work alliances offered to the whites a more formidable challenge than had the disciplined professional armies of 1893 or the Hehe wars?

In the Rhodesian case part of the answer certainly lies in the appeal back to traditions of past political centralization. But both in Rhodesia and in Tanzania the main answer lies in the emergence of a leadership which was charismatic and revolutionary rather than hereditary or bureaucratic.

The African societies of East and Central Africa could draw in times of emergency upon a number of traditions of such charismatic leadership. Two merge as particularly important in connection with the sort of large-scale resistance we are discussing. The first of these is the prophetic tradition. Many African societies of East and Central Africa had religious systems in which specialist officers played an institutionalized prophetic role, speaking with the voice of the divine either through possession or through dream or oracular interpretation. Such prophet officers have usually been regarded by scholars, in common with "traditional religion" as a whole, as conservative and normative forces. The prophet has been thought of as the ally of the established political order and as the guardian of its customary moral norms. But, as I have argued in a recent paper, the prophetic authority could not be so confined; the claim to speak with the voice of the divine was always potentially a revolutionary one, and if the prophet could invest the ordinary operations of a society with divine sanction he could also introduce new commandments. In his brilliant Malinowski Lecture for 1966, I.M. Lewis has suggested a typology and spectrum of possession and prophetic movements which throws a good deal of light on the point I am trying to make. His spectrum ranges from hysterical possession cults on the periphery of religious practice, to fully institutionalized tribal religions at the center, in which the messianic revelations of moral teaching shrink into creation myths and myth charters of the establishment. Lewis goes on to discuss the complex relationship of such establishment religions, "which celebrate an accepted code of public morality," with the messianic tradition. Establishment religions, he suggests, may have sprung from or may precede a messianic movement; there are nearly always within them "undercurrents" of messianism and nearly always also opportunities for the rise of "revitalizing prophets"; and often, where the establishment religion itself seems incapable of revitalization, it is surrounded by peripheral cults in which the innovatory vitality of prophetism is still present. "It seems probable," he writes, "that such displaced and peripherally relegated cults may provide the kind of institutional continuity which, in appropriate historical circumstances, enables new messianic cults to develop.

Something of the same pattern can be seen for the most striking mass primary resistances of East and Central Africa. Certainly it seems to hold for the two great risings already discussed—the Shona-Nedebele and the Maji Maji rebellions. I have argued at length elsewhere that what I described as the "traditional" religious authorities were the main coordinators, and in a real sense leaders, of the risings in Matabeleland and Mashonalond, and that the priests of the Mwari cult in the first province, and the spirit mediums of the Chaminuka-Nehanda hierarchies in the second, were the main vehicles of cooperation between the various elements engaged. Perhaps in these articles I have emphasized the "traditional" character of this religious leadership too much. Certainly it was important that they presented themselves as survivors from the imperial past of the Shona—the one cult so intimately identified with the old Rozwi empire and the other with the Mutapa dynasty and its outriders. But at the same time the emergence of these religious leaders as leaders also of a widespread rebellion constituted what Gann has described as a "theological revolution." Contemporary white observers stressed that the Mwari cult had previously been concerned with matters of peace and fertility and its militant, authoritarian character in 1896 took them by surprise; no doubt there was both ignorance and naivete in their idea of its earlier total severance from politics, but there seems no question that the power and the nature of the authority of Mwari priest-hood underwent significant development in 1896. Nor does there seem much question that this "theological revolution" took the form ascribed by Doutreloux to the prophet movements. The Mwari priests and the spirit mediums imposed new regulations and prohibitions upon their followers; to enter the rebellion was to enter a new society and to become subject to a new "law" the rebels were brought into the fellowship of the faithful by the dispensation of "medicine" and promised immunity from bullets; they were promised success in this world and a return from death to enjoy it. (When the religious leaders were attempting in 1897 to bring into being a Rozwi "front" in all the areas of Mashonaland as a means of coordinating the secular side of the rising after the withdrawal of the Ndebele aristocracy, they promised that all Rozwi who were killed should be resurrected and participate in the coming golden age.) The religious leaders move out of the limitations which, as well as the advantages, were implied by their connection with specific past political systems and speak to all black men. And they are to an extent successful. For a time the charismatic leadership of the prophets brings together Ndebele aristocrats, subject peoples, deposed Rozwi chiefs, Shona paramounts; as one scholar puts it, "the proud Matabele chieftains now agreed to operate under the supreme direction of an ex-serf, a remarkable man who in "normal" times would hardly have acquired much political influence." In the case of the Maji Maji rising, the evidence presented by Iliffe suggests a possible combination of both the prophetic and the witchcraft eradication elements in the inspiration and coordination of the rising. Clearly the Kolelo cult played an important part. It was influential over a wide area and provided centers to which large numbers of people went to receive medicine and instructions which they distributed on return. The evidence is perhaps sufficient to conclude that the Kolelo cult provided a machinery which could reach the peoples of the Rufiji complex and perhaps further afield. Like the Mwari cult, the Kolelo belief involved priest-interpreters of the oracle; like the Mwari cult also, its normal preoccupation was with fertility and the land. And, as Iliffe tells us, some "evidence suggests that in the period before the rebellion the Kolelo cult was transformed from its normal preoccupation with the land to a more radical and prophetic belief in a reversal of the existing order by direct divine intervention." The prophets of the new development commanded revolt in the name of the new God, who would come to live in the land. "He will change this world and it will be new. His rule will be one of marvels." They provided protective medicine; prescribed a new form of dress and imposed new prohibitions; they promised invulnerability or resurrection. The drinking of the holy water was a sign of entry into a rebel communion. The appeal was to all Africans. "Be not afraid," the message ran, "Kolelo spares his black children."

At the same time there seems evidence to suggest that the innovatory potentialities of witchcraft eradication movements were also being used. The Vidunda understood the *maji* in the context of an attack on sorcery, Iliffe tells us:

In southern Ubena a series of anti-sorcery movements had entered from the east, from Ungindo and the Kilombero. Maji Maji was also brought by Ngindo, and it seems that the pattern of Bena response followed that normal with a *mwavi* medicine, the hongo administering the maji to the assembled people in the presence of the chief. It seems very probable that both the rebellion and subsequent movements were drawing on an established pattern of indigenous millenarianism. Just as the rising in the Rufiji complex became associated with the cult of Kolelo, so its expansion appears to have taken place within the context of recurrent movements to eradicate sorcery.

My own work on subsequent witchcraft eradication cults in the Rufiji complex and in the Maji Maji area generally leads me to suppose that the ability of such movements to pass rapidly across clan and tribal boundaries, and to sweep people into a unity which overrides suspicions and allegations of sorcery, was indeed an important element in the 1905 rising.

In the first part of this article a number of possible connections between the last-ditch resisters and the earliest organizers of armed risings, and later leaders of opposition to colonial rule in East and Central Africa, were explored. It was argued that African "primary" resistance shaped the environment in which later politics developed; it was argued that resistance had profound effects upon white policies and attitudes; it was argued that here was a complicated interplay between manifestations of "primary" and of "secondary" opposition, which often overlapped with and were conscious of each other. Then the argument turned to a more ambitious proposition, namely that during the course of the resistances, or some of them, types of political organization or inspiration emerged which looked in important ways to the future; which in some cases are directly and in others indirectly linked with later manifestations of African opposition.

Half of the case for this assertion was set out in the first article, and the character of the organization and aspirations of the great resistance movements was discussed. It was argued that they attempted to create a larger effective scale of action; that they endeavored to appeal to a sense of Africanness; that they displayed an ambiguous attitude to the material aspects of white colonial society, often desiring to possess them without at the same time abandoning the values of their own communities; that they attempted to assert African ability to retain control of the world by means of a millenarian message. In all these ways, it was asserted, they were *similar* to later mass movements.

There is undoubtedly a link between these resistances and later mass movements of a millenarian character. Nor is this link merely a matter of *comparing* the Shona-Ndebele or Maji Maji risings with later prophet movements or witchcraft eradication cults. There is often a quite direct connection.

The most direct connections, of course, are provided by examples like that of Nyabingi, which provided the basis both of "primary resistance" and of persistent twentieth-century millenarian manifestations. Next come movements like that of the Mumbo cult in Nyanza province, Kenya. The Mumbo cult has recently been examined in a very interesting paper by Audrey Wipper. It arose among the Gusii, apparently around 1913, after the defeat of various "primary resistances." It reached peaks of activity in 1919, in 1933, and to a lesser extent in 1938 and 1947; it was one of the movements banned in 1954. Thus in point of time it bridged the period between the suppression of the Gusii risings of 1904, 1908 and 1916 and the emergence of modern mass nationalism. In character it was strikingly similar to the sort of movement we have already discussed. Although arising among the Gusii, it was "a pan-tribal pagan sect," creating its own society of true believers, whom it bound by its own codes of conduct and to whom it promised eventual triumph and reward. The colonial period, in its mythology was merely a testing period devised by the God of Africa to sort out the true believers from the fainthearted; before long those who remained true would enter into the wealth and power of the whites. Mumbo had the most direct links with the period of primary resistance. The Gusii's most venerated warriors and prophets, noted for their militant anti-British stance, were claimed by the movement, Miss Wipper tells us:

> Zakawa, the great prophet, Bogonko, the mighty chief, and Maraa, the *laibon* responsible for the 1908 rebellion, became its symbols, infusing into the living the courage and strength of past heroes. Leaders bolstered up their own legitimacy by claiming to be the mouth-piece of these deceased prophets.

Indeed, if Miss Wipper is right, we are close here to the idea of an "alternative leadership," stemming from traditions of resistance and opposed officially recognized authority. Especially successful in effecting such aims were the descendants of the prophets and chiefs concerned. Thus, with the progeny of the Gusii heroes supporting the sect, a physical as well as a symbolic link with the past was established. Here was a powerful symbolic group whose prestige and authority could well be used to arouse, strengthen and weld the various disunited cults into a solid anti-British position. Miss Wipper makes the important point that the cult looked back only to those figures who themselves stood out from and tried to transform traditional small-scale society; "it looks to the past for inspiration and to the future for living. Its goals are Utopian and innovative rather than traditional and regressive," involving attacks upon small-scale traditional values as well as upon European values. It would seem it is justifiable to apply the word "radical" to the cult, and to claim that "the history of African nationalism in the district must be traced back to its emergence."

Similar examples of direct "physical" and indirect "symbolic" connection with primary resistances can be given for Christian independent church movements. In the first category comes, for instance, Shembe's Nazarite Church in Zululand. This impressive manifestation of Zulu, rather than South African, nationalism referred back to one of the most dramatic occasions in the history of Zulu nationalism, the Bambata rising of 1906. It was physically linked to this rising through the person of Messen Qwabe, one of its leaders. Shembe himself proclaimed, "I am going to revive the bones of Messen and of the people who were killed in Bambata's rebellion." All five sons of Messen have joined the church, which was given posthumous spiritual approval by their dead father, and it is taken for granted that all members of the Qwabe clan will be members of it. In the second category comes Matthew Zwimba's church of the White Bird, established in 1915 in the Zwimba Reserve in Mashonaland, which appealed to the memory of the 1897 rising by regarding all those who died in the fighting in the Zwimba area as the saints and martyrs of the new church. It is important to note also that Zwimba regarded himself as very much a modernizer and succeeded, at least for a time, in establishing himself as the intermediary between the chiefs and people of Zwimba and representatives òf the modern world.

It can be shown, then, that some at least of the intermediary opposition movements of a millenarian character, which are usually by common consent given a place in the history of the emergence of nationalism, were loosely linked, as well as essentially similar, to some movements of primary resistance. Can we go further than this? It would be possible to argue, after all, that whatever may be the interest of such millenarian movements in the history of African politics, they have not in fact run into the mainstream of modern nationalism and in some instances have clashed with it. A movement like Dini Ya Msambwa might be cultivated for short-term purposes by a political party—as KANU is said to have cultivated it in order to find support in an otherwise KADU area—but it can hardly be thought to have had much future within the context of modern Kenyan nationalism.

It seems to me that there are a number of things to be said at this stage. I have argued that modern nationalism, if it is to be fully successful, has to discover how to combine mass enthusiasm with central focus and organization. This does not mean that it needs to *ally* itself with movements of the sort I have been describing which succeeded, on however limited a scale, in arousing mass enthusiasm. Indeed, it will obviously be in most ways a rival to them, seeking to arouse mass enthusiasm for its own ends and not for theirs. But it would be possible to present a triple argument at this stage. In the first place, one could argue, where nationalist movements do succeed in achieving mass emotional commitment, they will often do it partly by use of something of the same methods, and by appealing to something of the same memories as the movements we have been discussing. In the second place, where nationalist movements are faced with strong settler regimes in southern Africa, they will tend to move towards a strategy of violence which is seen by them as springing out of the traditions of "primary resistance." And in the third place, where nationalist movements fail, either generally or in particular areas, to capture mass enthusiasm, they may find themselves opposed by movements of this old millenarian kind, some of which will still preserve symbolic connections at least with the primary resistances.

The new mass party in East and Central Africa, as it spreads to the rural districts, comes to embody much of the attitude which has hitherto been expressed in less articulate movements of rural unrest. It often appears in a charismatic, almost millenarian role—the current phrase, "a crisis of expectations," which politicians from Kenya to Zambia employ to describe their relations with their mass constituents, is not a bad description of the explosive force behind all the movements we have described. Often the party locally—and nationally—appeals to the memories of primary resistance, and for the same reason as the millenarian cults did; because it is the one "traditional" memory that can be appealed to which transcends "tribalism" and which can quite logically be appealed to at the same time as tribal authorities are being attacked and undermined. My own experience of nationalist politics in Southern Rhodesia certainly bears out these generalizations. It was the National Democratic Party of 1961 which first really penetrated the rural areas and began to link the radical leadership of the towns with rural discontent. As it did so, the themes and memories of the rebellions flowed back into nationalism.

> In rural areas meetings became political gatherings and more, the past heritage was revived through prayers and traditional singing, ancestral spirits were evoked to guide and lead the new nation. Christianity and civilization took a back seat and new forms of worship and new attitudes were thrust forward dramatically. The spirit pervading the meetings was African and the desire was to put the twentieth century in an African context.

So Mr. George Nyandoro, grandson of a rebel leader killed in 1897, and nephew of a chief deposed for opposition to rural regulations in the 1930s, appealed in his speeches to the memory of the great prophet Chaminuka round whom the Shona rallied in the nineteenth century; so Mr. Nkomo, returning home in 1962, was met at the airport by a survivor of the rebellions of 1896-7,who presented him with a spirit axe as a symbol of the apostolic succession resistance; so the militant songs copied from Ghana were replaced by the Old tunes belonging to spirit mediums and rebel leaders.

It is natural that a nationalist movement which is still engaged in an increasingly violent struggle for independence will turn even more exclusively to the tradition of resistance. This has certainly happened in Southern Rhodesia, for example. The present phase of guerrilla activity in Rhodesia is called by the nationalists "Chimurenga," the name given by the Shona to the risings:

> What course of action will lead to the liberation of Zimbabwe?" asks a Zimbabwe African National Union writer. "It is not the path of appeasement. It is not the path of reformism. It is not the path of blocking thirds. It is the path of outright fearless defiance of the settler Smith fascist regime and fighting the current war for national liberation. It is the path of direct confrontation. It is the bath of Chimurenga.

The Maji Maji Rebellion
JOHN ILIFFE[3]

This article analyses the . . . organization of the Maji Maji rebellion of 1905-7 in the south and east of German East Africa. Perhaps a million people lived in the rebel area. The official guess was that 75,000 Africans died, mostly from famine and disease. An estimated 8,000 Pogoro and Mbunga assaulted Mahenge on 30 August 1905. Given these numbers, in an area without prior political unity, a crucial problem is to discover how the people were mobilized and organized for action. Three organizational principles require examination. First, the rebels may have organized according to prior political and cultural groupings, perhaps forming alliances between groups as often in past emergencies. Although the word has little meaning in the ethnic confusion of southern Tanzania, this method of organization may be called the "tribal" principle. Second the rebels may have utilized a sense of common grievance arising from the economic pressures of German rule. For reasons which must be explained, the economic status of some rebel peoples was moving towards that of a peasantry. The use of this common economic status may be called the "peasant" principle of organization. Third, an attempt to mobilize the southern peoples on a basis wider than the tribe might employ a "religious" principle of organization. It is probable that all three organizational principles were invoked at various times and places during the rising. As more evidence becomes available, a simple chronological sequence from one principle to another may become untenable, and any remaining pattern may be extremely complex, with wide regional variation. Yet, as a working hypothesis, it is perhaps worth while to set out a relatively simple pattern which is supported by much of the evidence now available.

It is therefore the thesis of this article that Maji Maji, as a mass movement, originated in peasant grievances, was then sanctified and extended by prophetic religion, and finally crumbled as crisis compelled reliance on fundamental loyalties to kin and tribe. Implicit in this thesis is the belief that the central historical problem of the rebellion is a conflict, common perhaps to all mass movements, between the ideology of revolt and economic, political and cultural realities.

The sequence of organizational principles may be correlated with the geographical expansion of the movement. If the rebellion is dated from the death of its first

[3]Iliffe, John, "The Organization of the Maji Maji Rebellion," *The Journal of African History* 8, no. 3, (1967). Excerpts taken from pages 495-512. John Iliffe is currently a professor at St. John's College in Cambridge. He is author of *A Modern History of Tanganyika* (Cambridge: Cambridge University, Press ,1979), and *Tanganyika under German Rule, 1905-12* (London: Cambridge University Press, 1969), among many other works.

victims, it began on the night of 31 July 1905, in the Matumbi Hills, and simultaneously (or even slightly earlier) in Madaba. From this nucleus, violence spread
north to Uzaramo (before 15 August), south to Liwale (somewhat earlier), and
north-west to Kilosa, Morogoro, and Kisaki (by late August). This complex, centering on the middle and lower Rufiji [Valley], was the first unit of revolt. The second was the Lukuledi Valley, whither the rebellion expanded, via Liwale, during the
last days of August. Simultaneously, the movement spread to the Kilombero Valley,
the Mahenge Plateau, and Uzungwa, probably carried by the Ngindo and Pogoro.
Finally, it was taken by the Ngindo to Ungoni early in September, whence it spread
to Upangwa and southern Ubena. The Bena, who attacked Yakobi mission on 19
September, were the last to join.

It is useful to distinguish between the first area—the Rufiji complex—and the
three other major areas of revolt. In the Rufiji complex, the rebellion began as a
peasant movement. It expanded elsewhere through its acquired religious content. In
the later areas, the tribal principle of organization quickly predominated. This article considers successively the peasant origins of the movement, the religious beliefs
through which it spread, and its acceptance and transformation by the peoples outside the original nucleus.

An analysis of the origins of Maji Maji must explain why it happened in that particular area at that precise moment. It is sometimes argued that post pacification
revolts are in reality delayed resistances, initiated by decentralized groups unable
either to offer effective resistance to the first European invasion or fully to comprehend its implications. Only after internal reorganization and experience of colonial
rule, it is said, are such peoples convinced of their need and ability to resist. Maji
Maji cannot be explained in this way. Several rebel peoples had previously offered
quite severe resistance to the Germans. . . . "Delayed resistance" is too simple a concept to explain the particularity of the rising. Nor can it easily be explained by general grievances against German rule—an explanation then common among
left-wing groups in Germany. The imposition of taxation and brutal methods of collection, forced labor on road construction or European plantations, the replacement
of indigenous leaders by alien agents (*akidas*)—all these were given as explanations. These were undoubtedly grievances, but they were shared widely in German
East Africa, and were experienced much more profoundly elsewhere in the colony,
especially in the north. More important, they were not new grievances in July 1905,
nor were they perhaps sufficiently burdensome to threaten the whole economy of
the rebel peoples. If the initial stage of the rising is to be explained as a reaction to
grievances, then the grievances must have been both more specific in time and place
and also more destructive in their impact.

Such grievances existed in this particular area at precisely this moment. In 1902
a new governor decided to initiate large-scale African cotton-growing. Since cotton
had failed on the northern coast, the experiment was confined to the south. Against
much official advice, the governor doubted whether individual cultivation could be
adequately supervised or produce worthwhile results. He therefore ordered that a

cotton plot be established in each neighborhood of the experimental area, under the control of the local headman. Each of the headman's subjects would work for a fixed number of days on this communal plot. The people of the Dar es Salaam district, the Zaramo, refused the thirty five cents they were each offered for their first year's work. Refusal to work on the plots became fairly general during 1903, and headmen either reported their loss of control or conscripted women and children as laborers.

[When the rebellion broke out, cotton everywhere was an object of attack,] yet the rebellion was not simply a protest against the introduction of commercial agriculture. Soon after the rising, to German surprise, cotton was widely grown by individuals in the Rufiji Valley. The protest had presumably been directed against obviously unacceptable methods of cultivation, against the consequent damage to the subsistence economy, and especially against the sheer unprofitability of the experiment.

Maji Maji was not "peasant revolt," if this implies that it was wholly the action of peasants for peasant ends. . . . It is more useful to seek the degree and character of peasant involvement in the various stages of a mass movement. Peasant involvement predominated in the early stakes of Maji Maji. Apart from the grievances specific to the outbreak area, there are two reasons for believing this. First any analysis of peasant involvement elsewhere suggests its amorphous, kaleidoscopic, essentially parochial character. The men of a locality hear that rebellion has broken out elsewhere. They congregate into a "band," leaders and spokesmen emerge, the property of notable local enemies is destroyed and the enemies, if available, are killed. If they escape the area, they are rarely pursued. The band may coalesce with another and march jointly on a more prominent provincial center, where the same process is repeated. Often the coalition dissolves and the men return home, wider action is likely only if charismatic leadership has emerged, or if some millennial belief has been evoked. The early phases of Maji Maji seem to follow this kaleidoscopic pattern.

If the origins and early character of the rising are to be found in peasant grievances and peasant action, its subsequent development falls more clearly into general pattern. In recent papers, Professor Ranger has argued that several rebellions and resistance movements in East and Central Africa sought new methods of organizing effective mass action. Their integrating principles were often ideological, and the agents of reorganization were religious leaders. Further, since the object was to organize anew, it was not sufficient merely to revitalize structures and beliefs which often reflected those divisions which had previously hindered effective action. Rather, it was necessary to enlarge the scale both of resistance and of religious allegiance. The central figure in such an enlargement was the prophet, proclaiming a new religious order to supersede the old, a new loyalty to transcend old loyalties of tribe and kinship. German observers saw in Maji Maji the signs of such a transformation. The *maji*—the water medicine accepted by each rebel—united in common action peoples with no known prior unity. Its power was believed to be religious, or in German terms was due to witchcraft. And it inspired its recipients with a passionate courage of which the Germans had believed their subjects incapable.

The Kolelo cult was influential over a wide area, and operated as German and other accounts of Maji Maji suggest. It provided centers to which large numbers of people went to receive medicine and instructions which they distributed on return. . . . The evidence stresses the role of the ministers of Kolelo cult [as being central to the expansion of the maji]. If the religious authorities who coordinated the Rhodesian risings of 1896-97 had counterparts in Maji Maji, these are the most likely. . . . The evidence is perhaps sufficient to conclude that the Kolelo cult provided a machinery which could reach the peoples of Rufiji complex. Yet there is no indication that it had political functions. It is curious and perhaps significant that the only area of Uluguru to join the rebellion—Mgeta—is on the opposite side of the mountains from Kolelo, and that for both the Luguru and Zaramo the source of medicine was the junior branch of the cult at Ngarambi. Nor do the accounts suggest that the cult had any role in warfare—until Maji Maji. . . . In the period before the rebellion the cult was transformed from its normal preoccupation with the land to a more radical and prophetic belief in a reversal of the existing order by direct divine intervention.

The Ngarambi branch of the [Kolelo] cult was deeply involved in Maji Maji. Very probably its ministers were the first to distribute the *maji,* and certainly its commitment to the rebellion became clear during the first days of violence. It remains, however, to discover whether the ministers were planning rebellion before violence began, whether they embodied and set the seal of ritual approval on the decision of the community as a whole, or whether they gave retrospective sanctification to violence already committed. On the present evidence, it seems more likely . . . that here was a "reciprocal action" between mass discontent and potentially prophetic leadership, their growing confidence in the *maji* impelling the people towards violence, and the increasing resolution of the people encouraging the religious leaders to expand their claims and objectives. The only indication of prior planning is that the *maji* was distributed some weeks before violence began. Against this is the lack of evidence of any decision of the community as a whole, the very loose coordination of actions within the Rufiji complex, the complete absence of preparatory organization elsewhere, and the fact that the precipitant of violence in many areas was the unexpected news of war in the Matumbi Hills. . . . The ministers of Kolelo had certainly taken new initiative, but there is little sign that it was designed as an initiative for war.

To this point, the argument has concentrated on the first area of revolt, where the cotton scheme provided a new and critical grievance, economic and cultural circumstances offered the possibility of intercommunication, and where the cult of Kolelo held authority. Yet the rising rapidly expanded far beyond this nucleus, among tribes whose economic and political systems were relatively little affected by German rule, and where—to judge from the silence of the accounts—Kolelo's name carried less weight. Here the normal precipitant of violence was the arrival of a *hongo* from the east with news and *maji*. To understand the sequence of events which followed, it is important to stress that by no means did all the peoples within the area of rebellion join. Even among those who did, there were invariably groups which either remained passive or actively joined the German side. Some explanation of these different responses issuggested by analysis of the actions of those peoples beyond the Rufiji complex for whom the evidence is most extensive. Those chosen are the Vidunda and Sangu, the Kibena-speaking peoples ruled by the Wakinamanga (Ubena of the Rivers), the Ndamba, the Mbeyela chiefdom in the south of highland Ubena, the Pangwa, and the Ngoni.

The factors which determined a decision to rebel are best illustrated by a one Father Schaegelen's account of the rising in Ovidunda. Maji Maji was brought to this area by a *hongo* whose identity is uncertain. He first approached a number of headmen and urged resistance. When they pointed to the power of European weapons, he sold them *maji*, with which he anointed them on face, chest, and legs. Although his claims and promises, as recorded, were remarkably similar to those made to Kibasila and others, three features of the Vidunda experience deserve special attention. First, the Vidunda understood the *maji* in the context of an attack on sorcery. . . . Second, the movement was denounced by the Vidunda chief, Ngwira. The chieftainship was a relatively recent institution which had emerged from nineteenth-century defensive measures. . . . [But] Ngwira [was] discredited, and *Hongo* appointed himself chief of the district. When *Hongo* saw that his strength was increasing he gathered them together to go and take Kilosa. The attack was a disaster. Several Vidunda were shot. Hongo had nothing to say. Now began a third phase, the "tribalization" of the movement in its later stages. After this they returned, to their houses with their spoils. On arriving home they began to break the taboos of *Hongo,* they killed cattle, goats and sheep and brewed beer for they knew that revenge was at hand. At this point the *hongo* disappeared . . . and instead, the Vidunda turned to guerrilla warfare in their mountains, as so often in their history. Simultaneously, Ngwira's authority revived.

In recent years, social anthropologists have described a number of popular movements designed to eradicate sorcery from African societies. One scholar has shown that among the Lele such periodic and short-lived movements are sharply opposed to routine measures to detect sorcerers and secure protection against them. Rather, they aim to rid the society of the possibility of sorcery by rendering its members unable either to practice or to suffer from it.

This makes it conceivable that the Maji Maji rebellion, in its expansion beyond the borders of the Rufiji complex, was also a millenarian movement. Schaegelen's narrative of events in Uvidunda supports such a description. Further evidence comes from the Mbeyela chiefdom of southern Ubena. Here, while the established cult of the ancestors, led by the chief, centered on Ukinga to the west, a series of antisorcery movements had entered from the east, from Ungindo and the Kilombero. Their apparent use of the mwari ordeal may imply witch-finding rather than eradication, but Maji Maji was also brought by Ngindo, and it seems that the pattern of Bena response followed that normal with mwari medicine, the hongo administering the *maji* to the assembled people in the presence of the chief. Yet the most persuasive reason for linking Maji Maji with a millennial assault on sorcery is the evidence of subsequent eradication movements within the same area. The greatest, in 1926-29, were inspired by Ngoja bin Kimeta, a Ngindo who lived in Segerea village near Dar es Salaam. Partly through his own travels, and partly through his licensed agents, Ngoja's water medicines were administered to thousands of Africans from the coast to Ungoni and Rilosa. As with Maji Maji, the main nuclei were Ungindo and the Matumbi Hills, and expansion across tribal borders was astonishingly swift. There were close similarities in methods of distribution, in the response of tribal authorities, and in associated beliefs. Ngoja was a respected Muslim, which accords with the undoubted participation of many Muslims in Maji Maji and the coastal prestige which seems to have aided the inland expansion of both movements. This is difficult evidence to evaluate. There is at present no indication of an eradication movement prior to 1905, and Ngoja's activities may have been modelled on Maji Maji. Yet it seems very probable that both the rebellion and the subsequent movements were drawing on an established pattern of indigenous millenarianism. Just as the rising in the Rufiji complex became associated with the cult of Kolelo, so its expansion appears to have taken place within the context of recurrent movements to eradicate sorcery.

The second notable aspect of the Vidunda experience is the conflict between established political authority and prophetic leadership. Whether or not a people chose to rebel probably depended largely on this struggle for power. Established leaders responded in very different ways. Some, like Ngwira, opposed the movement and were swept aside. Others opposed the movement successfully. Yet others put themselves at its head and sought to control and direct it. For example, of all the peoples within the rebel area, the Sangu had the most powerful and successful political leadership. After long conflict with the Hehe, the Merere dynasty had welcomed and allied with the Germans and had won back its homeland. Then came Maji Maji. On two occasions, it appears, the Sangu decision lay in the balance. During September, Merere refused to receive a missionary, fortified his capital, and failed to send the auxiliary warriors demanded by the local German officer. Only the appearance of a military force brought him to the German side. Again, in late January, he seems to have been in contact with the Ngoni leader Chaffruma. Missionaries reported a second crisis, but again a German force raced to Utengtile, and Merere once more provided auxiliaries. . . . A comparable situation existed in lowland Ubena. Although most of his people were anxious to rebel, the powerful and pro-German Kiwanga dealt with the threat by rallying immediately to the German side. "Kiwanga," reported a missionary, "simply cut the throat of every medicine man." Less dramatically, the chief's son and ultimate successor recalled how his father, rejecting the *hongo's* message, was ordered to follow this man *hongo* who had received the people and the elders, and to turn the hearts of the people back from their faith in his medicine. The *hongo,* however, refused to go before

Kiwanga, and the elders who followed *hongo* refused also. They would pretend to agree to follow Kiwanga, but they never meant it. They delayed and delayed and in the end never appeared. Early in October the Mbunga and Pogoro rebels in the area renewed their resistance by specifically attacking Kiwanga and Kalimoto, a loyalist Mbunga subchief. Kiwanga was eventually shot dead by the rebels. Here, as in Usangu, a disruption of the chiefdom followed the rebellion.

Particularly clear evidence of conflict caused by the arrival of the *maji* is available for the obscure Ndamba people of the Kilombero Valley, whose political organization was weak and most of whom were subject to Kiwanga. The leading family in this area was headed by Undole, who lived in Merera. The *hongo* first brought water to the neighboring Mgeta area. Undole sent the agent to investigate. Although the agent was persuaded, drank the *maji* and returned full of enthusiasm, Undole summoned the elders of the neighborhood and told them, "I do not want to hear that my people in my country are drinking *maji*. Similarly, I do not wish to welcome these people with *maji* into my country. Maji Maji is a false medicine brought by the Ngindo from Mponda's." The elders departed, but the movement was too strong. . . . When Undole heard that the elders had joined the rebels, he summoned them. They came and listened, but his authority over them was slight. The elders returned to join the rising; Undole sent messengers to Mahenge, who fought alongside the Germans. Undole's people were spared, but the remainder of the Ndamba suffered the normal fate. Thus the pattern suggested by Schaegelen's account is supported by evidence from other areas. Maji Maji spread as a millenarian revolt which threatened established authority. Only the strongest could reject it.

The Vidunda evidence also describes a third phase, in which the failure of the *maji* obliged the rebels to return to customary methods of tribal warfare. This was one means by which the movement was tribalized in its later stages. Alternatively, a different process could take place. . . . Movements to eradicate sorcery are able to adapt to local beliefs and circumstances until their original form is obscured. As Maji Maji expanded further south and west, it entered areas of strong political authority. In consequence, the revolutionary character of the movement declined while the element of tribal warfare grew. It has been seen that the Bena chief, Mbeyela, was willing and able to patronize and control the movement. Among the neighboring Pangwa, whose chief also sided with the rebels, Maji Maji was not brought by alien *hongo* but by Pangwa residents in Ungoni. In the southeast, it appears, the movement operated from the beginning within a tribal framework

Thus the paradox of later nationalist movements, the need to use old loyalties in order to popularize an effort to transcend them, also characterized this earlier attempt to enlarge political scale. The Maji Maji rebellion originated in peasant grievances, expanded through the dynamism of a millennial belief which challenged the old order, and finally came to reflect the cultural and political divisions of the past. Its changing organization demonstrates the tension within a mass movement between ideology and reality.

Nationalism in Sierra Leone
MARTIN KILSON[4]

A much neglected feature of the study of colonial change in Africa has been the transformation of the traditional *elite*. As a group they claimed a disproportionate share in modern social change, owing largely to their role in local colonial administration. Their position enabled them to retain traditional authority while simultaneously pursuing wealth and power in the modern sector of colonial society. Among the sources of new wealth available to chiefs were:

(1) direct money payments by governments

(2) tax extortion

(3) salary payments by native administrations, and

(4) the commercialization of chiefs' customary economic rights

The colonial transformation of traditional rulers had a considerable impact upon their relations with the peasantry. The chiefs, exposed to both colonial administration and the market economy, became a mediating agency through which much of modernity—specially its socio-political orientations—reached the masses in rural society. The particular use chiefs made of this function, especially the furtherance of their own modernization, influenced the changing political relationships between them and the peasantry.

The chiefs often abused local tax administration and perhaps the most important consequence of this was the emergence of a characteristically modern group conflict in local African society. This conflict was characterized by a form of rural "radicalism," which in some instances constituted a virtual peasant revolt against traditional rulers and authority.

In Sierra Leone this rural radicalism was evident in the 1930s, and it was particularly strong in the immediate postwar years (1946-51) and has sometimes flared up since then. On one occasion (October 1950) it took the form of a violent riot which involved some 5,000 peasants and hinterland town-dwellers in Kailahun District. Commenting on this riot in his annual report to the governor, the chief commis-

[4]Kilson, Martin, *Political Change in a West African State: A Study in Modernization Process in Sierra Leone* (Cambridge, MA: Harvard University Press, 1966). Excerpts taken from pages 53-4, 60-67, 68-72, and 89-93. Martin Kilson is a Professor of Political Science and author of *The Political Awakening of Africa* (Englewood Cliffs, NJ: Prentice Hall, 1965), and *New States in the Modern World* (Cambridge, MA: Harvard University Press, 1975), among other books.

sioner observed that "the extent and violence of the rioting, which spread from Kailahun to outlying towns and villages . . . with casualties and considerable damage to property, made it necessary to summon police help from Freetown." In late 1955 and early 1956 a recurrence of rural radicalism approximated a peasant revolt properly so-called; the commission of inquiry described it as a "mass disobedience to authority." The disturbances, known commonly as tax riots, involved "many tens of thousands" of peasants and hinterland town-dwellers and entailed widespread property destruction (especially chiefs' property—e.g., cattle, surplus crops, modern homes), with damages estimated at £750,000.

As regards the political meaning of this rural radicalism, it is perhaps best described . . . as peasant rebellion. The previously mentioned peasant riots seldom entailed demands for the destruction of the existing system of traditional authority . . . but instead were aimed at ameliorating aspects of its use. Such a distinction assists us in grasping the rather peculiar ambivalence of many Africans (literate and illiterate, rural and urban-dwelling) toward traditional rulers. In the words of Lucy Mair:

> In the eyes of the same persons the chiefs may be symbols of reaction, symbols of group unity, and symbols of pride in national history. That is why there has been no move to eliminate them from the political system altogether.

The chiefs' involvement in cash crop production and marketing created a competitive relationship between chiefs and the peasantry that had no precedent in tradition. The relationship was essentially modern or Western in nature. It stemmed from the money economy and related institutions established by colonial rule. It depended upon colonial legal and political support. Since there was no basis in the indigenous scheme of things for legitimizing this economic role of chiefs, the peasantry could not be expected to relate to it in traditional terms.

As it happened, the peasantry viewed the chiefs' role in the cash economy in modern competitive terms. It was seen as an unfair competitive advantage. As early as 1903 a Sierra Leone government report to the Colonial Office recognized this situation: "The chiefs cannot understand . . . that their young men prefer leaving their villages for work on the railway and in Freetown; but, considering that they got a good wage for their labor, from 9d. to 1s. a day, they naturally prefer it to unpaid labor in their villages under their chiefs." Similarly, a correspondence to the *Sierra Leone Weekly News* in 1930 related the economic relationships between chiefs and peasants in the following terms:

> The protectorate youths are forced to come to the Colony proper because of the almost inhuman oppression that seems to be going on. The natives are forced to make the chiefs' farms, to do all public buildings for the chiefs, all government buildings, and the monies for all

work done are paid to the chiefs; and if they refuse to turn up or are late, they are fined heavily; and they have to provide their food whilst doing these public works. Over and above that, they are fined heavily at court even beyond their means, and if they can manage a little time to make a small farm, the chiefs portion is also demanded. If you produce a good quantity of rice in your farm, the chief is sure to know it, and some charge is brought against you to take all that rice away. . . . Further, if you show any attitude of resistance or unwillingness to conform to the chiefs' dictates, you are either recommended for imprisonment or for deportation.

Although the average peasant's attitude toward the chiefs' advantage in the market economy was essentially economic in origin, it eventually became part of a wider outlook which would prove a basis for political action. A district commissioner's report for the year 1921, for instance, . . . mentioned that the "collection of tribute is the most fertile source of abuse and complaint."

The transmutation of specific economic grievances into a broader social and political consciousness, however, had to await the penetration of local African society by the middle-class nationalism of the post-World War II period.

The participation of chiefs in the colonial economic system has made it exceedingly difficult to categorize them simply as a "traditional *elite*." In reality they are both traditional and modern authorities. This situation has both weakened and strengthened their authority and power, depending upon the particular combination of modern circumstances confronted by chiefs at any given point in time.

As regards their authority, chiefs had superficially the best of both worlds: they freely invoked either traditional or modern justifications as circumstances required. In reality, however, this double standard was not easy to uphold unless the peasant masses remained unqualifiedly attached to traditional authority. The fact of the matter was that the same forces of change that made chiefs what may be called a traditio-modern *elite* equally influenced the peasantry and undercut or questioned allegiance to traditional authority. As we have shown, some peasants considered the chiefs' role in the modern economy an unfair competitive advantage and refused, often in violent ways, to accept it.

As regards their power—i.e., the physical means enabling chiefs to command or influence people—there is little doubt that traditional rulers became essentially modern. Most if not all of their traditional sources of power (e.g., slavery, war making, economic preemption) were either destroyed or regulated by the colonial state. What remained of these (e.g., customary rights of tribute, labor, land rights) was closely articulated to the colonial processes of social and economic change that they can scarcely be called "traditional."

The political implications of this situation are, I think, crucial for understanding the role of traditional rulers in African political change. The traditional rulers may be expected to support that political arrangement which will enable them (1) to maximize modern sources of their power and (2) simultaneously maintain as much as possible of traditional authority. Under colonial rule this political arrangement prevailed in its purest form: *ergo,* the accommodation by chiefs to the colonial system. Similarly, in the period of nationalist political change one can expect to find the traditional rulers shifting, especially as the central political power shifts, slowly but definitely away from accommodation to colonial rule toward a shrewd selection of political alliances among competing nationalist groups. Again, this shift will be governed by the chiefs' calculation of which nationalist group will best enable them to maximize modern sources of power and simultaneously retain much of their traditional authority.

Apart from the manner in which the chiefs' authority and power were modernized, a number of other circumstances enabled chiefs to pursue the political strategy I attribute to them. For one thing, the new *elite* nationalist leaders were frequently the direct kin of traditional rulers. They were thus disposed to assist chiefs in making the transition from traditional to modern society while at the same time upholding the traditional authority of chiefs. The fact that the kin of chiefs have become political leaders in emergent African societies is itself linked to the greater opportunities chiefs had to take advantage of social change. Their favored status under colonial administration and the wealth they derived from it enabled traditional rulers to provide their kin with the best education available. In the Sierra Leone Protectorate and elsewhere in Africa the educated kin of chiefs were among the first African professionals and the first senior African members of the colonial civil service. From these preferred positions they readily moved into nationalist political leadership.

Another factor that enabled traditional rulers to pursue the political strategy sketched here is that, though traditional values were shaken by social change, their hold on the rural masses did not dwindle completely. Despite the important occasions of peasant rebellion against certain uses of traditional authority in the context of modernization, the masses displayed the ambivalence toward chiefs and traditional authority that we have already noted. Thus there is still a real sense in which chiefs continue as the sole legitimate representatives of traditional values (especially as they relate to personal or group allegiances to authority) in the eyes of most people. In the context of modern political change this was a fact of considerable significance. The nationalistic new *elite* , in its attempt to secure mass political support beyond the urban centers of its own origin, normally accommodated its political organization, methods, and policies to the strategic position held by chiefs in local society, such was particularly the case for the Sierra Leone People's Party, the dominant party in the rise of postwar nationalism in Sierra Leone.

Usually the more advanced elements among the new African "social categories" arising under colonialism and afterward have been regarded as essentially a "new *elite* . . ." The new African *elite* was distinct from the lower strata of the *elite* as well as from the bulk of the African population. By virtue of their occupation, wealth, and prestige as senior civil servants, wealthy merchants or traders, wealthy planters, bankers, contractors, some manufacturers, African managers in European firms, the political *elite*, and members of the liberal professions constituted a veritable upper class. Those engaged in such occupations were not merely functionally distinct from the lower level of the new *elite* (e.g., junior civil servants, clerks, tailors, carpenters, seamstresses, masons, medium traders); they were equally distinguished by their affluence and style of life and by their significantly higher level of education. They were also differentiated from the lower level of the new *elite* insofar as they normally dominated the development of modern nationalist politics.

The new African *elite* . . . was a politically conscious group which entered politics to advance its overall position in society and ultimately to become a ruling or governing class. . . . It employed politics to become a ruling class or a politically effective group within the ruling community. In the context of colonial modernization, the African middle class's attempt to become a ruling class meant that it had to (1) replace the expatriate ruling oligarchy as the "standard setting" group, (2) appropriate for itself the prestige of the traditional *elite* as the most legitimate authority in the eyes of the black masses who still resided largely in traditional society.

The first of these requirements of ruling-class status was met by the upper level of the new *elite* through the political nationalism that they created and organized. To meet the second requirement, they often returned to traditional society in order to assume the symbols, titles, and other badges of prestige and rank which still carried weight with the common man.

It is not altogether correct to say that this group's success displaced the upper strata in traditional societies. Although there has certainly been a good measure of *elite* displacement under colonialism and since, traditional forces have qualified the process of displacement at several crucial points. First, traditional rulers have been able to modernize themselves to the point of assuming many new-*elite* attributes. Second, a not inconsiderable proportion of the professional and business elements among the new *elite* are the offspring of traditional rulers. Third, the new-*elite* persons of commoner origin have sought the symbols and badges of prestige, status and rank controlled by the traditional *elite*. This process has been particularly evident in West African states and in East Africa, especially Uganda.

Accordingly, what emerged in the new African societies was a legitimate ruling class which was a peculiar African amalgam of the traditional *elite* and upper level of the new *elite*. Marriages and the school system probably brought them together. Even more important perhaps was the sharing of political power.

The main phase of the development of the new *elite* in Sierra Leone coincided with the rise of anti-colonialism. World War I marked a watershed for both of these developments. The old middle class of the late nineteenth and early twentieth century, whose style of life may be described in terms of "bourgeois, old style," emphasizing thrift and hard work as the conditions for getting ahead in modern society, gave way at this time to a different type of middle-class outlook which focused upon the resources of the colonial government as the more effective means of advancement. This change in middle-class outlook was partly related to the fact that increasing numbers of professional Africans found government service the most suitable outlet for their skills. In 1925, for instance, 57 percent of the medical doctors in Sierra Leone were so employed. This, in turn, whetted the appetite of the new *elite* for more government jobs, as well as for direct government assistance in training and preparation for government posts.

Stripped to its essentials, the anti-colonial nationalism that emerged after World War I was merely the ideological projection of middle-class Africans for new jobs and related perquisites which only the government could provide. Inevitably, this nationalism confronted the sizable expatriate personnel who claimed the most desirable posts in the colonial establishment, as the main barrier to its goal. This barrier, it was soon discovered, could be overcome only with the demise of the colonial regime itself. Hence the anti-colonial orientation of African nationalism.

The National Congress of British West Africa founded in Accra, the Gold Coast, in March 1920, with branches in Sierra Leone, the Gambia, and Nigeria, was the major organizational expression of the new middle-class nationalism after World War I. The aims of the NCBWA covered the whole gamut of essentially middle-class needs, among which were greater African representation in central colonial government, expansion of the franchise, and the establishment of a British West African University to give British Africans technical and scientific training, and especially the training necessary for the holding of positions in the Colonial Service. Only a small portion of these aims was even partly achieved during the 1920s and 1930s. At the end of World War II, however, the authorities moved toward greater African representation in central government, which widened the possibilities for greater use of government resources for the development of the African *elite*.

This development, as the *elite* saw it, was basically a matter of the replacement of expatriate personnel at all levels of the colonial establishment. In Sierra Leone this policy of "Africanization" commenced in the late 1940s and by the end of the 1950s had no small achievement to its credit. . . . Professional Africans were the main beneficiary of this increase. By 1956 some 80 percent of the medical doctors were in government service, compared to 57 percent twenty-one years earlier, and in 1960 nearly 40 percent of the lawyers were so employed. Furthermore, a majority of the doctors and lawyers pursued private practice along with government employment. Africanization also applied to the training of professionals. Whereas the colonial government in Sierra Leone had sent fewer than one hundred students overseas for education in the period 1943-49, the Sierra Leone People's Party (SLPP) government, elected to office in 1951, had sent over three hundred students for higher education overseas by 1959. The SLPP government also assumed full financial responsibility for Fourah Bay College (now the University College of Sierra Leone) during this period; today most students at the College receive government scholarships.

The SLPP government has also extended wide assistance to the business community among the African *elite*. In the mid-1950s the government announced that it was government's policy to encourage private enterprise and by the end of the 1950s a number of measures bad been instituted to this end.

Manufacturing machinery was purchased and sold to African capitalists at less than original cost; African produce firms were given special consideration by the Sierra Leone Government Produce Marketing Board when purchasing cash crops for export; the Development of Industries Board was established to provide loans and easy credit to African businessmen; a variety of assistance, including credit, was extended to the large cash crop planters organized into cooperatives; and, finally, government pressure was brought to bear upon expatriate firms to expand their African managerial personnel and to upgrade it without let or hindrance.

With the establishment of the independent state of Sierra Leone in April 1961, the new *elite*, now with a governing class, obtained incomparable opportunities for further development. But it was no longer quite so easy for the new *elite* to justify claims upon government resources precisely in the same nationalistic mode that prevailed before independence. The range of self-serving policies that the new *elite* could have been accepted by the African majority in the pre-independence period as being in the public interest was much more limited in the post-independence era. Yet there will always be a lot of room for maneuver by the *elite* in this regard.

For instance, it is certainly arguable that the use of government resources to expand professional categories like that of medical doctors was as much in the public or national interest as it was in that of the new *elite*. Throughout West African states medical doctors shun many crucial areas of medicine because, as a report of the Nigerian government has noted, they "offer very little or no scope for remunerative practice."

In 1958 such important medical fields in Nigeria as pathology, dermatology, malariology, nutrition, anaesthetics, among others, had only a few or no practitioners. This situation necessarily affected the efficiency of any developing state in tropical Africa and cannot be left wanting; and to the extent that it is attended to, the result is as much in the public as in the new *elite*'s interest.

Yet every instance of government assistance to the professional and business categories of the *elite* could hardly be rationalized invariably in this way. Much of this assistance was purely and simply self-serving, with little or no gain for the public interest. Even so, it must be recognized that what we call public interest was a meaningless notion separate from specific group or class interest; the evaluation of the claims of both upon government resources must, therefore, take into consideration the relative nature of the relationship between them. As one scholar has put it:

> Private groups have a remarkable facility in the rationalization of private gain with the public interest. The principal driving forces in politics are class interests and group interests; they make themselves felt, regardless of the kind of government or social organization that exists. Yet the promotion of the public good cannot be accomplished apart from class or special interest. The public good is, after all, a relative matter.

Some Origins of Nationalism in East Africa

J.M. LONSDALE[5]

Historiographical controversies surrounding revolutions and other periods of rapid political change are concerned in part with the interactions of the "spontaneous element" of popular initiative and the "conscious element" of direction and control by intellectual and political leadership. Debate on the relative importance of these two elements is in most cases likely to prove sterile, for they are interdependent. Nevertheless there may well be such a debate with reference to African national revolutions, for emphasis on the one or the other element will derive from contrasting assumptions about the nature of African nationalism as a whole. Studies of the conscious element, the political *elite*, will tend to stress the extent to which a nationalist movement is a revolutionary exotic in its reaction to colonial rule, and its dependence on European ideas and organizational models. Analyses of popular spontaneity must on the other hand be concerned with the historical continuities of the specifically African contribution. This paper is a tentative attempt at probing both the sources of continuity—the patterns of precolonial society; resistance to the imposition of alien rule; the problems in the inter-war period of settled administration and incipient development—and the spontaneous contribution to revolutionary change after the Second World War.

The framework of this paper is more assured than its content warrants. Its main concern is the role of ordinary Africans in the emergence of national movements. In the first section, I try to outline the essential contribution of social change, concentrating on the shifts in African leadership and communication which it involved. There are in any society individuals who act as communicators of social needs within their locality and, if so activated, as communicators of political ideas between organizations wider than the locality and the people within it. It is tempting to suggest that there were definite stages whereby the old communicators within African society, the chiefs, became increasingly irrelevant not only socially, but also as political communicators with the colonial authority, so making way for a new type of communicating leadership. The background to this process seems to have been

[5]Lonsdale, J.M., "Some Origins of Nationalism in East Africa," *The Journal of African History* 9, no. 1, (1968): 119-146. Excerpts taken from pages 119-121, 123-126, 136, and 140-146. J.M. Lonsdale is a fellow of history at Trinity College in Cambridge, England. He is editor of *South Africa in Question* (Cambridge: African Studies Center, University of Cambridge, 1988).

the slow metamorphosis from tribesman to peasant in some East African communities. But this did not necessarily entail a corresponding move from tribalism to nationalism, for social change was not the sole determinant of political change. The focus of action for the emerging political associations was also influenced by the nature of the administrative framework and the extent of government interference in methods of production and marketing. In the second section, then, I discuss the political preoccupations of the inter-war years. They seem to have been concerned mainly with the competition between the old and the new communicators for leadership within, and external representation of, the localities. I then go on to suggest that while the old communicators were becoming less suited to these tasks, the new men themselves did not make real contact with their potential mass following in these years, save perhaps in Kikuyuland. This contact was essential for the development of mass nationalism. I discuss finally how this contact was made after 1945. To an important extent the initiative in its making seems to have lain with the mass of ordinary Africans. The potential communicators of the inter-war years now became both social leaders within their localities and communicators outside, no longer points of contact with the colonial authority, but with the nationalist *elite*, with some of them winning that status for themselves.

The belief that African nationalism is the political expression of social change may be summarized quite simply. In general the colonial period saw within each territory the creation of a single, if deeply divided, political and economic system out of the multitude of preexisting societies, tribes, peoples and kingdoms. For all but the most isolated of Africans there was a vast increase in social scale. With this there came the beginnings of proletarianization, especially in Kenya, and a growth of economic individualism through the introduction of marketable cash crops and outlets for food surpluses. On a lowly and obvious level, the social preconditions for a wider political consciousness—nationalism eventually—were provided. More importantly for this paper, the developing colonial situation was accompanied by a growing depersonalization of relations within African society. This process, with exceptions and variations, seems to have been marked by three broad phases.

There was the initial period in which the administrations were establishing themselves, finding or creating political communicators, points of contact with the subject peoples. In the ideal case the political communicator, king or chief, whether traditionally legitimate, traditionally recognizable as usurper, or jumped-up mercenary and buccaneer, remained also a social communicator, in close relationship with his tribesmen or peasants. His administrative duties, little more than tax collection and the maintenance of order, were not yet heavy enough to disrupt the known social pattern. Strains there were of course. But face-to-face relations were retained within the African societies, intrusion on the part of the British being confined to manipulation of the points of contact.

Then, with colonial authority firmly established, officials felt less dependent upon their African allies, being more preoccupied with administrative efficiency, development, and immigrant pressures. There was increasing economic and institutional change which tended to undercut the relationship between chief and people and between the people themselves.

In this second phase, then, governments were in some areas assisting in the social decline of the political communicators on whom their authority rested, a decline which was in any case likely with the widening influence of the market economy. To mark the third phase, in the 1930s a crucial new factor was added in each of the three mainland territories, namely increasing government intervention in the everyday business of life. There was proliferation of marketing controls, stricter supervision of the educational system and, most important of all, the first attempts to change African methods of land usage. All this government activity had two significant and related results. The more enterprising Africans, traders, teachers, improving farmers, came in increasing individual contact with the machinery of central government. Secondly, African authorities were either by-passed by departmental experts or, if efficient, became faceless coordinators of improvement schemes, much like the new breed of deskbound white officials themselves. The old communicators no longer occupied a sole focal point in local society.

The conclusion of this argument is vital. The combined effect of social change and the erosion of one form of African leadership was the emergence in some areas of groupings recognizable as peasantry. The term has been used already in this paper in contradistinction to tribesmen. There are difficulties in its application to the African situation, but if it is accepted that the distinguishing condition of a peasantry is its semi-autonomy or partial self-sufficiency in political, economic and cultural spheres, it seems clear that the introduction of the colonial authority structure, agricultural production in excess of subsistence requirements, and the spread of Christian and Islamic literary cultures together produced such a condition, certainly in those areas most exposed to change.

An independent landowning peasantry was emerging. Chiefs, the old communicators, were irrelevant to many of the peasants' dealings with economic agencies or new social communities; for example, the churches. And, as members of a stable bureaucracy, their prestige and wealth was less dependent upon such involvement in local society. . . . The way was clear for new communicators either to reknit the old society in relevant terms, or to join the new interests in new associations, in order to regain effective popular contact with the colonial authority, if necessary through the medium of open conflict. The choice of unifying symbols, whether tribe or peasant class and nation, was determined by the pressures, from above and from below, which developed within the colonial situation.

In the inter-war years the pressures from above, from the colonial authority, were still mediated almost exclusively through the official chiefs. The new opportunities for social mobility and status outside the chiefships were the most awkward signs of pressures from below. Together, they focused political attention on the possible alternatives for securing an effective African voice in the local councils of empire. The varied political focus employed by Africans was an index both of the changing nature of the colonial pressures and of the social confidence of their leaders. This focus was controlled by three factors: an estimate of the popular basis of support for a given action—an awareness of social change; an understanding of the enemy's most responsive and responsible point—a knowledge fostered by government action; and an appreciation of those features of the administrative and legal framework which could be turned to advantage. It defined political aims, tactics and organization.

There is an obvious difference between the political focus of the Gusii when in 1908 they tried to kill their district commissioner because he was looked upon as their sole aggressor and conqueror, and that of Bildad Kaggia, who in 1952 called for increased African representation in Kenya's Legislative Council in order to regain alienated land, on the ground that legislation rather than guns had been the means of alienation. The Gusii action illustrates what I call *diffuse* political focus. Such was typical of the early colonial period, when the social groupings in each territory were many and disparate, and when understanding of the colonial authority was as yet very personal. Kaggia's program on the other hand was *central* in focus. He was speaking at a mass meeting of 25,000 Africans drawn from many of Kenya's tribes; his and other speeches were translated into Kiswahili; he was demanding pressure on the colony's political center. Between these two poles of awareness was a third, local political focus, which seems to have dominated much of the political activity of the Kenya Africans during the inter-war years and to have been a factor in Uganda for very much longer.

Until the end of the First World War, the African political focus in Kenya remained diffuse in the sense suggested above. The hardships of the war itself, and immediately thereafter increased taxes, reduced wages, an influx of fresh settlers, their rising demands for labor, and the renewed threat to African lands implicit in the change of status from East Africa Protectorate to Kenya Colony—all these factors presented Africans with a clearly defined enemy.

To be effective and credible, nationalist leaders must appeal for mass support; but such an appeal brings into central focus those rivalries of tribe, language and culture which have hitherto been contained within their respective localities. In the inter-war years, the period of local focus, political argument had centered on the allocation of resources to the localities and the distribution of the ensuing benefits within them. The debates were conducted within fairly circumscribed groups of rival modernizers, African officials and those outside the mission or government hierarchies. These tended to present their conflicting claims to governments with but little attempt to mobilize popular followings.

Effective national movements could not emerge until the aspirant new communicators had realized their potential role. This was a difficult task. In the 1920s, educated men had tended to ally with the traditional communicators. The known unit, the tribe, was seen as the focal point of the desired independent society. For some the focus was the wider ethnic community of which neighboring tribes were but components. This wider scale of social endeavor was still more evident in the later phase of local political focus. The official nationalism of sectional chiefs was opposed by more radical movements demanding paramounts. More recently young nationalist movements have used locally traditional communicators, but for national ends. The focal point of the desired society was now the nation. The new men of the 1920s had made their alliances with the chiefs out of a sense of their own relative weakness. They recognized social facts. The nationalist politicians entered their alliances from a position of relative strength. They saw them as the prelude to social reform. But the politicians' freedom of action was not limitless. It depended rather on the continued exercise of diplomatic skill. And, in the words of one East African leader, the post-Independence strategy of development has still to use tradition in order to abolish tradition, to use the clan in order to create communities which are not clannish. Above all, nationalist parties were, and are, dependent on their local communicators whose political effectiveness depends on their social support.

Many accounts of African nationalism emphasize the role of the political party in creating this support, in rousing the people from the "inertia of loyalty" that attaches to any government in power, in this case the colonial regime. It seems possible to exaggerate this external moral-building function. For if in the inter-war period the mass of Africans were deprived of political communication by the lack of widely felt burdens and the minority attractions of western Christian culture, so from the late 1930s these conditions were reversed. As already suggested in the preliminary discussion of social change, purposive government action in economic, educational and agrarian spheres brought individual Africans, many of whom were now more peasants than tribesmen, into much closer and more irritating contact with the colonial regime. At the same time as many ordinary people were for this reason developing a more explicitly political interest, the potential new communicators, teachers, traders and clerks, were shedding their illusions. Improved education did not remove the color bar, but it did help to remove a sense of cultural inferiority. The secondary school-leaver was better equipped than the barely literate to distinguish between material and cultural aspects of the West. Concurrently, the new governmental pressures felt by the peasantry meant also the end of any hopes for effective local political focus. The expenditure of greater resources on economic development and social services brought with it more stringent central government control.

Such was the setting for the spontaneous contribution to nationalism. Of the many facets to this contribution, only four will be discussed here. Together they illustrate the shift in mass concerns from a political focus that was diffuse or local to one that was central. First there is the question of agrarian change generally, which focused attention on central government as a sometimes incompetent agent of reform. Secondly, the social philosophy which inspired governments' land tenure policies, namely the creation of a stable rural middle class, provoked a clearly radical social response. Thirdly, the cavalier treatment of elected local authorities by governments in a hurry forced the new communicators, often members of these authorities, into open opposition on a popular issue. Lastly, and perhaps most importantly, the development of producers' cooperatives gave to the peasantry organizations that were both locally based and centrally concerned with governments' economic policies.

Soil erosion had been recognized as a threat by the East African governments long before the Second World War. Customary land usage was increasingly destructive of the soil with the growth of population and commercial pressure on the land. Both physical anti-erosion measures were needed and, in the long term, changed methods of African farming. Improved husbandry was required if African cash crops were to be assured of a continuing welcome on the world market. The wartime emphasis on increased production, together with a shortage of the necessary departmental staff, meant that the agrarian problem had reached crisis proportions by 1945. More widely, the postwar era promised a new deal for the colonies from which both the dependent and metropolitan economies would benefit. In both the metropolitan and local contexts, the governments were in a hurry. In Kenya, urgency was added by the hope that economic development would silence political unrest. The 1954 Swynnerton Plan for the intensified development of African agriculture was a direct response to Mau Mau. Government hoped to solve a political problem by economic means: it was this very economic solution which precipitated the wider rural revolt which hastened the end of colonial rule.

Results were sought in the enactment of a multitude of orders affecting communal anti-erosion work, crop and animal husbandry. In the long term these were extremely effective in raising peasant and national incomes. But initially there were many failures. Insufficient time was allowed for experiment and demonstration. Risk-taking is anathema to subsistence farmers, and, in too many early improvement schemes, the risks, and the hard work they often involved, were clearly not worth taking. All over rural East Africa there were instances of local resistance to the changes. In these the peasants were committed against the officers of the central government, and their leadership combined traditional clan elders, intimately concerned with land usage, and the new men, traders and teachers. This was something new and portentous. Memories of earlier resistance to colonial occupation were revived as inspiration. As disturbing as the changes themselves was the environment in which they were implemented. Development entailed a great increase in European technical personnel in the rural areas at a time when there was further European settlement. The forcible removal of some of the Meru of northern Tanganyika to make way for European farmers in 1951 aroused alarm not only throughout that territory . . . but in Kenya also. It was unfortunate too that compulsory cattle culling appeared to be more immediately advantageous to European meat canners than to the African cattle owners.

Government motives were suspect. The social implications were disturbing too. One of the features of precolonial African history had been the existence of free cultivators, unencumbered by landlords or indebtedness. But, in Kenya especially, it was accepted that development must be empowered by the individual profit motive. Land must be consolidated, not only to give the secure tenure necessary for capital improvement, but to enable African farmers to mortgage their land against development loans. Hitherto, government had not interfered with customary conditions of tenure to limit the dangers of such indebtedness. In 1954 it was proposed that "former Government policy [should] be reversed, and able, energetic or rich Africans will be able to acquire more land, and bad or poor farmers less, creating a landed and a landless class. This is a normal step in the evolution of a country." The proposals were accepted. They were implemented, like all other government programs, through the official chiefs. These were in a position to reap disproportionate benefits in the land cases attendant on consolidation, and from the agricultural department's farm planning services. To the peasant, agrarian reform was not only change, but also another stage in the accretion of chiefly power and wealth, with individual land titles consolidating both. The danger was the greater where the peasantry were also migrant workers. On balance—it is a moot point—it seems that families whose heads were frequently away in European employment were less likely to change their farming methods. The rural modernizers were rather the old welfare association leadership and the chiefs—some of whom were retired agricultural instructors. These were the able, energetic or rich Africans, long associated with government departments. When land consolidation was started, it seemed likely that those already dispossessed in the towns or on European farms would be permanently dispossessed in their home areas also. Urban and rural radicalism nurtured each other. In Kikuyuland this situation led to something approaching civil war. More generally, this deepening alienation of the peasantry from their chiefs provided an open opportunity for a rural counter leadership.

This alternative leadership was present already in the elected . . . local government bodies [which] after the war were given more democratic form, greater authority and increased financial responsibility. The irony was that these new features were being inculcated by the same governments which, in their haste to solve agrarian problems, were resorting increasingly to enforcement rather than consultation. This was a long-standing African complaint. In 1935 the "loyalist" Kikuyu Provincial Association had asked agricultural officers to order their African subordinates, on going out "to advise other natives, [to] give their advice in the form of advice and not as a compulsory order. . . . Further they should explain the benefits of their advice." An African farmer's association near Dar es Salaam similarly complained of agricultural inspectors in 1948, that "instead of teaching us how to produce more crops etc., they tell us to clean our coconut shambas at once and in the case of failing to do so, . . . heavy fines and imprisonment are imposed." This same sentiment was expressed in the District Councils. In 1947, Oginga Odinga, then a union councillor, "emphasized that if the soil was to be preserved, it was the duty of the community to do the work on their own land rather than waiting or depending on someone else to come and do the work for them." Resentment of outside direction was combined with desire for improvement under African control, for African benefit. District Councils were quick to protest that their new powers were a sham. They had no say in the elaborate schemes of government departments. Early in 1959 the Luo African District Council of Central Nyanza, acting under strong local pressure, voted itself into dissolution rather than accept government terms for the management of an afforestation scheme. The government had to rely on nominated councils in Kikuyuland during the Mau Mau emergency. In Sukamuland, Tanganyika, there was the same story of council opposition to government instruction, even though the council was dominated by chiefs. Two points here must be emphasized. Most of the stimulus to such council opposition came from within the localities. Peasants and councilors knew like frustrations. This first observation is reinforced by the second. Many of the elected councilors, greatly increased in number with the extension of local democracy after the war, were already closely associated with the people by virtue of their leading positions in trading companies or cooperatives.

These too had a long history. In the inter-war years independent traders had been a minority group. They were often involved in the more radical movements within local political focus, resentful of the marketing advantages enjoyed by the chiefs. The generally increased peasant participation in the cash economy during the war, and the business aspirations of demobilized servicemen thereafter provided a much broader base for such commercial activity. African business careers were dogged by lack of capital and entrepreneurial experience, by Asian dominance in retail trade and produce marketing, by government marketing regulations and credit restriction. Many failed. Bitter experience taught the need for political assistance in the attack on economic privilege. Concurrently, there was a great expansion of producers' cooperatives, with which the majority of peasants in the more advanced areas had at least some connection. They were concerned with the whole range of central governments' economic policies. Each cooperative society was also a miniature cockpit of tension between the initiative of their African organizer and officials, and the paternalism of government cooperative officers. It is significant that cooperative or other commercial organizers were as prominent as the trade unionists in the national movements.

The passion of peasant resistance to government dictate had moved the inertia of loyalty to the colonial regimes. In many cases it had forced governments to admit failure, weakening colonial morale. Rural radicalism had in many areas provoked open opposition to the old communicators, the chiefs. The opportunities for an effective opposition leadership were confirmed in government treatment of elected local authorities. Rural economic enterprise joined peasant and new communicator in the cooperative society. A peasant revolt had thrown up its leaders—local men with central interests. As such the revolt was atypical. Peasant movements were historically anarchic. It was the function of the conscious element, the nationalist leaders, to maintain that centrality of focus. It remains their more exacting task after Independence.

The United States, European Disengagement, and African Nationalism
WILLIAM ROGER LOUIS AND
RONALD ROBINSON[6]

The fall of Europe's colonial empires in Africa has usually been attributed to a magpie's choice of African nationalism, shifts in national ideology, and changes in the international balance of power. Clearly a catalogue of such forces is not enough. The difficulty in assessing the collapse of the European regimes lies in relating the international, metropolitan, and colonial factors in a comprehensive framework that reveals both the chronology and the interacting forces. This chapter attempts to move the subject forward toward such an explanation by examining the problem through one particular but cardinally important aspect. It begins with the emergence of the United States as a global power—a global power that during the Second World War suddenly developed an intense interest in the British Empire, including its African components. When the center of world power shifted from London to Washington (and eventually to Moscow as well), the British felt the blow to their economy and their colonial position throughout the world. Did this shock trigger the changes of mind on the part of the British that eventually accelerated the transfer of power and the nationalization, or Africanization, of colonial administration?

A brief historical comment may help to explain the background of these remarks. After the partition of Africa at the turn of the century, the colonial powers of Europe supported each other against Africans. They only rarely interfered in each other's affairs. There was, in fact, what could be called an international colonial system

---

[6]Louis, William Roger, and Robinson, Ronald, "The United States and the Liquidation of British Empire in Tropical Africa, 1941-1951," in Gifford, Prosser, and Louis, William Roger, eds., *The Transfer of Power in Africa: Decolonization 1940-1960* (New Haven: Yale University Press, 1982). Excerpts taken from pages 31-2, 43-7, and 43-5. William Roger Louis received his D.Litt and D.Phil. from Oxford University and is Professor of History and Curator of Historical Collections at the Humanities Research Center, University of Texas. He is author of many works, including *Great Britain and Germany's Lost Colonies* (Oxford: Clarendon, 1967), and *The United States and the Decolonization of the British Empire, 1941-1945* (Oxford: Clarendon, 1978). Ronald Robinson received his Ph.D. from Cambridge University, is the former Smutts Reader in Commonwealth Studies at Cambridge, Beit Professor of Commonwealth History at Oxford, and a Fellow of Balliol College. He is perhaps most well-known for his co-authored work with the late John Gallagher *Africa and the Victorians* (London: Macmillam, 1961).

(interrupted, of course, by the First World War). Through international treaties the African powers of Europe accepted each other's colonies as exclusive spheres of influence—spheres recognized in international law. Though there were important protests against this system, notably on the part of Woodrow Wilson in 1919, the European powers administered their territories without fear of external intervention. So long as Europeans dominated the balance of power, colonial administrations could enjoy freedom of action without fear of international subversion. One way of looking at the beginning of the end of the "colonial system" is to analyze the impact which the emergence of the United States from isolation had on colonial affairs.

The momentous shifts in the bedrock of world politics during the Second World War raised one set of problems in Washington and another set in London. Should the Americans collaborate with British "imperialism" for purposes of winning the war and securing the peace? Or would their anticolonial tradition and expansive economic strategy bring them to insist on the liquidation of the empire? On the other side of the Atlantic, how could the British adjust to their unaccustomed dependence without giving up the empire?

In 1947 African nationalism was still in its infancy. Its leaders had not yet organized the *elite* and the people into a popular party, nor would they be able to do so until the British introduced the ballot box and democratized colonial government. Naturally the Labour government wished to show that the shibboleths for colonial reform, which had been applied in opposition, were being respected in office; but on the whole Labor's anti-imperialism, never strong, weakened further with experience. As Labour ministers grappled with the dollar crisis and learned the economic value of the African colonies to Britain, they became prouder of the feats of progress which they proposed to bring about under the Union Jack. Like earlier generations of British anti-imperialists, as they raised the standard of colonial trusteeship toward their ideals, most Labour leaders became more and more reluctant to give up the empire and the means to achieve their aspirations. Only by retaining the empire could they demonstrate the progressiveness of their colonial rule.

If neither the strength of nationalism in Africa nor the force of anti-imperialism in Britain seems fully to account for the new course of the postwar period, how far was the international or American factor responsible for it? It is generally true that after 1945 the fire of anticolonialism burned much less brightly within the United States government. By the time of the San Francisco conference, the American military had prevailed over those who sought to liquidate colonial empires by placing them under international supervision. In 1945 the United States had acquiesced in the return to their former rulers of many colonies which had been occupied by the common enemy. During the period of the loan and Marshall aid, the United States pledged its economic resources to the recover of its European allies with no conditions attached to colonies except that they should be more accessible to American trade and investment. During the early years of the Cold War there was very little question of American pressure to decolonize, though the dilemmas of orderly imperial liquidation persisted.

In the immediate postwar era, American involvement in European colonial affairs can be summed up in the names of Cyrenaica, Indochina, and Indonesia. Each of these carried a chilling message to the British. In the dispute over the future of the Italian colonies, Ernest Bevin, the foreign secretary in the Attlee government, hoped that Britain would be able to acquire trusteeship status over Cyrenaica and create a strategic base there in order to lessen British dependence on Egypt. When the negotiations for the renewal of an Anglo-Egyptian alliance broke down in 1946-7, and when it became clear that the Palestine problem could not be resolved to British advantage, the question of Britain's security in the Middle East became acute. To Bevin's dismay the Americans could not be counted on to back British trusteeship claims to Cyrenaica. American policy fluctuated in reaction to possible expansion into the eastern Mediterranean and in relation to the strength of the Communist movement in Italy. In 1945-8 the British were forced to turn to Iraq as the linchpin of British defense in the Middle East. What the British learned from the episode of the Italian colonies was that American policy toward colonial areas in North Africa and the Middle East would change according to the fortunes of the Cold War and would not necessarily accommodate the strategic requirements of the British Empire.

Postwar American policy favored the European colonial regimes rather than the nationalist movements. The French and the Dutch would not have been able to combat colonial nationalism as effectively as they did had it not been for the economic and military resources provided by the United States through the use of lend-lease and indirect economic assistance. Publicly the Truman administration disassociated itself from French and Dutch counterrevolutionary activities, but privately American officials were quite aware that considerable amounts of financial aid under the Marshall Plan were being siphoned off into Southeast Asia. In the case of Indonesia, however, the American government feared that the Dutch flouting of the United Nations good-offices committee would weaken the United Nations organization itself, and that Dutch intransigence with the moderate or Republican nationalists would lead to a Communist revolution. In December 1948 the American government suspended an unexpended balance of Marshall Plan aid of about five million dollars designated for the Netherlands East Indies. The United States made it clear that economic assistance to the Netherlands itself might be in jeopardy. The Dutch capitulated. No move by the Americans could have been more dramatic to the British: it became apparent that the United States was prepared to cut off economic aid to a European ally in order to promote colonial independence.

Dependence on the United States since 1941 and the witnessing of the American response to such crises as the one in Indonesia profoundly influenced the official mind of British imperialism. The course of American anticolonialism in the 1940s helped to undermine the confidence and shatter the traditional perspectives of British colonial rulers. It also armed British liberal reformers with compelling arguments that reform was vital in order to preserve the American alliance. There were powerful reasons for the belief that the anticolonial sentiment of the American public might yet provoke the United States government to interfere if the British did not continue with a progressive colonial policy. Above all, dependence on the United States was probably the one experience humiliating enough to convince the British psychologically that the age of empire was ending. The change of perspective resulting from this reversal of international roles encouraged a new spirit and direction in British policy that favored the eventual transfer of power in Africa.

As far as officials in Washington were concerned, the dismantling of the British Empire led to balkanization and local instability. They were confronted with a lengthening series of local crises similar to those faced by the British in the nineteenth century. In one way or another these crises compelled the Americans to extend their "responsibilities" in order to fill the vacuum left by the contraction of the British Empire. In Africa the rapid fragmentation was a phenomenon the United States neither planned nor welcomed, but to some extent it was the logical outcome of the goal of the American government to save as much as possible of the non-Western world from communism and to do so in the historic American tradition of anticolonialism.

How can the appeasement of American anticolonialism be assessed in relation to the decline of the British Empire as a world power, the rise of the Labour party in domestic politics, and the advent of the nationalist movements in Asia and Africa? In answering that question (which has a bearing on the French, Dutch, Belgian, and Portuguese colonial empires as well), it may help to advance certain propositions concerning the transfer of power. The viability of empire depended upon a substantial accommodation at three different levels: in the colony itself, in the metropolitan power, and in the international sphere. More explicitly, the maritime colonial empires of western Europe could continue to exist only so long as three requirements were fulfilled: (1) that their colonial subjects acquiesced in their authority; (2) that the politicians and electorates of the metropolitan countries accepted colonial commitments as not entirely unethical and on the whole worthwhile; and (3) that these empires received international recognition. The colonial regimes could not survive the breach of these conditions.

In international politics—with which this essay has been especially concerned—conditions became more exacting as the imperial nations lost their domination of the world balance of power; at the metropolitan and colonial levels, attitudes hardened as ideologies changed and political movements and parties became more assertive. In these circumstances the terms for the acceptance of colonial rule could still be found on some levels, but it became increasingly difficult to achieve compatible terms on all three levels at once. Indeed, readjustment or renegotiating of the terms for the acceptance of empire on one level or another tended to disrupt the agreements already concluded on other levels by making them unattractive or impracticable. In other words, the practical politics of retaining a colonial empire consisted not only in finding viable "bargains" in colonial, metropolitan, and international politics, but also in keeping them compatible with each other.

The interdependence of terms for the toleration of colonial empires became sharply apparent in the mid-twentieth century. For example, the decline of the European powers in world politics tempted not only the Soviet Union but also the United States to stiffen the conditions for acquiescing in the continued existence of the overseas colonial regimes; the international balance of power, in turn, encouraged nationalists in the colonies to organize support and demand more concessions. Increasing international pressure together with growing resistance from colonial subjects thus tended to test the willingness of the metropolitan peoples to tolerate the burden of colonial empires. The extent of that toleration varied with the financial and military cost of colonial upkeep, the supposed economic benefit, and the prevailing ethic or ideology. In the British case, so few politicians knew enough about colonial economics that most were forced to rely on ethical yardsticks to trusteeship to measure the value of empire and hence their own willingness to tolerate the burden. As the humane values of democracy, pacifism, and social welfare increasingly pervaded a war-weary Europe, the limits of metropolitan toleration tended to shrink from coercion to concession; in other words, where once the colonial power coerced its subjects, it now made concession to them. The increased reluctance of the metropole to pay the cost of retaining colonies in turn diminished the imperial administrators' power to bargain for the acquiescence of their colonial subjects.

Just as international and metropolitan conditions reflected in part the tensions in the colonies, so the circumstances in the colonies themselves were profoundly affected by the changing balance of forces at the international and metropolitan levels. Colonial governments have always stood or fallen as the rulers and the ruled have accommodated or resisted each other's major interests. The rulers usually came to the negotiating table with the idea of retaining imperial authority up the brink of a crisis in which they would have to "shoot or get out"; subjects, on the other hand, came with the intention of enlarging their share of governing power up to the point of "getting shot or backing down." For the proconsul the colonial problem was how much power to share with subjects in exchange for their cooperation; for the subject the question was how much noncooperation would elicit the maximum share of power. Between the two extremes the terms for obtaining acquiescence in colonial rule depended on several variables: for example, the expenditure of finance and use of force which the peoples of the metropolitan country would tolerate for purposes of keeping a colony; the extent of a colonial government's demands on its subjects for land, labor, and produce and of the resistance thus provoked; the volume of metropolitan investment offering partnerships to subjects in the profits of the international economy; and the extent of power-sharing with indigenous *elites*.

In short, the existence of the Western overseas empires depended on conditions which made them acceptable to the politics of the metropolitan countries, and these terms also had to be practicable both in international relations and in the local politics of colonial or quasi-colonial societies. Empires eventually fall when the conditions necessary for their survival at one of these levels become impossible to translate acceptable at the other two levels. If this thesis holds good, it would be futile to debate the question whether the main cause of the fall of empires is to be found either in shifts in the international balance, or in the vicissitudes of metropolitan politics, or in the rise of colonial nationalism. No simple, single-cause explanation can be found. Change at any one level caused changes in others. In the British case, Colonial Office planners ultimately concluded that there could be no resolution of the tensions—international, metropolitan, and colonial—other than by swift transfers of power. The "transfers of power" were intended to sustain British influence through African agents.

Suggested Readings

Auma-Osolo, Agola, *Cause-Effects of Modern African Nationalism on the World Market* (Lanham: University Press, 1983).

Balandier, George, "Messianism and Nationalism in Black Africa," in Van den Berghe, *Social Problems of Change and Conflict* (San Francisco: Chandler Publishing, 1965).

Beach, D.N., "Chimurenga: The Shona Uprising of 1896-7," *Journal of African History* 20, no. 3, (1979), 395-420.

Clough, Marshall, *Fighting Two Sides: Kenya Chiefs and Politicians, 1918-1940* (Nimot, CO: University of Colorado Press, 1990).

Cobbing, Julian, "The Absent Priesthood: Another Look at the Rhodesian Rising of 1896-7," *Journal of African History* 18, no. 1, (1977), 61-84.

Coleman, James, "Nationalism in Tropical Africa," *American Political Science Review* 48, no. 2, (1954), 404-14.

Nigeria: Background to Nationalism (Berkeley: University of California Press, 1963).

Egerton, Roger, *Mau Mau: An African Crucible* (New York: Free Press, 1989).

Emerson, Rupert, *From Empire to Nation: The Rise of Self-Assertion of Asian and African Peoples* (Cambridge, MA: Harvard University Press, 1960).

Gifford, Prosser, and Louis, Roger, eds., *The Transfer of Power in Africa: Decolonization, 1940-60* (New Haven: Yale University Press, 1982).

Harbeson, John, *Nation Building in Kenya: The Role of Land Reform* (Evanston: Northwestern University Press, 1973).

Henderson, Ian, "The Origins of Nationalism in East and Central Africa: The Zambian Case," *The Journal of African History* 11, no. 4, (1970), 591-603.

Kanoga, Tabitha, *Squatters and the Roots of Mau Mau* (Athens: Ohio University Press, 1987).

Kedourie, Elie, ed., *Nationalism in Africa and Asia* (London: Weidenfeld and Nickolson, 1970).

Kitching, Gavin, *Class and Economic Change in Kenya: The Making of an African Bourgeoisie, 1905-1970* (New Haven: Yale University Press, 1980).

Kohn, Hans, *African Nationalism in the Twentieth Century* (Princeton: Van Nostrand, 1965).

Linden, Jane and Ian, "John Chilembwe and the New Jerusalem," *Journal of African History* 12, no. 4, (1971), 629-51.

Muzrui, Ali, *Nationalism and New States in Africa from about 1935 to the Present* (Nairobi: Heineman, 1984).

Olusanya, O., *The West African Students' Union and the Politics of Decolonization, 1925-58* (Ibadan: Daystar Press, 1982).

Ranger, T.O., *Revolt in Southern Rhodesia* (Evanston: Northwestern University Press, 1967).

Rosberg, Carl, and Nottingham, John, *The Myth of Mau Mau: Nationalism in Kenya* (Nairobi: East African Publishing House, 1966).

Rotberg, Robert, and Mazrui, Ali, eds., *Protest and Power in Black Africa* (New York: Oxford University Press, 1970).

Rotberg, Robert, *The Rise of Nationalism in Central Africa* (Cambridge, MA: Harvard University Press, 1966).

Shepperson, George, and Price, Thomas, *Independent Africa: John Chilembwe and the Origins, Setting, and Significance of the Nyasaland Native Rising of 1915* (Edinburgh: University Press, 1958).

Sithole, Ndabaningi, *African Nationalism* (London: Oxford University Press, 1968).

Thorp, David, *Economic and Social Origins of Mau Mau* (London: James Curry, 1987).

Turton, E.R., "Somali Resistance to Colonial Rule and the Development of Somali Political Activity in Kenya, 1893-1960," *The Journal of African History* 13, no. 4, (1972), 117-43.

Wilson, Henry, *Origins of West African Nationalism* (London: Macmillan, 1969).

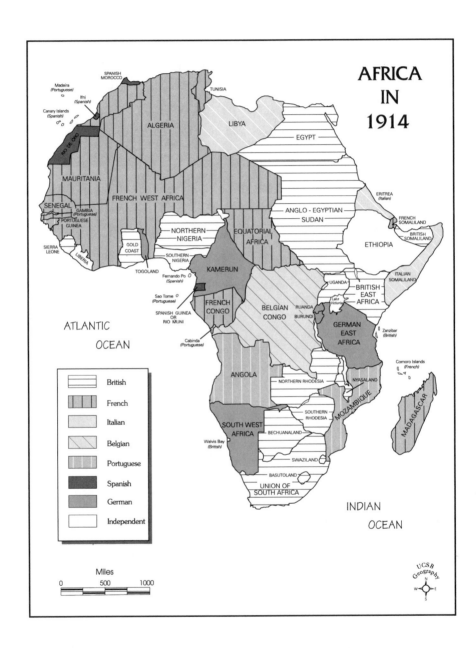

AFRICA
IN
1914

SPANISH MOROCCO
Madeira *(Portuguese)*
Ifni *(Spanish)*
Canary Islands *(Spanish)*
RIO DE ORO
ALGERIA
TUNISIA
LIBYA
EGYPT

MAURITANIA
FRENCH WEST AFRICA
ERITREA *(Italian)*
ANGLO - EGYPTIAN SUDAN
FRENCH SOMALILAND
BRITISH SOMALILAND
SENEGAL
GAMBIA *(Portuguese)*
PORTUGUESE GUINEA
SIERRA LEONE
LIBERIA
GOLD COAST
NORTHERN NIGERIA
SOUTHERN NIGERIA
TOGOLAND
EQUATORIAL AFRICA
ETHIOPIA
ITALIAN SOMALILAND

Fernando Po *(Spanish)*
KAMERUN
Sao Tome *(Portuguese)*
SPANISH GUINEA OR RIO MUNI
FRENCH CONGO
BELGIAN CONGO
RUANDA
BURUNDI
UGANDA
Lake Victoria
BRITISH EAST AFRICA
GERMAN EAST AFRICA
Zanzibar *(British)*

ATLANTIC
OCEAN
Cabinda *(Portuguese)*

ANGOLA
NORTHERN RHODESIA
NYASALAND
Comoro Islands *(French)*
MADAGASCAR

SOUTHERN RHODESIA
MOZAMBIQUE
SOUTH WEST AFRICA
BECHUANALAND
Walvis Bay *(British)*
SWAZILAND
BASUTOLAND
UNION OF SOUTH AFRICA

INDIAN
OCEAN

British
French
Italian
Belgian
Portuguese
Spanish
German
Independent

Miles
0   500   1000

UCSB
Geography
N
W — E
S

PROBLEM VI
EXPLOITATION OR DEVELOPMENT

The occupation of Africa at the end of the nineteenth century by the Europeans resulted in a clash between economic life of the industrial, colonial nations of the West and the agrarian, pastoral, and trading societies of Africa. Economic motives frequently personified as greed were a principal but not the only motivation for the European seizure of the African continent. King Solomon's mines, fertile soil, plentiful labor, and the beauty of the continent excited the adventurers and entrepreneurs of Europe, whether they were men of probity or charlatans, to Africa in search of wealth. To the colonial administrator, Africa measured in pay and pensions beyond that which they could expect in the hum-drum life of their homelands. Their positions usually provided them with a great deal of autonomy, particularly in isolated regions, which they could exploit by sloth, autocracy, or drink, but most recognized a certain sense of responsibility for the "natives" by planning and executing, often under difficult circumstances, schemes to improve the Africans' standard of living. There was a commitment by many colonial administrators, frequently associated with a Christian belief, to spread the civilizing mission. To the cynic any such schemes of development whether it be a road or a dam were regarded as merely generating revenue for the administration of the colony or the metropole rather than an attempt to regenerate the "primitive" economic life of the Africans. To them these good intentions were by design or coincidence advantageous to the enrichment of imperial rule or the administrative bureaucracy and only peripheral to improving the Africans economic life. This "white man's burden" has been described as the exploitation of the resources of Africa, a condemnation of colonial rule with its forced labor, taxation, and land policies designed for the benefit of the rulers rather than the ruled.

The imperialist would argue that what Africans regarded as exploitation of them and their resources, land and labor, were in fact to their benefit, bringing them into the modern world, providing all the infrastructure for which they were paying—schools, hospitals, railways, roads, government buildings and above all education which not only created an intellectual elite but the leaders of nationalism who ironically overwhelmed the imperialists in little more than a century, transferring governance of Africans from Europeans to themselves. To the colonialists and the Africans who benefitted from their education and association with the Europeans, the century of colonial rule was one of enlightenment and development that laid the foundation for the participation of the independent African states in a wider and increasingly interdependent world. Finally the question of exploitation or development in Africa cannot be divorced from the moral issue of right or wrong, good or bad, implied and explicit in the rule of an alien people, but that is a decision which only the individual can make within the privacy of his or her own conscience.

L.H. Gann and Peter Duignan have long been advocates that colonialism in Africa was not all that bad—indeed more constructive than destructive. Rejecting those who regard European colonialism in Africa as exploitive and historically unsound as the Edwardian novelists who wrote of the need to civilize the "barbarians" of Africa, Gann and Duignan argue that colonialism was actually a burden upon Europe to the advantage of Africa. Many scholars have glorified the African past as an egalitarian and agrarian or pastoral society in which equality and freedom were much more prevalent than in the Africa of the imperialists. Gann and Duignan respond that in actuality, precolonial Africa was a continent of social diversity and inequality like any other society in history. European penetration did not bring social degradation, nor did it take away from African tribesmen any form of wealth that they had previously enjoyed. Rather, Europeans provided the infrastructure of twentieth century Africa—roads, ports, and hydroelectric plants—that allowed for the more efficient extraction of Africa's resources for the improvement of European and African alike. They argue that those areas of white settlement—South Africa, the Rhodesias, and Kenya—are the most advanced in education, medical care, and facilities for the Africans which could have only been achieved by European intervention.

D.K. Fieldhouse is more cautious. On the one hand Africa has suffered from a disparate economic position relative to Europe. On the other Europe has played an exploitive role in its relationship with Africa, but European colonialism was not responsible for this predicament. Rather the continent's problems are the result of Africa's failure to possess the tools that would allow it to compete effectively in the world market. Western capital, technology, and markets were necessary to unearth Africa's untapped resources. After Africa's occupation, Europe received only limited economic advantages from Africa that it did not already possess. The independent state of Liberia brings a perspective to the economic benefits or deficits of colonialism. While never formerly occupied by an imperial power, Liberia exhibits conditions of underdevelopment similar to those regions that were under European tutelage. In Liberia and Africa "exploitation" was a consequence of the already underdeveloped economic position of Africa prior to European intervention and would have occurred whether Europe colonized Africa or not.

Michael Crowder regards the economic impact of colonial rule on African society as much less significant than either Gann, Duignan, or Fieldhouse demonstrate. In his examination of West Africa under colonial rule, Crowder acknowledges that in certain areas, European incursions had dramatic consequences. But, this was limited to those regions that the Europeans found specifically important economically—the cocoa of Gold Coast and the coffee and palm regions of Nigeria. For those peasants that produced crops for the European market, the social transformations that emerged as a result of taxation and the construction of railways, ports, and roads were profound. Nevertheless, even in these areas the colonial powers did little to improve growing techniques, and the money the Africans earned from the colonial economy did little to improve their standard of living. For those Africans who lived outside the regions of European economic interest, the changes from colonial rule were limited, while the greatest source of frustration came from that small group of African businessmen who were excluded from a share in the profits being made by Europeans.

Walter Rodney totally disagrees. According to Rodney, European colonialism was the penultimate conclusion to over 400 years of Europe's exploitive interventionism in Africa. Starting with the slave trade and ending with the political and economic degradation of African society under colonialism, Europe must bear the moral and economic shame for African underdevelopment. Rodney defines "underdevelopment" as the creation of economic poverty under exploitive rule, but also it represents the reversal of all previous social and economic development that Africa had achieved prior to the European presence. What Gann and Duignan describe as Europe's beneficial economic intervention in Africa—the production of such primary commodities as coffee, rubber, and cocoa—Rodney regards as the pinnacle of exploitation since such commodities were exchanged for Europe's manufactured goods, the terms of trade always being to the detriment of the Africans. Such endeavors may have speeded up economic growth, but at the cost of economic exploitation and the deterioration of the social values associated with "traditional" African life.

Bade Onimode, in his case study of the financial policy of colonial rule in Nigeria, agrees with Walter Rodney. Rather than creating development, the colonial financial system was designed to transfer Nigeria's economic surplus to Great Britain. The most effective method by which this was accomplished was through loans. Colonial administrators forced Nigeria to take out a number of loans at interest rates well above that of the British capital market. Moreover, since it was demanded that Nigeria maintain a 100 percent external reserve for foreign currency, Nigeria essentially leant money to Great Britain interest free. When such policies as these were combined with the growth of cash crops at the expense of food production for Nigeria's populace, colonialism in Nigeria meant the development of Great Britain at the expense of Nigeria.

A. Adu Boahen takes a much more balanced approach. Colonialism is certainly a watershed in the history of the African continent, and the future of Africa will undoubtedly be bound to the legacies of colonialism. But colonialism's impact on Africa has both debits and credits, for while it exploited and scarred, colonialism also created and developed. According to Boahen there is no easy answer, and one must examine both the positive and the negative aspects of colonial rule, a conclusion which may very well satisfy no one.

The Burden of Empire
L.H. GANN AND PETER DUIGNAN[1]

The history of Africa, the argument goes, is obviously the history of Africans, not that of its conquerors, and against the vast time span of Africa's past, the imperial period is but a brief interlude. Western conquest in Africa, starting in the 1870s and 1880s, therefore formed but an episode. The "new imperialism" arose from the inner needs of an overripe capitalist system which called for protected markets and even more for new opportunities for Western investors' growing stock of capital. Relying on their temporary military superiority, the whites conquered Africa and introduced new techniques of government and economic exploitation. Under the imperial aegis Africa nevertheless remained poor. Its economy, where not deliberately distorted to suit the victor's purse, was stagnant. African living standards were stationary or declined.

Western man, the argument continues, used the peoples of Africa and their natural riches for his own selfish purpose. His activities therefore help to account for Africa's present backwardness. Empires in Africa greatly contributed to the accumulation of Western capital resources and present-day Western prosperity. One continent's loss was another's gain. But Africa, at long last, revolted against the white conqueror and has achieved its political liberation, with the exception of a few remaining bastions of Western rule. This victory forms only one of the many struggles in the emancipation of underprivileged classes and races all over the world. African political independence, however, is meaningless without economic independence. Economic, or even cultural, colonialism continues to threaten emergent Africa, and the battle must continue until the levers of financial, commercial, and industrial power pass into black hands and until the last remnants of Western colonialism are liquidated.

We believe that many of these views are wrong and that others stand in need of modification. We are critical of what seems an unduly philanthropic approach to world affairs, of an outlook which springs from a justifiable attempt at cultural self-

---

[1]Gann, L.H., and Duignan, Peter, *Burden of Empire: An Appraisal of Western Colonialism in Africa South of the Sahara* (New York: Frederick A. Praeger, 1967). Excerpts taken from pages v-vii, 229-31, 234, and 236-52. L.H. Gann and Peter Duignan are both senior fellows at the Hoover Institute. Together they have authored many books on African history and have come to be renowned for their interpretations. Some of their many influential publications include *Africa and the World* (San Francisco: Chandler, 1972), the two volume edited collection of *Colonialism in Africa 1870-1960*, (Cambridge: Cambridge University Press, 1972), *White Settlers in Tropical Africa,* (London: Penguin, 1962), *The Rulers of British Africa* (Stanford: Stanford University Press, 1978), and *The Rulers of German Africa* (Stanford: Stanford University Press, 1977).

criticism—commendable within limits—but which nevertheless is as much a distortion as the old-fashioned flag-waving view of history.

We hold that cultures differ objectively in the number of choices which their members can make and in their ability to develop man's potentialities. Matabele society, for instance, possessed some admirable features. Warriors belonging to the ruling stratum were trained to display courage, fortitude, and self-respect. But the number of effective alternatives open to a Matabele fighting man . . . was very limited. He might earn renown in battle. He could accumulate wealth in the shape of horned beasts. He could marry many wives and, if successful, gather a large following of kinsmen and captives. But these achievements exhausted the limits of his choice. This is hardly surprising; the resources of Matabele society were small. Drought might destroy the crops, disease might strike down the cattle, and war and pestilence might wipe out a whole community. The margin of survival remained small even at the best of times, and there was relatively little room for innovation or experiment. It is our contention that imperial rule helped to bring about major social, economic, and ideological changes which in turn vastly extended social opportunity. The Matabele warriors' modern descendant can make a living as a teacher, a trader, a bus owner, a civil servant, a farmer, or a tailor. This advance was not only relative, but absolute. It was made possible by a great cultural transfusion in which the West took the leading part and which was not limited to technical factors alone.

In the race for development, the Union of South Africa had many advantages. The country contained more people of European ancestry than all the rest of the continent together; the young dominion therefore commanded the greatest reservoir of human skills and capital existing in Africa. South Africa had a developed transport system. There was an efficient public service and, by African standards, a fairly productive agriculture; there were some excellent ports; there was a developed system of trade and finances. South Africa moreover possessed great mineral riches; the country's gold resources kept their value during periods of depression, when the price of commodities such as copper, maize, or peanuts rapidly dropped. Not surprisingly, South Africa attracted more than twice as much money as all the rest of British Africa. From the mid-1920s to the mid-1930s, South Africa thus nearly doubled the value of its gold output. Mining supplied the government with an enormous amount of revenue and also provided funds for development of other industries.

Copper production in the Belgian Congo made similar progress. Development began in a small way during the first decade of the 1900s. Organized mineral production was incompatible with a "robber economy" based on the export of ivory and wild rubber. The original abuses practiced under the Congo Free State administration disappeared, and after 1908 a more orderly Belgian colonial administration enforced a more sensible policy of economic development. In 1910 a southern railway reached Elisabethville, provided the mines with an outlet for their products to Beira in Portuguese East Africa and enabled the Belgian mines to import coal from

Southern Rhodesia and stores and mining equipment from South Africa. World War I stimulated activities, and in 1918 over 20,000 tons of copper were turned out. The slump occasioned a serious setback, but world capitalism surmounted the crisis. In 1936 output reached well over 100,000 tons, and by 1958 copper output amounted to 237,000 tons. The Congo also became the world's greatest producer of industrial diamonds and one of Africa's largest suppliers of hydroelectric power. Mining development went with improved social legislation; the Belgians proved intelligent employers, and after thorough investigation during the late 1920s, the Belgian administration came out with model labor laws for its territory.

South and South Central Africa thus developed into major mineral exporters. Mining dominated the local economy, and minerals from the southern portion of the continent accounted for most of sub-Saharan Africa's foreign trade. In addition, other territories as well made advances. The proclamation of imperial rule over the Gold Coast encouraged an influx of European capital. Foreign entrepreneurs imagined that deep-level mining might also create a second Rand on the West Coast. British and South African investors, however, suffered many disappointments. The gold-bearing strata proved insufficiently rich, and the African people were too numerous and tenacious to give up long-established rights. Gold mining nevertheless made some advance; by 1935 about 41 percent of the country's, exports consisted of minerals, mainly gold and diamonds. Gold mining, together with the need to secure a firm hold over the Ashanti, also caused the government to embark on railway building. The opening of the forest by railways and later by motor roads in turn gave great stimulus to the production of cocoa on the part of individual peasant owners.

All Marxist and many non-Marxist economists believe that a country which makes a living by selling raw materials to foreigners necessarily stays poor. Prosperity supposedly cannot be gained without factories, especially steel mills and machine-tool manufactures. There is, however, no justification for this belief. The doctrine rests in the highly ethnocentric assumption that the chronological pattern of the British industrial revolution must prevail all over the world. . . . The question of priority also needs to be considered. Modern Zambia may well make money in manufactures, but this does not mean that Northern Rhodesia would have done better in the 1920s and 1930s, at an early stage in its development, by directing funds into factories. Thirty years ago the country lacked an economic infrastructure; manufacturing would have been expensive in social as well as economic terms and might merely have led to a dead end.

The next point concerns the general relationship between colonial capitalism and secondary industry. Marxist arguments notwithstanding, a capitalist economy does not necessarily preclude industrial development in colonial or ex-colonial territories. South Africa and Southern Rhodesia both started as mining and farming countries. In time they built up factories and steelworks with money made in primary industries, an economic policy which they shared with countries as diverse as Australia and the United States.

Large-scale mining, moreover, was not confined to purely extractive processes, but also set off development in what might be called the "nonmetallic" sectors of the economy. Here a distinction must be made between simpler forms of enterprise, such as alluvial gold washing, and complex ventures, such as the deep-level excavation of copper, vanadium, or gold. The technology of alluvial gold production is comparatively simple and requires little capital. Many African communities in countries as widely separated as Ghana and the ancient kingdom of Zimbabwe knew the art of washing the yellow metal and worked this natural resource. That does not mean that mining of this type, needing little capital and often stopping short of processing the extracted raw material, did not contribute to economic well-being. In East and Central Africa, indigenous miners sold their gold to Arab or Portuguese traders and thereby acquired more consumer goods than they would otherwise have enjoyed. Large-scale mining, however, made for much greater changes. The mines created markets for more agricultural produce. The flow of investment was not confined just to sinking shafts and driving tunnels. Smelters and electrolytic plants went up in the bush. Mining gave rise to railway development, to road construction, and to the provision of port facilities. Money went into workshops, electric power plants, waterworks, and cement factories. The concentrations of population created a demand for permanent housing. The emergence of townships, large and small, required public utilities and public services. Development in turn attracted a multitude of people eager to meet the growing demand for building material, food, fuel, clothing, and all kinds of services. Banks and trading stores opened their doors. White and black farmers alike found new opportunities for selling their grain and cattle, and "the basis was thus laid for a multiplier-accelerator process of economic growth."

[Some scholars] express indignation over the figures devoted to African wages. [They] point out that only £2 million in money and rations went to Africans working on the mines, out of a gross value of output amounting to £36,742,000. The mineowners, however, also had a case. The mines . . . paid £3,600,000 into the public coffers. The government spent some of this on projects benefiting Africans on the Copper Belt, a contribution to African living standards ignored by the conventional Marxist argument. Wages for unskilled men were small because the supply of such labor was large and its competence was low. But African copper miners went to work because they wanted to; in Northern Rhodesia there was no compulsory labor of the type practiced under the fully collectivist system that then prevailed in the Soviet Union. The Central African mines, with their high level of technology and their paternalistic outlook, also eschewed the kind of underground labor on the part of women and children that was utilized during the early industrial revolution in Great Britain. The African proletariat in some ways, therefore, paid a lower price for incipient industrialization than did the British workers in the eighteenth century. African mine workers on the Copper Belt enjoyed a higher standard of living than they did in their native villages; they received better housing and food than at home, so much so that their average physical well-being consistently improved in employment.

For many decades mining dominated the cash economy of sub-Saharan Africa. From the first decade of the 1900s, however, agricultural exports began to rise sharply, and agriculture rapidly increased in relative importance. Much of this development centered on South Africa, by far the most advanced country and the most important pioneer on the African continent. Yet economic growth in many other parts of Africa also went forward at a rapid pace. There is, accordingly, no justification at all for the view, fashionable among critics of the colonial system in the 1920s and 1930s, which saw Africa as nothing but a stagnant pool, whose people, under the imperial aegis, either stood still or were retrogressing. Africa's agricultural progress was all the more surprising in view of the many natural obstacles faced by cultivators black and white alike. Many parts of Africa suffer from alternating cycles of drought, followed by heavy tropical downpours which leach the soils. Erosion forms an everpresent threat to inexpert farmers. The peoples of Africa faced all kinds of human, plant, and animal diseases peculiar to tropical areas. Development was desperately hampered until Western research found means of coping with afflictions such as malaria, sleeping sickness, and parasites attacking cattle. The lack of transportation facilities further impeded development. Most parts of Africa lacked good riverine communications; because of the great distances, inland producers in the past could rarely market their crops. The imperial impact vastly changed this situation. The period from 1880 to 1920 was the great age of railway building in Africa. By the end of the 1930s about 32,000 miles of railroad track were in operation, about two-thirds of which served South Africa, the Rhodesias, the Congo, and the Portuguese colonies.

The steam locomotive helped bring about a social revolution. An ordinary freight train used nowadays in Africa will do the work of 15,000 to 20,000 carriers for one-fifth to one-tenth the cost. The steam engine thus relieved the sweating African porter from his age old labors; for the first time in the continent's history farmers could produce economic crops away from coastal and river ports. Africa's scarce manpower could at last be used in pursuits more profitable to the economy than head porterage. In the 1920s and 1930s motortrucks and bicycles also began to make their appearance in the bush. The new means of locomotion might in some ways be called "markets on tires," providing backward farmers with new incentives for turning out more and better crops.

Agricultural development in twentieth-century Africa stood, so to speak, on three legs. There was cultivation by African peasants; there was farming by European settlers; there were some large-scale plantations run by big concessionary companies. Of all these, African enterprise was by far the most important, but it was also the form of enterprise that varied most extensively in methods, technical skill, and output. African peasants faced many obstacles. They had to contend not only with the difficulties of nature, but also with lack of physical and social capital. Throughout most of Africa their work continued to depend on hoes and axes and on the unaided power of the human muscle. In most parts of Africa tribesmen lacked incentives for intensive cultivation. Land was plentiful; whenever cultivators had exhausted the fertility of their gardens, they moved on, allowing nature to restore the fertility of the soil. As long as the supply of land seemed unlimited and storage facilities and markets few or nonexistent, African cultivators would only have wasted time and effort by producing more specialized crops. Where conditions became favorable, however, African farmers did make use of new opportunities and in some areas made astonishing progress.

One of the best-known success stories concerns the development of cocoa in the Gold Coast (now Ghana). The Gold Coast had an ancient tradition of overseas trade. The commerce in palm oil and other commodities had created a certain amount of capital. Long-standing links with the Western world and improved railway and port facilities created under British aegis put bush farmers in touch with metropolitan customers. Contacts with other countries also introduced new cultivable plants, including the cacao tree. The colony's agricultural department provided valuable help [for cocoa production], and by 1935-1936 output amounted to 285,351 tons, that is, nearly half the world's supply. Cocoa enabled the Gold Coast to pay for substantial imports of cement, machinery, flour, and so forth, commodities unknown to the country in the 1890s. Carriers and canoes gradually gave way to steam locomotives, trucks, and bicycles, and conditions of life underwent a major transformation.

African society at the same time experienced a new kind of social differentiation. The old pattern of a small family farm, run entirely by the labor of the peasant's own kinsfolk, gradually disintegrated. The majority of growers came to rely on hired labor; some accumulated great wealth, but others fell into poverty. West Africa as a whole now had to face the problem of migrant labor, with the additional disadvantage that small proprietors could not afford welfare facilities remotely comparable to those provided by big European-owned mining companies. The growers also believed that foreign buyers combined to keep down cocoa prices. In 1937 most of the big European firms entered into an agreement to restrict competition and to prevent local prices from rising above the world market level. The African growers, to their good fortune, were not then tied down by any official distribution monopoly, and they retaliated by refusing to sell to the buyers' combine. Some European firms, moreover, remained aloof from the restriction scheme, and in the end the two parties to the dispute concluded a truce which once again allowed cocoa to be sold abroad. There were many other difficulties, but by and large African agricultural enterprise made considerable progress, especially on the West Coast; the black farmer became what he had never been before in the history of his continent—a factor of some importance in the world economy.

In relation to the enormous size of the African landmass, white agricultural enterprise remained restricted in extent, being confined to a few relatively limited areas. . . . [In its early days] South Africa never experienced any large-scale white immigration, and economic progress remained relatively slow. Cape farmers turned out limited quantities of grain, fruit, vegetables, wine, and livestock for local consumption and for ships plying the Indian trade. But the settlers who pushed inland had to rely largely on grazing of a simple type, requiring many acres. Territorial expansion in most parts of South Africa thus owed its primary impetus to cattlemen rather than to capitalists with land as the prize of victory. Technically backward as the settlers might have been, their economic and military potential nevertheless remained far superior to that of the Bantu. The black tribesmen thus lost control over most of the available land, and South Africa became the only region on the continent where the overwhelmingly greater part of the available acreage passed into white ownership.

After about the middle of the nineteenth century, moreover, European farmers at the Cape strengthened their economic potential and found a modest kind of prosperity. Growing ports and expanding mining compounds furnished farmers with additional markets. Engineers put up roads, bridges, railways, and dockyards. The growth of shipping and banking helped to put the country in touch with new customers overseas. Some farmers began to work out more intensive methods, and various technological improvements made their appearance in the countryside. Landowners experimented with new products such as mohair and ostrich feathers, while South African Merino wool acquired a recognized place on the world markets. In the twentieth century, technological change acquired increasing momentum. Agricultural mechanization and progress in agricultural processing industries such as fruit canning, tobacco manufacture, and meat refrigeration vastly added to the country's wealth. Farmers developed better methods of plant selection, stockbreeding, and soil management. Veterinary surgeons learned how to cope with various kinds of animal diseases. Despite large remaining islands of backwardness, South Africa developed into the most skilled and most versatile of Africa's agricultural exporters.

[Another] instrument of progress was company enterprise. Big business preferred to put its resources into mines and railways and, in South Africa, into factories. There were, however, some notable exceptions. Unilever in the Congo and the Cameroons Development Corporation in West Africa promoted extensive agricultural enterprises. Liberia also owed much of its development to similar foreign initiative. In 1926 the Finance Corporation, a Firestone subsidiary, concluded an agreement with the Liberian government and advanced money to the small, financially unstable republic. . . . The Liberians secured sufficient cash to satisfy some of their creditors and attained the unusual distinction of being one of the few nations to repay their war debts to the United States in full. Firestone received extensive land and tax concessions and in turn initiated the world's largest rubber undertaking. Furthermore, the company acquired a good reputation as an employer. It paid its workmen much more adequately than the government and other local entrepreneurs and also subsidized wages by bonuses for increased output and by selling low-priced food to its employees. Plantation labourers could work their own plots in spare-time hours; debt peonage was strictly avoided. The company put up hospitals, built roads, and established a public radio service and other undertakings. Firestone had sufficient perception to encourage independent rubber production in Liberia, proving thereby that company enterprise need not necessarily conflict with private initiative. The company provided free rubber seeds to independent growers, as well as high-yielding clones, or buds, and trained instructors to advise on methods.

In summary, the inter-war period saw tremendous economic growth in Africa. There is, accordingly, no justification for the view of this period of African history as one of imperial neglect in contrast with Communist progress. True enough, development was uneven. Large areas of Africa were little affected by change; only South Africa, the oldest white-settled area on the continent, managed to build up substantial industries, while the continent as a whole remained a primary producer which devoted its resources to the export of minerals and crops. Africa did, however, see vast additions to its real resources in the shape of railway lines, roads, mines, plantations, hydroelectric plants, and other assets. These economic changes came about without large-scale liquidations and without forced labor of the Stalinist variety. Imperial rule indeed shielded sub-Saharan Africa from other foreign pressures and prevented internecine struggles; colonial Africa bore but a minor military burden; it operated with a relatively small and inexpensive state machinery, so that comparatively few resources were diverted into civil service and defense expenditure (the Gold Coast had fewer than 150 civil servants in the 1930s).

The new enterprise, by the very speed of its impact, created a host of social tensions. The clash of black peasant agriculture, white farming, and company ventures, for instance, might engender sharp competition for labor and natural resources. Competition, on the other hand, might also imply cooperation. Firestone's activities to a certain degree assisted indigenous Liberian rubber producers; white Rhodesian tobacco farmers bought native-grown maize. The various new enterprises in some ways complemented one another. Critics of existing colonial practices often erred, therefore, when they advocated reforms in terms of a rigid either-or choice and contrasted black with white farming or primary with secondary industries as mutually exclusive categories.

Contact with the white man, whether as merchant, mineowner, farmer, or manufacturer also brought about economic changes of a more intangible kind. Europeans taught African villagers the art of storing ideas. In the past, tradition had depended on memory and word of mouth; the old knew most and the young least. Now missionaries and others showed how words might be committed to paper and permanently preserved. Not only were labor migrants enabled to communicate with their fellow villagers back home by means of inky marks on paper, but also they were enabled to read books and newspapers. Of equal significance was the creation of a vernacular literature which began, as in Europe, with translations of the Scriptures and the compilation of hymnbooks in indigenous languages. Cash-books and catechisms both demand literacy of their users, and these skills in turn helped to speed up economic transformation.

In addition, economic change spread new ways of measuring time and space. The Africans, of course, could reckon time quite adequately for their purposes; they divided the year into months and seasons, or they used the growth cycle of a crop, with the day further subdivided by the sun's position or what people would normally be doing at that hour. But in villages there were neither printed calendars nor mechanical clocks. Time was an everlasting stream. The white man's beliefs, however, were very different. Time to the European was something that could be minutely subdivided, a commodity for sale. . . . The new space-time concept slowly influenced African thought in general and in turn contributed to the great economic transformation that was beginning to change the face of Africa.

The Myth of
Economic Exploitation
D.K. FIELDHOUSE[2]

The most commonly held and dangerous myth connected with the modern empires is that they were great machines deliberately constructed by Europe to exploit dependent peoples by extracting economic and fiscal profit from them. Its corollary is that the new states had a moral claim to be compensated for losses suffered in the past by being helped to become advanced industrial economies. None denied that it was desirable for wealthy industrial states to help those with primitive economies, but to base their claim to assistance on the premise that they were exploited in the past was wrong. The myth of imperial profit making is false.

To start with, the modern empires were not artificially constructed economic machines. The second expansion of Europe was a complex historical process in which political, social and emotional forces in Europe and on the periphery were more influential than calculated imperialism. Individual colonies might serve an economic purpose; collectively no empire had any definable function, economic or otherwise. Empires represented only a particular phase in the ever changing relationship of Europe with the rest of the world, analogies with industrial systems or investment in real estate were simply misleading.

Yet, though the colonial empires were undoubtedly functionless in origin, this is not to say that they did not later provide an economic return, a "profit," to their owners. Certainly many colonial enthusiasts in Europe alleged that they could and did. Were they right?

To answer this question requires a careful analysis of its meaning. It is, in fact, highly theoretical. An industrial company exists to produce profits, colonies were human societies belonging to a different order of things. It is really as meaningless to ask whether a colony such as Nigeria was "profitable" to Britain as to ask whether Wales or England was. In each case some form of "advantage" was obvious. But this was not necessarily economic; and if it was it cannot necessarily be called

[2]Fieldhouse, D.K., *The Colonial Empires: A Comparative Survey from the Eighteenth Century* (New York: Delacorte Press, 1967). Excerpts taken from pages 380-7 and 389-94. D.K. Fieldhouse received his M.A. and D.Litt. from Oxford University and is the Vere Harmsworth Professor of Imperial and Naval History and fellow of Jesus College, Cambridge University. He is recognized as a leading scholar on empire and colonialism. He is author of Colonialism, 1870-1945 (New York: St. Martin's Press, 1981), *Economics and Empire, 1830-1914* (Ithaca, NY: Cornell University Press, 1973), and *The Theory of Capitalist Imperialism* (New York: Barnes and Noble, 1967).

"profit" and need not result from "exploitation." In short, such concepts reflect a perverted form of thinking about colonies which derived from the "mercantile" theories of the first empires. The fact that they were commonly held does not make them true. The task of the historian is to analyze the various forms of "profit" Europe may have gained from her colonies; to compare these with countervailing disadvantages; and to decide whether on balance empire gave economic advantages which Europe would not otherwise have obtained.

The crux of the matter is to define what empire meant in economic terms. A colony differed from an independent state only in that it was governed by an alien power, colonial status was primarily a political phenomenon. This immediately limits the field of inquiry, for it excludes all those influences exerted by Europe which fell short of full political control: "economic imperialism" and "informal empire," for example. If empire generated "profit" this must be directly attributable to alien rule. The question can therefore be redefined: what economic advantages did Europe extract from her colonies which she could not have gained from other countries, however similar in other ways?

There were at least six obvious ways in which this might be done. The first was simply to loot an occupied country of its treasures. This was very rare in the modern empires. Few new colonies possessed hoarded wealth on the scale of Mexico, Peru or India in the past: there was little that could profitably be seized from African or Polynesian chiefs. Moreover, although "pacifying" armies were often barbarous in their methods, they were normally under direct metropolitan control, and conquest was quickly followed by civilized methods of government. The rape of Bengal in the 1760s was not repeated after 1815.

A more sophisticated way of extracting profit before 1815 was to transfer colonial revenues to the metropolitan treasury. This also became very rare. From 1831 to 1877 the Dutch transferred Indonesian surpluses through the "Culture System"; the British East India Company and other chartered companies sometimes paid dividends out of colonial taxation; but no normal colonial government ever did so. Some demanded contributions to defence costs; the French confused things by integrating the accounts of some colonies with their own. But most colonies were left to use their own revenues and were more likely to receive subsidies than to be robbed of surpluses.

A third possible source of imperial advantage was to transfer money or goods from colony to metropolis as interest on loans, payment for services rendered, the pensions and savings of colonial officials and the profits made by business firms. Much has been made of this "drain," particularly by Indian historians; but the Indian case is misleading. The greater part—interest charges, profits of alien enterprises, etc.—would have been equally due from independent states which borrowed in the British capital market or in which British firms operated. The net "drain" was therefore the cost of services, such as the Indian army, which Britain controlled and which India might not otherwise have chosen to pay for, and the transferred salaries of alien officials. The damage to India was not the absolute cost but the loss of currency and international exchange by a country short of both.

A fourth possible form of exploitation was the imposition of "unfair" terms of trade on a colony. This had been the basic device of the "mercantile" empires, and, in its pre-nineteenth century form, may well have provided artificially high profit levels for metropolitan merchants and producers. But no modern empire operated a comparable system of monopoly. By the 1860s the old controls had been dismantled. Although tariff preferences, shipping subsidies, navigation acts and import quotas were soon disinterred, no country ever entirely closed colonial ports to foreign competition. Even the proportion of colonial trade which fell to the parent states was unimpressive. Britain's share of her empire's trade fell from an average of 49 per cent in the decade after 1854 to 36 per cent in 1929-33, thereafter, even revived protection only increased it slightly. France kept a larger share, always more than half, of the trade of her colonies; even so, the proportion declined with time. Most other empires had a similar experience, only the United States and Russia, which entirely enclosed their colonies within domestic tariff systems, really had a commercial monopoly; and this probably benefitted the dependencies as much as the metropolis. Although modern protectionism harmed the interests of colonial subjects as much as it did metropolitan consumers, it was at least reasonably impartial and the losses of colonial consumers were compensated by guaranteed and preferential markets in Europe. It is therefore unlikely that "neo-mercantilism" produced substantial net "profits" for metropolitan countries.

By a curious paradox, however, it has been argued that during their era of free trade the British "exploited" colonies by making it impossible for them to protect their own industries against her exports, so holding back their industrial progress. This did not apply to the settlement colonies, which were allowed their own protectionist policies from 1859, but may have been true of others. India was again the test case, since she was the only British dependency in the nineteenth century with the evident capacity to develop large-scale mechanized industry. There is no doubt that free trade had serious consequences for her. In the early nineteenth century free import of British cottons destroyed Indian hand-loom weaving on a commercial scale, thereafter the British ban on protective tariffs held back mechanized cotton production and kept the market open for Lancashire. Indian cottons were not protected until about 1926, and textile imports from Britain then dropped significantly. India consumed £40,729,000 out of total British manufactured textile exports of £195,805,000 in 1913, but only £11,373,000 in 1934. To some extent enforced free trade may have had similar effects on other nascent Indian industries and on the economic growth of other British dependencies.

Yet it is impossible to be certain that these disadvantages were specifically the result of British imperial authority, for other and totally independent states were also forced, during the nineteenth century, to reduce or abolish import duties in the interests of British exports. China, for example, was restricted by treaty after 1842 to a maximum tariff of 5 percent on all imports. An "open door" might, in fact, have been imposed on any weak state by European powers, an independent India might have been as unable as China was to protect her own industries against foreign demands for freedom of access. Thus the "open door" was a typical product of Europe's general preponderance. Formal empire was one way of imposing it, but by no means the only way; and the benefits resulting from free commercial access to non-European states cannot be regarded as an exclusively imperial "profit."

The most commonly alleged form of imperial profiteering was to "exploit" the natural endowments of dependencies—oil, minerals, natural rubber, ivory, etc. If these were extracted without giving compensating advantages, an ex-colony might hypothetically find itself robbed of assets which might otherwise have financed the creation of a modern industrial economy. . . . Examples of "exploitation" on this scale are, however, difficult to find. Extractive industries were never entirely insulated from their environment. All had to use local labor. They paid wages lower than they paid to Europeans but vastly higher than those normal in subsistence economies. All had to build modern communications and other amenities which benefitted the colony as a whole. Some part of company profits were always spent locally, lubricating the colonial economy. Most overseas companies had to pay taxes to the colonial government. Thus no extractive industry failed to provide some advantages to the dependency in which it operated. The question is whether these were enough: whether an independent state could have gained more.

The question was pragmatic rather than moral. The value of natural endowments was for the most part created by demand elsewhere, in most cases only alien capital and skills could give them commercial value. What tax was due to the indigenous owners of the soil? The only useful yardstick was what happened in comparable independent countries; and evidence provided by states such as Persia and the Latin American republics suggests that this would have been small simply because their bargaining power also was small. Independence enabled ex-colonies to impose stricter terms on foreign companies, but these were matched by the higher demands also made by previously independent states after 1945. If neither was able to undertake such complex economic operations on its own account, its demands were limited by the fact that Europeans might cease to operate altogether.

It is impossible, therefore, to measure the "profit" Europe gained from "exploiting" the natural resources of her dependencies because they were formal colonies. By mid-twentieth-century standards Europeans showed a cavalier disregard for the interests of other societies, taking what was profitable and putting back only what was necessary. Yet this had little to do with political empire and was not limited to it. One-sided use of natural resources reflected an imbalance of power between the west and the nonindustrialized areas of the world; and while this lasted no non-European society had sufficient bargaining power to impose fully equitable terms.

The last and most sophisticated way in which empires have been alleged to give economic profit was through the higher return Europeans could obtain by investing capital in colonies than they could get at home. . . . This theory was based on the Marxist principle of "surplus value," and turned on the greater profitability of using capital in tropical lands where labor was cheaper than in industrialized Europe.

Lenin, for example, argued in 1916 that the growth of industrial monopoly and "finance-capitalism" in western states created an enormous "superabundance of capital." This could not profitably be invested at home without raising wage levels, and therefore reducing profits, simply because the labor supply could not be expanded. The rest of the world lacked capital but had ample labor and raw materials. European capital could generate a higher surplus value there than at home, and this enabled metropolitan capital to go on accumulating. If it could not go abroad, capital would stagnate and capitalism would crack. Lenin predicted that in course of time the nonindustrial world would be entirely absorbed by European "imperialists" (finance-capitalists), and that this would lead to wars for imperial redivision which would destroy capitalist society and usher in the socialist revolution.

Shorn of its ideological trimmings, Lenin's theory simply asserted that the combination of cheap labor, political power to make it work at subsistence wages, and commercial monopoly to exclude foreign rivals, generated excess profits for European empires. The desire for these advantages led to tropical colonization. Was he right?

He was wrong on one point at least, for, as has already been seen, it is impossible to explain the expansion of European empires after 1815 in terms of economic need: there simply was no correlation between the time-scale of European "finance-capitalism" and imperial expansion, nor between colonies and areas of greatest investment.

The advantages which Lenin thought European capital engaged in the colonies received from imperial political power were in fact of little significance. Labor was certainly cheap by European standards: otherwise many of these enterprises would have been unprofitable. But low wages were not created by political power, they reflected the social environment of a subsistence economy. In the period before about 1906 many colonial governments provided forced or semi-forced labor; but this was also a period of generally low company profits. Thereafter colonial governments tended to impose restrictions on labor contracts and conditions of work, both tending to raise labor costs. Europeans could have "exploited" native labor more effectively if they had not been policed by imperial administrations sensitive to humanitarian public opinion at home, and they often did so in independent Latin America and the Middle East. Nor did empire provide a degree of commercial monopoly sufficient to enable capitalists to sell at monopolistic prices at home or in the colonies. European investors showed no marked preference for their own colonies, and often got higher returns by operating in foreign empires. Conversely, the really artificial prices were those set by agreement between companies of different nationalities, especially the oil companies, which transcended imperial systems. Thus, while colonial governments often provided a convenient framework of political security within which private companies could work satisfactorily, formal empire was in no sense necessary for profitable European activity overseas.

Second, the relative profitability of investment in Europe and in tropical dependencies was determined by many complex factors and varied immensely from time to time. Changing economic and political conditions within Europe sometimes encouraged investment at home, sometimes overseas. Another important influence was the relative demand for the products of the advanced economies and those of primary producing countries in which a large proportion of "colonial" investment was made. When the terms of trade favored primary producers, investment in tropical colonies was obviously more profitable than when the terms favored manufacturing states. During the half century before 1914 European demand for minerals, tropical vegetable oils, and food increased considerably, and the terms of trade normally favored primary producers. This enabled the more fortunate European companies producing such goods to make spectacular profits. Between 1914 and 1939, however, the terms of trade normally favored industrial producers, with the result that the relative advantage of investing in primary-producing countries was less. After 1939 the war and postwar demand for primary products again favored the overseas investor, though by the later 1950s his advantage was declining. Such trends cannot confidently be translated into statistics, but some indication of their importance can be gained from estimates of the relative percentage rate of profit gained from investment in industrial concerns operating in Britain and in British companies operating overseas between 1953 and 1961. In 1953 British industrialists gave an average net profit of 12.5 percent on their capital (ordinary capital plus capital and revenue reserves), as against 21.5 percent from overseas companies. In 1961 British industrials were yielding 12.4 percent but overseas companies only 13.7 percent. In the same years the terms of trade, taking 1937-8 as 100, had moved in Britain's favor from 119 to 103.

Such figures are far too limited to prove anything; but they do suggest, in conjunction with other evidence, that the profitability of investment in primary-producing non-European economies, many of which were colonies, depended more on international economic factors than on the special advantages which Lenin thought colonies provided for their masters. By comparison the political status of nonindustrialized countries was of little importance, and empire could not of itself generate super profit for European capital.

If Europe benefitted economically from other parts of the world by "exploiting" them, it was because of her immense military and economic preponderance. Empire in the formal sense was merely one form in which this was expressed, and had no colonial empires been created in the nineteenth century Europe would still have taken whatever economic assets she needed and dictated the terms on which she did so.

In fact, no meaningful balance sheet can be constructed, even in economic terms. One or two small or short-lived empires almost certainly cost their owners more than they repaid. Certainly the German and Italian empires did so, because their colonies lacked natural resources, and because they were in any case destroyed before high initial expenditure could be written off against long-term advantages. All other empires were too complex for such definite verdicts to be made. Most colonies were "unprofitable" during the period of initial conquest and while later internal rebellions lasted. But there were few such expenses between about 1920 and 1939; and apart from obvious metropolitan expenditure (grants-in-aid, payment for services in particular colonies, etc.) the cost of colonies depends on what proportion of total imperial expenditure (on defence, for example) is debited to them. Hence no one can determine whether the accounts of empire ultimately closed with a favorable cash balance.

This is unimportant, for the value of the colonial empires was not to be measured in money. Colonies were seldom deliberately acquired to produce wealth, and they were retained irrespective of their "profitability." Empire in the modern period was the product of European power: its reward was power or the sense of power. The end of empire did not mean economic loss to the onetime imperial states, on the contrary, it meant that the economic advantage of operating in other parts of the world was no longer offset by the cost and inconvenience of political responsibilities. Only the minority of private investors and others, whose assets or business concerns were hampered, destroyed, or taken over without proper compensation by the new states, actually lost through decolonization. The West retained its economic preponderance: some even held that the margin of wealth between advanced and "developing" countries widened as empire ended. If Europe in fact derived her wealth from her colonies, their loss made remarkably little difference to her.

Yet the West undoubtedly suffered from the end of empire, for Europe and America lost some part of their political power and self-assurance. The world no longer consisted of colonies unable to complicate international politics, the United Nations provided a forum in which the new states could challenge overwhelming power by appealing to alleged moral standards and the principle of one state one vote. The powers were no longer free to use their military power to support their interests, the Suez crisis of 1956-7 marked the end of "informal empire" in its nineteenth-century form. The world was no longer ringed by the western bases and colonial armies which had enabled it to impose its will on all continents. Europeans had lost the freedom of movement and economic activity which empire had given them. They were now dependent on a multiplicity of small and often chauvinistic states who needed western enterprise but also resented it and complicated its operations. But above all the end of empire deprived the West of status. The countries of Europe were no poorer than they had been before, but they were infinitely smaller. They had been the centers of vast empires, now they were petty states preoccupied with parochial problems. Dominion had gone and with it the grandeur which was one of its main rewards.

The Economic Impact of Colonial Rule in West Africa

MICHAEL CROWDER[3]

The economic impact of colonial rule on African society was much less profound than colonial administrators liked to think. The period 1919-39 was one of *immobilisme* in which what little change there was did not stand comparison with what was taking place in the outside world. The railway systems had for the most part been completed by 1918—only the introduction of the motor vehicle was a significant factor for change in this period. The African found himself the simple producer of raw materials for which Lebanese were the agents of sale and European companies the exporters. Conversely these same companies imported the goods which the African bought, mainly at the shops or through the agencies of Lebanese traders, with the money he earned from the sale of his crop. Only in rare cases did the African survive as an importer, almost never as an exporter, and in neither role was he significant after 1920. Except in the cocoa-producing areas of the Gold Coast and Nigeria, the African was squeezed out of his precolonial role of middleman between peasant producer and expatriate exporter by the Lebanese. This meant that the African's role in the colonial economy became almost exclusively that of petty trader and primary producer of cash crops on his own account or as labourer on the farms of others, African or European, in the case of the few plantations that existed in French West Africa. A small number were employed in mining industries in Ashanti, Jos, and Enugu on the railways and as casual labourers in the urban centers. The income they derived from the colonial economy was for the most part so low that it brought about no significant change in their standard of living. Only cocoa and coffee fetched high enough prices to affect the traditional socioeconomic structure of the peoples producing it. The other cash crops, most of which had, like palm products, groundnuts and cotton, been exported before the imposition of colonial rule fetched such low prices that the peasant produced just enough to pay taxes and satisfy his immediate needs for imported cloths, utensils and foodstuffs like sugar. The narrow range of goods in the Lebanese stores was not substantially

[3]Crowder, Michael, *West Africa under Colonial Rule* (Evanston: Northwestern University Press, 1968). Excerpts taken from pages 345-53. Michael Crowder was a former professor of history at the University of Ibadan and fellow at the Commonwealth Institute. He†is recognized as having been one of the leading historians of West Africa. He is author of *The Story of Nigeria* (London: Faber and Faber, 1978), *West African Resistance* (London: Hutchinson, 1978), *Senegal* (London: Oxford University Press, 1962), and *Revolt in Bussa* (London: Faber and Faber, 1973).

different from those which the African middleman used as the basis of barter in pre-colonial times.

For the African peasant the growing of cash crops during the colonial period was, except in the cocoa- and coffee-producing areas, primarily geared to paying taxes and supplementing the subsistence economy with imported luxuries. If the price for cash crops was low, his marginal propensity to produce cash crops for sale over and above those necessary for the purposes of paying taxes fell also. For the peasant could provide most of his basic needs from internal sources. Even when the price for crops was high, immense effort was required in labor terms to produce larger quantities. This problem was solved, partially, by the importation of labor from other areas. This migratory labor was available, as we have seen, because of taxes imposed on peoples inhabiting areas on which no cash crops would grow. In certain areas the peasant would involve himself in commitments based on the previous year's price for a crop, and be forced to produce greater quantities of his cash crop in order to meet them if it fell. Where immigrant labor was scarce, he would have to transfer labor from the subsistence crops to the cash crops. In parts of Senegambia this situation, aggravated by the long-standing dependence on imported goods, reached the point where peasants were importing rice which they could grow themselves, and going without food for nearly two months a year, because they had neglected the subsistence economy in favor of the cash crops. Counteracting the propensity of the peasant to abandon cultivation of the cash crop in favor of subsistence crops, was his tendency to incur debts to the Lebanese traders, who were quite aware that indebtedness was one of the only ways over and above taxation which could force him to produce for a low price. The French, however, resorted to the introduction of compulsory production of crops in areas where the peasant would otherwise have refused to grow them because of the low price. Thus, anxious to be independent of cotton supplies from outside the French empire, the administration in French West Africa forced the peasant to produce it under threat of imprisonment if the quality was not good enough or the quantity insufficient. The ease with which people moved out of the cash economy into a purely subsistence economy also related to the dependence their society had built up on imported goods. In Senegal, where by the time of the Depression many families had been involved in the export of groundnuts to Europe for over seventy years, imported cloths, utensils and rice had become part of their way of life. But even they, despite predictions of famine and political upheaval, were able to revert to subsistence production in 1932. Millet, manioc and taro were substituted for imported rice. Home-grown tobacco replaced imported varieties. Honey was gathered in place of sugar, and local soap and perfumes were produced again; thus stimulating the subsistence economy.

The extent of the involvement of the peasant in the cash crop economy was limited by the extent of the colonial transportation system. Vast areas, such as Bornu in Nigeria, remained largely untouched by it because no railway passed through them, and until after the Second World War long-distance road haulage of the low-priced cash crops did not pay. Even the term cash applied to these crops is inappropriate, for in many areas the exchange of "cash" crop for imported goods was largely by barter. It was the migrant labourer rather than the peasant farmer who became the pioneer of currency as a means of exchange.

Just how little the bulk of the people were affected by the European-dominated import-export economy is brought out by Governor Clifford's report to the Nigerian Council in 1923:

> The vast majority of the indigenous population are still independent of the outside world for all their essential supplies. They can and do spin their own thread, weave their own garments, provide their own foodstuffs, and even, when the necessity arises, forge their own tools, and make their own pottery. For them imports from Europe are still, in the main, luxuries with which, if needs must, they can wholly dispense; and the sole exception to this in pre-war days, was imported spirits of European manufacture.

And for these latter they had "illicit" substitutes. Twenty years later, with regard to the whole of British West Africa, the Leverhulme Trust Commission reported that "all Africans are, to a very large extent, and very many of them wholly, outside the system of money economy which dominates the economic life of Europe and the rest of the world." The African, encouraged in times of good prices to produce cash crops, and ignorant of the fluidity of prices on the world commodity markets, was easily convinced that he was being robbed and deceived by the whites if they offered him a low price, and refused to continue production unless under pressure of taxation, indebtedness or force.

The African Peasant and New Crops

The colonial regime did little to improve the growing techniques of low-value export crops: they remained the same as in precolonial times. For most peasants the European agricultural officers were an irrelevance. There was of course no attempt to improve the methods of production of subsistence crops, as the Germans had done in Togo. Thus the peasant, whether farming for himself or working on the farms of others, did not gain any new knowledge of agricultural techniques under colonial rule. Even the labourer in European plantations used for the most part his traditional instruments, and stayed there as short a time as possible, learning nothing about improvement. Rather the peasant was allowed to exhaust the land. In Senegal, for instance, large areas, like the Baol, have been reduced to semi-desert by the cultivation of groundnuts. As early as 1925 certain areas of Senegal like Thies and Diourbel were exhausted and the peasants had to move eastwards, following the railway to earn enough money to pay taxes and buy imported goods.

The colonial administration did nothing to prevent situations such as that in Gambia where rice that could have been grown by the peasant more cheaply was imported, and to pay for it he devoted more of his energies in the cultivation of groundnuts. Indeed it favored the colonial economic system, for French rice exporters in Indochina could find a market in Senegal. Only when Indochina became independent of France did France make efforts to develop Senegal's own rice potential. Similarly, Cardinall, commenting on the imports of foodstuffs in Gold Coast in 1930, noted that the country could have produced itself half "the fresh fish, rice, maize and other meal, beans, salted and fresh meat, edible oils, spices and fresh vegetables (imported), or in other words would have saved 200,000 pounds."

The only crops that did radically alter the standard of living of their producers were cocoa and coffee in the Gold Coast, Ivory Coast and Western Nigeria. For both these crops the price was consistently sufficiently high for the farmer safely to depend on imported goods in substitution for domestically produced goods. Under the stimulus of a crop whose value increased in the Gold Coast from £4,764,067 in 1921 to £11,229,000 in 1928 on the eve of the Depression, great tracts of new land were opened to cocoa cultivation by immigrant "rural capitalists" who used the profits from their first crops to purchase further farm land. It has often been thought that the revolutionary aspect of the Gold Coast cocoa industry was the fact that Africans sold land which was supposed to have been communally owned. But . . . the sale of land had been common in some areas for fifty years or so before the introduction of cocoa into the Akwapim and Akim-Abuakwa area. What was an innovation was not the idea of sale of land itself but the intensity of its application.

In Ivory Coast the Abe found no difficulty in selling land, but the Agni strongly resisted it. The cocoa boom in the Gold Coast and later in the Ivory Coast stimulated migrations of farmers into new lands. Those who could not buy land, worked for the owners. In the case of the Gold Coast two systems of tenant-farmer relation have been [documented.] The first was that of *abusa,* whereby the labourer was paid one third of the cocoa he plucked for his employing farmer, the second that of *nto-tokano,* whereby the labourer was paid a fixed sum per load for the cocoa he plucked for his employing farmer.

The cocoa industry in Ghana created a rich class of farmers who were able to undertake social innovations at their own initiative, and who showed that the African peasant, if prices were good, did not have to be forced into production. . . . The same was true of the Ivory Coast cocoa industry which grew from a mere 1,000 tons in 1920 to 52,714 tons in 1938, and the coffee industry which grew from 248 tons in 1928 to 14,076 tons in 1938.

Of the peasant-farmers in West Africa, only those producing cocoa and coffee were significantly involved in the money economy and experienced substantial social change as a result. In Larteh, Akwapim, in Ghana, cocoa-farming and the wealth it brought had far-reaching effects on all aspects of economic and social life. The farmers of Larteh on their own initiative built roads and bridges to link their farms with the government road and the main cocoa-collecting centers. In 1914 they even employed a Swiss engineer to build a wooden bridge, still standing today, for which nine of them and one other subscribed £2,000. Between 1914 and 1930 the people of Akwapim spent at least £30,000 on roads to connect with the government-built road. One such road, built entirely without government assistance, was actually opened in 1926 by the acting governor, to whom the chief responsible addressed a request for government assistance with the debt of £2,600 still outstanding to the contractor. The chief, the Benkumhene, also asked that government "appoint a town engineer to lay and carry out the construction of streets and other works of public utility" in Larteh. These demands for development were refused and a warning given against the construction of further roads. As it was, apart from the railway the communications system of the area was built by the local people with little or no assistance and encouragement from government.

Over half Larteh's completed houses in 1963—some 1,000—were built with profits from the cocoa trade before 1910. Apart from investment in communications, housing, education and funerals became the main items of expenditure of the cocoa farmers. Unfortunately, . . . the acquisition of wealth did not mean a necessary improvement in basic standards of living and nutrition, for far too much money was spent on luxuries, and at the same time concentration on cocoa farming led to neglect of subsistence farming. No other group was brought into the money economy in the way the cocoa and coffee farmers were. The migrant labourer depended on currency, but he earned very little, and most of it was taken in taxes and by his family on his return.

The African Labourer

Those employed on the European plantations of the Ivory Coast or Guinea were little affected by their experience. Their terms of labor were seasonal for the most part, and they were not only underpaid, but not given, as we have seen in Ivory Coast, all that they earned in cash. No rural proletariat arose from among the workers on the European plantations. Before 1940 only the railways employed a large number of regular workers, among whom many were, or were trained as, skilled artisans. The only comparable industries to the railways as employers of labor were the mines. But much of the labor on the mines was irregular. In Jos, the tin mines employed for the most part daily paid unskilled and illiterate labor to dig at the faces of the open mines. In the gold mines of Ashanti the main problems were the shortage of labor and its irregularity. And most of those employed were immigrants who intended returning home eventually. In Enugu labourers were press-ganged by unscrupulous chiefs into work on the coal mines in the early years from 1915 until 1922. After that labor flowed freely into the mines so that by 1930 the management, which was a government agency, was able to be selective in the employment policy. The peoples of the area in which the mines were situated tended to be less educated than those from neighboring divisions, and management deliberately pursued a policy of recruiting illiterate locals rather than their neighbors who were

relatively more educated and could voice their grievances and were therefore
regarded as trouble makers.

The mines, then, employed a labor force which was either of temporary immigrant nature as in the case of the Gold Coast gold mines, or, where locally recruited as in the case of the Jos and Enugu mines, largely illiterate. Wages on all three
mines were low for the ordinary labourer: in the coal mines in 1929 they were about
7d.-1s. 6d. per day; in 1930 in the gold mines they were 1s. a day for unskilled surface labourers and between 1s. 3d. and 1s. 9d. for unskilled underground labourers;
on the tin mines 1s. 6d. per day for unskilled labourers.

The wages for these labourers were too low to alter their standard of living significantly. Before 1940 none of the mine workers had organized themselves into
effective trade unions, though wildcat strikes had taken place before that time. For
instance in 1925, pit boys in the Enugu mines downed tools in protest against the
failure of management to raise their pay to 1922 levels. They were dismissed. In
1937 after the recovery of the colliery from the Depression, workers undertook considerable but uncoordinated agitation for an increase in their rates of pay. In
September of that year the tub boys struck when a European overman assaulted one
of their fellows. In 1924 there was a strike at Obuasi on the Ashanti goldfields
against the introduction of time clocks. None of these strikes were organized by a
union. Indeed until the Second World War trade unions were of no real significance
in either British or French West Africa. In the latter they were illegal until the
advent of the Popular Front Government in 1937. In the former they were tolerated
but not recognized until about the same time. Trade Union Ordinances were passed
for Gambia in 1932, Sierra Leone in 1939, Nigeria in 1939 and Gold Coast in 1941.
The attitude of the Sierra Leone Government to Trade Unions was not much different from that of the Southern Nigerian Government with respect to employment on
the Enugu mines. In 1921 it refused to recognize a union on the grounds that:

> A tribal ruler is elected for each tribe in Freetown by the members of
> the tribe themselves. These tribal rulers are recognized by law and form
> the intermediaries between the members of the tribe and the govern-
> ment, and it is not possible for the government to deal with or recognize
> any rival authority introduced by strangers to the colony.

Only some ten trade unions of any importance seem to have been formed and to
have survived any length of time in West Africa before 1940. Significantly of these
five were African Civil Servants unions, and two were railway workers unions.

Civil servants and railway employees formed the only two major coherent
groups of workers among whom there was an educated elite in any way capable of
organizing workers against government. Thus in 1919 daily-paid workers on the
Sierra Leone railway went on strike from 15th-22nd July, because they had not been
paid their "war bonus." The railway was brought to a standstill, and work was only
resumed when they were promised payment of their war bonus as soon as possible.

Daily-paid staff of the Public Works Department also went on strike at the same time. In 1926 the unrecognized Sierra Leone Railway Workers' Union led a strike for improved conditions of service, which led to a slowdown of service. Government took a very tough line against the strikers who returned to work on its terms. The 1926 strike, in contrast to those in 1919, had the active support of the Sierra Leone members of the National Congress of British West Africa.

In French West Africa the railways too were the main focus of strikes. In 1925 railway workers on the Dakar-St. Louis line went on strike, and in the same year Bambara conscripted for work on the Thies-Kayes line provoked a general strike after three of their leaders were arrested as a result of discontent among them. The troops, many of whom were Bambara, refused to be involved in any action against the strikers and the administration had to release the Bambara leaders to bring an end to the strike.

From a social point of view, then, the impact of the colonial economy was much less than has usually been supposed. Perhaps the most important effect was the ousting and consequent frustration of the African businessman from a share in the profits from the expansion of the economy that took place under colonial rule.

How Europe
Underdeveloped Africa
WALTER RODNEY[4]

The . . . benefits from colonialism were small and they were not gifts from the colonialists, but rather fruits of African labor and resources for the most part. Indeed, what was called "the development of Africa" by the colonialists was a cynical shorthand expression for "the intensification of colonial exploitation in Africa to develop capitalist Europe." The analysis has gone beyond that to demonstrate that numerous false claims are made purporting to show that Europe developed Africa in the sense of bringing about social order, nationalism, and economic modernization. However, all of that would still not permit the conclusion that colonialism had a negative impact on Africa's development. In offering the view that colonialism was negative, the aim is to draw attention to the way that previous African development was blunted, halted, and turned back. In place of that interruption and blockade, nothing of compensatory value was introduced.

The decisiveness of the short period of colonialism and its negative consequences for Africa spring mainly from the fact that Africa lost power. Power is the ultimate determinant in human society, being basic to the relations within any group and between groups. It implies the ability to defend one's interests and if necessary to impose one's will by any means available. In relations between peoples, the question of power determines maneuverability in bargaining, the extent to which one people respect the interests of another, and eventually the extent to which a people survive as a physical and cultural entity. When one society finds itself forced to relinquish power entirely to another society, that in itself is a form of underdevelopment.

During the centuries of precolonial trade, some control over social, political, and economic life was retained in Africa, in spite of the disadvantageous commerce with Europeans that little control over internal matters disappeared under colonialism. Colonialism went much further than trade. It meant a tendency towards direct appropriation by Europeans of the social institutions within Africa. Africans ceased to set indigenous cultural goals and standards, and lost full command of training

---

[4]Rodney, Walter, *How Europe Underdeveloped Africa* (Washington, D.C.: Howard University Press, 1982). Originally published in 1972 by Bogle-L'Overture Publications, London and Tanzanian Publishing House. Excerpts taken from pages 223-238. Dr. Rodney's biography is listed beneath his reading in the preceding problem on "Educating the African."

young members of the society. Those were undoubtedly major steps backward. The Tunisian, Albert Memmi, puts forward the following proposition:

> The most serious blow suffered by the colonized is being removed from history and from the community. Colonization usurps any free role in either war or peace, every decision contributing to his destiny and that of the world, and all cultural and social responsibility.

Sweeping as that statement may initially appear, it is entirely true. The removal from history follows logically from the loss of power which colonialism represented. The power to act independently is the guarantee to participate actively and *consciously* in history. To be colonized is to be removed from history, except in the most passive sense. A striking illustration of the fact that colonial Africa was a passive object is seen in its attraction for white anthropologists, who came to study "primitive society." Colonialism determined that Africans were no more makers of history than were beetles—objects to be looked at under a microscope and examined for unusual features.

The negative impact of colonialism in political terms was quite dramatic. Overnight, African political states lost their power, independence, and meaning—irrespective of whether they were big empires or small polities. Certain traditional rulers were kept in office, and the formal structure of some kingdoms was partially retained, but the substance of political life was quite different. Political power had passed into the hands of foreign overlords. Of course, numerous African states in previous centuries had passed through the cycle of growth and decline. But colonial rule was different. So long as it lasted, not a single African state could flourish.

To be specific, it must be noted that colonialism crushed by force the surviving feudal states of North Africa; that the French wiped out the large Moslem states of the Western Sudan, as well as Dahomey and kingdoms in Madagascar; that the British eliminated Egypt, the Mahdist Sudan, Asante, Benin, the Yoruba kingdoms, Swaziland, Matabeleland, the Lozi, and the East African lake kingdoms as great states. It should further be noted that a multiplicity of smaller and growing states were removed from the face of Africa by the Belgians, Portuguese, British, French, Germans, Spaniards, and Italians. Finally, those that appeared to survive were nothing but puppet creations. For instance, the Sultan of Morocco retained nominal existence under colonial rule which started in 1912; and the same applied to the Bey of Tunis; but Morocco and Tunisia were just as much under the power of French colonial administrators as neighboring Algeria, where the feudal rulers were removed altogether.

Sometimes, the African rulers who were chosen to serve as agents of foreign colonial rule were quite obviously nothing but puppets. The French and the Portuguese were in the habit of choosing their own African "chiefs"; the British went to Iboland and invented "warrant chiefs"; and all the colonial powers found it convenient to create "superior" or "paramount" rulers. Very often, the local population hated and despised such colonial stooges. There were traditional rulers such as the Sultan of Sokoto, the Kabaka of Buganda, and the Asantehene of Asante, who retained a great deal of prestige in the eyes of Africans, but they had no power to act outside the narrow boundaries laid down by colonialism, lest they find themselves in the Seychelles Islands as "guests of His Majesty's Government."

One can go so far as to say that colonial rule meant the effective eradication of African political power throughout the continent, since Liberia and Ethiopia could no longer function as independent states within the context of continent-wide colonialism. Liberia in particular had to bow before foreign political, economic, and military pressures in a way that no genuinely independent state could have accepted; and although Ethiopia held firm until 1936, most European capitalist nations were not inclined to treat Ethiopia as a sovereign state, primarily because it was African, and Africans were supposed to be colonial subjects.

The pattern of arrest of African political development has some features which can only be appreciated after careful scrutiny and the taking away of the blinkers which the colonizers put on the eyes of their subjects. An interesting case in point is that of women's role in society. Until today, capitalist society has failed to resolve the inequality between man and woman, which was entrenched in all modes of production prior to localism. The colonialists in Africa occasionally paid lip service to women's education and emancipation, but objectively there was deterioration in the status of women owing to colonial rule.

A realistic assessment of the role of women in independent precolonial Africa shows two contrasting but combined tendencies. In the first place, women were exploited by men through polygamous arrangements designed to capture the labor power of women. As always, exploitation was accompanied by oppression; and there is evidence to the effect that women were sometimes treated like beasts of burden, as for instance in Moslem African societies. Nevertheless, there was a countertendency to insure the dignity of women to greater or lesser degree in all African societies. Mother-right was a prevalent feature of African societies, and particular women held a variety of privileges based on the fact that they were the keys to inheritance.

More important still, some women had real power in the political sense, exercised either through religion or directly within the politico-constitutional apparatus. In Mozambique, the widow of an Nguni king became the priestess in charge of the shrine set up in the burial place of her deceased husband, and the reigning king had to consult her on all important matters. In a few instances, women were actually heads of state. Among the Lovedu of Transvaal, the key figure was the Rain-Queen, combining political and religious functions. The most frequently encountered role of importance played by women was that of "Queen Mother" or "Queen Sister." In practice, that post was filled by a female of royal blood, who might be mother, sister, or aunt of the reigning king in places such as Mali, Asante, and Buganda. Her influence was considerable, and there were occasions when the "Queen Mother" was the real power and the male king a mere puppet.

What happened to African women under colonialism is that the social, religious, constitutional, and political privileges and rights disappeared, while the economic exploitation continued and was often intensified. It was intensified because the division of labor according to sex was frequently disrupted. Traditionally, African men did the heavy labor of felling trees, clearing land, building houses, apart from conducting warfare and hunting. When they were required to leave their farms to seek employment, women remained behind burdened with every task necessary for the survival of themselves, the children, and even the men as far as foodstuffs were concerned. Moreover, since men entered the money sector more easily and in greater numbers than women, women's work became greatly inferior to that of men within the new value system of colonialism: men's work was "modern" and women's was "traditional" and "backward." Therefore, the deterioration in the status of African women was bound up with the consequent loss of the right to set indigenous standards of what work had merit and what did not.

One of the most important manifestations of historical arrest and stagnation in colonial Africa is that which commonly goes under the title of "tribalism." That term, in its common journalistic setting, is understood to mean that Africans have a basic loyalty to tribe rather than nation and that each tribe still retains a fundamental hostility towards its neighboring tribes. The examples favored by the capitalist press and bourgeois scholarship are those of Congo and Nigeria. Their accounts suggest that Europeans tried to make a nation out of the Congolese and Nigerian peoples, but they failed, because the various tribes had their age-long hatreds; and, as soon as the colonial power went, the natives returned to killing each other. To this phenomenon, Europeans often attach the word "atavism," to carry the notion that Africans were returning to their primitive savagery. Even a cursory survey of the African past shows that such assertions are the exact opposite of the truth.

All of the large states of nineteenth-century Africa were multi-ethnic, and their expansion was continually making anything like "tribal" loyalty a thing of the past, by substituting in its place national and class ties. However, in all parts of the world, that substitution of national and class ties for purely ethnic ones is a lengthy historical process; and, invariably there remains for long periods certain regional pockets of individuals who have their own narrow, regional loyalties, springing from ties of kinship, language, and culture. In Asia, the feudal states of Vietnam and Burma both achieved a considerable degree of national homogeneity over the centuries before colonial rule. But there were pockets of "tribes" or "minorities" who remained outside the effective sphere of the nation-state and the national economy and culture.

Colonialism blocked the further evolution of national solidarity, because it destroyed the particular Asian or African states which were the principal agents for achieving the liquidation of fragmented loyalties. Because ethnic and regional loyalties which go under the name of "tribalism" could not be effectively resolved by the colonial state, they tended to fester and grow in unhealthy forms. Indeed, the colonial powers sometimes saw the value of stimulating the internal tribal jealousies so as to keep the colonized from dealing with their principal contradiction with the

European overlords—i.e., the classic technique of divide and rule. Certainly, the Belgians consciously fostered that; and the racist whites in South Africa had by the 1950s worked out a careful plan to "develop" the oppressed African population as Zulu, as Xhosa, and as Sotho so that the march towards broader African national and class solidarities could be stopped and turned back.

The civil war in Nigeria is generally regarded as having been a tribal affair. To accept such a contention would mean extending the definition of tribe to cover Shell Oil and Gulf Oil! . . . What came to be called tribalism at the beginning of the new epoch of political independence in Nigeria was itself a product of the way that people were brought together under colonialism so as to be exploited. It was a product of administrative devices, of entrenched regional separations, of differential access by particular ethnic groups into the colonial economy and culture.

Pre-colonial trade had started the trend of the disintegration of African economies and their technological impoverishment. Colonial rule speeded up that trend. The story is often told that in order to make a telephone call from Accra in the British colony of the Gold Coast to Abidjan in the adjacent French colony of Ivory Coast it was necessary to be connected first with an operator in London and then with an operator in Paris who could offer a line to Abidjan. That was one reflection of the fact that the Gold Coast economy was integrated into the British economy, and the Ivory Coast economy was integrated into the French economy, while the neighboring African colonies had little or no effective economic relations. The following conclusion reached by the United Nations Economic Commission for Africa in 1959 goes directly to the point:

> The most outstanding characteristic of the transportation systems of Africa is the comparative isolation in which they have developed within the confines of individual countries and territories. This is reflected in the lack of links between countries and territories within the same geographical sub-region.

Africa was denied the opportunity of developing healthy trade links with parts of the world other than Europe and North America. Some trade persisted across the Indian Ocean, but on the whole it is fair to say that the roads in Africa led to the seaports and the sea lanes led to Western Europe and North America. That kind of lopsidedness is today part of the pattern of underdevelopment and dependence.

The damaging impact of capitalism on African technology is even more clearly measurable in the colonial period than in the earlier centuries. In spite of the slave trade and of the import of European goods, most African handicraft industries still had vitality at the start of the colonial period. They had undergone no technological advance and they had not expanded, but they had survived. The mass production of the more recent phase of capitalism virtually obliterated African industries such as cloth, salt, soap, iron, and even pottery-making.

In North Africa, handicraft industries had made the greatest advances before colonialism, in spheres ranging from brasswork to woolens. As in the towns of feudal Europe, craft workshops flourished in Algerian towns like Oran, Constantine, Algiers, and Tlemcen. But French colonialism destroyed the handicraft industries and threw thousands out of work. The same thing had happened in Europe itself when new machines had thrown artisans out of employment in places like Lancashire and Lyons, but in that instance the new machines became the basis of the prevailing mode of production, and formerly independent artisans returned to factories as proletarians to master different skills and expand the productive capacity of their society. In Africa it was simply destruction without redress. By the time political independence was achieved, surviving craftsmanship had been turned towards attracting tourists rather than meeting the real needs of African people.

Besides, as was true of the European slave trade, the destruction of technology under colonialism must be related to the barriers raised in the path of African initiative. The vast majority of Africans drawn into the colonial money economy were simply providing manual labor, which stimulated perspiration rather than scientific initiative. Africans connected to the trading sector were sometimes successful in a limited way. The resourcefulness of West African market women is well known, but it was put to petty purposes. The problem posed to capitalists and workers in Europe while making insecticide from African pyrethrum was one requiring that resourcefulness be expressed in a technical direction. But the problem posed to an African market woman by the necessity to make a penny more profit on every tin of imported sardines was resolved sometimes by a little more vigor, sometimes by a touch of dishonesty, and sometimes by resort to *juju*.

Colonialism induced the African ironworker to abandon the process of extracting iron from the soil and to concentrate instead on working scraps of metal imported from Europe. The only compensation for that interruption would have been the provision of modern techniques in the extraction and processing of iron. However, those techniques were debarred from Africa, on the basis of the international division of labor under imperialism. As was seen earlier, the non-industrialization of Africa was not left to chance. It was deliberately enforced by stopping the transference to Africa of machinery and skills which would have given competition to European industry in that epoch.

In the period of African development preceding colonialism, some areas moved faster than others and provided the nuclei for growth on a wide regional basis. Northern Nigeria was one of those; and it virtually went to sleep during the colonial period. The British cut it off from the rest of the Moslem world and fossilized the social relations, so that the serfs could not achieve any change at the expense of the ruling aristocracy.

Instead of speeding up growth, colonial activities such as mining and cash-crop farming speeded up the decay of "traditional" African life. In many parts of the continent, vital aspects of culture were adversely affected, nothing better was substituted, and only a lifeless shell was left. The capitalist forces behind colonialism were interested in little more than the exploitation of labor. Even areas that were not directly involved in the money economy exploited labor. In extracting that labor, they tampered with the factor that was the very buttress of the society, for African "traditional" life when deprived of its customary labor force and patterns of work was no longer "traditional."

During the colonial era, many thinly populated villages appeared in Central and Southern Africa, comprising women, children, and old men. They practiced subsistence agriculture which was not productive enough, and colonialists contrasted them with cash-crop areas, which in comparison were flourishing. However, it was precisely the impact of colonialism which left so many villages deserted and starving, because the able-bodied males had gone off to labor elsewhere. Any district deprived of its effective laboring population could not be expected to develop.

There were several spots within different colonies which were sufficiently far removed from towns and colonial administration that they neither grew cash crops nor supplied labor. In southern Sudan, for instance, there were populations who continued to live a life not dissimilar to that which they had followed in previous centuries. Yet, even for such traditional African societies the scope for development no longer existed. They were isolated by the hold which the colonialists had on the rest of the continent. They could not interact with other parts of Africa. They were subject to increasing encroachment by the money economy and were more and more to be regarded as historical relics. The classic example of this type of obstructed historical development is to be found in the U.S.A., where the indigenous population of Indians who survived slaughter by the whites were placed in reservations and condemned to stagnation. Indian reservations in North America are living museums to be visited by white tourists who purchase curios.

In South Africa and Rhodesia, the policy of establishing "native reserves" was openly followed. Inside a reserve, the major means of production was the land. But the quantity and fertility of the land allocated was entirely inadequate to support the numbers of Africans who were driven in. The reserves were reservoirs of cheap labor, and dumping grounds for those who could not be accommodated within the money economy of the racist southern section of Africa. Further north, there were no areas named as reserves except in colonial Kenya and to a very limited extent in Tanganyika. But the money economy was constantly transforming the traditional sector into one which was just as deprived as any reserve.

The money economy of colonialism was a growing sector. That is not to be denied. However, it has already been indicated how limited that growth was, viewed over the continent as a whole. The growth in the so-called modern sector exercised adverse effects on the non-monetary sector. What remains is to emphasize that the character of growth in Africa under colonialism was such that it did not constitute development—i.e. it did not enlarge the capacity of the society to deal with the natural environment, to adjudicate relations between members of the society, and to protect the population from external forces. Such a statement is already implicitly borne out in the inability of capitalism to stimulate skilled labor in colonial Africa. A system which must stand in the way of the accumulation of skills does not develop anything or anybody. It is implicit, too, in the manner in which Africa was cut into economic compartments having no relation one to another, so that, even though the volume of commercial activity within each compartmentalized colony may have increased, there was no development comparable to that which linked together the various states of the U.S.A.

In recent times, economists have been recognizing in colonial and postcolonial Africa a pattern that has been termed "growth without development." That phrase has now appeared as the title of books on Liberia and Ivory Coast. It means that goods and services of a certain type are on the increase. There may be more rubber and coffee exported, there may be more cars imported with the proceeds, and there may be more gasoline stations built to service the cars. But the profit goes abroad, and the economy becomes more and more a dependency of the metropoles. In no African colony was there economic integration, or any provision for making the economy self-sustained and geared to its own local goals. Therefore, there was growth of the so-called enclave import-export sector, but the only things which developed were dependency and underdevelopment.

A further revelation of growth without development under colonialism was the overdependence on one or two exports. The term "monoculture" is used to describe those colonial economies which were centered around a single crop. Liberia (in the agricultural sector) was a monoculture dependent on rubber, Gold Coast on cocoa, Dahomey and southeast Nigeria on palm produce, Sudan on cotton, Tanganyika on sisal, and Uganda on cotton. In Senegal and Gambia, groundnuts accounted for 85 to 90 percent of money earnings. In effect, two African colonies were told to grow nothing but peanuts!

Every farming people have a staple food, plus a variety of other supplements. Historians, agronomists, and botanists have all contributed to showing the great variety of such foods within the precolonial African economy. There were numerous crops which were domesticated within the African continent, there were several wild food species (notably fruits), and Africans had shown no conservatism in adopting useful food plants of Asian or American origin. Diversified agriculture was within the African tradition. Monoculture was a colonialist invention.

There was nothing "natural" about monoculture. It was a consequence of imperialist requirements and machinations, extending into areas that were politically independent in name. Monoculture was a characteristic of regions falling under imperialist domination. Certain countries in Latin America such as Costa Rica and Guatemala were forced by United States capitalist firms to concentrate so heavily on growing bananas that they were contemptuously known as "banana republics." In Africa, this concentration on one or two cash crops for sale abroad had many harmful effects. Sometimes, cash crops were grown to the exclusion of staple foods—thus causing famines. For instance, in Gambia rice farming was popular before the colonial era, but so much of the best land was transferred to groundnuts that rice had to be imported on a large scale to try to counter the fact that famine was becoming endemic. In Asante, concentration on cocoa raised fears of famine in a region previously famous for yams and other foodstuff.

Yet the threat of famine was a small disadvantage compared to the extreme vulnerability and insecurity of monoculture. When the crop was affected by internal factors such as disease, that amounted to an overwhelming disaster, as in the case of Gold Coast cocoa when it was hit by swollen-shoot disease in the 1940s. Besides, at all times, the price fluctuations (which were externally controlled) left the African producer helpless in the face of capitalist maneuvers.

From a capitalist viewpoint, monocultures commended themselves most because they made colonial economies entirely dependent on the metropolitan buyers of their produce. At the end of the European slave trade, only a minority of Africans were sufficiently committed to capitalist exchange and sufficiently dependent upon European imports to wish to continue the relationship with Europe at all costs. Colonialism increased the dependence of Africa on Europe in terms of the numbers of persons brought into the money economy and in terms of the number of aspects of socio-economic life in Africa which derived their existence from the connection with the metropole. The ridiculous situation arose by which European trading firms, mining companies, shipping lines, banks, insurance houses, and plantations all exploited Africa and at the same time caused Africans to feel that without those capitalist services no money or European goods would be forthcoming, and therefore Africa was in debt to its exploiters!

The factor of dependency made its impact felt in every aspect of the life of the colonies, and it can be regarded as the crowning vice among the negative social, political, and economic consequences of colonialism in Africa, being primarily responsible for the perpetuation of the colonial relationship into the epoch that is called neocolonialism.

In the light of the prevailing balance-sheet concept of what colonial rule was about, it still remains to take note of European innovations in Africa such as modern medicine, clinical surgery, and immunization. It would be absurd to deny that these were objectively positive features, however limited they were quantitatively. However, they have to be weighed against the numerous setbacks received by Africa in all spheres due to colonialism as well as against the contributions Africa made to Europe. European science met the needs of its own society, and particularly those of the bourgeoisie. The bourgeoisie did not suffer from hunger and starvation. Bourgeois science therefore did not consider those things as needs which had to be met and overcome-not even among their own workers and least of all on behalf of Africans. This is just a specific application of the general principle that the exploitation of Africa was being used to create a greater gap between Africa and capitalist Europe. The exploitation and the comparative disadvantage are the ingredients of underdevelopment.

Imperialism and
Underdevelopment in Nigeria
BADE ONIMODE[5]

Free-trade imperialism under British hegemony was a system of international division of labor for global accumulation by Britain and her allies of Western Europe. Under this global division of labor, the imperialist metropoles monopolized manufacturing and forced the colonies to specialize in primary production of raw materials for their factories, and cheap food for their labor force. While this primary production chained the colonial population to the land in abysmal ignorance, poverty and backwardness, their cheap food supply helped to maximize the exploitation of the European labor force with low wages, while their abundant cheap raw materials ensured enormous profits for the exploiters who dumped shoddy manufactures on the colonies. This squalid fraud was wrapped in the intellectual garb of the so-called theory of comparative advantage and free trade.

This summary of the British economic philosophy of free-enterprise capitalism for the colonial economy reflects the classical economic thought of Adam Smith, whose reactionary ideas still dominated imperial thinking, even during the new-classical era of the 1920s. It explains why, throughout the colonial era, until 1946, when political circumstances forced it to embark on patched-up economic planning, the imperial administration neither directly undertook any large-scale productive enterprises, nor evolved a coherent development strategy for the colonies.

Consequently, the motives and processes of primary production in the colonial economy were dictated by private capitalist calculations for which the colonial administration provided a propitious environment. In Nigeria, the dominant motives were simply to use the country as an agricultural estate to produce raw materials for British factories, and thereby generate some purchasing power to enable Nigerians to buy the manufactured products of these same factories. Both objectives would ensure the transfer of economic surplus from Nigeria to Britain. The actual process

[5]Onimode, Bade, *Imperialism and Underdevelopment in Nigeria: The Dialectics of Mass Poverty* (London: Zed Press, 1982). Excerpts taken from pages 42-3, 48-9, 51-2, 91-3, and 103-4. Bade Onimode is an economist at the University of Ibadan and is one of Nigeria's foremost progressive scholars. He has written many works addressing the political economy of underdevelopment in Africa. These include *Economic Development in Nigeria* (Ibidin: Nigeria Academy of Arts, Sciences, and Technology, 1975), *MNC's in Nigeria: Multinational Corporations in Nigeria* (Ibidin: L. Shynden, 1983), *An Introduction to Marxist Political Economy* (London: Zed Books, 1985), and his most recent work, *A Political Economy of the African Crisis* (London: Zed Books, 1988).

of primary production included cash-cropping, forestry and mining. The production of cash crops was left largely to peasant farmers, both because they were more efficient than the few plantation planters, and because Lugard's indirect rule required minimal disruption of traditional land tenure. But forestry and mining, which were less tedious, more lucrative and more capital intensive, were dominated by British imperialists.

The production of "cash crops" in Nigeria for export spearheaded the incorporation of the majority of Nigerians into the colonial capitalist economy, constituted the springboard for the series of factors that led to the entrenchment of capitalist relations of production and dominated the sources of transfer of economic surplus to Britain. The principal cash crops were palm oil and kernels, cocoa, cotton, groundnuts and rubber. Some hides and skins, citrus, kola nuts, beni-seed, shea butter and bananas were also produced for export, especially towards the end of the colonial era. Palm oil and kernels were required for soap, candles, tin plate, nut butters and cattle cake. Cocoa was needed for chocolate and confectionery, cotton for textiles, groundnuts for oils and soap, rubber for tires and other products, and hides and skins for leather. The introduction of taxes to be paid in cash, payment of money for these cash crops and direct government stimulus encouraged their production by peasants, almost to the neglect of food crops.

Huge export values represented only part of the economic surplus from capitalist agriculture in colonial Nigeria. The shamelessly unfavorable terms of trade for these exports, which fell as low as twenty-two, meant that much of the surplus was transferred to Britain through exploitively monopolistic pricing. Producer incomes associated with these export values under the Marketing Board system were generally much below world prices.

The use of money in payment for these export crops, the existence of produce-buying agents, plantations, plot registration, hired labor and monetary taxes meant that commercial agriculture was one of the critical bridgeheads for the infiltration of capitalist relations of production into Nigeria. This was particularly the case the tree crop culture in palm produce, cocoa and rubber in the south. This in part explains the longer survival of feudal relations in the groundnut and cotton culture of the north.

Technologically, even though agrarian capitalism experienced some innovations involving new seeds, crop research, insecticides, harvesting and oil extraction machines, the basic techniques for land clearing and cultivation remained stagnated under the hoe-and-cutlass culture. Modern agricultural machinery like tractors, ploughs, harvesters, milk processors etc. of the Agrarian Revolution were never introduced into the country.

Food crops constituted the much maligned "traditional" or "subsistence" production. The production organization for these consisted of household peasant cultivation on small plots under a mixture of communal and feudal land tenure. Feudal land relations were reflected in payments called *isakole* in the western parts and *kurdin kasa* in the northern emirates. The extended family system provided most of the labor, seeds were provided by the peasants, while the production techniques consisted of the hoe and cutlass. After deducting the share for family consumption and feudal tribute, the surplus was sold in the local markets, and sometimes transported by head, canoes, donkeys, and later lorries and trains, to other parts of the country in the predominantly north-south trade.

The static nature of food production and its backward technology were part of the cumulative consequence of near total neglect of food production by the imperialists. Indeed, under such conditions, it was a miracle that the indigenous labour force was able to feed its rising population as well as pay oppressive taxes. This is particularly true after 1900, when the export boom led to an increasing transition from food to export production.

In terms of relative size, unexported agricultural production engaged some 85 percent of the Nigerian population during most of the colonial era, though the percentage dropped slightly from the beginning of the twentieth century. But even during the 1900-29 boom, food output rose by only about 10 percent, whereas agricultural export production rose by about 500 percent in this period. Consequently, in spite of huge differences in input employment, both the absolute and relative increase in the production of "cash crops" exceeded that of food products. By the 1950s, the performance gap was much wider, given the continuing innovations for export crops involving new seeds, planting instruction, research, processing machines, and so on.

The associated rising prices and incomes from export production led to a continuing switch from the largely static food production to commercial agriculture. These conversions were particularly frequent and significant during 1900-29 and 1945-60; the opposite switch, from commercial to food cropping, was much less, even during the slack years from 1929-45, because land under export tree crops could not easily be transferred to food production.

The colonial financial system was supposed to be self-sufficient, but in reality it was neither self-supporting nor autonomous. Throughout its existence, it was merely an appendage of the British imperialist financial structure. Consequently, it had neither the dynamism for internal growth, nor the external assistance for any international recognition. . . . In particular . . . the financial system was the organized purveyor of credit and the creator of money, which were the taproots of capitalist exchange and accumulation.

Seven fundamental characteristics distinguish the colonial financial system. First, it was a thoroughly exploitative conduit system designed specifically for the transfer of Nigeria's enormous economic surplus for the development of imperial Britain. This process was in turn facilitated by some critical features of the functioning of the system. One of these was the fact that the colonial government and the imperialist firms used this financial system for the continuous transfer of annual surpluses like those of the Marketing Boards and the so-called foreign profit—under frequently dubious practices. Another was the 100 percent external reserve demanded for colonial currency in Nigeria, which in effect meant continuous zero interest loans by Nigeria to Britain for several decades. Moreover, while export and budget surpluses at nominal interest rates were piled up by Nigeria for the development of Britain, Nigeria was forced by colonial administrators to borrow at a higher interest rate from the British capital market. This meant, on net, that Nigeria borrowed her own funds from Britain at positive interest rate. Instead of employing the funds obtained from Nigeria to further development there the policy of colonial financial institutions was to invest abroad, or make loans to fellow expatriate exploiters.

Second, the colonial financial infrastructure was really an extension of the British financial system. Nigeria's colonial currency was tied to the Sterling Exchange Standard, external reserves were largely in sterling, held in London, and London determined the exchange rate. The main commercial banks were overseas branches of British multinational financial oligarchies like Bank of British West Africa (B.B.W.A.) and Barclays (now Union) Bank, while the credit offered by these financial houses went largely to Britain. Consequently, the colonial financial system was the nerve of the umbilical cord, which, until 1960, tied Nigeria bilaterally to British imperialism. Since then, the link has become increasingly multilateral with all the industrialized capitalist countries. Indeed, until the last year of its existence in 1959, the hub of this colonial financial apparatus was the extra-territorial West African Currency Board whose sole agent in West Africa was the B.B.W.A.

Third, foreign domination crippled the colonial financial system. Until 1929, there was no indigenous bank in Nigeria, and by 1945 there were only two indigenous financial institutions. In the same year, foreign balances due to other British banks accounted for over 80 percent of total assets of commercial banks in Nigeria whose foreign investment was 79 percent of total investment. By 1960, out of 195 commercial bank branches, 130 were owned by expatriate banking houses, while the imperialist banks controlled over 80 percent of all loans and advances. Thus, throughout the colonial era, these imperialist banks are accused of ruinous competition designed to destroy all indigenous banks and exclude Nigerians from the banking industry.

Fourth, the competitive structure of these financial institutions was distinctly monopolistic and oligopolistic at various times. Between 1894 and 1917 the B.B.W.A., which swallowed the Bank of Nigeria in 1912, was the only bank in the country. Then from 1917 to 1960, the B.B.W.A. and Barclays Bank controlled over 60 percent of commercial banking activities in the country, accounting for 118 of the 195 bank branches in the country. Moreover, from 1912 to 1959 the B.B.W.A. was the sole agent of the West African Currency Board and the colonial administration. This market control also enhanced the exploitative activities of these banks.

Fifth, unbridled *laissez-faire,* bordering on anarchy, was another characteristic of the colonial financial structure. There was no real central bank throughout the period, so there was no real control over the monetary system, especially over the predominantly expatriate commercial banks. Even when the Central Bank of Nigeria was established in 1959, it was required by its ordinance to cooperate with the commercial banks, rather than to control them. For this same reason, monetary policy rested largely on "moral persuasion." There was no banking examiner until 1959, no minimum liquid-asset reserve requirement for bank loans until 1958, no banking ordinance until 1952 after the bankruptcies of the "banking mania" of the late 1940s, and no published banking statistics until 1943. These facts meant that for several decades Nigerians had no protection against the excesses of the imperialist banks, thus constituting the country into a financial jungle for Adam Smith's avaricious "invisible hand." Hence, Nigeria had barely one decade of organized commercial banking "under law," during a total colonial tutelage of 100 exploitative years.

Sixth, financial conservatism, which imperialist scholars gleefully flog to demonstrate their "critical" view of colonial financial arrangements, was in reality only an offshoot of the predatory primitiveness and intellectual backwardness of capitalist economics and imperialist social thought generally, and of British empiricist philosophy in particular. Earl Grey's insistence on financial self-sufficiency, which was ignored in the accumulation of Nigerian surpluses in London, was pursued in the reactionary obsession with "sound money" and "balanced budgeting" was perverted into persistent budget surpluses, . . . with surpluses for all but one year during 1946 to 1960. In spite of these surpluses, Nigeria was forced to borrow from London at exorbitant interest rates.

Finally, the collective consequence of these characteristics of the imperialist financial system in Nigeria was to burden the country with a weak, largely amorphous and ruthlessly exploitative set of financial institutions after 1960. With neither money nor capital market, no tradition of monetary control, and only a nominal Central Bank, this colonial financial apparatus was a veritable Trojan horse which performed only one function too well—to serve as a conduit for the transfer of Nigeria's economic surplus to develop imperialist Britain and simultaneously underdevelop Nigeria.

The colonial fiscal system was distinguished by nondevelopmental, oppressive, externally oriented, conservative and divisive features. Developmental expenditure, especially on capital projects, typically accounted for less than 30 percent of total annual budgets. Even during the exceptional railway construction era from about 1890 to 1920, revenue for the railways was usually raised externally, as if it were outside the annual budget. During 1943-45, for example, public works, education and agriculture were allocated barely 10 percent, 5 percent and 5 percent each of the budget respectively. By contrast, the civil establishment involving colonial salaries, pensions and the coercive apparatus together swallowed up over 50 percent of the budget from 1860-90, and more than 40 percent thereafter. This was partly a consequence of capitalist *laissez-faire* policy.

Colonial taxes were usually oppressive and exploitative with respect to their absolute rates relative to Nigerian incomes, coercive methods of collection, their functional distribution among social classes and the minimal benefits of taxation. In an age when incomes were derived in kind for some 80 percent of the largely agricultural population, and when, even by 1947, wages were as low as 1s.6d. per day, the imposition of regressive poll taxes on both men and women often led to anti-tax riots, such as the Aba women's riot of 1929. The violent tax-raids, together with the colonial objective of forcing peasants into the nascent capitalist labor force by imposing taxes to be paid in cash, were equally repressive. Multiple taxation of the peasantry through poll, income, produce, export, land and cattle taxes, etc., were really ruinous to the peasants and destroyed their productive energies.

In addition, the imperialist orientation of the colonial fiscal system was reflected in its heavy and continuous reliance on exploitative foreign loans, as well as import duties. Even when the country was piling up export surpluses in London at very low interest rates, especially during the export booms of 1900-29 and 1946-54, the colonialists imposed huge foreign debts on Nigeria at exorbitant interest rates. For example, the total loan of £24.9 million in 1946-47 was external, while in 1955-56, £16.8 million out of the total loan of £20.0 million was external. And, except for a small deficit in 1949, there were budget surpluses from 1946 to 1960. Import duties similarly accounted for about 45 percent of total revenue from 1930-45, and about 60 percent from 1946-60 with 78 percent in 1960. Such heavy reliance on import duties meant a built-in commitment to imperialist manufactures and the dominance of the foreign trade sector, both of which exposed the colony to further imperialist exploitation and negated any internal dynamics for manufacturing and development.

No indirect rule anchored to imperialism and feudalism could ever serve, or was even meant to serve, "the public interest." The dual fiscal system of the colonial administration and local authorities degenerated into a tripartite system under the explosively divisive and centrifugal regional system of government after 1951. That meant multiple tiers of taxation by different authorities with all the arbitrariness this implies, including the imposition of "warrant chiefs" in such areas as Eastern Nigeria where feudalism had no historical roots, regressive poll taxes levied lump-sum on whole communities, taxes without receipt, and similar abuses. Predictably, the revenue garnered through these repressive methods was frequently put to fraudulent use by the traditional rulers, and lapped up in expenditure on the "civil establishment" of the colonial D.O. and his cohorts.

The Colonial Impact

A. ADU BOAHEN[6]

Nowhere in Africa did the colonial system last more than a hundred years—from the 1890s to the 1970s. In the history of a continent, a hundred years is a very brief span indeed, a mere episode or interlude in the life of the peoples. Yet, short and episodic as it was, there is no doubt that colonialism made an impact on the continent. . . . I would like to examine the nature of the legacies that colonialism has bequeathed to Africa, as well as assess the significance of colonialism for Africa and Africans.

The first obvious positive political legacy was undoubtedly the establishment of continuous peace and stability in Africa, especially after the First World War. Let me hasten to add, first, that Africa was certainly not in a Hobbesian state of nature at the dawn of the colonial era and, [that colonialism] . . . introduced into Africa far more violence, instability, anarchy, and loss of African lives than probably any other period in its history. The population of the Belgian Congo fell by 50 percent, and that of the Herero by 80 percent, as a result of the oppressive and inhuman treatment of the Africans by the colonizers during the period. There is no doubt, however, that after the wars of occupation and the repression of African opposition and resistance, an era of continuous peace, order, and stability set in. This certainly facilitated and accelerated the economic and social changes that occurred on the continent during the colonial period.

The second positive political impact has been the very appearance of the independent African states of today. The partition of Africa by the imperial colonial powers led ultimately to the establishment of some forty-eight new states, most of them with clearly defined boundaries, in place of the existing innumerable lineage and clan groups, city-states, kingdoms, and empires without any fixed boundaries. It is significant that the boundaries of these states have been maintained ever since independence.

However, the Creation of the states has proved to be more of a liability than an asset to the present independent African nations. Had the boundaries of these states been laid down in accordance with any well-defined, rational criteria and in full

[6]Boahen, A. Adu, *African Perspectives on Colonialism* (Baltimore: Johns Hopkins University Press, 1987). Excerpts taken from pages 94-112. A. Adu Boahen was former professor of history and the former vice-chancellor at the University of Ghana. He was also President of the UNESCO International Scientific Committee for the drafting of a General History of Africa. In addition to authoring *Topics in West African History,* and Ghana, he is the editor of the 7th Volume of UNESCO's history of Africa, entitled *Africa under Colonial Rule.*

cognizance of the ethnocultural, geographical, and ecological realities of Africa, the outcome would have been wholesome. Unfortunately, many of these boundaries were arbitrarily drawn on African maps in the chancelleries of the imperial powers in Europe. The result has been that most of these states are artificial creations, and this very artificiality has created very serious problems, many of which have still not been solved.

A second problem has been that of interstate boundary disputes. Not only did these artificial boundaries create multiethnic states, but worse still, they often run across preexisting nations, ethnicities, states, kingdoms, and empires. The Bakongo, for instance, are divided by the boundaries of the Congo, Zaire, Angola, and Gabon. Some of the Ewe live in Ghana, some in Togo, and others in Benin, while the Akan are found in the Ivory Coast and Ghana. The Somali are shared among Ethiopia, Kenya, and Somalia. The Senufo now live in Mali, the Ivory Coast, and Burkina Faso.

A third problem has been the uneven sizes and unequal natural resources and economic potentialities of these states. Some of the states that emerged from the partition were really giants; . . . others were midgets. Moreover, some states have miles and miles of coastline, while others are landlocked, with no access to the sea. . . . Some have very fertile lands and several mineral resources, but others . . . are mere desert. Finally, while some states . . . have only a border or two to police, others have four or more, and Zaire has seven.

The third positive political impact of colonialism was its introduction into Africa of two new institutions—a new bureaucracy of civil servants and a new judicial system. On the first score, the contribution of the Europeans was uneven: the British bequeathed a far better trained and numerically stronger civil service to its former colonies than the French, while the record of the Belgians and the Portuguese is the worst in this field. However, the judicial systems, bequeathed by the colonial administrations, have not undergone any fundamental changes in any of the independent African states.

Another positive colonial impact was the generation of a sense of nationalism as well as the intensification of the spirit of Pan-Africanism. The colonial system generated a sense of identity and consciousness among the different ethnic groups of each colonial state, while the anticolonial literary activities of some of the educated Africans and more especially the Fascist attack on Ethiopia and the connivance of the other European imperial powers diffused and strengthened the spirit of Pan-Africanism throughout the black world.

But it should be immediately pointed out that African nationalism was one of the accidental by-products of colonialism. No colonial power ever deliberately set out to generate or promote that consciousness. Moreover, the nationalism that was generated by colonialism was not a positive but a negative one, arising out of the sense of anger, frustration, and humiliation produced by the oppressive, discriminatory, and exploitative measures and activities of the colonial administrators.

Another political legacy bequeathed to independent African states was the professional army. . . . These armies were among the most conspicuous legacies apart from physical structures bequeathed to independent African states. . . . In retrospect, they have become nothing but a chronic source of instability, confusion, and anarchy as a result of their often unnecessary and unjustifiable interventions in the political processes of African countries. Indeed, African armies are the greatest millstones around the necks of African leaders.

The final political impact and a very negative and regrettable one is the delay that colonialism caused in the political development and maturity of African states. If colonialism meant anything at all politically, it was the loss of sovereignty and independence by the colonized peoples. This loss of sovereignty, in turn, implied the loss of the right of a state to control its own destiny; to plan its own development; to decide which outside nations to borrow from or associate with or emulate; to conduct its own diplomacy and international relations; and above all, to manage or even mismanage its own affairs, derive pride and pleasure from its successes, and derive lessons, frustrations, and experience from its failures.

The impact of colonialism in the economic field, as in the political field, was clearly a mixed one. The most important economic benefit was the provision of an infrastructure of roads, railways, harbors, the telegraph and the telephone. The basic infrastructure of every modern African state was completed during the colonial period, and in most countries, not even a mile of railroad has been constructed since independence. A second important economic impact was the development of the primary sector of Africa's economy. It was during this period that the mineral potential of many African countries was discovered and modern scientific mining introduced. Above all, it was during this period that the production of such cash crops as cotton, peanuts, palm oil, coffee, tobacco, rubber, and cocoa, became the main feature of the political economy of many an African state.

These fundamental economic changes, in turn, had some far reaching consequences. In the first place, land acquired great commercial value and assumed far greater importance than it had ever had before. Secondly, the spread of cash-crop agriculture enabled Africans of whatever social status, and especially rural Africans in many regions, to acquire wealth and raise their standard of living. Another significant impact was the spread and consolidation of the money economy in Africa and with it not only a change in the traditional standards of wealth and status but also a phenomenal increase in the class of wage earners and salaried persons. In the wake of the money economy came the banking activities which have become such a feature in the economies of independent African states. The sum total of all these colonial economic reforms was what has been described by economists as the completion of the integration of the African economy into the world economy in general and into the capitalist economy of the former colonial powers in particular.

But the economic changes introduced by colonialism had a negative side also. First, the transportation and communications infrastructure that was provided was not only inadequate but was also very unevenly distributed in nearly all the colonies. The roads and railways were by and large constructed to link areas with the potential for cash crops and with mineral deposits with the sea or the world commodity market. In other words, the infrastructures were meant to facilitate the exploitation of the natural resources but not to promote the accessibility and development of all regions of the colony. The outcome of this has been uneven regional economic development in most African countries, still a major stumbling block in the way of nation-building in Africa today.

Secondly, the colonial system led to the delay of industrial and technological developments in Africa. As has been pointed out already, one of the typical features of the colonial political economy was the total neglect of industrialization and of the processing of locally produced raw materials and agricultural products in the colonies. . . . Preexisting industries were almost all eradicated by the importation of cheap and even better substitutes from Europe and India, while Africans were driven out of the mining industry as it became an exclusive preserve of Europeans. This neglect of industrialization, destruction of the existing industries and handicrafts in Africa, and elimination of Africans from the mining field further explain Africa's present technological backwardness.

Thirdly, colonialism saddled most colonies with monocrop economies. During the colonial period, as may be recalled, each colony was made to produce a single cash crop or two, and no attempts were made to diversify the agricultural economy. The habit of producing these single cash crops appears to have become so ingrained that it has not been changed to any appreciable degree since independence. The other consequence of this concentration on the production of cash crops for export was the neglect of the internal sector of the economy and, in particular, of the production of food for internal consumption, So that rice, maize, fish, and other foods had to be imported. Thus, during the colonial period, Africans were encouraged to produce what they did not consume and to consume what they did not produce, a clear proof of the exploitative nature of the colonial political economy.

Finally, the monetary policies pursued by all the colonial powers must be held partly responsible for the present underdeveloped state of the continent. Under these policies, all the colonial currencies were tied to those of the metropolitan countries, and all their foreign exchange earnings were kept in the metropolitan countries and not used for internal development. The expatriate commercial banks and companies were also allowed to repatriate their deposits, savings, and profits instead of reinvesting them in the colonies for further development. The consequence of all this was that at the time of independence, no African state apart from the Union of South Africa had the strong economic or industrial base needed for a real economic takeoff. And if this base could not be provided during the eighty-year period of colonial rule, should we expect it to have been done in twenty years of independence, especially in the light of the changing international economic order?

What about the impact in the social field? Here again, there are both credit and debit sides. In the first place, there is no doubt that after the initial decline, population growth resumed after the First World War. Caldwell has estimated that the population of Africa increased by 37 percent during the colonial period. The increase was undoubtedly due to some of the policies and activities of the colonial administrators—such as the provision of roads and railways, which made for mobility; the campaign launched against such epidemic diseases as sleeping sickness, bubonic plagues, yellow fever, and yaws; and the provision of some medical facilities.

A second important benefit was urbanization. Not only did preexisting towns expand, but completely new urban centers emerged following the establishment of the colonial system. . . . There is no doubt that the quality of life for Africa's population was relatively improved through the provision of piped water, hospitals and dispensaries, better housing and sanitary facilities.

A third important social benefit of colonialism was the spread of Christianity and Islam and especially of Western education. During the colonial period Christianity gained far more converts and penetrated farther, especially in East and Central Africa, than it had in all the previous three or four centuries put together. Islam also gained a lot of ground thanks to the patronage especially of the French and British colonial administrators. It should be emphasized that traditional African religion maintained its position in the face of all the inroads by these foreign religions.

The spread of Western education was due mainly to the activities of the Christian missionaries. . . . Education . . . was mainly responsible for producing the educated African *elite* which not only spearheaded the overthrow of the colonial system but also constitutes the backbone of the civil service of independent African states.

The other beneficial result of the spread of Western education was the provision of a lingua franca for each colony or cluster of colonies. In all the colonies, the mother tongue of the metropolitan country became the official language as well as the main medium of communication among the multi-ethnic populations of each colony.

The final social benefit was the new social order that emerged in Africa as a result of the operation of the colonial system. Though there was social mobility in the traditional African social order, undue weight was given to birth. The colonial system, on the other hand, emphasized individual merit and achievement rather than birth, and this greatly facilitated social mobility.

It would appear that the positive contribution of colonialism in the social field was quite considerable. Unfortunately, so also—and probably more so—was the negative impact. In the first place, it was the colonial system that initiated the gap that still exists between the urban and rural areas. All of the modern facilities— schools, hospitals, street lights, radio, postal services—and above all most of the employment opportunities were concentrated in the urban centers. The combination of modern life and employment pulled rural dwellers, especially the young ones and those with schooling, in the direction of the cities.

Secondly, the social services provided by colonialism were grossly inadequate and unevenly distributed. For instance, while in Nigeria by the 1930s, twelve modern hospitals had been built for Europeans, who numbered only 4,000, there were only fifty-two for Africans, numbering 40 million. In Dar es Salaam the ratio of beds to population by 1920 was approximately 1 to 10 for the European hospital and

1 to 400-500 for the African hospital.

There was even greater deficiency, uneven distribution, and in this case even misdirected orientation in the educational facilities that were provided in colonial Africa. University education was totally ignored in all the colonies until the 1940s, and only one university was subsequently established for each colony. In Portuguese Africa, there were no universities. Moreover, most of the secondary schools were in the major cities and the coastal areas of the colonies and seldom in the interior and rural regions. Thirdly, in no colony was the demand for education at all levels ever adequately met.

The effects of colonial education were really unfortunate. First, because of its inadequacy, large numbers of Africans remained illiterate and illiteracy is still widespread. Secondly, the *elite* produced by these colonial educational institutions were with few exceptions people who were alienated from their own society in terms of their dress, outlook, and tastes in food, music, and even dance. They were people who worshiped European culture, equating it with civilization, and looked down upon their own culture. Radical African scholars are now talking of colonial miseducation rather than education. Unfortunately, it is this very alienated and badly oriented *elite* that have dominated both the political and the social scene in Africa since independence. Above all, the neglect of technical education and the emphasis on liberal education created in educated Africans a contempt for manual work and an admiration for white-collar jobs which have still not left them. Finally, the use of the metropolitan language as the lingua franca also had the most regrettable effect of preventing the development of an official African language as a lingua franca in each colony or even in a cluster of colonies.

Another negative social impact of colonialism was the downgrading of the status of women in Africa. During the colonial period, there were far fewer facilities for girls than for boys. Women could therefore not gain access into the professions—medicine, law, the civil service, and the bench. Very few women were ever appointed to any "European post," while there was never a female governor of a colony.

The colonial administrators and their allies, the European missionaries, condemned everything African in culture—African names, music, dance, art, religion, marriage, the system of inheritance—and completely discouraged the teaching of all these things in their schools and colleges. Even the wearing of African clothes to work or school was banned. All this could not but retard the cultural development of the continent.

But the last and the most serious negative impact of colonialism has been psychological. This is seen, first, in the creation of a colonial mentality among educated Africans in particular and also among the populace in general. This mentality manifests itself in the condemnation of anything traditional, in the preference for imported goods to locally manufactured goods (since independence), and in the style of dress—such as the wearing of three-piece suits in a climate where temperatures routinely exceed eighty degrees Fahrenheit.

The final and worst psychological impact has been the generation of a deep feeling of inferiority as well as the loss of a sense of human dignity among Africans. Both complexes were surely the outcome not only of the wholesale condemnation of everything African already referred to but, above all, of the practice of racial discrimination and the constant humiliation and oppression to which Africans were subjected throughout the colonial period. The sense of human dignity seems to have been regained, but the feeling of inferiority has not entirely disappeared even after two decades of independence.

It should be obvious from the above, then, that all those historians who see colonialism as a "one-armed bandit" are totally wrong. Equally guilty of exaggeration are those colonial apologists who see colonialism as an unqualified blessing for Africa as well as those who see its record as a balanced one. Colonialism definitely did have its credit and debit sides, but quite clearly the debit side far outweighs the credit side. Indeed, my charge against colonialism is not that it did not do anything for Africa, but that it did so little and that little so accidentally and indirectly; not that the economy of Africa under colonialism did not grow but that it grew more to the advantage of the colonial powers and the expatriate owners and shareholders of the companies operating in Africa than to the Africans; not that improvements did not take place in the lives of the African peoples but that such improvements were so limited and largely confined to the urban areas; not that education was not provided but that what was provided was so inadequate and so irrelevant to the needs and demands of the African themselves; not that there was no upward social mobility but that such a relatively small number of Africans did get to the top. In short, given the opportunities, the resources, and the power and influence of the colonial rulers, they could and should have done far more than they did for Africa. And it is for this failure that the colonial era will go down in history as a period of wasted opportunities, of ruthless exploitation of the resources of Africa, and on balance of the underdevelopment and humiliation of the peoples of Africa.

Suggested Readings

Atmore, A.E. "The Credit Balance of Imperialism," A Review of L.H. Gann and Peter Duignan's *Burden of Empire,* in *The Journal of African History* 10, no. 2, (1969), 333-6.

Austen, Ralph, *African Economic History: Internal Development and External Dependency* (London: J. Currey, 1987). Davidson, Basil, *Modern Africa: A Social and Political History* (London: Longman, 1989).

————, *Which Way Africa? The Search for a New Society* (Baltimore: Penguin Books, 1964).

Falola, Toyin, ed., *Britain and Nigeria: Exploitation or Development* (London: Zed Press, 1987).

Fanon, Frantz, *Wretched of the Earth* (New York: Grove-Weidenfeld, 1991).

Gann, L.H., and Duignan, Peter, *White Settlers in Tropical Africa* (Harmoundsworth: Penguin Books, 1962).

Howard, Rhoda, *Colonialism and Underdevelopment in Ghana* (London: Groom Helm, 1978).

Huttenback, Robert, *Mammon and the Pursuit of Empire: The Economics of British Imperialism* (New York: Cambridge Press, 1988).

Huxley, Elspeth, *Race and Politics in Kenya: A Correspondence between Elspeth Huxley and Margery Perham* (Westport: Greenwood Press, 1975).

Johnston, Sir Harry, *A History of Colonization of Africa by Alien Races* (London: Cambridge, 1913).

Kabwegyere, Tarris, *The Politics of State Formation: The Nature and Effects of Colonialism in Uganda* (Nairobi: East African Literature Bureau, 1974).

Kitching, Gavin, *Development and Underdevelopment in Historical Perspective* (London: Routledge, 1989).

Lloyd, Peter, *Africa in Social Change* (New York: Praeger, 1968).

————, *Classes, Crises and Coups* (London: MacGibbon and Kee, 1971).

McCarthy, Dennis, *Colonial Bureaucracy and Creating Underdevelopment: Tanganyika, 1919-1940* (Ames: Iowa State University Press, 1982).

Memmi, Albert, *The Colonizer and the Colonized* (Boston: Beacon Press, 1967).

Offiong, Daniel, *Imperialism and Dependency: Obstacles to African Development* (Washington, D.C.: Howard University Press, 1982).

Perham, Margery, *The Colonial Reckoning* (New York: Knopf, 1962).

————, *The Economics of Tropical Dependency* (London: Faber and Faber, 1946).

Strachey, John, *The End of Empire* (London: Gollancz, 1959).

Suret-Canale, Jean, *French Colonialism in Tropical Africa,* 1900-1945 (New York: Pica Press, 1971).

Wallerstein, Immanuel, *Africa and the Modern World* (Trenton: Africa World

Press, 1986).

Williams, Eric, *Capitalism and Slavery* (Chapel Hill: University of North Carolina Press, 1944).

Woddis, Jack, *Africa: The Roots of Revolt* (New York: Citadel Press, 1962).

Woolf, Leonard, *Empire and Commerce in Africa: A Study of Economic Imperialism* (New York: H. Fertig, 1968).

Acknowledgments

The editor gratefully acknowledges the following authors and publishers: Humanities Press International, Inc., Atlantic Highlands, NJ, for permission to reprint "Egypt and the Partition of Africa" from *Africa and the Victorians,* by Robinson and Gallagher, pp. 163, 166, 168-74, 274, 281-89, 376-78; Cambridge University Press for permission to reprint from the *The Journal of African History* the following articles: "King Leopold, Savorgnan de Brazza, and the Scramble for Africa" by Jean Stengers, Vol. 3, No. 3, pp. 49, 91; "French Policy and the Origins of the Scramble for Africa" by C.W. Newbury and A. S. Kanya-Fostner, Vol. 10, No. 2, pp. 170-75; "Connections between Primary Resistance Movements" by T.O. Ranger, Vol. 9, No. 4, pp. 437-53, 631-37; "The Organization of the Maji Maji Rebellion" by John Illiffe, Vol. 8, No. 3, pp. 495-512; "Some Origins of Nationalism in East Africa" by J.M. Lonsdale, Vol. 9, No. 1, pp. 119-21, 123-26, 135, 140-46; The Macmillan Press Ltd. for permission to reprint *Germany's First Bid for the Colonies,* by A.J.P. Taylor, pp. 1-7; Yale University Press for permission to reprint from *Britain and Germany in Africa* by Roger Louis, Prosser Gifford, and Alison Smith, eds., pp. 49-53; Edinburgh University Press for permission to reprint *England, Europe and the Upper Nile,* by G.N. Sanderson, pp. 386-92; Columbia University Press for permission to reprint *The Economic History of West Africa,* by A.G. Hopkins, pp. 135, 143-47.

Grateful appreciation is also expressed to Cambridge University Press for permission to reprint *The New Cambridge Modern History,* Vol. XI, ch. 22, pp. 639-40; Penguin Books for permission to reprint *A Short History of Africa* by Roland Oliver and J.D. Gage, pp. 202-3; Cambridge University Press for permission to reprint *Colonialism in Africa,* Vol. I, by John D. Hargreaves, pp. 199-200, 205-16; Princeton University Press for permission to reprint *Conflict and Collaboration: Kingdoms of Uganda,* by Edward Steinhart, pp. *vii, viii,* 256-60, 266-69; Frank Cass Publishers for permission to reprint *The Dual Mandate in Tropical Africa,* by John Frederick Lugard, pp. 94-97, 102-5, 199-218; Waterlow and Sons, Ltd. for permission to reprint *Revisions of Instruction to Political Officers on Subjects Chiefly Political and Administrative,* by John Frederick Lugard, pp. 296-305; Oxford University Press for permission to reprint *Buganda and British Overrule: 1900-1955,* by D. Anthony Low and R. Cranford Pratt, pp. 163-76; Cambridge University Press for permission to reprint "One Hundred Million French Men: The Assimilation Theory in French Colonial Policy" in *Comparative Studies in Society and History,* Vol. 4, by Martin D. Lewis, pp. 129-49; Columbia University Press for permission to reprint *Assimilation and Association in French Colonial Theory,* by Raymond Betts, pp. 106-28; International African Institute, London School of Enconomics for permission to reprint "Et Maintenant, Lord Lugard," by Hubert

Jules Deschamps, that appeared in *Africa* 33 (4), pp. 293-305 and "Indirect Rule—French and British Style," by Michael Crowder, that appeared in *Africa* 34 (3), pp. 197-205 which is reprinted by permission of the copyright holder, Q.N. Parsons.

Also to Faber and Faber Limited for permission to reprint *The Anglo-Egyptian Sudan,* by Harold MacMichael, pp. 269-70; Phelps Stokes for permission to reprint *Education in Africa: A Study of West, South and Equatorial Africa by the African Education Commission, under the Auspices of the Phelps-Stokes Fund and Foreign Mission Societies of North America and Europe,* by Thomas Jesse Jones, pp. 57-60, 65, 69-79; Royal Institute of International Affairs, Oxford University Press for permission to reprint *An African Survey: A Study of the Problems Arising in Africa South of the Sahara,* by William Malcolm Hailey, pp. 1278-83; Teachers College Press for permission to reprint *Education and Changing West African Culture,* by John Wilson, pp. 34, 38-43; Howard University Press for permission to reprint *How Europe Underdeveloped Africa,* by Walter Rodney, pp. 223-38, 240-41, 243, 245-47, 249-53; Greenwood Publishing Group for permission to reprint *Education in Africa,* by Abdan Maumouni, pp. 50-53; Harvard University Press for permission to reprint *Political Change in a West African State: A Study in Modernization Process in Sierra Leone,* by Martin Kilson, pp. 53-54, 60-67, 68-72, 89-93; Yale University Press for permission to reprint *The Transfer of Power in Africa: Decolonization, 1940-1960,* by William Roger Louis and Ronald Robinson, pp. 31-32, 43-47, 53-55; L.H. Gann and Peter Duignan for permission to reprint *Burden of Empire: An Appraisal of Western Colonialism in Africa South of the Sahara,* pp. v-vii, 229-31, 234, 236-52; George Weidenfeld & Nicholson for permission to reprint *The Colonial Empires: A Comparative Survey from the Eighteenth Century,* by D.K. Fieldhouse, pp. 380-87, 389-94; Northwestern University Press for permission to reprint *West Africa under Colonial Rule,* by Michael Crowder, pp. 345-53; Zed Press for permission to reprint *Imperialism and Underdevelopment in Nigeria: The Dialectics of Mass Poverty,* by Bade Onimode, pp. 42-43, 48-49, 51-52, 91-93, 103-4; and Johns Hopkins University Press for permission to reprint *African Perspectives on Colonialism,* by A. Boahen, pp. 94-112.